EXPLORING RESEARCH

EIGHTH EDITION

Neil J. Salkind
University of Kansas

PEARSON

Boston   Columbus   Indianapolis   New York   San Francisco   Upper Saddle River
Amsterdam   Cape Town   Dubai   London   Madrid   Milan   Munich   Paris
Montreal   Toronto   Delhi   Mexico City   Sao Paulo   Sydney
Hong Kong   Seoul   Singapore   Taipei   Tokyo

Executive Editor: Stephan Frail
Editorial Assistant: Madelyn Schricker
Marketing Manager: Nicole Kunzmann
Marketing Assistant: Jessica Warren
Production Assistant: Caitlin Smith
Production/Manufacturing Manager: Pat Brown
Cover Administrator: Jayne Conte
Editorial Production and Composition Service: Hemalatha/
   Integra Software Services Pvt. Ltd.
Cover Designer: Bruce Kenselaar
Printer and Binder: Bind-Rite Graphics
Cover Printer: Lehigh-Phoenix Color
Cover image: Shotterstock

Credits and acknowledgments borrowed from other sources and reproduced, with permission, in this textbook appear on the appropriate page within the text. Appendix A screenshots are all from SPSS, Inc.

Many of the designations by manufacturers and seller to distinguish their products are claimed as trademarks. Where those designations appear in this book, and the publisher was aware of a trademark claim, the designations have been printed in initial caps or all caps.

Library of Congress Cataloging-in-Publication Data
Salkind, Neil J.
  Exploring research / Neil J. Salkind.—8th ed.
    p. cm.
  Includes bibliographical references and index.
  ISBN-13: 978-0-205-09381-6 (alk. paper)
  ISBN-10: 0-205-09381-7 (alk. paper)
  1. Psychology—Research—Methodology.
  2. Education—Research—Methodology.   I. Title.
  BF76.5.S24 2012
  150.72—dc22

                                    2011008869

10 9 8 7 6 5 4 3 2 1—14 13 12 11 10

ISBN-10:   0-205-09381-7
ISBN-13: 978-0-205-09381-6

ISBN 10:   0-205-09390-6
ISBN 13: 978-0-205-09390-8

ISBN 10:   0-205-10877-6
ISBN 13: 978-0-205-10877-0

For Sara, Micah and Ted and my fellow
Sharks . . . Happy Laps

At a Glance

Contents

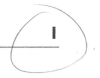

Chapter 3B: The Importance of Practicing Ethics in Research   83

Chapter 6: Methods of Measuring Behavior   133

Chapter 7: Data Collection and Descriptive Statistics   155

odq 10&13
Que 5/19

Chapter 8: Introducing Inferential Statistics   177

Chapter 9: Nonexperimental Research: Descriptive
and Correlational Methods   197

Chapter 10: Nonexperimental Research: Qualitative Methods   213

Chapter 11: Pre- and True Experimental Research Methods   229

Chapter 12: Quasi-Experimental Research: A Close Cousin to Experimental Research   245

Chapter 13: Writing a Research Proposal   259

Chapter 14: Writing a Research Manuscript   273

Appendix A: An Introduction to SPSS 19.x   301

Appendix B: Sample Data Set   363

Preface

I've been very lucky. For more than 35 years, I have had the privilege of teaching introductory research methods and have been able to share all that I know and continue to learn about this fascinating topic. This eighth edition of *Exploring Research* reflects much of what has taken place in my classrooms over those years.

This book is intended for upper-level undergraduate students and graduate students in their first research methods course in the social, behavioral, and health sciences fields. These students are the primary audience. But, lately, other disciplines have been introducing research methods courses to their curriculum, such as public policy, government, journalism, and related fields, and students there have been using *Exploring Research* as well. And, recently, even such fields as American Studies and Ethnomusicology have started incorporating the types of methods we talk about here.

Exploring Research is intended to provide an introduction to the important topics in the general area of research methods and to do so in a nonintimidating and informative way. The existence of an eighth edition of *Exploring Research* means that the audience for a straightforward and unassuming presentation of this material still exists, and I believe that audience is growing. I'm grateful for those who have chosen to use this book.

What's New in This Edition?

Many of the changes are the result of suggestions from students and faculty and the capable reviewers who reviewed the seventh edition and although they will be thanked later in this preface, it's none too early to tell you how much I appreciate their efforts.

- More coverage of ethics because this is becoming increasingly important as a topic that beginning researchers need to know about. There's more on the history of how ethical practices have progressed as well as a brief coverage of some important case studies.
- After lots of discussion with faculty who have adopted this book, it was decided that the answers to the end-of-chapter questions should go at the end of the book in a separate appendix (Appendix C) of its own.
- The online sources for more exploration are increased by about 50% as well.
- Updated and new coverage of software for dealing with qualitative data and the development and refinement of bibliographies.
- Inserted after many sections are questions that will help the reader summarize the content in that part of the chapter and serve, if so desired, as a taking-off point for discussion. These "Test Yourself" questions don't necessarily have a right or a wrong answer—they are there to help facilitate thinking and discussion about the topic at hand.
- Each chapter has about 50% more, new end-of-chapter exercises so readers can practice the skills they have learned through their reading of the chapter.
- The material on the use of the Internet for research is updated with more information about conducting research and literature reviews online and including an introduction to how social media can be used in a research context. I am assuming that most students who are using this book have basic computer skills and have access to the Internet either at home or at school. I also assume they know about e-mail and how to use it, so information on that topic has been significantly reduced to allow room for other material such as expanded and updated coverage.

- Appendix A, which covers the basic features of SPSS, is part of this new edition. This appendix serves as an introduction to the basic features of SPSS (version 19.x) including entering and analyzing data, doing simple analyses, and creating graphs. If you have an earlier version of SPSS, your screens might not match exactly, but you should certainly be able to follow the instructions.
- The last chapter contains information about the use of the latest, sixth, edition of the *Publication Manual of the American Psychological Association*.

How This Book Is Organized

Exploring Research is organized into 14 chapters (with a big and little Chapters 3A and 3B, respectively) and three appendices. Chapter 1, "The Role and Importance of Research," covers the basics about the scientific method and includes a brief description of the different types of research that are most commonly used in the social and behavioral sciences.

Chapter 2 "The Research Process: Coming to Terms," focuses on some of the basic terms and concepts in research methods, including variables, samples, populations, hypotheses, and the concept of significance.

The first step for any researcher is the selection of a problem, which is what Chapter 3A "Selecting a Problem and Reviewing the Research," is all about. Here you will learn how to use the library and its vast resources to help you focus your interests and actually turn them into something you want to know more about! You will also be introduced to the use of electronic sources of reference material, such as online searches, and how using the Internet can considerably enhance your research skills.

A new Chapter 3B "The Importance of Practicing Ethics in Research," talks about the ethical practices and ethical concerns in research.

The content of Chapter 4, "Sampling and Generalizability," is critical to understanding the research process. How you select the group of participants and how and when the results of an experiment can be generalized from this group to others are a fundamental premise of all scientific research. In this chapter, you will read all about this process.

What is research without measuring outcomes? Not much, I'm afraid. Chapter 5, "Measurement, Reliability, and Validity," introduces you to the measurement process and the important concepts of reliability and validity. You need to understand not only the principles of measurement but also the methods used to measure behavior. That is what you will learn in Chapter 6, "Methods of Measuring Behavior," which discusses different types of tests and their importance.

Once you understand what you want to study and the importance of measuring it, the only thing left to do is to go out and collect data! Chapter 7, "Data Collection and Descriptive Statistics," takes you through the process step by step and includes a summary of important descriptive statistics and how they can be used.

One of the reasons data are collected is to make inferences from a smaller group of people to a larger one. In Chapter 8, "Introducing Inferential Statistics," you will find an introduction to the discipline of the same name and how results based on small groups are inferred to larger ones.

Chapter 9 "Nonexperimental Research: Descriptive and Correlational Methods," is the first of four chapters that deal with different types of research methods. In this chapter, you will learn about descriptive and correlational methods.

Chapter 10 "Nonexperimental Research: Qualitative Methods," provides the reader with an introduction to various qualitative tools, including case studies, ethnographies, and historical methods, and talks a bit about the advantages and disadvantages of each. I hope that you find this new chapter helpful and that it will give you another set of tools to answer important and interesting questions.

Chapter 11 "Pre- and True Experimental Research Methods," and Chapter 12, "Quasi-Experimental Research: A Close Cousin to Experimental Research," continue the overview of research methods by introducing you to the different types of research designs that explore the area of cause and effect. Developmental research is discussed in Chapter 12.

Chapter 13 "Writing a Research Proposal," reviews the steps involved in planning and writing a proposal and includes an extensive set of questions that can be used to evaluate your proposal. If your research methods course does not include the preparation of a proposal as a requirement, this chapter can be used as a stand-alone instructional tool.

Exploring Research ends with Chapter 14, "Writing a Research Manuscript," a step-by-step discussion of how to prepare a manuscript for submission to a journal for publication using the format prescribed by the sixth edition of *Publication Manual of the American Psychological Association*. Appendix A is an introduction to version 19.x of SPSS. Appendix B contains a sample data set that is used in certain examples throughout the book, and this data set is also contained on the Internet site. Appendix C contains the answers to the exercises found at the end of each chapter.

What's Special About This Book?

I have included several features in this edition that I hope will help make this book more useful and the learning of the material more interesting. These features have not changed because the feedback from both faculty and students has been so positive.

- "What You'll Learn About in This Chapter" is a listing of the major points that will be covered in each chapter. This listing acts not only as a set of advanced organizers but also as a summary of the primary topics covered in the chapter.
- You will find marginal notes that highlight important points contained in the text. These can be used for review purposes and help to emphasize especially important points. There's also room for your own notes in the margins.
- Those "Test Yourself" questions mentioned earlier.
- Last, but not least, is a Glossary of important terms found at the end of the book. The terms that you find in the glossary appear in boldface in the text.

A Note to the Instructor

All teachers tend to use teaching materials in different ways and I tried to complete this edition in such a way that the chapters can be read through in an order different from what is contained in the table of contents. For example, some instructors tell me that they start with Chapter 14 because a central element in their course is writing a research report. Others start with Chapter 4 on sampling and others go right from descriptive statistics to correlational methods. There is, of course, some mention of materials from previous and upcoming chapters throughout, but these are relatively few and will not bear on your students' access to the information they need to understand the ideas under discussion.

Also, if you want to know more about SPSS, you might want to look at the newly released SPSS Quick Start (2010) from Prentice Hall by Salkind and Green. And, if you are looking for a fun introductory stat book, you might want to look at *Statistics for People Who Think They Hate Statistics* (fourth edition from Sage) by me. And, of course, e-mail me at njs@ku.edu should you have any questions.

Finally, you can learn more about ancillaries that are available for this book by going to *www.pearsonhighered.com*.

How to Use This Book

I have tried to write this book so that it is (you guessed it) user friendly. Basically, what I think this means is that you can pick it up, understand what it says, and do what it suggests. One reviewer and user of an earlier edition was put off at first by the easy-going way in which the book is written. My philosophy is that important and interesting ideas and concepts need not be written about in an obtuse and convoluted fashion. Simple is best. You see, your mother was right!

Whether you are using this book as the main resource in a research methods course or as a supplemental text, here are some hints on how to go about using the book to make the most out of the experience.

- Read through the "At a Glance" table of contents (page v–vi) so you can get an idea of what is in the book.
- If you find a chapter that seems particularly interesting, turn to that page and take a look at "What You'll Learn About in This Chapter".
- Take your time and do not try to read too much at one sitting. You will probably be assigned one chapter per week. Although it is not an enormous task to read the 20–30 pages that each chapter contains in one sitting, breaking your reading up by main chapter sections might make things a little easier. Too much too soon leads to fatigue, which in turn leads to frustration, and then no one is happy!
- Do the exercises at the end of each chapter. They will give you further insight into the materials that you just read and some direct experience with the techniques and topics that were covered.
- Write down questions you might have in the margins of pages where things seem unclear. When you are able, ask your professor to clarify the information or bring your questions to your study group for discussion.

A *Big* Thanks

All textbooks have the author's name on the cover, but no book is ever the work of a single person. Such is also the case with *Exploring Research*.

Many people helped make this book what it is, and they deserve the thanks that I am offering here. Chris Cardone, way back at Macmillan, was the inspiration for this book. She remains the best of editors and a close friend. At Pearson, thanks to editors Jeff Marshall, Susan Hartman and finally Stephen Frail who became editor for this book at the end of the project and assured its timely completion. Great thanks as well to Pat Brown, production editor (and his entire team including Murugesh and Hema), Courtney M. Elezovic, and Alexandra Mitton for unfailing help. And special thanks to Kristin Teasdale for her superb help on every aspect of the revision, from new questions at the end of each chapter to proofing and finding typos in the previous edition. Thank you, thank you, thank you. To people I do not know about or have inadvertently forgotten to mention, my sincere thanks to you as well.

Second, outside reviewers Annette Taylor, University of San Diego; Dawn M. McBride, Illinois State University; Kristy A. Nielson, Marquette University; Nina Coppens, University of Massachusetts Lowell; Karen Schmidt, University of Virginia; Andrew Supple, UNC Greensboro; Sharon L. Hill, University of Tennessee at Chattanooga; Brad Chilton, Tarleton State University; Notis Pagiavlas, Embry-Riddle Aeronautical University; Sara Goldstein, Montclair State University; Isaac Mizelle, Concordia University Chicago; Susan Ruppel, University of South Carolina Upstate; James Spencer, West Virginia State University; and Katja Wiemer-Hastings, Northern

Illinois University-DeKalb, offered invaluable suggestions, all of which improved the quality of the finished manuscript. They deserve a great deal of thanks.

I take full responsibility for the errors and apologize to those students and faculty who might have used earlier editions of the book and had difficulty because of the mistakes. As many of those screwups (that is exactly the phrase) have been removed as is humanly possible.

Finally, as always, words cannot express my gratitude to Leni for her support and love that see projects like this through to the end. And to Sara, Micah and Ted, my deepest admiration and respect as they continue to build professional and personal lives of their own. These young adults are making the world a better place.

So, now it is up to you. Use the book well. Enjoy it and I hope that your learning experience is one filled with new discoveries about your area of interest as well as about your own potential. I would love to hear from you about the book, including what you like and do not like, suggestions for changes, or whatever. You can reach me through snail mail or e-mail.

Neil J. Salkind
University of Kansas
Lawrence, KS 66045

Chapter 1

The Role and Importance of Research

Say Hello to Research!

Walk down the hall in any building on your campus where social and behavioral science professors have their offices in such departments as psychology, education, nursing, sociology, and human development. Do you see any bearded, disheveled, white-coated men wearing rumpled pants and smoking pipes, hunched over their computers and mumbling to themselves? How about disheveled, white-coated women wearing rumpled skirts, smoking pipes, hunched over their computers, and mumbling to themselves?

Researchers hard at work? No. Stereotypes of what scientists look like and do? Yes. What you are more likely to see in the halls of your classroom building or in your adviser's office are men and women of all ages who are hard at work. They are committed to finding the answer to just another piece of the great puzzle that helps us understand human behavior a little better than the previous generation of scientists.

Like everyone else, these people go to work in the morning, but unlike many others, these researchers have a passion for understanding what they study and for coming as close as possible to finding the "truth." Although these truths can be elusive and sometimes even unobtainable, researchers work toward discovering them for the satisfaction of answering important questions and then using this new information to help others. Early intervention programs, treatments of psychopathology, new curricula, conflict resolution techniques, effective drug treatment programs, and even changes in policy and law have resulted from evidence collected by researchers. Although not always perfect, each little bit of evidence gained from a new study or a new idea for a study contributes to a vast legacy of knowledge for the next generation of researchers such as yourself.

You may already know and appreciate something about the world of research. The purpose of this book is to provide you with the tools you need to do even more, such as

- develop an understanding of the research process.
- prepare yourself to conduct research of your own.
- learn how to judge the quality of research.
- learn how to read, search through, and summarize other research.
- learn the value of research activities conducted online.
- reveal the mysteries of basic statistics and show you how easily they can be used.

WHAT YOU'LL LEARN ABOUT IN THIS CHAPTER:

- Who does research and why
- How research is defined and what some of its purposes are
- What a model of scientific inquiry is and how it guides research activities
- Some of the things that research is and some of the things that it isn't
- What researchers do and how they do it
- The characteristics of good research
- How a method of scientific inquiry guides research activity
- The different types of research methods and examples of each

Today, more than ever, decisions are evidence based, and what these researchers do is collect evidence that serves as a basis for informed decisions.

1

- measure the behaviors, traits, or attributes that interest you.
- collect the type of data that relate to your area of interest.
- use a leading statistical package (SPSS) to analyze data.
- design research studies that answer the question that you want answered.
- write the type of research proposal (and a research report) that puts you in control—one that shows you have command of the content of the research as well as the way in which the research should be done.

Sound ambitious? A bit terrifying? Exciting? Maybe those and more, but boring is one thing this research endeavor is not. This statement is especially true when you consider that the work you might be doing in this class, as well as the research proposal that you might write, could hold the key to expanding our knowledge and understanding of human behavior and, indirectly, eventually helping others.

So here you are, beginning what is probably your first course in the area of research methods and wondering about everything from what researchers do to what your topic will be for your thesis. Relax. Thousands of students have been here before you and almost all of them have left with a working knowledge of what research is, how it is done, and what distinguishes a good research project from one that is doomed. Hold on and let's go. This trip will be exciting.

What Research Is and What It Isn't

Research is, among other things, an intensive activity that is based on the work of others and generates new ideas to pursue and questions to answer.

Perhaps it is best to begin by looking at what researchers really do. To do so, why not look at some of the best? Here are some researchers, the awards they have won, and the focus of their work. All of these people started out in a class just like the one you are in, reading a book similar to the one you are reading. Their interest in research and a particular issue continued to grow until it became their life's work.

The following awards were given in 2009 by the American Psychological Association in recognition of outstanding work.

Susan E. Carey from the psychology department at Harvard University was honored for her contributions to the field of cognitive development and developmental psychology. The work that she did early in her career focused on understanding how children learn language, and she coined the term "fast mapping" for how children can learn the meaning of a new word with very little experience with that word.

Nancy E. Adler from the University of California won the Distinguished Scientific Award for the Applications of Psychology for her work in health. Her early research focused on the health behaviors in adolescence, and she explained the incredibly interesting question of why individuals engage in health-damaging behaviors and how their understanding of risk affects their choices.

Finally, one of several Distinguished Scientific Awards for Early Career Contributions to Psychology went to Jennifer A. Richeson from Northwestern University for her work on stereotyping, prejudice, discrimination, and inter-group conflict. This focus examined the experiences and behaviors both of members of devalued groups and of members of dominant groups.

The American Educational Research Association (AERA) also gives out awards that recognize important contributions.

The 2009 E. F. Lindquist award was given to Wim J. van der Linden for his contributions to the field of testing and measurement, including optimal test design and adaptive testing. The award is named after E. F. Lindquist, who was a founder of The American College Testing Program, and is given for outstanding applied or theoretical research in the field of testing and measurement.

AERA has an extensive award program including the Distinguished Contributions to Gender Equity in Education Research Award, given to Sandra Harding from the University of California–Los Angeles in recognition of her research that helps to advance public understanding of gender and/or sexuality in the education community.

And, as with many other organizations, AERA also offers awards for researchers still early in their careers, such as the Early Career Award won by Michele Moses from the University of Colorado–Boulder and Nell Duke from Michigan State University.

What all these people have in common is that at one time or another during their professional careers, they were active participants in the process of doing research. **Research** is a process through which new knowledge is discovered. A **theory**, such as a theory of motivation, or development, or learning, for example, helps us to organize this new information into a coherent body, a set of related ideas that explain events that have occurred and predict events that may happen. Theories are an important part of science. It is at the ground-floor level, however, that the researcher works to get the ball rolling, adding a bit of new insight here and a new speculation there, until these factors come together to form a corpus of knowledge.

High-quality research is characterized by many different attributes, many of which tend to be related to one another and also tend to overlap. High-quality research

- is based on the work of others,
- can be replicated,
- is generalizable to other settings,　　*We do this every day*
- is based on some logical rationale and tied to theory,
- is doable,
- generates new questions or is cyclical in nature,
- is incremental, and
- is an apolitical activity that should be undertaken for the betterment of society.

Let's take a closer look at each of these.

First, *research is an activity based on the work of others.* No, this does not mean that you copy the work of others (that's plagiarism), but you always look to the work that has already been done to provide a basis for the subject of your research and how you might conduct your own work. For example, if there have been 200 studies on gender differences in aggression, the results of those studies should not be ignored. You may not want to replicate any one of these studies, but you certainly should take methodologies that were used and the results into consideration when you plan your own research in that area.

It is a guide & does not formulate a step by step treatment plan — those are taylored to the individual & the gardener tabors ferterlizer to different gardens

A good example of this principle is the tremendous intellectual and scientific effort that went into the creation of the atomic bomb. Hundreds of top scientists from all over the world were organized at different locations in an intense and highly charged effort to combine their knowledge to create this horrible weapon. What was unique about this effort is that it was compressed in time; many people who would probably share each other's work in any case did so in days rather than months because of the military and political urgency of the times. What was discovered one day literally became the basis for the next day's experiments (see Richard Rhodes' Pulitzer Prize–winning book, *The Making of the Atomic Bomb*, for the whole story).

Second, while we're talking about other studies, *research is an activity that can be replicated*. If someone conducts a research study that examines the relationship between problem-solving ability and musical talent, then the methods and procedures (and results) of the experiment should be replicable with other groups for two reasons. First, one of the hallmarks of any credible scientific finding is that it can be replicated. If you can spin gold from straw, you should be able to do it every time, right? How about using a new method to teach children to read? Or developing early intervention programs that produce similar results when repeated? Second, if the results of an experiment can be replicated, they can serve as a basis for further research in the same area.

Third, *good research is generalizable to other settings.* This means, for example, that if adolescent boys are found to be particularly susceptible to peer pressure in one setting, then the results would probably stand up (or be generalizable) in a different but related setting. Some research has limited generalizability because it is difficult to replicate the exact conditions under which the research was carried out, but the results of most research can lend at least something to another setting.

Fourth, *research is based on some logical rationale and tied to theory.* Research ideas do not stand alone merely as interesting questions. Instead, research activity provides answers to questions that help fill in pieces to what can be a large and complicated puzzle. No one could be expected to understand, through one grand research project, the entire process of intellectual development in children, or the reason why adolescents form cliques, or what actually happens during a midlife crisis. All these major areas of research need to be broken into smaller elements, and all these elements need to be tied together with a common theme, which more often than not is some underlying, guiding theory.

Fifth, and by all means, *research is doable*! Too often, especially for the young or inexperienced scientist (such as yourself), the challenge to come up with a feasible idea is so pressing that almost anything will do as a research topic. Professors sometimes see thesis statements from students such as, "The purpose of this research is to see if the use of drugs can be reduced through exposure to television commercials." This level of ambiguity and lack of a conceptual framework makes the statement almost useless and certainly not doable. Good research poses a question that can be answered, and then answers it in a timely fashion.

Sixth, *research generates new questions or is cyclical in nature.* Yes, what goes around comes around. The answers to today's research questions provide the foundation for research questions that will be asked tomorrow. You will learn more about this process later in this chapter when a method of scientific inquiry is described.

Seventh, *research is incremental.* No one scientist stands alone; instead, scientists stand on the shoulders of others. Contributions that are made usually take place in small, easily definable chunks. The first study ever done on the development of language did not answer all the questions about language acquisition, nor did the most recent study put the icing on the cake. Rather, all the studies in a particular area come together to produce a body of knowledge that is shared by different researchers and provides the basis for further research. The whole, or all the knowledge about a particular area, is more than the sum of the parts, because each new research advance not only informs us but it also helps us place other findings in a different, often fruitful perspective.

Finally, at its best, *research is an apolitical activity that should be undertaken for the betterment of society.* I stress "at its best," because too often various special-interest groups dictate how research funding should be spent. Finding a vaccine for acquired immunodeficiency syndrome (AIDS) should not depend on one's attitudes toward individual lifestyles. Similarly, whether early intervention programs should be supported is independent of one's personal or political views. And should research on cloning be abandoned because of its potential misuse? Of course not. It's how the discovery of new knowledge is used that results in its misuse, not the new knowledge itself.

Although it should be apolitical, research should have as its ultimate goal the betterment of society. Researchers or practitioners do not withhold food from pregnant women to study the effects of malnutrition on children. To examine the stress–nutrition link, researchers do not force adults to eat particular diets that might be unhealthy. These unethical practices would not lead to a greater end, especially because there are other ways to answer such questions without resorting to possibly harmful practices.

If these attributes make for good research, what is bad research? It takes the opposite approach of all the things stated earlier and then some. In sum, bad research is the fishing trip you take looking for something important when it simply is not to be found. It is plagiarizing other people's work, or falsifying data to prove a point, or misrepresenting information and misleading participants. Unfortunately, there are researchers whose work is characterized by these practices, but they are part of an overall minority.

TEST YOURSELF

Note: At the end of every major heading in each chapter of *Exploring Research,* we'll have a few questions for you that we hope will help you understand the content and guide your studying.

Provide an example of how research is incremental in nature and what advantage is this to both future and past researchers?

Think of an example of how knowledge about a certain topic can lead to new questions about that, or a related, topic.

A Model of Scientific Inquiry

In the past 20 years, the public has been exposed to the trials and tribulations of the research process as described through hundreds of books by and about the everyday work of scientists around the world.

Regardless of the specific content of these books, they all have one thing in common. The work was accomplished through adherence to guidelines that allowed these researchers to progress from point A to point Z while remaining confident that they were on the trail of finding (what they hoped was) an adequate answer to the questions they had posed.

Their methods and their conclusions are not helter-skelter because of one important practice: They share the same general philosophy regarding how questions about human behavior should be answered. In addition, for scientists to be able to trust their colleagues, in the sense of having confidence in the results produced by their studies, these scientists must have something in common besides good intentions. As it turns out, what they share is a standard sequence of steps in formulating and answering a question.

When you read in a journal article that Method A is more effective than Method B for improving retention or memory, you can be pretty sure that the steps described next were followed, in one form or another. Because there is agreement about the general method used to answer the question, the results of this comparison of Method A and Method B can be applied to the next study. That study would perhaps investigate variations of Method A and how and why they work. The research efforts of developmental psychologists, gerontologists (specialists in aging), linguists, and experts in higher education all depend on the integrity of the process.

Figure 1.1 shows a set of such steps as part of a model of scientific inquiry. The goal of this model is to find the truth (whatever that means) or, in other words, to use a **scientific method** that results in a reasonable and sound answer to important questions that will further our understanding of human behavior.

An interesting and timely topic, *the effects of using social media on adolescents' social skills,* will be used as an example of the different steps followed in this model.

"Doing science" means following a model that begins with a question and ends with asking new questions.

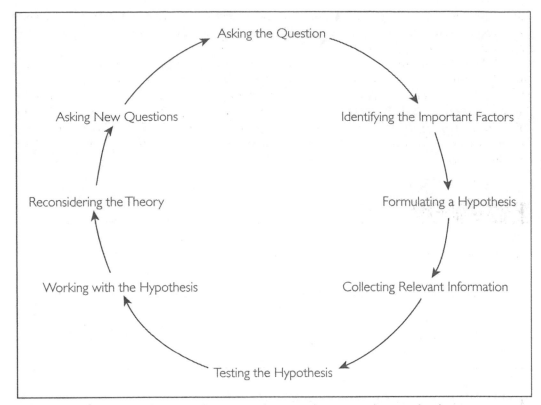

Figure 1.1 The steps in the research process, wherein each step sets the stage for the next.

Asking the Question

Remember the story of *The Wizard of Oz*? When Dorothy realized her need to get to the Emerald City, she asked Glinda, the good witch, "But where do I begin?" Glinda's response, "Most people begin at the beginning, my dear," is the case in almost any scientific endeavor.

Our first and most important step is asking a question (I wonder what would happen if . . . ?) or identifying a need (We have to find a way to . . .) that arises as the result of curiosity, and to which it becomes necessary to find an answer. For example, you might be curious about how the use of social media such as Twitter and Facebook affects relationships between children and their peers. You also might feel an urgency to find out how to use various types of media most effectively for educating children and adults about the dangers of using drugs.

Such questions are informally stated and often are intended as a source of discussion and stimulation about what direction the specific research topic should take. Where do such questions come from? They rarely come from the confines of a classroom or a laboratory. Rather, questions spring (in the fullest sense of the word) from our imagination and our own experiences, enriched by the worlds of science, art, music, and literature. It is no coincidence that many works of fiction (including science fiction) have a basis in fact. The truly creative scientist is always thinking about everything from solutions to existing questions to the next important question to ask. When Louis Pasteur said that *chance favors the prepared mind*, he was really saying, "Take advantage of all the experiences you can, both in and out of school." Only then can you be well prepared to recognize the importance of certain events, which will act as a stimulus for more rigorous research activity.

Questions can be as broad as inquiring about the effects of social media on peer groups, or as specific as the relationship between the content of social media transactions and acceptance by peers. Whatever their content or depth of inquiry, questions are the first step in any scientific endeavor.

Identifying the Important Factors

Once the question has been asked, the next step is to identify the factors that have to be examined to answer the question. Such factors might range from the simplest, such as an adolescent's age or socioeconomic status, to more complicated measures, such as the daily number of face-to-face interactions.

For example, the following list of factors have been investigated over the past 10 years by various researchers who have been interested in the effects of social media:

- age and gender of the adolescent,
- ethnicity,
- level of family education,
- access to types of social media,
- number of self-identified close friends,
- parental attitude toward social media,
- family configuration,
- family communication patterns.

And these are only ten of hundreds of factors and associated topics that could be explored. But of all the factors that could be important and that could help us to understand more about the effects of social media, which ones should be selected as a focus?

In general, you should select factors that

- have not been investigated before,
- will contribute to the understanding of the question you are asking,
- are available to investigate,
- hold some interest for you personally or professionally,
- lead to another question.

It is hard enough to define the nature of the problem you want to study (see Chapter 3) let alone generate questions that lead to more questions, but once you begin the journey of becoming a scientist, you are a member of an elite group who has the responsibility to contribute to the scientific literature not only by what you do but also by what you see that needs to be done.

Formulating a Hypothesis

When asked what she thought a hypothesis was, a 9-year-old girl said it best: "An educated guess." A **hypothesis** results when the questions are transformed into statements that express the relationships between variables such as an "if . . . then" statement.

For example, if the question is, "What effects does using Facebook have on the development of friendships?" then the hypothesis could be, adolescents who use Facebook as their primary means of maintaining social contact have fewer close friends. Several characteristics make some hypotheses better than others, and we will talk about those in Chapter 2.

For now, you should realize that a hypothesis is an objective extension of the question that was originally posed. Although all questions might not be answerable because of the way in which they are posed—which is fine for the question stage—a good hypothesis poses a question in a testable form. Good questions lead to good hypotheses, which in turn lead to good studies.

Collecting Relevant Information

Hypotheses should posit a clear relationship between different factors, such as a correlation between number of followers on Twitter and quality of social skills. That is the purpose of the hypothesis. Once a hypothesis is formulated, the next step is the collection of information or empirical data that will confirm or refute the hypothesis. So, if you are interested in whether or not participating in social media has an impact on adolescent's social skills, the kinds of data that will allow the hypothesis to be tested must be collected.

For example, you might collect two types of data to test the hypothesis mentioned in the previous paragraph. The first might be the number of friends an adolescent might have. The second might be the quality of those relationships.

An important point about testing hypotheses is that you set out to *test* them, not to *prove* them. As a good scientist, you should be intent on collecting data that reveal as much of the truth about the world as is possible and letting the chips fall where they may, whether you agree or disagree with the outcomes. Setting out to prove a hypothesis can place scientists in the unattractive position of biasing the methods for collecting data or the way in which study results are interpreted. If bias occurs, then the entire sequence of steps can fall apart. Besides, there's really no being "wrong" in science. Not having a hypothesis supported means only that there are additional questions to ask or that those which were asked should be reformulated. That is the beauty of good science—there is always another question to ask on the same topic—one that can shed just a bit more light. And who knows? That bit more light might be the tipping point or just the amount needed to uncover an entirely new and significant finding.

Testing the Hypothesis

Is it enough simply to collect data that relate to the phenomena being studied? Not quite. What if you have finished collecting data and find that adolescents who spend more than 10 hours a week involved in social media have 50% fewer qualitatively "good" relationships with peers than those who spend less than 10 hours? What would your conclusion be?

On one hand, you could say the adolescents who used social media more than 10 hours per week were one-half as sociable as other adolescents or had one-half the quality of relationships of the children who used social media less than 10 hours per week. On the other hand, you might argue that the difference between the two groups of adolescents is too large enough for you to reach any conclusion. You might conclude that in order for a statement about social media use and quality of friendships, you would have to have much greater differences in the quality of relationships.

Say hello to inferential statistics (see Chapter 8 for more), a set of tools that allows researchers to separate the effects of an isolated factor (such as time spent on Facebook) from differences between groups that might be owing to some other factor or to nothing other than **chance**. Yes, luck, fate, destiny, the wheels of fortune, or whatever you want to call what you cannot control, sometimes can be responsible for differences between groups.

For example, what if some of the adolescents participating in your study went to some kind of social function where there was a particularly strong emphasis on social media methods of communicating such as texting. Or, what if one of the adolescents just was afraid to truthfully report how much time he or she spent on Facebook during study time?

The job of all the tools that researchers have at their disposal (and the ones you will learn about throughout *Exploring Research*) is to help you separate the effects of the factors being studied (such as amount of time spent on Facebook) from other unrelated factors (such as the number of years a family has lived at its current address). What these tools allow researchers to do is assign a probability level to an outcome so that you can decide whether what you see is really due to what you think it is due to or something else which you leave for the next study.

Working with the Hypothesis

Once you have collected the required data and have tested the hypothesis, as a good scientist you can sit down, put up your feet, look intellectual, and examine the results. The results may confirm or refute the hypothesis. In either case, it is off to the races. If the data confirm your hypothesis, then the importance of the factors that were hypothesized to be related and conceptually important were borne out and you can go on your merry way while the next scientific experiment is being planned. If the hypothesis is not confirmed, it may very well be a time for learning something that was not known previously. In the example used earlier, it may mean that involvement in social media has no impact on social skills or social relationships. Although the researcher might be a bit disappointed that the initial hunch (formally called a hypothesis) was not supported, the results of a well-run study always provide valuable information, regardless of the outcome.

Reconsidering the Theory

Finally, it is time to take stock and relate all these research efforts to what guides our work in the first place: theory. Earlier in this chapter, a theory was defined as a set of statements that predict things that will occur in the future and explain things that have occurred in the past. But the very nature of theories is that they can be modified according to the results of research based on the same assumptions on which the theory is based.

For example, a particular approach to understanding the development of children and adults is known as social learning theory, which places special importance on the role of modeling and vicarious, or indirect, learning. According to this theory, exposure to aggressive behavior would lead to aggressive behavior once the environment contains the same kinds of cues and motivation that were present when the initial aggressive model (such as particularly unkind Facebook postings) was observed.

If the hypothesis that observing such models increases lack of civility is confirmed, then another building block, or piece of evidence, has been added to the house called social learning theory. Good scientists are always trying to see what type of brick (new information) fits where, or if it fits at all. In this way, new knowledge can change or modify the way the theory appears and what it has to say about human behavior. Consequently, new questions might be generated from the theory that will help contribute further to the way in which the house is structured.

Asking New Questions

In any case, the last step in this simple model of scientific inquiry is to ask a new question. It might be a simple variation on a theme (Do males use social media in a different way than females?) or a refinement of the original question (How might the use of social media differentially affect the social relationships of males and females?).

Whether or not the hypothesis is supported, good research leaves you farther along the trail to answering the original question. You just might be at a different place than you thought or intended to be.

TEST YOURSELF

Hypothesis plays a very important role in scientific research, with one of them being the objective testing of a particular question that a scientist might want to ask. What are some of the factors that might get in the way of the scientist remaining objective and what impact might that have on a fair test of the hypothesis of interest? What is the danger of not being aware of these biases?

Different Types of Research

By now, you have a good idea what research is and how the research process works. Now it is time to turn your attention to a description and examples of different types of research methods and the type of questions posed by them.

The types of research methods that will be discussed differ primarily on three dimensions: (1) the nature of the question asked, (2) the method used to answer it, and (3) the degree of precision the method brings to answering the question. One way in which these methods do not necessarily differ, however, is in the content or the focus of the research.

In other words, if you are interested in the effects of the use of social media on adolescents' friendships, your research may be experimental, where you artificially restrict access to social media and look at friendship outcomes, or nonexperimental, where you survey a group of adolescents to determine the frequency of use of social media tools.

A summary of the two general categories of research methods (nonexperimental versus experimental), which will be discussed in this volume, is shown in Table 1.1. This table illustrates the purpose of each category, the time frame that each encompasses, the degree of control the different method has over competing factors, "code" words that appear in research articles that can tip you off as to the type of research being conducted, and an example of each. Chapters 9–12 discuss in greater detail each of these research methods.

There is one very important point to keep in mind when discussing different methods used in research. As often as not, as research becomes more sophisticated and researchers (like you in the future) become better trained, there will be increased reliance on mixed methods models, where both experimental and nonexperimental methods are combined. Some researchers feel that this type of approach lacks clarity and precision, but others feel it is the best way to look at a phenomenon of interest from a variety of perspectives and thereby be more informative.

Nonexperimental Research

Nonexperimental research examines the relationship between variables, without any attention to cause-and-effect relationships.

Nonexperimental research includes a variety of different methods that describe relationships between variables. The important distinction between nonexperimental methods and the others you will learn about later is that nonexperimental research methods do not set out, nor can they test, any causal relationships between variables. For example, if you wanted to survey the social media–using behavior of adolescents, you could do so by having them maintain a diary in which they record what tools they use and for how long.

	Types of Research					
	Nonexperimental				Experimental	
	Descriptive	Historical	Correlational	Qualitative	True Experimental	Quasi-experimental
Purpose	Describe the characteristics of an existing phenomenon	Relate events that have occurred in the past to current events	Examine the relationships between variables	To examine human behavior and the social, cultural, and political contexts within which it occurs	To test for true cause-and-effect relationships	To test for causal relationships without having full control
Time frame	Current	Past	Current or past (correlation) Future (prediction)	Current or past	Current	Current or past
Degree of control over factors or precision	None or low	None or low	Low to medium	Moderate to high	High	Moderate to high
Code words to look for in research articles	Describe Interview Review literature	Past Describe	Relationship Related to Associated with Predicts	Case study Evaluation Ethnography Historical Research Survey	Function of Cause of Comparison Between Effects of	Function of Cause of Comparison between Effects of
Example	A survey of dating practices of adolescent girls	An analysis of Freud's use of hypnosis as it relates to current psychotherapy practices	An investigation that focuses on the relationship between the number of hours of television watching and grade-point average	A case study analysis of the effectiveness of policies for educating all children	The effect of a preschool language program on the language skills of inner-city children	Gender differences in spatial and verbal abilities

Table 1.1   Summary of research methods covered in *exploring research*.

This descriptive study provides information about the *content* of their online behaviors but tells you little about *why* they may do what they do. In this type of a research endeavor, you are not trying to understand the motivation for using what online tools are used nor are you trying to manipulate their use or content of the communication or any other outcome. This is nonexperimental in nature because no cause-and-effect relationships of any type are being hypothesized or investigated.

Nonexperimental research methods that will be covered in this volume are descriptive, correlational, and qualitative. Descriptive and correlational methods will be covered in Chapter 9, and qualitative methods will be discussed in Chapter 10. The following is a brief overview of each.

Descriptive Research

Descriptive research describes the characteristics of an existing phenomenon. The every 10-year U.S. Census is an example of descriptive research as is any survey that assesses the current status of anything from the number of faucets in a house to the number of adults over 60 years of age who have grandchildren.

What can be done with this information? First, it provides a broad picture of a phenomenon you might be interested in exploring. For example, if you are interested in learning more about the reading process in children, you might want to consult *The Reading Report Card* (at http://nces.ed.gov/nationsreportcard/reading/). This annual publication summarizes information about the reading achievement of children ages 9, 13, and 17 years. Or you might want to consult a publication of the Centers for Disease Control and Prevention, the *Morbidity and Mortality Weekly Report* (at http://www.cdc.gov/mmwr/), to determine the current incidence of measles cases in the Midwest, or the Bureau of Labor Statistics (at http://www.bls.gov/) to determine the current unemployment rate and the number of working single parents who have children under age 5 (about 60%). If you want to know it, there is a place to find it. Descriptive research demands this type of information.

In another example, Eleanor Hanna, Hsiao-ye Yi, Mary Dufour, and Christine Whitmore (2001) examined the relationship of early smoking to alcohol use, depression, and drug use in adolescence. They used descriptive statistics and other statistical techniques to find that in comparison with those who never smoked, or those who simply experimented, early smokers were those most likely to use alcohol and other drugs as well as have school problems and early sexual experiences culminating in pregnancy.

Descriptive research can stand on its own, but it can also serve as a basis for other types of research in that a group's characteristics often need to be described before the meaningfulness of any differences can be addressed. And almost always descriptive data is collected but as the first step of many on the way to a more complex study. Want to describe an outcome? Learn about descriptive techniques.

Correlational Research

Descriptive and **historical research** provide a picture of events that are currently happening or have occurred in the past. Researchers often want to go beyond mere description and begin discussing the relationship that certain events might have to one another. The most likely type of research to answer questions about the relationship among variables or events is called correlational research.

What **correlational research** does, which neither descriptive nor historical research does, is to provide some indication as to how two or more things are related to one another or, in effect, what they share or have in common, or how well a specific outcome might be predicted by one or more pieces of information.

Correlational research uses a numerical index called the **correlation coefficient** (see Chapter 9 for a complete discussion) as a measure of the strength of this relationship. Most correlational studies report such an index when available.

Descriptive research focuses on events that occur in the present.

Correlational research examines the relationship between variables.

If you were interested in finding out the relationship between the number of hours that first-year students spend studying and their grade-point averages, then you would be doing correlational research, because you are interested in the relationship between these two variables. If you were interested in finding out the best set of predictors of success in graduate school, you would be doing a type of correlational research that includes prediction.

For example, in a study of culture, obesity stereotypes, self-esteem, and the "thin ideal," Klaczynski, Goold, and Mudry (2004) examined the relationships among negative stereotypes of obesity, and other variables such as perceptions of the causes of obesity and of control over weight and self-esteem. They found a negative correlation between beliefs in control over one's weight and self-esteem.

One of the most important points about correlational research is that while it examines relationships between variables, it in no way implies that one causes changes in the other. In other words, correlation and prediction examine associations but not causal relationships, wherein a change in one factor directly influences a change in another.

For example, it is a well-established fact that as the crime rate in a community increases, so does the level of ice cream consumption! What's going on? Certainly, no rational person would conclude that the two are causally related such that if ice cream were banned, no more crimes would occur. Rather, another variable, temperature, better explains the increased ice cream consumption and the increased crime rate (both rise when it gets warm). It might seem ridiculous that people would identify causality just because events are related, but you do not have to read far in the daily newspaper to discover that politicians can reach just such unwise conclusions.

Qualitative Research

Qualitative research methods (see Chapter 10) are placed in this general category of nonexperimental methods because they do not directly test for cause and effect and, for the most part, follow an entirely different paradigm than the experimental model.

> Qualitative research studies phenomena within the social and cultural context in which they occur.

The general purpose of qualitative research methods is to examine human behavior in the social, cultural, and political contexts in which they occur. This is done through a variety of tools, such as interviews, historical methods, case studies, and ethnography, and it usually results in qualitative (or nonnumerical) primary data. In other words, the qualitative researcher is more (but not only) interested in the contents of an interviewee's speech than in the number of times (frequency) a particular comment is made.

Qualitative research is relatively new to the social and behavioral sciences and, to a large extent, its increasing popularity is due to a degree of dissatisfaction with other available research methods. Some scientists feel that the traditional experimental model is too restrictive and narrow, preventing underlying and important factors and relationships from being revealed. What's so valuable about this set of tools is that it allows you to answer a whole new set of questions in a whole new way.

Experimental Research

You already know that correlational research can help to establish the presence of a relationship among variables, but it does not provide any reason to believe that variables are causally related to one another. How does one find out if characteristics, behaviors, or events are related in such a way that the relationship is a causal one? Two types of research can answer that question: true experimental research and quasi-experimental research.

> Experimental research examines the cause-and-effect relationship between variables.

True Experimental Research

True experimental research examines direct cause-and-effect relationships.

In the **true experimental research method**, participants are assigned to groups based on some criterion, often called the treatment variable or treatment condition. For example, let us say that you are interested in comparing the effects of two different techniques for reducing obsessive-compulsive behavior in adults. The first technique includes behavioral therapy, and the second one does not. Once adults are assigned to groups and the programs are completed, you will want to look for any differences between the two groups with regard to the effects of the therapy on the frequency of obsessive-compulsive behaviors. Because the nature of the groups is determined by the researcher, the researcher has complete control over the factors to which the adults are exposed.

This is the ideal model for establishing a cause-and-effect relationship because the researcher has clearly defined the possible cause (if indeed it results in some effect) and can keep very close tabs on what is happening. Most important, however, the researcher has complete control over the treatment.

In a quasi-experimental study, the researcher does not have such a high degree of control because people have already been indirectly assigned to those groups (e.g., social class, type of abuse, gender, and type of injury) for which you are testing the effects.

The distinction between experimental and other methods of research boils down to a matter of control. True experimental research designs (discussed in Chapter 11) isolate and control all the factors that could be responsible for any effects except the one of most interest.

For example, Fleming, Klein, and Corter (1992) examined the effects of participation in a social support group on depression, maternal attitudes, and behavior in new mothers. As part of the experimental design, the researchers divided 142 mothers into three groups. Group 1 received the intervention, Group 2 received the no-intervention condition, and Group 3 received a special group-by-mail intervention. The key point here is the manipulation (the key word in experimental designs) of the condition for each of the three groups. This research is true experimental because the researchers determined the nature of the treatment and who is assigned to each group. As you will learn, in a quasi-experimental study, the researcher has no control over the origin of group membership (male or female, black or white, etc.). The primary difference between quasi-experimental and true experimental research is that in the former, subjects are preassigned to groups. It's that simple.

Quasi-Experimental Research

Quasi-experimental studies also focus on cause and effect, but they use preassigned groups.

In **quasi-experimental research**, participants are *preassigned* to groups based on some predetermined characteristic or quality. Differences in gender, race, age, grade in school, neighborhood of residence, type of job, and even experiences are examples. These group assignments have already taken place *before the experiment begins*, and the researcher has no control over who is assigned to which group.

Let us say that you are interested in examining voting patterns as a function of neighborhood. You cannot change the neighborhood people live in, but you can use the quasi-experimental method to establish a causal link between residence and voting patterns. In other words, if you find that voting pattern and residence are related, then you can say with some degree of confidence (but not as much as with an experimental study) that there is a causal relationship between where one resides and how one votes.

The most important use of the quasi-experimental method occurs where researchers cannot, in good conscience, assign people to groups and test the effects of group membership on some other outcome. For example, researchers who are interested in reducing the impact of child abuse cannot "create" groups of abusers, but rather have to look at already established groups of people who are abusive. That's exactly what Mark Chaffin and his colleagues (2004) did when they assigned already (and that's the key word) physically abusive parents to one of three intervention conditions. They found a reduction in abusive behavior by parents who were assigned to parent–child interaction therapy.

Quasi-experimental research is also called *post hoc*, or after the fact, research because the actual research takes place after the assignment of groups (e.g., abusive versus nonabusive, employed versus unemployed, malnourished versus nonmalnourished, and male versus female). Because assignment has already taken place, the researcher has a high degree, but not the highest degree, of control over the cause of whatever effects are being examined. For the highest degree of control to occur, the true experimental model must be followed.

> Another phrase for *quasi-experimental research* is *post-hoc*, or after the fact.

TEST YOURSELF

We have briefly defined and discussed the different research methods that you will learn about later in *Exploring Research* in much greater detail. For now, answer this question. What determines the research method that a scientist should use to answer a question or test a hypothesis? Which research method described here best lends itself to questions you want answered?

What Research Method to Use When?

This is a beginning course and no one would expect you to be able to identify what type of research method was used in a particular study—at least not yet. You may have a very good idea if you understand what you just read about nonexperimental and **experimental research methods**, but it takes some experience to become really good at the identification process.

So, here is a little jump start in the form of a "cheat" sheet (shown in Figure 1.2). This is not a substitute for learning how to distinguish nonexperimental from experimental **research designs**—it's just a good way to get started and a bit of a help when you need it. Note that an alternative to any nonexperimental method is a qualitative approach (which is not shown in Figure 1.2).

Basic Research Versus Applied Research

> Both basic and applied research are critical parts of studying and understanding a wide range of phenomena.

Sometimes in the research world, distinctions must be made not only about the type of research but also about the most general category into which the implications or utility of the research might fall. This is where the distinction between basic and applied research comes in. But beware! This distinction is sometimes used as a convenient way to classify research activity rather than to shed light on the intent or purpose of the researcher and the importance of the study.

The most basic distinction between the two types of research is that **basic research** (sometimes called pure research) is research that has no immediate application at the time it is completed, whereas **applied research** does. If this appears to be a somewhat ambiguous distinction, it is, because almost all basic research eventually results in some worthwhile application over the long term. In fact, the once easy distinction between the two is slowly disappearing.

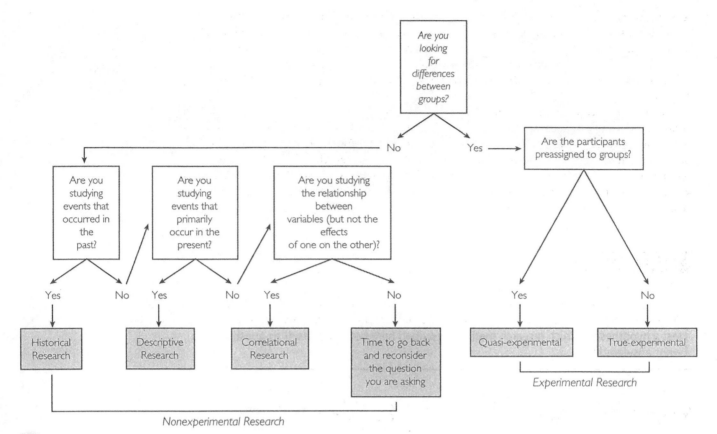

Figure 1.2 Research design "cheat" sheet.

For example, for every dollar spent on the basic research that supported the lunar missions during the 1960s and 1970s, $6 were returned in economic impact. Data from basic research that hypothesizes a relationship between Alzheimer's disease in older people and Down's syndrome (a genetic disorder) in younger people could eventually prove to be the critical finding that leads to a cure for both conditions. Another example: Who cares if some children have a more difficult time than others do in distinguishing between two very similar stimuli? You do, if you want to teach these children how to read. Many different reading programs have grown directly from such basic research efforts.

Never judge the quality of either the finished product or the worth of supporting a research project by branding it as basic or applied research. Rather, look closely at its content and judge it on its merit. This approach obviously has been used, because more and more reports about basic research (at one time beyond the interests of everyday practitioners) appear in such practitioner-oriented professional journals as *Phi Delta Kappan* and the *APA Monitor*, as well as the Sunday *New York Times Magazine*, *Newsweek*, *Science News*, and *American Scientist*. And the results of applied research are those that policy makers look to when formulating position papers.

TEST YOURSELF

Why are both basic and applied research essential to the scientific community as well as to the public community that it serves? What do you think an educated or informed citizen should know about how the research process works? What five questions might he or she be able to answer?

Summary

Great! You have finished the first chapter of *Exploring Research*, and hopefully you now have a good idea about what research is (and isn't), what the purpose of research is, and some of the different ways in which research can be carried out. With this new information under your belt, let's turn to the next chapter, which focuses on some "researchese," or the language used by researchers, and how these new terms fit together with what you have learned here.

Exercises

1. The process of research never stands independently from the content of the research. As a student new to the field of research, and perhaps even to your own discipline (such as education, psychology, sociology, or nursing), answer the following questions:
   (a) What areas within your discipline especially interest you?
   (b) Who are some of the outstanding researchers in your field, and what is the focus of their work?
   (c) Of the different types of research described and discussed in this chapter, which one do you think best fits the type of research that is done in your discipline?

2. At this point in your studies, what do you find most intimidating about the research process? What is one thing you could do to make this part of the research process a little bit easier or more comfortable? In which part of conducting research are you most confident?

3. How do the terms "hypothesis" and "theory" differ in meaning?

4. Visit your college or university library and locate an article from a professional journal that describes a research study. Access it online, or as a hard copy. From the description of how scientific inquiry takes place (which you read about in this chapter), answer the following:
   (a) What is the primary question posed by the study?
   (b) What important factors are identified?
   (c) Is there a hypothesis stated? If so, what is it?
   (d) Describe how the information was collected.
   (e) How do the results of the study affect the original hypothesis?

5. Interview an active researcher on your campus and ask about this person's research activities, including:
   (a) The focus of this person's research interests.
   (b) Why this individual is interested in this area.
   (c) What the most exciting part of the research is.
   (d) What the least exciting part of the research is.
   (e) What impact the results of the research might have on this individual's particular discipline.
   (f) What studies this individual would like to see as follow-up studies to the research.

6. Select a discipline within the social and behavioral sciences, such as child development, social psychology, higher education, or health psychology. For the discipline you select, find a representative study that is quasi-experimental or experimental in nature. Write a one-paragraph description of the study. Do the same for a historical study.

7. This chapter contains several examples of preassigned groups used in quasi-experimental research (e.g., groups based on preassignment such as gender, race, grade in school, etc.). Name three more examples of preassigned groups appropriate for quasi-experimental research.

8. Research questions come from imagination and can be enriched by science, art, music, and literature. Identify a book you have read or a television show or movie you have watched. What kind of research question can you pull from this work? Here are some examples to get you started:

   "Pride and Prejudice" (Jane Austen): In what ways do perceptions of social status relate to choices in a relationship partner?

   "Clueless" (Amy Heckerling): How does an intervention involving vocabulary lessons, a new wardrobe, and instructions on which social groups to befriend affect ratings of popularity from fellow high school students?

9. Find a normal part of your daily routine about which to ask an "I wonder if . . ." question. For example, "I wonder if the amount of text messaging in the hour before bedtime affects the amount of time needed to fall asleep in adolescents."

10. In a fictitious correlational study, the results showed that age was related to strength, that is, as children get older, their strength increases. What is the problem with the statements that increased strength is caused by increasing age, or that the stronger you get the older you get?

11. Write down your definition of science. How would your definition of science differ from a student's in a similar class 25 years ago? How would your definition differ from that put forth by a physical (e.g., physics, chemistry) scientist, if it differs at all?

12. When trying to decide which scientific method to use when exploring a question, what is the best rule of thumb to go by?

13. Look for examples of editorials or research articles that present correlational evidence. Do the authors infer a cause-and-effect relationship in the correlation? Why might it be difficult for even seasoned researchers to avoid making this mistake?

14. Research often replicates findings made by others. What is the value in this process?

15. We live in a very complex world just filled with economic and social challenges. How can the research process help us solve or better understand some of those problems and issues?

16. Identify five attributes that characterize high-quality research.

17. A researcher who hypothesized that 6-year-old children of nonworking mothers have more advanced reading skills than those of 6-year-old children of working mothers found insignificant results. Based on this information and what you have learned about the field of research, answer the following questions:
    (a) What is a new research question the researcher could ask?
    (b) What is one step in between examining the results and asking the new research question that might point the researcher in the right direction?

18. Two characteristics of high-quality research are generalizability and the ability to contribute to the betterment of society. In other words, results from high-quality research, particularly applied research, can provide a meaningful answer to the question, "So What?" Read a research article and describe in one or two sentences how the research addresses the "So What?" question.

19. Explain the difference between historical, correlational, and quasi-experimental research.

20. Here's the question . . .
    What is the difference between achievement scores for a group of children born in Peoria and a group born in Croatia?
    Use Figure 1.2 to determine the method you should use.

Online. . .

Professional Organizations

Because someday you'll be a professional, there's no time like the present to get information about some professional societies and join as a student—it will never be cheaper. Here are some of the largest organizations and their Internet addresses:

- American Anthropology Association at http://www.aaanet.org/
- American Educational Research Association at http://www.aera.net/
- American Medical Association at http://www.ama-assn.org/
- American Psychological Association at http://www.apa.org/
- American Public Health Association at http://www.apha.org/
- National Association for the Education of Young Children at http://www.naeyc. org/
- American Nurses Association at www.nursingworld.org/
- American Association for the Advancement of Science at www.aaas.org/
- American Statistical Association at http://www.amstat.org
- American Psychiatric Association at http://www.psych.org
- American Pharmacists Association at http://www.pharmacist.com
- Council for Exceptional Children at http://www.cec.sped.org

❖ ❖ ❖ Chapter 2 ❖ ❖ ❖

The Research Process: Coming to Terms

From Problem to Solution

All you need to do is to identify an interesting question, collect some data, and poof!—instant research! Not quite. The model of scientific inquiry (discussed in Chapter 1) does a nice job of specifying the steps in the research process, but there is quite a bit more to the process than that.

At the beginning of this chapter, we will provide a real-life example of how the process actually takes place and how researchers begin with what they see as a problem (to be solved) and end with a solution (or the results) to that problem. Keep in mind, however, that the meanings of the words "problem" and "solution" go beyond solving a simple problem of the $2 + 2 = 4$ variety. Rather, the questions that researchers ask often reflect a more pressing social concern or economic issue. In addition, the results from a research study often provide the foundation for the next research endeavor.

We will look at an interesting study entitled "Maternal Employment and Young Adolescents' Daily Experiences in Single-Mother Families" (Duckett & Richards, 1989), which examines the impact of maternal employment on adolescent development. Although the study is more than 30 years old, it continues to effectively illustrate many of the ideas and concepts covered in this chapter.

One of the most creative things about this study is the way in which these researchers collected their data. They did not sit down and ask adolescents how they felt about this or that, but instead they tried to get an overall picture of their feelings outside of the laboratory setting. And as you will see, it's an early use of technology that provides some insight into how people were using new tools (no cell phones then, but pagers) to answer interesting questions.

Duckett and Richards studied 436 fifth through ninth graders and their mothers to determine the effects of a combination of issues that continue to receive considerable attention in the media. The general goal of the research (and the problem) was to understand better some of the factors and consequences that surround the large number of working mothers of adolescents.

To narrow their investigation, the researchers set out to learn about the general nature of the adolescents' experiences as a function of having a mother who works, as well as the quality of time that the adolescents spent with their mothers. Given that so many mothers (more than 50% of those with children under 18 years of age) from both single-parent and dual-parent families work outside the home, answers to questions like those posed by this study are becoming increasingly important in the formation of social and economic policies.

To obtain their answers, the researchers compared adolescents living with two parents (382, or 88%) with those adolescents who live with only their

WHAT YOU'LL LEARN ABOUT IN THIS CHAPTER:

- The path from formulating questions to seeking and finding solutions

- The difference between dependent and independent variables

- What a hypothesis is and how it works

- The importance of the null hypothesis

- The difference between the null hypothesis and the research hypothesis

- The characteristics of a good hypothesis

- The importance of samples and populations in the research process

- The definition of statistical significance

There are many different ways to answer a question, but often the simplest, most clever research plan is the best one.

mother (54, or 12%). However, to reach fully their goal of better understanding the effects of maternal employment, the researchers had to break down the group of children and parents even further into those children whose mothers worked part-time, those children with mothers who worked full-time, and those children with mothers who were unemployed.

When the groups were separated on these two factors (family configuration and employment status), the researchers could make a comparison within and between the six groups (all combinations of single-parent and two-parent families, with part-time employed, full-time employed, and unemployed mothers) and get the information they needed to answer the general questions posed.

Now comes the really creative part of the study. Duckett and Richards used a method called the experience sampling method previously developed by M. Csikszentmihalyi and R. Larson (1987). In accordance with this method, the adolescents participating in the study would carry electronic beepers. On an unpredictable schedule, they would receive a beep from "beep central" and would then stop what they were doing and complete a self-report form. They would do this for 1 week.

TEST YOURSELF

It's really interesting when new technologies have been adopted by social scientists to help them collect and analyze data. For example, there are few adolescents who don't have cell phones, and the capabilities of these cell phones are no longer limited to sending and receiving calls; cell phones are, in and of themselves, small computers that have GPS and multimedia capabilities. We'll discuss technology and the research process later in *Exploring Research*, but for now, what other new types of technology can you think of that might play a role in completing research? Any ideas as to what the future might bring? What other new technology can you think of that might also play a role in research?

A signal telling the participant to stop and complete the form was sent on an average of every 2 hours between 7:30 A.M. and 9:30 P.M., with a total of 49 signals sent for the week for each participant. In the course of 1 week, 49 separate forms were completed, which provided information about how participants felt at any particular moment. For 436 participants at 49 forms each, a total of 21,364 forms were completed, which is a hefty sample of adolescents' behavior!

What was contained on these self-report forms? The adolescents had to report on what the researchers call *affect* (happy–sad, cheerful–irritable, friendly–angry) and *arousal* (alert–drowsy, strong–weak, excited–bored). Each of these six items was rated on a scale of 1–7. For example, the participants might indicate a 4, meaning they felt "right in the middle of happy and sad at that moment in time." These six items could be completed in a short period of time, and an accurate picture of the adolescents' daily life could then be formed. Adolescents also had to respond to "What were you doing?" and "Whom were you with?" as well as to some questions about their perceptions of their parents' friendliness and their feelings while they were with their parents.

Duckett and Richards had an interesting comparison (single-parent versus dual-parent mothers who are unemployed or employed part-time or full-time) and a good-sized set of reactions from adolescents on which to base their analysis and discussion. To make sense of all this information, the researchers compiled and then applied some statistical tests (you will learn more about these later) to reach their conclusions, including the following:

- Children of working single mothers benefit in ways other than just in the provision of income.
- Maternal employment is related to positive parent–child interactions.
- Children of single mothers employed full-time felt friendliest toward their fathers.

This well-designed, straightforward study examined a question that bears on many issues that everyone from schoolteachers to employers needs to have answered. The study involved a more than adequate number of participants and used methods that directly focused on the type of information the researchers wanted. Although they did not answer every question about the relationship between maternal employment and adolescent development, the researchers did provide an important piece to the puzzle of understanding the effects of employment on growing children and changing families.

The researchers seemed to take a logical approach of going from a question that has some import for many groups in today's society and articulating it in such a way that it can be answered in a reasonable and efficient manner.

The issue of how children are affected by working parents is certainly still an important one, but the results of research, such as that summarized earlier, bring us closer to a solution to some of the questions posed by such work arrangements. To be the kind of researcher you want to be, you need to know the rules of the game (and the lingo) and follow them as did Duckett and Richards. This knowledge begins with an understanding of some basic vocabulary and ideas.

TEST YOURSELF

Think about how these two scientists used technology (in this case beepers) to help them collect data. Now, think of the technology that you use every day for a variety of personal communications and to access information, and see if you can think of a way that those tools could be used in a research setting.

The Language of Research

Significance levels. Null hypotheses. Independent variables. Factorial designs. Research hypotheses. Samples. Populations. Yikes!—that's a lot of new terms. But these and other new words and phrases form the basis for much of the communication that takes place in the research world. As with any endeavor, it is difficult to play the game unless you learn the rules. The rules begin here, with a basic understanding of the terminology used by researchers in their everyday activities. The rest of this chapter offers a language lesson of sorts. Once you become familiar with these terms, everything that follows in *Exploring Research* will be easier to understand and more useful. Each of the terms described and defined here will be used again throughout the book.

Many different terms are used in the research community, and the faster you become familiar with them, the easier the entire process will be to understand.

All About Variables

The word *variable* has several synonyms, such as *changeable* or *unsteady*. Our set of rules tells us that a **variable** is a noun, not an adjective, and represents a class of outcomes that can take on more than one value.

For example, hair color is a variable that can take on the values of red, brown, black, blond, and just about any other combination of primary colors as well. Other examples of variables would be height (expressed as short or tall, or 5 feet, 3 inches or 6 feet, 1 inch), weight (expressed as heavy or light, 128 pounds or 150 pounds), age at immunization (expressed as young or old, 6 weeks or 18 months), number of words remembered, time off work, political party affiliation, favorite type of M&Ms™, and so on. The one thing all these traits, characteristics, or preferences have in common is that the variable (such as political party affiliation) can take on any one of several values, such as Republican, Democrat, or Independent.

However, the more precisely that a variable is measured, the more useful the **measurement** is. For example, knowing that Rachael is taller than Gregory is useful, but knowing that Rachael is 5 feet, 11 inches and Gregory is 5 feet, 7 inches is even more useful.

Interestingly, variables that might go by the same name can take on different values. You could measure height in inches (60) or in rank (the tallest), for example—or be defined differently, depending on a host of factors, such as the purpose of the research or the characteristics of the participants. For example, consider the variable called intelligence. For one researcher, the definition might be scores on the Stanford–Binet Intelligence Test, whereas for another it might be scores on the Kaufman Assessment Battery. For Howard Gardner (1983), who believes in the existence of multiple intelligences, the definition might be performance in mathematics, music, or some physical activity. All of these variables represent the same general construct of intelligence, albeit assessed in different ways.

Variables are used for different purposes as well. For example, a variable such as average number of days hospitalized following surgery might be used as a measure of recovery from surgery. But, this same variable might be used to equalize initial differences in patients when the question becomes, "How much post-operative pain did patients experience?" Statistically removing (or controlling for) how long they stayed in the hospital after their surgery is a fancy and very cool technique for taking differences in length of hospital stay out of the equation.

The following paragraphs describe several types of variables, and Table 2.1 summarizes these types and what they do.

Dependent Variables

A **dependent variable** represents the measure that reflects the outcomes of a research study. For example, if you measure the difference between two groups of adults on how well they can remember a set of 10 single digits after a 5-hour period, the number of digits remembered is the dependent variable. Another example: If you are looking at the effect of parental involvement in school on children's grades, the grades that the children received would be considered a dependent variable.

> The dependent variable is that which is examined as the outcome of an experiment or a research project.

Think of a dependent variable as the outcome that may depend on the experimental treatment or on what the researcher changes or manipulates.

Type of Variable	Definition	Other Terms You Might See
Dependent	A variable that is measured to see whether the treatment or manipulation of the independent variable had an effect	• Outcome variable • Results variable • Criterion variable
Independent	A variable that is manipulated to examine its impact on a dependent variable	• Treatment variable • Factor • Predictor variable
Control	A variable that is related to the dependent variable, the influence of which needs to be removed	• Restricting variable
Extraneous	A variable that is related to the dependent variable or independent variable that is not part of the experiment	• Threatening variable
Moderator	A variable that is related to the dependent variable or independent variable and has an impact on the dependent variable	• Interacting variable

Table 2.1 Different types of variables.

Independent Variables

An **independent variable** represents the treatments or conditions that the researcher has either *direct* or *indirect* control over to **test** their effects on a particular outcome. An independent variable is also known as a *treatment variable*—it is within this context that the term is most often used. An independent variable is manipulated in the course of an experiment to understand the effects of this manipulation on the dependent variable.

For example, you might want to test the effectiveness of three different reading programs on children's reading skills. This design is illustrated in Figure 2.1. Method A includes tutoring, Method B includes tutoring and rewards, and Method C includes neither tutoring nor rewards (these kids just spend some time with the teacher). In this example, the method of reading instruction is manipulated, and it is the independent variable. The outcome or dependent variable could be reading scores. This experiment includes three levels of one independent variable (method of teaching) and one dependent variable (reading score).

The direct and indirect distinction has to do with whether the researcher actually creates the levels (such as Method A, Method B, or Method C) or the levels are already naturally occurring and cannot be manipulated directly but can only be tested, such as differences in gender (we cannot very well assign that trait to people) or age groupings (we cannot make people younger or older).

So, what if you wanted to investigate whether there is a difference between males and females in their mathematics scores on some standardized test? In this example, the independent variable is gender (male or female), and the outcome or dependent variable is the mathematics score.

Or, you could look at the effects of the number of hours of weekly television-watching time (less than 25 hours for group A or 25 or more hours for group B) on language skills. Here, the amount of time watching television is the independent variable, and the level of language skills is the dependent variable.

The general rule to follow is that when the researcher is manipulating anything or assigning participants to groups based on some characteristic, such as age or ethnicity or treatment, that variable is the independent variable. When researchers look to some outcome to determine whether the grouping had an effect, then they look to the dependent variable.

In some cases, when researchers are not interested in looking at the effects of one thing on another, but only in how variables may be related, there are no independent variables. For example, if you are interested only in the relationship between the amount of time a father spends with his children and his job performance, nothing is manipulated, and, in a sense (but not everyone agrees), there are no variables that are independent of one another nor are there variables that are dependent upon others.

Independent variables must take on at least two levels or values (because they are variables) and variables, by definition, vary. For example, if a researcher were studying the effects of gender differences (the independent variable) on language development (the dependent variable), the independent variable would have two levels, male and

> The independent variable is that which is manipulated or changed to examine its effect upon the dependent variable.

Figure 2.1   Research designs can take on many different configurations. Here, the researcher is examining the effects of three different methods or levels of teaching reading on reading scores. Note that in the last method neither treatment is implemented, making it the control condition.

		Age (years)								
		3			5			7		
Social Class		High	Med.	Low	High	Med.	Low	High	Med.	Low
Gender	Male									
	Female									

Figure 2.2 Many experiments in the social and behavior sciences use more than one independent variable. In this particular example, there are three independent variables: two (what else?) levels of gender, three levels of age, and three levels of social class.

female. Similarly, if a researcher were investigating age differences in stress for people aged 30–39 years, 40–49 years, and 50–59 years, then the independent variable would be age, and it would have three levels.

What happens if you have more than one independent variable like we just described? Look at Figure 2.2, which represents a factorial design wherein gender, age, and social class are independent variables. **Factorial designs** are experiments that include more than one independent variable. Here are two levels of gender (male and female), three levels of age (3, 5, and 7 years), and three levels of social class (high, medium, and low), accounting for a 2 by 3 by 3 design for a total of 18 separate combinations of treatment conditions, or cells, of levels of independent variables. You can see that, as independent variables are added to a research design, the total number of cells increases rapidly.

Here's the key in understanding this way of noting variables and their levels.

If you see something like this . . .

$$3 \times 4$$

you can rest assured there are the same number of independent variables as there are numerals separated by the "x" which stand for "times" just as in simple multiplication. You can ignore the value of the number. So, for a 3×4, there are two independent variables (one for the "3" and one for the "4"). For each of these independent variables, the value of the number represents the number of levels. So, for this example, there are two independent variables, one having 3 levels and the other having 4. And, the total number of separate conditions? That's right, it's 12 since $3 \times 4 = 12$.

The Relationship Between Independent and Dependent Variables

This is really important and sure to be a question on your next test or quiz.

The best independent variable is one that is independent of any other variable that is being used in the same study. In this way, the independent variable can contribute the maximum amount of understanding beyond what other independent variables can offer. When variables compete to explain the effects, it is sometimes called **confounding**.

The best dependent variable is one that is sensitive to changes in the different levels of each independent variable; otherwise, even if the treatment had an effect, you would never know it.

TEST YOURSELF

Go back to the Duckett and Richards study and define what the independent and dependent variables are. According to the last paragraph in this section, why are the two independent variables a good choice?

Other Important Types of Variables

Independent and dependent variables are the two kinds of variables that you will deal with most often throughout *Exploring Research*. However, there are other variables that are important for you to know about as well, because an understanding of what they are and how they fit into the research process is essential for you to be an intelligent consumer and to have a good foundation as a beginning producer of research. The following are other types of variables that you should be familiar with (see Table 2.1).

A **control variable** is a variable that has a potential influence on the dependent variable; consequently, the influence must be removed or controlled. For example, if you are interested in examining the relationship between reading speed and reading comprehension, you may want to control for differences in intelligence, because intelligence is related both to reading speed and to reading comprehension. Intelligence must be held constant for you to get a good idea of the nature of the relationship between the variables of interest.

An **extraneous variable** is a variable that has an unpredictable impact upon the dependent variable. For example, if you are interested in examining the effects of television watching on achievement, you might find that the type of television programs watched is an extraneous variable that might affect achievement. Such programs as *Discovery, Nova,* and *Sesame Street* might have a positive impact on achievement, whereas other programs might have a negative impact.

A **moderator variable** is a variable that is related to the variables of interest (such as the dependent and independent variable), masking the true relationship between the independent and dependent variable. For example, if you are examining the relationship between crime rate and ice cream consumption, you need to include temperature because it moderates that relationship. Otherwise, your conclusions will be inaccurate.

Hypotheses

In Chapter 1, a hypothesis was defined as "an educated guess." Although a hypothesis reflects many other things, perhaps its most important role is to reflect the general problem statement or the question that was the motivation for undertaking the research study. That is why taking care and time with that initial question is so important. Such consideration can guide you through the creation of a hypothesis, which in turn helps you to determine the types of techniques you will use to test the hypothesis and answer the original question.

The "I wonder . . . " stage becomes the problem statement stage, which then leads to the study's hypothesis. Here is an example of each of these.

The Stage	An Example
"I wonder"	It seems to me that several things could be done to help our employees lower their high absentee rate. Talking with some of them tells me that they are concerned about after-school care for their children. I wonder what would happen if a program were started right here in the factory to provide child supervision and activities?
The hypothesis	Parents who enroll their children in after-school programs will miss fewer days of work in 1 year and will have a more positive attitude toward work as measured by the Attitude Toward Work (ATW) survey than parents who do not enroll their children in such programs.

A good hypothesis provides a transition from a problem statement or question into a form that is more amenable to testing using the research methods we are discussing. The following sections describe the two types of hypotheses—the null hypothesis and the research hypothesis—and how they are used, as well as what makes a good hypothesis.

The Null Hypothesis

The null hypothesis is a statement of equality.

A **null hypothesis** is an interesting little creature. If it could talk, it would say something like, "I represent no relationship between the variables that you are studying." In other words, null hypotheses are statements of equality such as,

- There will be no difference in the average score of ninth graders and the average score of twelfth graders on the ABC memory test.
- There is no relationship between personality type and job success.
- There is no difference in voting patterns as a function of political party.
- The brand of ice cream preferred is independent of the buyer's age, gender, and income.

A null hypothesis, such as the ones described here, would be represented by the following equation:

$$H_0 : \mu_9 = \mu_{12}$$

where: H_0 = the symbol for the null hypothesis

μ_9 = the symbol (the Greek letter *mu*) for the theoretical average for the population of ninth graders

μ_{12} = the symbol (the Greek letter *mu*) for the theoretical average for the population of twelfth graders.

The four null hypotheses listed earlier all have in common a statement of two or more things being equal or unrelated to each other.

What are the basic purposes of the null hypothesis? The null hypothesis acts as both a starting point and a benchmark against which the actual outcomes of a study will be measured. Let's examine each of these purposes.

First, the null hypothesis *acts as a starting point* because it is the state of affairs that is accepted as true in the absence of other information. For example, let's look at the first null hypothesis stated earlier in the list: There will be no difference in the average score of ninth graders and the average score of twelfth graders on the ABC memory test. Given no other knowledge of ninth and twelfth graders' memory skills, you have no reason to believe there will be differences between the two groups. You might speculate as to why one group might outperform another, but if you have no evidence a priori (before the fact), then what choice do you have but to assume that they are equal? This lack of a relationship, unless proved otherwise, is a hallmark of the method being discussed. In other words, until you prove that there is a difference, you have to assume that there is no difference.

Furthermore, if there are any differences between these two groups, you have to assume that the differences are due to the most attractive explanation for differences between any groups on any variable: chance! That's right; given no other information, chance is always the most likely explanation for differences between two groups. And what is chance? It is the random variability introduced as a function of the individuals participating as well as many unforeseen factors.

For example, you could take a group of soccer players and a group of football players and compare their running speeds. But who is to know whether some soccer players practice more, or if some football players are stronger, or if both groups are receiving additional training? Furthermore, perhaps the way their speed is being measured leaves room for chance; a faulty stopwatch or a windy day can contribute to differences unrelated to *true* running speed.

As good researchers, our job is to eliminate chance as a factor and to evaluate other factors that might contribute to group differences, such as those that are identified as independent variables.

The second purpose of the null hypothesis is to *provide a benchmark against which observed outcomes can be compared* to determine whether these differences are caused by chance or by some other factor. The null hypothesis helps to define a range within which any observed differences between groups can be attributed to chance (which is the contention of the null hypothesis) or whether they are due to something other than chance (which perhaps would be the result of the manipulation of the independent variable).

Most correlational, quasi-experimental, and experimental studies have an implied null hypothesis; historical and descriptive studies may not. For example, if you are interested in the growth of immunization during the last 70 years (historical) or how people feel about school vouchers (descriptive), then you are probably not concerned with positing a null hypothesis.

The Research Hypothesis

Whereas a null hypothesis is a statement of no relationship between variables, a **research hypothesis** is a definite statement of the relationship between two variables. For example, for each of the null hypotheses stated earlier, there is a corresponding research hypothesis. Notice that I said "a" and not "the" corresponding research hypothesis, because there can certainly be more than one research hypothesis for any one null hypothesis. Here are some research hypotheses that correspond with the null hypotheses mentioned earlier.

> Research hypotheses are statements of inequality.

- The average score of ninth graders is different from the average score of twelfth graders on the ABC memory test.
- There is a relationship between personality type and job success.
- Voting patterns are a function of political party.
- The brand of ice cream preferred is related to the buyer's age, gender, and income.

Each of these four research hypotheses has one thing in common: They are all statements of *inequality*. Unlike the null hypothesis, these research hypotheses posit a relationship between variables, not an equality. The nature of this inequality can take two different forms: directional and nondirectional.

If the research hypothesis posits no direction to the inequality (such as "different from"), then the research hypothesis is a nondirectional research hypothesis.

If the research hypothesis posits a direction to the inequality (such as "more than" or "less than"), then the research hypothesis is a directional research hypothesis.

The Nondirectional Research Hypothesis

A **nondirectional research hypothesis** reflects a difference between groups, but the direction of the difference is not specified. For example, the research hypothesis *The average score of ninth graders is different from the average score of twelfth graders on the ABC memory test* is nondirectional in that the direction of the difference between the two groups is not specified. The hypothesis states only that there is a difference and says nothing about the *direction* of that difference. It is a research hypothesis because a difference is hypothesized, but the nature of the difference is not specified.

A nondirectional research hypothesis such as the one described here would be represented by the following equation:

$$H_1 : \overline{X}_9 \neq \overline{X}_{12}$$

where: H_1 = the symbol for null hypothesis

$\overline{X}_{12}$ = the average memory score for twelfth graders

$\neq$ = the inequality symbol or the not equal symbol

$\overline{X}_{12}$ = the average memory score for ninth graders

The Directional Research Hypothesis

A **directional research hypothesis** reflects a difference between groups, and the direction of the difference is specified. For example, the research hypothesis *The average score of twelfth graders is greater than the average score of ninth graders on the ABC memory test* is directional, because the direction of the difference between the two groups is specified—one group's score is hypothesized to be greater than the other.

Directional hypotheses can take the following forms:

- A is greater than B (or A > B)
- B is greater than A (or B > A)

These both represent inequalities. A directional research hypothesis, such as the one described earlier wherein twelfth graders are hypothesized to score better than ninth graders, would be represented by the following equation:

$$H_1 : \overline{X}_{12} > \overline{X}_9$$

where: H_1 = the symbol for (the first of possible) research hypothesis

$\overline{X}_{12}$ = the average memory score for twelfth graders

$>$ = the greater-than sign

$\overline{X}_9$ = the average memory score for ninth graders

What is the purpose of the research hypothesis? It is this hypothesis that is tested directly as one step in the research process. The results of this test are compared with what you expect by chance alone (reflecting the null hypothesis) to see which of the two explanations is the more attractive one for observed differences between groups.

But do beware of one thing. Beginning researchers often start out to *prove* a research hypothesis. As good scientists, we are not to be swayed by our own too personal beliefs and prejudices. Rather than setting out to prove anything, we set out to *test* the hypothesis.

Differences Between the Null Hypothesis and the Research Hypothesis

Other than the fact that the null hypothesis represents an equality and the research hypothesis represents an inequality, there are several important differences between these two types of hypotheses.

First, the null hypothesis states that there is *no relationship between variables* (an equality), whereas the research hypothesis states that there is a relationship (an inequality).

Second, null hypotheses *always refer to the population*, whereas research hypotheses always refer to the *sample*. As you will read later in this chapter, researchers select a sample of participants from a much larger population. It is too expensive, and often impossible, to work with the entire population and thus directly test the null hypothesis.

Third, because the entire population cannot be directly tested (again, it is impractical, uneconomical, and often impossible), *you can never really say that there is actually no difference between groups* (or an inequality) on a specified dependent variable (if you accept the null hypothesis). Rather, you have to infer it (indirectly) from the results of the test of the research hypothesis, which is based on the sample. Hence, the null hypothesis is indirectly tested, whereas the research hypothesis is directly tested.

Fourth, null hypotheses are always stated using Greek symbols (such as μ or *mu* for the average), whereas research hypotheses are always stated using Roman symbols (such as $\overline{X}$ for the average), as illustrated just a few pages ago.

Finally, because you cannot directly test the null hypothesis (remember that you rarely will have access to the total population), it is an implied hypothesis. The research hypothesis, on the other hand, is explicit. It is for this reason that you rarely see null hypotheses stated in research reports, whereas you almost always see the research hypothesis.

What Makes a "Good" Hypothesis?

Hypotheses are educated guesses. Some guesses are better than others right from the start. I cannot stress enough how important it is to ask the question you want answered and to keep in mind that any hypothesis you present is a direct extension of the original question you asked. This question will reflect your own personal interests as well as previous research.

> Good hypotheses are declarative in nature and posit a very clear and unambiguous relationship between variables.

With that in mind, here are some criteria you might use to decide whether a hypothesis you read in a research report or the ones you formulate are acceptable. Let's use an example of a study that examines the effects of after-school child-care programs for employees who work late on the parents' adjustment to work. The following is a well-written hypothesis:

> *Parents who enroll their children in after-school programs will miss fewer days of work in one year and will have a more positive attitude toward work as measured by the Attitude Toward Work (ATW) Survey than parents who do not enroll their children in such programs.*

Here are the criteria we want to apply to a "good" hypothesis:

1. A good hypothesis is *stated in declarative form*, not as a question. Hypotheses are most effective when they make a clear and forceful statement.
2. A good hypothesis *posits an expected relationship between variables*. The example hypothesis clearly describes the relationship between after-school child care, the parents' attitude, and the absentee rate. These variables are being tested to determine whether one (enrollment in the after-school program) has an effect upon the others (absentee rate and attitude).

   Notice the word "expected" in the second criterion? Defining an expected relationship is intended to prevent the "fishing-trip approach" (sometimes called the "shotgun approach") which may be tempting to take but is not very productive. In the fishing-trip approach, you throw out your line and pull in anything that bites. You collect data on as many things as you can, regardless of your interest or even whether collecting the data is a reasonable part of the investigation. Or, put another way, you load up the guns and blast away at anything that moves. You are bound to hit something. The problem is that you may not want what you hit and, worse, you may miss what you want to hit—even worse (if possible), you may not know what you hit!

Good researchers do not want just anything they can catch or shoot—they want specific results. To get such results, researchers must formulate their opening questions and hypotheses in a manner that is clear, forceful, and easily understood.

3. Hypotheses *reflect the theory or literature upon which they are based.* As you read in Chapter 1, the accomplishments of scientists can rarely be attributed to their hard work alone. Their accomplishments also are due to the work of many other researchers who have come before them and laid a framework for later explorations. A good hypothesis reflects this; it has a substantive link to existing literature and theory. In the previous example, let's assume that the literature indicates that parents who know their children are being cared for in a structured environment can be more productive at work. Knowledge of this would allow a researcher to hypothesize that an after-school program would provide parents the security they are looking for, which in turn allows them to concentrate on work rather than on awaiting a phone call to find out whether Max or Sophie got home safely.

4. A hypothesis should be *brief and to the point.* Your hypothesis should describe the relationship between variables in a declarative form and be as succinct (to the point) as possible. The more succinct the statement, the easier it will be for others (such as your master's thesis committee members) to read your research and understand exactly what you are hypothesizing and what the important variables are. In fact, when people read and evaluate research (as you will learn more about later in this chapter), the first thing many of them do is read the hypotheses so they can get a good idea of the general purpose of the research and how things will be done. A good hypothesis defines both these things.

5. Good hypotheses are *testable* hypotheses. This means that you can actually carry out the intent of the question reflected in the hypothesis. You can see from the sample hypothesis that the important comparison is between parents who have enrolled their child in an after-school program with those who have not. Then, such things as attitude and number of workdays missed will be measured. These are both reasonable objectives. Attitude is measured by the ATW Survey (a fictitious title, but you get the idea), and absenteeism (the number of days away from work) is an easily recorded and unambiguous measure. Think how much harder things would be if the hypothesis were stated as *Parents who enroll their children in after-school care feel better about their jobs.* Although you might get the same message, the results might be more difficult to interpret given the ambiguous nature of words such as "feel better."

In sum, complete and well-written hypotheses should:

- be stated in declarative form
- posit a relationship between variables
- reflect a theory or a body of literature upon which they are based
- be brief and to the point
- be testable

When a hypothesis meets each of these five criteria, then it is good enough to continue with a study that will accurately test the general question from which the hypothesis was derived.

TEST YOURSELF

Hypotheses are absolutely critical to the scientific process, and we reviewed several reasons why and reviewed the hypothesis' relationship to chance. What is that relationship and in general why is it important to the scientific process?

Samples and Populations

As a good scientist, you would like to be able to say that if Method A is better than Method B, this is true forever and always and for all people. Indeed, if you do enough research on the relative merits of Methods A and B and test enough people, you may someday be able to say that, but it is unlikely. Too much money and too much time (all those people!) are required to do all that research.

However, given the constraints of limited time and limited research funds which almost all scientists live with, the next best strategy is to take a portion of a larger group of participants and do the research with that smaller group. In this context, the larger group is referred to as a **population**, and the smaller group selected from a population is referred to as a **sample**.

Samples should be selected from populations in such a way that you maximize the likelihood that the sample represents the population as much as possible. The goal is to have the sample resemble the population as much as possible. The most important implication of ensuring similarity between the two is that, once the research is finished, the results based on the sample can be generalized to the population. When the sample does represent the population, the results of the study are said to be generalizable or to have **generalizability**.

The various types of sampling procedures are discussed in Chapter 4.

> Our goal is to select a sample from a population that most closely matches the characteristics of that population.

TEST YOURSELF

It's important that samples be representative of the populations from which they came. Provide an example of a population and a sample from that population. How would you know that the sample is representative?

The Concept of Significance

There is probably no term or concept that represents more confusion for the beginning student than that of **statistical significance**. This term is explained in detail in Chapter 8, but it is important to be exposed to the term early in *Exploring Research* because it is a basic and major component of understanding the research process.

At the beginning of this chapter, you read a simple overview of a study wherein two researchers examined the differences between adolescents whose mothers work and adolescents whose mothers do not (as well as family status, but for this example let's stick with the employed and not employed groups).

Let's modify the meaning of "differences" to include the adjective "significant." Here, significant differences are the differences observed between adolescents of mothers who work and of those who do not that are due to some influence and do not appear just by chance. In this example, that influence is whether the mothers work. Let's assume that other factors that might account for any differences were controlled for. Thus, the only thing left to account for the differences between adolescents is whether or not the mothers work. Right? Yes. Finished? Not quite.

Because the world and you and I and the research process are not perfect, one must allow for some leeway. In other words, you need to be able to say that, although you are pretty sure the difference between the two groups of adolescents is due to the mothers' working, you cannot be absolutely, 100%, positively, unequivocally, indisputably (get the picture?) sure.

Why? There are many different reasons. For example, you could just be wrong (horrors!). Maybe during this one experiment, differences were not due to the group the

> Significance is a measure of how much risk we are willing to take when reaching a conclusion about the relationship between variables.

adolescents were in but to some other factor that was inadvertently not accounted for, such as out-of-home experiences. What if the people in one group were mostly adolescent boys and reacted quite differently than the people in the other group, mostly adolescent girls? If you are a good researcher and do your homework, such differences between groups are unlikely outcomes, but possible ones nonetheless. This factor (gender) and others certainly could have an impact on the outcome or dependent variable and, in turn, have an impact on the final results and the conclusion you reach.

So, what to do? In most scientific endeavors that involve proposing hypotheses and examining differences between groups, there is bound to be a certain amount of error that simply cannot be controlled. **Significance level** is the risk associated with not being 100% confident that the difference is caused by what you think and may be due to some unforeseen factor. If you see that a study resulted in significant findings at the .05 level (it looks like this in journal articles and scientific reports $p < .05$), the translation is that a chance of less than 1 in 20 (or .05 or 5%) exists that any differences found between the groups were not due to the hypothesized reason (the independent variable in the case of a comparison between two groups) but to some other unknown reason or reasons. This number is actually an indirect measure of chance. As you will see in Chapter 8 new data analysis computer programs have gone a step further and rather than defining a range of probability (such as less than .05 or less than 5%), they assign a specific probability (such as .042 or 4.2%).

As a good scientist, your job is to reduce this likelihood as much as possible by accounting for all the competing reasons, other than the one you are testing, for any differences that you observed. Because this is possible in theory only and you cannot fully eliminate the likelihood of other factors, you account for these other factors by assigning them a level of probability and report your results with that caveat.

So even if you are quite sure that your findings reflect the "truth," the good scientist is neither so arrogant nor so confident that he or she cannot admit there is a chance of error. The probability that error may occur is what we mean by significance. We get into a much more detailed discussion of this in Chapter 8.

TEST YOURSELF

You're going to see the word *significance* a lot in *Exploring Research* and learn a good deal more about it. What is the relationship between a significant finding and the likelihood that the finding is due to chance?

Summary

That wraps up some vocabulary and provides you with a basic knowledge for understanding most of the important terms used in the research process, terms that you will see and use throughout the rest of *Exploring Research*. Being familiar with these terms will provide a foundation for a better understanding during subsequent chapters. If you are unsure about the meaning of a certain term, refer back to this chapter for a refresher course or consult the glossary at the end of the book.

Exercises

1. In the following examples, identify the independent and dependent variable(s):
   (a) Two groups of children were given different types of physical fitness programs to determine whether the programs had an effect on their strength.

    (b)   A group of 100 heavy smokers was divided into five groups, and each group participated in a different smoking-cessation program. After 6 months of program participation, the number of cigarettes each participant smoked each day was counted.

    (c)   A university professor was interested in determining the best way to teach introductory psychology and ensure that his students would learn the material.

2. For the following situations name at least one independent variable (and the levels of that variable) and one dependent variable.

    (a)   A research project where the topic of interest is achievement.

    (b)   A research project where the topic of interest is voting preferences in the presidential election.

    (c)   A research project where the topic is recovery rate in a drug and alcohol rehabilitation program.

3. What is another name for "outcome variable"?

4. Why is the null hypothesis always a statement of equality? Why can the research hypothesis take on many different forms?

5. Write the null and research hypotheses for the following description of a research study:

      A group of middle-aged men was asked to complete a questionnaire on their attitudes toward work and family. Each of these men is married and has at least two children. Another group of men with no children also completed the same survey.

6. Write the null and a directional research hypothesis for the following description of a research study:

      A pediatrician was comparing the effects of an early intervention program during children's first 3 years of life and the impact that program might have on academic achievement on grade school competency tests.

7. Name two advantages of having a hypothesis that is linked to existing literature and theory.

8. Why is having a hypothesis with an expected outcome better practice than a "fishing-trip" approach?

9. No one would argue that defining variables clearly and in an unambiguous manner is critical to good research. With that in mind, work as a group and define the following variables. Keep track of how different people's definitions reflect their personal views of what the variable represents, and note how easy it is to define some variables and how difficult it is to define others.

    (a)   Intelligence

    (b)   Height

    (c)   Social skills

    (d)   Age

    (e)   Aggressiveness

    (f)   Conservatism

    (g)   Alcohol consumption

    (h)   Street smarts

    (i)   Personality

Be sure to note that even those variables that appear to be easy to define (e.g., height) can take on different meanings and definitions (tall, 5 feet 1 inch, awesome) as well.

10. What is statistical significance and why is it important?

11. A researcher spent 5 years on a project, and the majority of the findings were not significant. How can the lack of significant results still make an important contribution to the field?

12. A researcher interested in the use of energy in Howard County households makes survey phone calls to every 10th household listed in the county phonebook. In this example, assuming every household contacted participates in the survey:
    (a) What is the sample?
    (b) What is the population?

13. Indicate which of the following are variables and which are constants:
    (a) Lew's hair color
    (b) Age in years
    (c) Number of windows in your residence
    (d) Color of the late-model car parked in front of the building
    (e) What time it is right now
    (f) Number of possible correct answers on this week's quiz
    (g) Number of signers of the Declaration of Independence
    (h) Name of the fifth girl in the third row
    (i) Today's date
    (j) Number of words remembered on a memory test

14. The principal of an elementary school wants to know how well her 600 students like the school. She hires a researcher, who gives a "satisfaction with school" survey to three different third-grade classes.
    (a) How could the use of a sample like this threaten the value of the study's outcomes??
    (b) How might the flawed sample affect the usefulness of the results?

15. Two researchers complete projects looking at the relationship between the amount of time studied and performance on a science test. Researcher A's results state that "John performed better than Lisa, who performed better than Drew." Researcher B's results state that "John earned a 97%, Lisa earned a 96%, and Drew earned a 71%." Between Researcher A and Researcher B, who has the best way of measuring the dependent variable of test performance? Why?

16. A researcher from Louisiana hypothesizes that people living out in the country display fewer avoidance strategies under stress than do people living in large cities. To test his hypothesis, he completes research with a group of participants from New Orleans and a group of participants from Church Point, Louisiana, and finds support for his hypothesis. However, he later learns that most of the participants from New Orleans were there during Hurricane Katrina. In this example, the experience of Hurricane Katrina is considered what type of variable?

17. Go to the library and locate three journal articles in your area of interest which are experimental in nature (where groups are compared). Do the following:
    (a) Identify the independent and dependent variables.

(b) For each dependent variable, specify how it is going to be measured and whether it is clearly defined.

(c) For each independent variable, identify the number of levels of that variable. What other independent variables would you find of interest to study?

18. What makes a good hypothesis?

Online . . .

Seven Golden Steps

The librarians at Cornell University bring you the Seven Steps of the Research Process at http://www.library.cornell.edu/okuref/research/skill1.htm. These steps are similar to those outlined in this chapter but just a bit different, and they give you another view of what's important and why.

The Research Process Helper

The Research Process Helper at http://www3.sympatico.ca/sandra.hughes/sandra. hughes/research/default.html brings you Sandra Hughes' four-step approach to the research process, including preparing, accessing, professing, and transferring information and data. It's a nice place to begin your quest for the project that's just right for you.

How to Conduct Research
wikiHow has outlined the research process with steps, tips, tools, and potential barriers at http://www.wikihow.com/Conduct-Scientific-Research

Research 101
The University of Washington Libraries has created a tutorial, complete with exercises to quiz you on your knowledge about the research process. The tutorial is available at http://www.lib.washington.edu/uwill/research101/index.html

❖ ❖ ❖ Chapter 3A ❖ ❖ ❖

Selecting a Problem and Reviewing the Research

So here you are, in the early part of a course that focuses on research methods, and now you have to come up with a problem that you are supposed to be interested in! You are probably so anxious about learning the material contained in your professor's lectures and what is in this volume that you barely have time to think about anything else.

If you stop for a moment and let your mind explore some of the issues in the behavioral and social sciences that have piqued your interest, you will surely find something that you want to know more about. That is what the research process is all about—finding out more about something that is, in part, already known.

Once you select an area of interest, you are only part of the way there. Next comes the statement of this interest in the form of a research question followed by a formal hypothesis. Then it is on to reviewing the literature, a sort of fancy phrase that sounds like you will be very busy! A literature review involves library time online or actually there, note taking, and organizational skills (and of course writing), but it provides a perspective on your question that you cannot get without knowing what other work has been done as well as what new work needs to be done.

But hold on a minute! How is someone supposed to have a broad enough understanding of the field and spew forth well-formed hypotheses before the literature is reviewed and then become familiar with what is out there? As poet John Ciardi wrote, therein "lies the rub."

The traditional philosophers and historians of science would have us believe that the sequence of events leading up to a review of what has been done before (as revealed in the literature) is as shown in Figure 3A.1a. This sequence of steps is fine in theory, but as you will discover, the actual process does not go exactly in the manner shown in the figure.

The research question and research hypothesis are more an outgrowth of an interaction between the scientist's original idea and an ongoing, thorough review of the literature (good scientists are always reading), as you can see in Figure 3A.1b. This means that once you formulate a hypothesis, it is not carved in stone but can be altered to fit what the review of the literature may reflect, as well as any change in ideas you may have. Remember, our work "stands on the shoulder of grants."

For example, you might be interested in how working adults manage their time when they are enrolled in graduate programs. That's the kernel of the idea you want to investigate. A research question might ask what the effects of enrollment in graduate school and full-time work are on personal relationships and personal growth. For a hypothesis, you might predict that

> **WHAT YOU'LL LEARN ABOUT IN THIS CHAPTER:**
>
> - How to select a research problem
>
> - Defining and sorting out idea after idea until one fits your interests
>
> - The importance of personal experience in selecting a problem
>
> - The steps in reviewing the literature
>
> - Different sources of information and how to use them
>
> - How to use journals, abstracts, and indices
>
> - The difference between primary and secondary resources
>
> - Using a synthesis of literature
>
> - How scholarly journals work
>
> - Using the Internet to complete your literature review

39

Figure 3A.1a   From idea to literature review, with the research hypothesis on the way.

Figure 3A.1b   From idea and literature review to research hypothesis.

those adults enrolled in school and who work full time and who participate in a time management support group have more meaningful personal relationships than those who do not.

You might consider the hypothesis to be finished at this point, but in reality your ongoing review of the literature and your changing ideas about the relationship between the variables will influence the direction your research will take. For example, suppose the findings of a similar previous study prompt you to add an interesting dimension (such as whether the employer subsidizes the cost of tuition) to your study, because the addition is consistent with the intent of your study. You should not have to restrict your creative thinking or your efforts to help you understand the effects of these factors just because you have already formulated a hypothesis and completed a literature review. Indeed, the reason for completing the review is to see what new directions your work might take. The literature review and the idea play off one another to help you form a relevant, conceptually sound research question and research hypothesis.

In sum, you will almost always find that your first shot at a hypothesis might need revision, given the content of the literature that you review. Remember, it is your idea that you will pursue. The way in which you execute it as a research study will be determined by the way in which you state the research question and the way in which you test the research hypothesis. It is doubtful that a review of the relevant literature would not shed some light on this matter.

This chapter begins with some pointers on selecting a problem worth studying, and then the focus moves to a description of the tools and the steps involved in preparing a review of the literature.

> Use the results of previous studies to fine-tune your research ideas and hypothesis.

Selecting a Problem

> Select a problem which genuinely interests you.

People go to undergraduate and graduate school for a variety of reasons, including preparing for a career, the potential financial advantages of higher education, and even expanding their personal horizons and experiencing the sheer joy of learning (what a radical thought!). Many of you are in this specific course for one or more of these reasons.

The great commonality between your course work and activities is your exposure to a wealth of information which you would not otherwise experience. That is the primary purpose of taking the time to select a research problem that makes sense to you and that interests you, while at the same time makes a contribution to your specific discipline. The selection of the area in which to work on is extremely important for two reasons. First, research takes a great deal of time and energy, and you want to be sure that the area you select interests you. You will work so hard throughout this project that continuing to work on it, even if it's the most interesting project, may at times become overwhelming. Just think of what it would be like if you were not interested in the topic!

Second, the area you select is only the first step in the research process. If this goes well, the remaining steps, which are neither more nor less important, also have a good chance of going well.

Just as there are many different ways to go about selecting a research problem, there are also some potential hazards. To start you off on the right foot, the following briefly reviews some of these almost fatal errors.

It is easy to do, but *falling in love with your idea* can be fatal. This happens when you become so infatuated with an idea and the project and you invest so much energy in it that you cannot bear to change anything about it. Right away someone is going to say, "What's wrong with being enthusiastic about your project?" My response is a strong, "Nothing at all." As does your professor, most researchers encourage and look for enthusiasm in students (and scientists) as an important and essential quality. But enthusiasm is not incompatible with being objective and dispassionate about the actual research process (not the content). Sometimes—and this is especially true for beginning research students—researchers see their question as one of such magnitude and importance that they fail to listen to those around them, including their adviser, who is trying to help them formulate their problem in such a way as to make it more precise and, in the long run, easier to address. Be committed to your ideas and enthusiastic about your topic but not so much that it clouds your judgment as to the practical and correct way to do things.

Next, *sticking with the first idea* that comes to mind isn't always wise. Every time the 1930s cartoon character Betty Boop had a problem, her inventor grandfather would sit on his stool, cross his legs (taking a Rodin-like pose), and think about a solution. Like a bolt from the blue, the light bulb above his head would go on, and Grampy would exclaim, "I've got it!," but the idea was never exactly right. Another flash would occur, but once again the idea was not perfect. Invariably, it was the third time the light went on that he struck gold.

Do you like your first idea for a research study? Great, but don't run out and place an advertisement for research participants in the newspaper quite yet. Wait a few days and think about it, and by no means should you stop talking to other students and your adviser during this thinking stage. Second and third ideas are usually much more refined, easier to research, and more manageable than first ones. As you work, rewrite and rethink your work . . . constantly.

Do you want to guarantee an unsuccessful project that excites no one (except perhaps yourself)? *Doing something trivial* by selecting a problem that has no conceptual basis or apparent importance in the field can lead to a frustrating experience and one that provides no closure. Beginning students who make this mistake sometimes over-intellectualize the importance of their research plans and don't take the time to ask themselves, "Where does this study fit in with all that has been done before?" Any scientific endeavor has as its highest goal the contribution of information that will help us better to understand the world in general and the specific topic being studied in particular. If you find out what has been done by reading previous studies and use that information as a foundation, then you will surely come up with a research problem of significance and value.

Ah, then there are researchers who *bite off more than they can chew*. Sound silly? Not to the thousands of advisers who sit day after day in their offices trying to convince well-intentioned beginning students that their ideas are interesting but that (for example) it may be a bit ambitious to ask every third adult in New York City about their attitudes toward increasing taxes to pay for education. Grand schemes are fine, but unless you can reduce a question to a manageable size, you might as well forget about starting your research. If these giant studies by first-timers ever do get done (most of the time they don't in their original form), the experiences are usually more negative than positive. Sometimes these students end up as **ABD**s (all but dissertation). Although you may not be seeking a doctorate right now, the lesson is still a good one. Give yourself a break from the beginning—choose a research question that is doable.

Finally, if you *do something that has already been done,* you could be wasting your time. There is a fine line between what has been done and what is important to do next based on previous work. Part of your job is to learn how to build and elaborate on the results of previous research without duplicating previous efforts. You might remember from the beginning of this chapter that I stressed how replication is an important component of the scientific process and good research. Your adviser can clearly guide you as to what is redundant (doing the exact same thing over without any sound rationale) and what is an important contribution (doing the same thing over but exploring an aspect of the previous research or even asking the same question, while eliminating possibly confounding sources of variance present in the first study).

TEST YOURSELF

Perhaps one of the most interesting dimensions of being a scientist is how the questions they ask are modified as they review the literature and learn more about the topic they are interested in. It's a constant give and take—hence the importance of being well informed. Ask your advisor or some other faculty how they keep themselves informed in their own field of study.

Defining Your Interests

Never disregard personal experience as an important source of ideas.

It is always easy for accomplished researchers to come up with additional ideas for research, but that is what they are paid and trained to do (in part, anyway). Besides, experienced researchers can put all that experience to work for themselves, and one thing (a study) usually leads to another (another study).

But what about the beginning student such as yourself? Where do you get your ideas for research? Even if you have a burning desire to be an experimental psychologist, a teacher, a counselor, or a clinical social worker, where do you begin to find hints about ideas that you might want to pursue?

In some relatively rare cases, students know from the beginning what they want to select as a research area and what research questions they want to ask. Most students, however, experience more anxiety and doubt than confidence. Before you begin the all-important literature review, first take a look at the following suggestions for where you might find interesting questions that are well worth considering as research topics.

First, *personal experiences and firsthand knowledge* more often than not can be the catalyst for starting research. For example, perhaps you worked at a summer camp with disabled children and are interested in knowing more about the most effective way to teach these children. Or, through your own personal reading, you have become curious about the aging process and how it affects the learning process. A further example: At least three of my colleagues are special educators because they have siblings who were not offered the special services they needed as children to reach their potential. Your own experiences shape the type of person you are. It would be a shame to ignore your past when considering the general area and content of a research question, even if you cannot see an immediate link between these experiences and possible research activities. Keep reading and you will find ways to help you create that link.

You may want to take complete responsibility for coming up with a research question. On the other hand, there is absolutely nothing wrong with consulting your advisor or some other faculty member who is working on some interesting topic and asking, "What's next?" *Using ideas from your mentor or instructor* will probably make you very current with whatever is happening in your field. Doing so also will help to establish and nurture the important relationship between you and your adviser (or some other faculty member), which is necessary for an enjoyable and successful experience. These are the people doing the research, and it would be surprising not to find that they have more ideas than time to devote to them and would welcome a bright, energetic student (like you) who wants to help extend their research activities.

Next, you might *look for a research question that reflects the next step in the research process*. Perhaps A, B, and C have already been done, and D is next in line. For example, your special interest might be understanding the lifestyle factors that contribute to heart disease, and you already know that factors such as personality type (for example, Type A and Type B) and health habits (for example, social drinking) have been well studied and their effects well documented. The next logical step might be to look at factors such as work habits (including occupation and attitude) or some component of family life (such as quality of relationships). As with research activities in almost all disciplines and within almost all topics, there is always that next logical step that needs to be taken.

Last, but never least, is that you may have to *come up with a research question because of this class*. Now that is not all that bad either, if you look at it this way: People who come up with ideas on their own are all set and need not worry about coming up with an idea by the deadline. Those people who have trouble formulating ideas need a deadline; otherwise, they would not get anything done. So although there are loftier reasons for coming up with research questions, sometimes it is just required. Even so, you need to work very hard at selecting a topic that you can formulate as a research question so that your interest is held throughout the duration of the activity.

Test Yourself

You'd be surprised how many important scientific breakthroughs were the result of informal talk (aka "bull") sessions between people interested in the same or similar topics. Just sitting around and talking about ideas is one of the great pleasures when it comes to learning and scientific discovery. Be a bit creative and list five ideas you have or questions you find particularly interesting about any topic. Don't worry at this point how you would answer the question but take a few intellectual risks and see what you come up with.

Ideas, Ideas, Ideas (and What to Do with Them)

Even if you are sure of what your interest might be, sometimes it is still difficult to come up with a specific idea for a research project. For better or worse, you are really the only one who can do this for yourself, but the following is a list of possible research topics, one of which might strike a chord. For each of these topics, there is a wealth of associated literature. If one topic piques your interest, go to that body of literature (described in the second part of this chapter) and start reading.

aggression	child care	conflict
AIDS	children of war	cooperative learning
autism spectrum disorder	circadian rhythms	creativity
bilingual education	classical conditioning	delusions
biofeedback	cognitive development	depression
biology of memory	color vision	déjà vu
birth control	competition	development of drawing
body image	compliance	diets
central nervous system	computer applications	divorce

dreams	identity	obesity
drug abuse	imagery	optimism
early intervention	intelligence	pain
egocentrism	language development	parenting
elder care	learning disabilities	perception
endocrine system	mediation	prejudice
epilepsy	memory	public policy
ethics	menarche	racial integration
exercise	mental sets	reinforcement
fat	middle adulthood	relaxation
fetal alcohol syndrome	motivation	REM sleep
fluid intelligence	narcolepsy	self-esteem
gender differences	neural development	violence in schools
Head Start	nightmares	
homeschooling	nutrition	

From Idea to Research Question to Hypothesis

Research ideas lead the
way to hypotheses.

Once you have determined what your specific interest might be, you should move as quickly as possible to formulate a research question that you want to investigate and begin your review of literature.

There is a significant difference between your expressing an interest in a particular idea and the statement of a research question. Ideas are full of those products of luxurious thinking: beliefs, conceptions, suppositions, assumptions, what if's, guesses, and more. Research questions are the articulation, best done in writing, of those ideas that at the least imply a relationship between variables. Why is it best done in writing? Because it is too easy to "get away" with spoken words. It is only when you have to write things down and live with them (spoken words seem to vanish mysteriously) that you face up to what has been said, make a commitment, and work to make sense out of the statement.

Unlike a hypothesis, a research question is not a declarative statement but rather is a clearly stated expression of interest and intent. In the pay-me-now or pay-me-later tradition, the more easily understood and clearer the research question, the easier your statement of a hypothesis and review of the literature will be. Why? From the beginning, a clear idea of what you want to do allows you to make much more efficient use of your time when it comes to searching for references and doing other literature review activities.

Finally, it is time to formulate a hypothesis or a set of hypotheses that reflects the research question. Remember from Chapter 2 the set of five criteria that applies to the statement of any hypothesis? To refresh your memory, here they are again. A well-written hypothesis

1. is stated in declarative form
2. posits a relationship between variables
3. reflects a theory or body of literature upon which it is based
4. is brief and to the point
5. is testable

When you derive your hypothesis from the research question, you should look to these criteria as a test of whether what you are saying is easily communicated to others and easily understood. Remember, the sources for ideas can be anything from a passage that you read in a novel last night to your own unique and creative thoughts. When you get to the research question stage, however, you need to be more scientific and clearly state what your interest is and what variables you will consider.

Research Interest or Ideas	Research Problem or Questions	Research Hypothesis
Open Classroom and Academic Success	What is the effect of open versus traditional classrooms on reading level?	Children who are taught reading in open classroom settings will read at a higher grade level than children who are taught reading in a traditional setting.
Television and Consumer Behavior	How does watching television commercials affect the buying behavior of adolescents?	Adolescent boys buy more of the products advertised on television than do adolescent girls.
Effectiveness of Checklists in Preventing Hospital Infections	Does the use of checklists when preparing patients for surgery help reduce the level of infection in the hospital?	Those hospitals that regularly use checklists in patient preparation for surgery will have a lower rate of infection per 1,000 patients then these hospitals, which do not.
Food Preference and Organic Foods	Do consumers prefer food that is organic?	There will be a difference in preference level as measured by the I ♥ Food scale between those consumers who are offered organic food and those who are offered non-organic food.
Use of Energy by Home Owners	Will a home owners' energy usage change as a function of his or her knowledge of his or her neighbor's usage?	Those people who know how much energy their neighbors use on a monthly basis will use less energy.
Adult Care	How have many adults adjusted to the responsibility of caring for their aged parents?	The number of children who are caring for their parents in the child's own home has increased over the past 10 years.

Table 3A.1   Research ideas and questions and the hypothesis that reflect them

Table 3A.1 lists five research interests, the research questions that were generated from those ideas, and the final hypotheses. These hypotheses are only final in the sense that they more or less fit the five criteria for a well-written hypothesis. Your literature review and more detailed discussion may mean that variables must be further defined and perhaps even that new ones will need to be introduced. A good hypothesis tells what you are going to do, not how you will do it.

TEST YOURSELF

As Pasteur said, chance does favor the prepared mind and you will never know where the best information will come from. So, even if some class seems to contain material unrelated to your specialty or your interests, you never know what insight you might gain from reading widely and discussing ideas with your fellow students. What five things might you read (that you have not) that are related to your interests?

Reviewing the Literature

The review of literature provides a framework for the research proposal.

Here it comes again. Today's research is built on a foundation of the hard work and dedication of past researchers and their productive efforts. Where does one find the actual results of these efforts? Look to scholarly journals and books and other resources, which are located in the library and online.

Although all stages in the research process are important, a logical and systematic review of the literature often sets the stage for the completion of a successful research proposal and a successful study. Remember one of the fatal mistakes mentioned at the beginning of the chapter about selecting a research question that has been done before? Or one that is trivial? You find out about all these things and more when you see what has already been done and how it has been done. A complete review provides a framework within which you can answer the important question(s) that you pose. A review takes you chronologically through the development of ideas, shows you how some ideas were left by the wayside because of lack of support, and tells you how some were confirmed as being truths. An extensive and complete review of the literature gives you that important perspective to see what has been done and where you are going—crucial to a well-written, well-documented, well-planned report.

So get out your yellow (or recyclable white) writing pads, index cards, pens or pencils, laptop computer, or iPad and let's get started. Also, don't forget your school ID card so you can check out books at the campus library.

The literature review process consists of the steps listed in Figure 3A.2. You begin with as clear an idea as possible about what you want to do, in the form either of a clear and general statement about the variables you want to study or of a research hypothesis. You should end with a well-written, concise document that details the rationale for why you chose the topic you did, how it fits into what has been done before, what needs to be done in the future, and what is its relative importance to the discipline.

There are basically three types of sources that you will consult throughout your review of the literature (see Table 3A.2). The first are **general sources**, which provide clues about the location of references of a general nature on a topic. Such sources certainly have their limitations (which we will get to in a moment), but they can be a real asset because they provide a general overview of, and introduction to, a topic.

Define your idea in as general terms as possible by using general sources.

↓

Search through the secondary sources.

↓

Search through the primary sources.

↓

Organize your notes.

↓

Write your proposal.

Figure 3A.2   The steps in reviewing the literature. It is a formidable task, but when broken down step by step, it is well within your reach.

Information Source	What It Does	Examples
General Sources	Provides an overview of a topic and provides leads to where more information can be found	Daily newspaper, news weeklies, popular periodicals and magazines, trade books, Reader's Guide to Periodical Literature, New York Times Index
Secondary Sources	Provides a level of information "Once removed" from the original work	Books on specific subjects and reviews of research
Primary Sources	The original reports of the original work or experience	Journals, abstracts and scholarly books, Educational Resources Information Center (ERIC), movies

Table 3A.2   What different sources can do for you in your search for relevant material about an interesting research question

For example, let's say you are interested in the general area of sports psychology but have absolutely no idea where to turn to find more information. You could start with a recent article that appeared in the *New York Times* (a general source) and find the name of the foremost sports psychologist and then go to more detailed secondary or primary sources to find out more about that person's work.

The second source type, **secondary sources**, are "once removed" from the actual research. These include review papers, anthologies of readings, syntheses of other work in the area, textbooks, and encyclopedias.

Finally, the most important sources are **primary sources**. These are accounts of the actual research that has been done. They appear as journal articles or as other original works including abstracts. Table 3A.2 summarizes the functions of general, secondary, and primary resources and provides some examples. These three different types of sources are also covered in Chapter 9 in a discussion of historical methods of doing research.

Before you get started, let me share my own particular bias. There is no substitute for using every resource that your library has to offer, and that means spending lots of time turning the pages of books and journals and reading their contents. In many cases, however, there's no substitute for exploring and using electronic resources such as online databases. You'll learn about both printed and electronic resources here, but you should remember that you won't find everything you need online (and much of it is not verifiable), yet online is where the most recent material appears. There is even material now being posted online that will not show up in the library—a new and very interesting development owing to the appearance of online (only) journals and e-books. However, at least for now, begin developing your library as well as your online skills. The online world of literature may someday be the only world of literature, but that surely will not be the case this semester.

One last note before we get started. Your university has an absolute ton of online resources available to you and probably more than you can imagine. How do you find out what might be available? Well, you can access your library online and find out, or follow these steps:

1. Go to any of the libraries on your campus.
2. Ask for where the reference librarians sit.
3. Ask one for a short tour of what's online (or enroll in one of many classes that most libraries offer at the beginning of the semester to address these skills especially).

General, secondary, and primary resources are all important, but very different, parts of the literature review.

One of the best kept secrets on any college campus is how smart and resourceful reference librarians are. Reference librarians are the original search engines. Get to know them (individually)—it will serve you very well.

Using General Sources

General sources of information provide two things: (1) a general introduction to areas in which you might be interested and (2) some clues as to where you should go for the more valuable or useful (in a scientific sense, anyway) information about your topic. They also provide great browsing material.

Any of the references discussed below, especially the indices of national newspapers and so on, can offer you 5, 10, or 50 articles in a specific area. In these articles, you will often find a nice introduction to the subject area and a mention of some of the people doing the research and where they are located. From there, you can look through other reference materials to find out what other work that person has done or even how to contact that person directly.

There are loads of general sources in your college or university library as well as in your local public library and online as well. The following is a brief description of just a few of the most frequently used sources and a listing of several others you might want to consult. Remember to use general sources only to orient yourself to what is out there and to familiarize yourself with the topic.

All of what follows can be accessed online, but the **URL** (or the Uniform Resource Locator) will differ since you may be accessing it through your university or college.

Readers' Guide, Full Text Mega Edition is by far the most comprehensive available guide to general literature. Organized by topic, it is published monthly, covering hundreds of journals (such as the *New England Journal of Medicine*) and periodicals or magazines (such as *Scientific American*). Because the topics are listed alphabetically, you are sure to find reading sources on a selected topic easily and quickly.

New to the *Readers' Guide* world is now the *Readers' Guide Retrospective,* which allows access to more than 100 years of coverage from 375 U.S. magazines with indexing of leading magazines back as far as 1890 and citations to more than 3,000,000 articles. If you can't find something about your interests or related topics here, it's time to reassess the topic you want to focus on.

Another very valuable source of information is the Facts on File Online Databases with content first published in New York in 1940. Facts on File presents a collection of databases that include tens of thousands of articles and other resources (such as video and audio files) in a multitude of areas. The following list shows you what just some of these databases are and a brief description of each:

- *U.S. Government Online* presents in-depth information on the structure and function of the U.S. government.
- *American History Online* covers more than 500 years of political, military, social, and cultural history.
- *African-American History Online* provides cross-referenced entries, covering African American history.
- *Curriculum Video on Demand* provides a video subscription to more than 5,000 educational programs.
- *Science Online* contains information on a broad range of scientific disciplines.
- *Ferguson's Career Guidance Center* provides profiles of more than 3,300 jobs and 94 industries.
- *Bloom's Literary Reference Online* contains information on thousands of authors and their works, including an archive of 38,000 characters.
- And, the grandparent of them all, *Facts On File World News Digest*, which is the standard resource for information on U.S. and world events

The *New York Times Index* lists by subject all the articles published in the *Times* since 1851. Once you find reference to an article that might be of interest, you then go to the stacks and select a copy of the actual issue or view it on microfilm. The originals are seldom available because they are printed on thin paper which was designed to hold up only for the few days that a newspaper might be read.

Instead, contents are recorded on microfilm or some other medium and are available through your library. Many libraries now have microfilm readers that allow you to copy directly from the microfilm image and make a print or hardcopy of what you are viewing. The full text of many newspapers is also now available electronically (discussed later in this chapter). And, although the index is not available online, you can search through the archives of the *New York Times* online at http://www.nytimes.com—most articles are free to access, but as of this writing, future users are likely to be charged (unless you subscribe to the print edition individually) and of course, probably still free at your local library or institution's libraries.

Nobody should take what is printed as the absolute truth, but weekly news magazines such as *Time* (http://www.time.com/time/), *Newsweek* (http://www.msnbc. msn.com/id/3032542/site/newsweek/), and *U.S. News and World Report* (http://www. usnews.com/) offer general information and keep you well informed about other related events as well. You may not even know that you have an interest in a particular topic (such as ethical questions in research), but a story on that topic might be in a current issue, catch your eye, and before you know it you will be using that information to seek out other sources.

There are two other very comprehensive electronic general source databases: Lexis/Nexis Academic (there are other versions as well) and the Expanded Academic ASAP, both of which are probably available online through your library.

Lexis/Nexis Academic is the premier database. It is absolutely huge in its coverage and contains information on current events, sports, business, economics, law, taxes, and many other areas. It offers full text of selected newspaper articles. Figure 3A.3 shows you the results of a search on the general term "school finance." You can print this information, e-mail it (to yourself of course if you are in the library and have no other way to record it), and sort in various ways (such as by date).

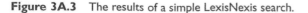

Figure 3A.3 The results of a simple LexisNexis search.

The Expanded Academic ASAP is a multidisciplinary database for research, which provides information on disciplines such as the humanities, communication studies, social science, the arts, science, technology and many more disciplines. It covers from 1980 to the present and contains well over 18 million articles.

As the electronic world of resources and reference tools charges long, Google has shown its value in at least two different ways.

First there is Google Scholar, which provides a tool to broadly search for scholarly literature. You can search across disciplines and sources to find articles and books (and other types of publications such as abstracts) and it is the ideal way to locate works by a particular scholar. For example, if you are interested in learning more about what Ron Haskins, a noted expert on policy and families, has done, go to Google Scholar and search; you'll find works completed by Professor Haskins as well as works in which he is referenced. What a terrific help!

Also, there is Google Books, where Google has undertaken the process of digitizing and making available for no charge millions of books in libraries and other institutions around the world. In Google Books, you can find everything from a limited preview of a book you need for class or the full text of other books that may, or may not, be in the public domain.

Google Books is an absolutely invaluable tool for any researcher, but its use is not without controversy. After all, an author's work is appearing with no charge to the user and no benefit to the author (such as a royalty payment). The years to come will sort out how tools such as Google Books can be used and still be fair to the author as well as to the researchers.

Then, there is the wealth of information you can dig out of everyday sources such as your local newspaper, company newsletters, and other publications. Thousands of newspapers can be accessed through http://www.newspapers.com, and newspapers often carry the same Associated Press articles as major papers such as the *New York Times* and the *Washington Post*. And, please, do not forget the U.S. Government Printing Office (GPO), which regularly publishes thousands of documents on everything from baseball to bees, and the majority of these documents are free—your tax dollars at work. Do you want to know more about the GPO? Visit http://www.gpo.gov for a catalog of what is available.

Finally, there's the hugely popular and successful Wikipedia (at http://www.wikipedia.org/), an encyclopedia that is almost solely based on the contributions of folks like you and me. At this writing, Wikipedia contains over 3,000,000 articles on absolutely everything you can think of. This may be the perfect online place to start your investigations.

Trustworthy? To a great extent, yes. Wikipedia is monitored by content experts, and a recent study found that the venerable *Encyclopedia Britannica* had more factual errors than did Wikipedia. And, of course, the great thing about any wiki (and it is a general term for anything built on the contributions of many people and open for editing by anyone as well) is that the facts, if incorrect initially, will surely be changed or modified.

The Wikipedia site also contains other wikis, including Wiktionary (a dictionary), Wikinews, Wikiquotes, and more. Just exploring the encyclopedia and these ancillaries is fun.

Finally, one especially useful source that you should not overlook is *The Statistical Abstract of the United States,* published yearly by the U. S. Department of Commerce (http://www.census.gov/statab/www). This national database about the United States includes valuable, easily accessible information on demographics and much more.

Major syntheses of information such as reviews can be a terrific foundation for your review.

Using Secondary Sources

Secondary sources are those that you seek out if you are looking for a scholarly summary of the research that has been done in a particular area or if you are looking for further sources of references.

Reviews and Syntheses of Literature

These are the BIG books you often find in the reference section of the library (not in the stacks). Because so many people want to use them, they must always be available. The following is a summary of some of the most useful. More and more of these books are being published as encyclopedias.

A general secondary source of literature reviews is the *Annual Reviews* (published since 1930 by Annual Reviews in about 40 disciplines), containing about 20 chapters and focusing on a wide variety of topics such as medicine, anthropology, neuroscience, biomedical engineering, political science, psychology, public health, and sociology. Just think of it—you can go through the past 10 years of these volumes and be very up-to-date on a wide range of general topics. If you happen to find one chapter on exactly what you want to do, you are way ahead of the game. You can find out more about these volumes and see sample tables of contents at http://www.annualreviews.org/.

Another annual review that is well worth considering is the *National Society for the Study of Education* (or *NSSE*) Yearbooks (also available at http://nsse-chicago.org). Each year since 1900, this society has published a two-volume annual that focuses on a particular topic, such as adolescence, microcomputers in the classroom, gifted and talented children, and classroom management. The area of focus is usually some contemporary topic, and if you are interested in what is being covered, the information can be invaluable to you. The 2009 yearbook has as its focus "localism."

The Condition of Education in Brief 2007 (available at http://nces.ed.gov/pubsearch/pubsinfo.asp?pubid=2007066) contains a summary of 20 of the 48 indicators in the Condition of Education 2007, including public and private enrollment in elementary/secondary education, the racial/ethnic distribution of public school students, students' gains in reading and mathematics achievement through third grade, trends in student achievement from the National Assessment of Education Progress in reading and mathematics, international comparisons of mathematics literacy, annual earnings of young adults by education and race/ethnicity, status dropout rates, immediate transition to college, availability of advanced courses in high school, inclusion of students with disabilities in regular classrooms, school violence and safety, faculty salary and total compensation, early development of children, expenditures per student in elementary and secondary education, and public effort to fund postsecondary education. The files are available for downloading.

If you are interested in child development, seek out the *Handbook of Child Psychology* (Wiley 2006), which is often used as the starting point (for ideas) by developmental and child psychology students, early childhood education students, medical and nursing students, and many others. The four individual volumes are

- Volume 1: *Theoretical Models of Human Development*
- Volume 2: *Cognition, Perception and Language*
- Volume 3: *Social, Emotional and Personality Development*
- Volume 4: *Child Psychology in Practice*

Finally, there's the eight-volume *Encyclopedia of Psychology* from Oxford University Press (2000), which includes 1,500 articles on every aspect of psychology.

Also, do not forget the large number of scholarly books that sometimes have multiple authors and are edited by one individual or that are written entirely by one person (which, in the latter case, is sometimes considered a primary resource, depending on its content). Use the good old card catalog (or your library's computerized search system) to find the title or author you need.

Using Primary Sources

Primary sources are the meat and potatoes of the literature review. Although you will get some good ideas and a good deal of information from reading the secondary sources, you have to go to the real thing to get the specific information to support your points and make them stick.

Get to know your library and where you can find journals related to your field of study. Most libraries offer tours on a regular basis.

In fact, your best bet is to include mostly primary sources in your literature review, with some secondary sources to help make your case. Do not even think about including general sources. It is not that the information in *Redbook* or the *New Jersey Star Ledger* is not useful or valuable. That information is secondhand, however, and you do not want to build an argument based on someone else's interpretation of an idea or concept.

Journals

Journals? You want journals? Table 3A.3 lists journals arranged by category. This should be enough for you to answer your professor when he asks, "Who can tell me some of the important journals in your own field?" This list is only a small selection of what is available. The print version of *Ulrich's Periodicals Directory* (first published in 1932) lists information on thousands of periodicals, including journals, consumer magazines, and trade publications (at http://www.ulrichsweb.com/ and at your library as well).

Psychology	
Adolescence	Journal of Experimental Child Psychology
American Journal of Family Therapy	Journal of Experimental Psychology, Human
American Journal of Orthopsychiatry	Perception and Performance
American Psychologist	Journal of Experimental Psychology, Learning,
Behavioral Disorders	Memory, and Cognition
Child Development	Journal of Genetic Psychology
Child Study Journal	Journal of Humanistic Psychology
Developmental Psychology	Journal of Personality and Social Psychology
Contemporary Educational Psychology	Journal of Psychology
Educational and Psychological Measurement	Journal of Research in Personality
Journal of Abnormal Child Psychology	Journal of School Psychology
Journal of Applied Behavioral Analysis	Perceptual and Motor Skills
Journal of Autism and Development Disorders	Psychological Bulletin
Journal of Child Psychology and Psychiatry and	Psychological Review
Allied Disciplines	Psychology in the Schools
Journal of Consulting and Clinical Psychology	Psychology of Women Quarterly
Journal of Counseling Psychology	Small Group Behavior
Journal of Educational Psychology	Transactional Analysis Journal

Special Educational and Exceptional Children	
Academic Therapy	Journal of Learning Disabilities
American Annals of the Deaf	Journal of Mental Deficiency Research
American Journal of Mental Deficiency	Journal of Special Education
Behavioral Disorders	Journal of Special Education Technology
Education and Training of the Mentally Retarded	Journal of Speech and Hearing Disorders

Table 3A.3   A sample of the thousands of journals being published in all different fields

Education of the Visually Handicapped	Journal of Speech and Hearing Research
Exceptional Children	Journal of Visual Impairment and Blindness
Exceptional Education Quarterly	Learning Disability Quarterly
Exceptional Parent	Mental Retardation
Gifted Child Quarterly	Sightsaving Review
Hearing and Speech Action	Teaching Exceptional Children
International Journal for the Education of the Blind	Teacher Education and Special Education
Journal for the Education of the Gifted	Teacher of the Blind
Journal of The Association for the Severely Handicapped	Topics in Early Childhood Special Education
	Volta Review

Health and Physical Education

Journal of Health Education	Journal of School Health
Journal of Alcohol and Drug Education	Journal of Sport Health
Journal of Leisure Research	Physical Educator
Journal of Motor Learning	Research Quarterly of the American Alliance
Journal of Nutrition Education	for Health, Physical Education, Recreation
Journal of Outdoor Education	and Dance
Journal of Physical Education, Recreation and Dance	School Health Review

Child Psychology

Adolescence American Journal of Family Therapy	American Psychologist Behavioral Disorders
American Journal of Orthopsychiatry	Child Development
Child Study Journal	Journal of Experimental Psychology, Learning, Memory, and Cognition
Contemporary Educational Psychology	
Developmental Psychology	Journal of Genetic Psychology
Educational and Psychological Measurement	Journal of Humanistic Psychology
Journal of Abnormal Child Psychology	Journal of Personality and Social Psychology
Journal of Applied Behavioral Analysis	Journal of Psychology
Journal of Autism and Development Disorders	Journal of Research in Personality
Journal of Child Psychology and Psychiatry and Allied Disciplines	Journal of School Psychology
	Perceptual and Motor Skills
Journal of Consulting and Clinical Psychology	Psychological Bulletin
Journal of Counseling Psychology	Psychological Review
Journal of Educational Psychology	Psychology in the Schools
Journal of Experimental Child Psychology	Psychology of Women Quarterly
Journal of Experimental Psychology, Human Perception and Performance	Small Group Behavior
	Transactional Analysis Journal

Special Education and Exceptional Children

Academic Therapy	Journal of Learning Disabilities
American Annals of the Deaf	Journal of Mental Deficiency Research
American Journal of Mental Deficiency	Journal of Special Education
Behavioral Disorders	Journal of Special Education Technology
Education and Training of the Mentally Retarded	Journal of Speech and Hearing Disorders
Education of the Visually Handicapped	Journal of Speech and Hearing Research
Exceptional Children	Journal of Visual Impairment and Blindness
Exceptional Education Quarterly	Learning Disability Quarterly
Exceptional Parent	Mental Retardation
Gifted Child Quarterly	Sightsaving Review

Table 3A.3 *(Continued)*

Hearing and Speech Action	Teaching Exceptional Children
International Journal for the Education of the Blind	Teacher Education and Special Education
Journal for the Education of the Gifted	Teacher of the Blind
Journal of The Association for the Severely	Topics in Early Childhood Special Education
Handicapped	Volta Review

Health and Physical Education

Journal of Alcohol and Drug Education	National Elementary Principal
Journal of Health Education	Negro Education Review
Journal of Leisure Research	Peabody Journal of Education
Journal of Motor Learning	Phi Delta Kappan
Journal of Nutrition Education	Physical Educator
Journal of Outdoor Education	Research Quarterly of the American Alliance for Health, Physical Education, Recreation and Dance
Journal of Physical Education, Recreation and Dance	Review of Educational Research
Journal of School Health	School Health Review
Journal of Sport Health	School Library Media Quarterly
Library Research	School Psychology Review
Lifelong Learning: The Adult Years	School Science Review
Mathematics and Computer Education	Science and Children
Mathematics Teacher	Science Education
Modern Language Journal	Science Teacher
Music Education Journal	Secondary School Theatre Journal
National Education Association Research Bulletin	Social Education
Studies in Art Education	Theory Into Practice
Studies in Educational Evaluation	Today's Education
Teachers College Record	Voc Ed
Theory and Research in School Education	Young Children

Sociology and Anthropology

American Anthropologist	Journal of Marriage and the Family
American Behavioral Scientist	Rural Sociology
American Journal of Sociology	Sex Roles: A Journal of Research
American Sociological Review	Social Work
Anthropology and Education Quarterly	Sociology and Social Research
Child Welfare	Sociology of Education
Family Relations	Urban Anthropology
Group and Organization Studies	Urban Education
Human Organization	Urban Review
Human Services in the Rural Environment	Youth and Society
Journal of Correctional Education	

Analytical Research

Administration and Society	Daedalus
American Historical Review	Economics of Education Review
American Political Science Review	Education and Urban Society
Annals of the American Academy of Political and	Education Forum
Social Science	Educational Studies
Civil Liberties Law	Educational Theory
Comparative Education Review	Harvard Civil Rights

Nursing	
AACN Advanced Critical Care	Journal of Infusion Nursing
Advanced Emergency Nursing Journal	Journal of Neuroscience Nursing
Advances in Neonatal Care	Journal of Nursing Care Quality
Advances in Nursing Science - Featured Journal	The Journal of Nursing Research
Advances in Skin & Wound Care: The Journal for	Journal of Perinatal and Neonatal Nursing
Prevention and Healing	Journal of Public Health Management & Practice
AJN, American Journal of Nursing	Journal of the Dermatology Nurses' Association
Alzheimer's Care Today	Journal of Trauma Nursing
Cancer Nursing	MCN, The American Journal of Maternal/Child
CIN: Computers, Informatics, Nursing	Nursing
Critical Care Nursing Quarterly	Men in Nursing
Dimensions of Critical Care Nursing	Nurse Educator
Family & Community Health	Nursing 2010
Gastroenterology Nursing	Nursing 2010 Critical Care
Health Care Food & Nutrition Focus	Nursing Administration Quarterly
Health Care Management Review	Nursing Made Incredibly Easy!
The Health Care Manager	Nursing Management
Holistic Nursing Practice	Nursing Research
Home Healthcare Nurse	Nutrition Today
Infants & Young Children	Oncology Times
Journal for Nurses in Staff Development	OR Nurse 2010
Journal of Ambulatory Care Management	Orthopaedic Nursing
Journal of Cardiovascular Nursing	Outcomes Management
Journal of Christian Nursing	Plastic Surgical Nursing
Journal of Head Trauma Rehabilitation	Professional Case Management
Journal of Hospice and Palliative Nursing	Quality Management in Health Care

Table 3A.3   *(Continued)*

Journals are by far the most important and valuable primary sources of information about a topic because they represent the most direct link among the researcher, the work of other researchers, and your own interests.

What actually is a journal, and how do papers or manuscripts appear? A journal is a collection (most often) of research articles published in a particular discipline. For example, the American Educational Research Association (AERA) publishes more than six journals, all of which deal with the general area of research in education. The American Psychological Association (APA) publishes many journals including the *Journal of Experimental Psychology* and the *Journal of Counseling Psychology*. The Society for Research in Child Development (SRCD) publishes *Child Development* and *Child Development Monographs,* among others. Membership in these professional groups entitles you to a subscription to the journals as part of the package, or you can subscribe separately.

Most often, these professional organizations do not do the actual publishing themselves, but only the editorial work where the manuscripts are reviewed and considered for publication. For example, *Child Development,* sponsored by the SRCD, is published by Wiley Publishers/ Blackwell.

How do most respectable journals work? First, a researcher writes an article within the province of the particular journal to which it is being submitted. The manuscript is prepared according to a specific format (such as the one shown in Chapter 14), and then usually three copies are submitted to the journal editor. Guidelines for preparing manuscripts are usually found on the front or back covers of most journals in the social and behavioral sciences. Often the journal requires that the author follow guidelines stated in the sixth edition of the *American Psychological Association Publication Manual* (2009).

The peer review process of reviewing journal submissions ensures that experts review and comment on a research manuscript before it is published.

Second, once the article has been received by the editor, who is an acknowledged expert in that particular field, the article is sent to at least three reviewers who are also experts in the field. Note that today, almost all of the submission and review process occurs online. These reviewers participate in a process known as **peer review**, in which the reviewers do not know the identity of the author (or authors) of the paper. The author's name appears only on a cover sheet, which is removed by the editor. A social security number, or some other coded number, is used for identification on the rest of the manuscript. This makes the process quite fair (what is called "**blind**")—the reviewer's chance of knowing the identity of the author is greatly reduced, if not eliminated. The possibility that personalities might get in the way of what can be a highly competitive goal—publishing in the best journals—is thus minimized. Each reviewer makes a recommendation regarding suitability for publication. The options from which the reviewers select can include

- Accept outright, meaning that the article is outstanding and can be accepted for publication as is
- Accept with revisions, meaning that some changes need to be made by the author(s) before it is accepted (and is of course reviewed again)
- Reject with suggestions for revisions, meaning that the article is not acceptable as is, but after changes are made the author(s) should be invited to resubmit it
- Reject outright, meaning that the article is completely unacceptable and is not welcome for resubmission

Finally, when a consensus is reached by the reviewers, the editor of the journal conveys that decision to the author(s). If a consensus cannot be reached, the editor makes a decision or sends the article to another reviewer for additional comments. Editors work very hard to ensure that the review process and the journal publication process are fair.

By the way, you might be interested to know that the average rejection rate for the top journals is about 80%. Yes, 80% of the articles submitted never get in, but those rejected by the top journals usually find their way into other journals. Just because these articles are not accepted by the journals with the highest rejection rate does not mean they cannot make a significant contribution to the field. In fact, several studies have shown that there is little consistency among reviewers, and what one might rank high, another might rank quite low. However, in general, it's safe to say that the better scientific reports are published by the better journals.

One more note about primary sources in general. If you know of a journal or a book that you might need and your library does not have it (and it is not available online), do not despair. First, check other libraries within driving distance or check with some of the professors in your department. They might have it available for loan. If all else fails, use the interlibrary loan system, with which your reference librarian will be glad to help you. This service helps you locate and physically secure the reference materials you want for a limited amount of time from another library. The system usually works quickly and is efficient.

Abstracts

If journals are the workhorses of the literature review, then collections of abstracts cannot be very far behind with regard to their convenience and usefulness. An **abstract** is a one- (or at most two-) paragraph summary of a journal article which contains all the information readers should need to decide whether to read the entire journal article.

By perusing collections of abstracts, researchers can save a significant amount of time compared with leafing through the journals from which these abstracts are drawn. Most abstracts also include subject and author indexes to help readers find what they are looking for, and abstracts of articles routinely appear in more than one abstract resource.

Abstracts help you save the time it would take to locate potentially important sources of information.

For example, a study on the benefits of long-distance learning might appear in PsychINFO from the *International Journal of Simulation and Process Modelling.*

The following is a brief description of some abstract collections you might find useful.

One well-known collection of abstracts is PsycINFO (at http://www.apa.org/pubs/databases/psycinfo/index.aspx). PsycINFO (for members of APA) and PsycINFO Direct (for nonmembers) provide an electronic database that contains abstracts and summaries of psychological literature from the 1800s to the present. Some facts about PsycINFO: It contains articles and abstracts from more than 2,500 journals, is updated weekly, offers chapters from scholarly books, contains material from 49 different countries, covers dissertations, and much more. No doubt—on your research travels, it is a great resource.

There is an unlimited amount of information in PsycINFO, and the online nature enables you to search electronically. Figure 3A.4 shows you a sample PsycINFO screen for a journal article. Screens for books and chapters and dissertations look quite similar.

One other way to use PsycINFO is to look up the key word "bibliography." Under this heading, you will find a list of bibliographies that have already been published. You might be lucky and find one that focuses on your area of interest.

One index that is especially useful is Educational Resources Information Center, or ERIC. ERIC (http://www.eric.ed.gov/) is a nationwide information network that acquires, catalogs, summarizes, and provides access to education information from all sources. It currently contains more than 1.3 million education-related documents and adds about 30,000 per year. The database and ERIC document collections are housed in about 3,000 locations worldwide, including most major public and university library systems.

ERIC produces a variety of publications and provides extensive user assistance with several different ways to search the database. As with PsycINFO, the ERIC system works with a set of descriptive terms found in a thesaurus, the Thesaurus of ERIC Descriptors (see Figure 3A.5), which should be your first stop. Once you find the search words or descriptors, you can use the subject index (published monthly) until you find the number of a reference focusing on what you want. Finally, you are off to the actual

Database	Aerospace & High Technology Database
Title	Learning Operations Research online: benefits, challenges, and experiences
Author	Faulin, Javier; Juan, Angel A.; Fonseca, Pau; Pla, Lluis M.; Rodriguez, Sara V.
Source	International Journal of Simulation and Process Modelling. Vol. 5, no. 1, pp. 42-53. 24 May 2009
ISSN	1740-2123
Descriptors	☐ Learning ☐ Distance education ☐ Computer programs ☐ Students ☐ Operations research ☐ Education ☐ Distance learning ☐ Computer simulation
	New Search Using Marked Terms: ⊙ Use AND to narrow ○ Use OR to broaden Add to Current Search: ○ Use AND to narrow ○ Use OR to broaden (Go)
Abstract	Information technologies offer new ways to teach and learn Operations Research (OR): on the one hand, they have driven the growth of distance learning opportunities; on the other hand, they facilitate the shifting to an emergent educational paradigm, which considers students as active and central actors in their learning process. The use of computer software and collaborative e-learning as methodological policies to increase students' motivation for OR are also discussed in this paper. Thus, we describe lessons learned in some real experiences, developed during the last years at four different universities in Spain, regarding the teaching and learning of OR.
Publisher	Inderscience Publishers Ltd , PO Box 735
Language	English
Publication Year	2009
Publication Type	Journal Article
Classification	63 Mathematics and Computation (CE); 63 Mathematics and Computation (MT); 67 Theoretical Mathematics (AH); 52 Numerical Analysis, Simulation, and Modeling (CI)
DOI	10.1504/IJSPM.2009.025826
Update	201001
Accession Number	201001-63-0232635 (CE); 201001-63-1449937 (MT); A09-67-1824172 (AH); 201001-52-0149926 (CI)
Journal Volume	5
Journal Issue	1
Journal Pages	42-53
Subfile	Civil Engineering (CE); Mechanical & Transportation Engineering (MT); Aerospace & High Technology (AH); Computer & Information Systems (CI)

Figure 3A.4 The results of a PsycINFO search. Screenshot is reprinted with permission of the American Psychological Association, publisher of the PsycINFO database, All rights reserved.

description of the reference, as you see in Figure 3A.6. Most of the time, these ERIC documents are in PDF (portable document format) and you can access the entire document. Other times, although rare, you may have to order directly from the ERIC clearinghouse. If your library has a government documents department, it might already have the document on hand. Also, you might be able to contact the original author as listed in the résumé.

ERIC has been in business since 1966 and has regional clearinghouses that archive, abstract, and disseminate educational articles and documents. Education is broadly defined, so many disciplines in the social and behavioral sciences are covered quite adequately.

Do you think that this is enough to get started? PsycINFO and the ERIC sets of abstracts are major resources, but there are others that are a bit more specialized and also very useful.

Figure 3A.5   The set of ERIC terms in the thesaurus you start with when conducting an ERIC search.

Figure 3A.6   Once you have identified areas through the ERIC thesaurus, it's time to turn to key words that produce ERIC entries like these.

Titles of other abstracts, such as *Sociological Abstracts, Exceptional Child Education Resources, Research Related to Children,* and *Dissertation Abstracts,* reveal the wide variety of available reference material.

Finally, there's ProQuest Dissertations and Theses (which replaces Dissertation Abstracts at many libraries) at http://www.proquest.com/en-US/catalogs/databases/detail/pqdt.shtml, which contains over 2.7 million dissertations and theses dating from 1861, with full text online from 1997. More than 75,000 new entries are added every year and it contains the abstracts of over 2,000,000 dissertations from 1861 to the present, in the following areas:

- Agriculture
- Astronomy
- Biological and Environmental Sciences
- Business and Economics
- Chemistry
- Education
- Engineering
- Fine Arts and Music
- Geography and Regional Planning
- Geology
- Health Sciences
- History and Political Science
- Language and Literature
- Library and Information Science
- Mathematics and Statistics
- Philosophy and Religion
- Physics
- Psychology and Sociology

Indices

Journals and abstracts provide the substance of an article, a conference presentation, or a report. If you want a quick overview of where things might be located, turn to an index, which is an alphabetical listing of entries by topic, author, or both.

> Indices help you locate the sources of important information.

The widely used and popular *Social Sciences Citation Index* (SSCI) and *Science Citation Index* (SCI) work in an interesting and creative way. SSCI (at http:// thomson-reuters.com/products_services/science/science_products/a-z/social_sciences_citation_index) provides access to bibliographic information, author abstracts, and citations from more than 2,400 journals in more than 50 disciplines. SCI (now part of the Web of Science at http://thomsonreuters.com/products_services/science/ science_products/a-z/science_citation_index) provides researchers access to over 3,700 scientific and technical journals across 100 disciplines.

Let's say you read an article that you find to be very relevant to your research proposal and want to know what else the author has done. You might want to search by subject through abstracts, as we have talked about, but you might also want to find other articles by the same author or on the same general topic. Tools like SSCI and SCI allow you to focus on your specific topic and access as much of the available information as possible. For example, do you want to find out who has mentioned the classic article "Mental and Physical Traits of a Thousand Gifted Children," written by Louis Terman and published in 1925? Look up Terman, L., in SSCI year by year, and you will find more references than you may know what to do with.

Finally, you can consult the *Bibliographic Index Plus* online (at http://www.hwwilson.com/Databases/biblio.htm), a compilation of bibliographies that results from a search of more than 530,000 bibliographies. Just think of the time you can save if you locate a relatively recent bibliography on what interests you.

What is the best use to which you can put a general, secondary, and primary source and name one of each which you might use in better understanding the most important questions in your own field of study?

Reading and Evaluating Research

Research articles and reports must always be carefully evaluated and the results never taken at face value.

Almost any research activity that you participate in involves reading research articles that appear in journals and textbooks. In fact, one of the most common faults of beginning researchers is not being sufficiently familiar with the wealth of research reports available in their specific area of interest. It is indeed rare to find a research topic about which nothing (or nothing related) has been done. You may not be able to find something that addresses the exact topic you wish to pursue (such as changes in adolescent behavior in Australian children who live in the outback), but there is plenty of information on adolescent behavior and plenty on children who live in Australia. Part of your job as a good scientist is to make the argument why these factors might be important to study.

You can do that by reading and evaluating research that has been done in various disciplines on the same topic.

What Does a Research Article Look Like?

The only way to gain expertise in understanding the results of research studies is to read and practice understanding what they mean. Begin with one of the journals in your own area. If you don't know of any, do one of two things:

- Visit your adviser or some faculty member in the area in which you are interested and ask the question, "What are the best research journals in my area?"
- Visit the library and look through the index of periodicals or search online some of the resources we just identified. You are bound to find hundreds of journals, most online.

For example, for those of you interested in education and psychology and related areas, the following is a sample of 10 research journals that would be a great place for you to start:

- *American Educational Research Journal*
- *American Psychologist*
- *Educational Researcher*
- *Educational and Psychological Measurement*
- *Harvard Educational Review*
- *Journal of Educational Research*
- *Journal of Educational Psychology*
- *Journal of Educational Measurement*
- *Phi Delta Kappan*
- *Review of Educational Research*

Here are 10 more that focus primarily on psychology:

- *Child Development*
- *Cognition*
- *Human Development*

- *Journal of Applied Developmental Psychology*
- *Journal of Experimental Psychology*
- *Journal of Personality and Social Psychology*
- *Journal of School Psychology*
- *Perceptual and Motor Skills*
- *Psychological Bulletin*
- *Sex Roles*

And, don't forget our previous discussion of Ulrich's periodical guide (over 300,000 entries).

Criteria for Judging a Research Study

Judging anyone else's work is never an easy task. A good place to start might be the following checklist, which is organized to help you focus on the most important characteristics of any journal article. These eight areas can give you a good start in better understanding the general format of such a report and how well the author(s) communicated to you what was done, why it was done, how it was done, and what it all means.

> Research articles take all kind of shapes and forms, but their primary purpose is to inform and educate the reader.

1. Review of Previous Research
   - How closely is the literature cited in the study related to previous literature?
   - Is the review recent?
   - Are there any seminal or outstanding references you know of that were left out?

2. Problem and Purpose
   - Can you understand the statement of the problem?
   - Is the purpose of the study clearly stated?
   - Does the purpose seem to be tied to the literature that is reviewed?
   - Is the objective of the study clearly stated?
   - Is there a conceptual rationale to which the hypotheses are grounded?
   - Is there a rationale for why the study is an important one to do?

3. Hypothesis
   - Are the research hypotheses clearly and explicitly stated?
   - Do the hypotheses state a clear association between variables?
   - Are the hypotheses grounded in theory or in a review and presentation of relevant literature?
   - Can the hypotheses be tested?

4. Method
   - Are both the independent and dependent variables clearly defined?
   - Are the definitions and descriptions of the variables complete?
   - Is it clear how the study was conducted?

5. Sample
   - Was the sample selected in such a way that you think it is representative of the population?
   - Is it clear where the sample came from and how it was selected?
   - How similar are the participants in the study to those who have been used in similar studies?

6. Results and Discussion
   - Does the author relate the results to the review of literature?
   - Are the results related to the hypothesis? Is the discussion of the results consistent with the actual results?
   - Does the discussion provide closure to the initial hypothesis presented by the author?

7. References
    • Is the list of references current?
    • Are they consistent in their format? Are the references complete?
    • Does the list of references reflect some of the most important reference sources in the field?

8. General Comments About the Report
    • Is the report clearly written and understandable?
    • Is the language biased?
    • What are the strengths and weaknesses of the research?
    • What are the primary implications of the research?
    • What would you do to improve the research?
    • Does the submitted manuscript conform to the editor's or publisher's specifications?

Using Electronic Tools in Your Research Activities

Imagine this if you will: You are in your apartment and it is late at night. You find that you need one more citation on the development of charter schools to complete your literature review. You are tired. It is snowing. The library is about to close, and it might not have what you need anyway.

Zoom, you're on the Internet and you're on the way. Log on to your library and access one of their many databases to search for the information you need. In 20 seconds you have the reference to read or print. Is this for real? You bet, and since the printing of the last edition of *Exploring Research* (some staggering 3 years ago), online tools and databases are even more dominant forces in preparing, conducting, and disseminating research.

Whether at home, in your office, or in the confines of the library—and now using wireless technology at the mall or in front of the student union—the use of technology for completing literature searches and reviews is booming, and blooming with new databases to search becoming available each day.

In a moment we'll start our explanation of some of this, but first a few words of "this can't be true, but it is." Many of you who are using this book may have never taken advantage of what your library services have to offer. You may not, for whatever reason, access these from off campus, but what is not understandable is why you are not accessing these resources on campus. All colleges and universities (and, of course, the local public library) provide free access to all these resources for students. The personal computers you can use may be located in the computer center, in the library, in academic buildings, or even in all three and more—but they are surely there for the using. It is likely that a hefty chunk of the fees that you pay each semester goes toward purchasing new equipment and paying for these services, so use them!

And just a few more words about libraries in general. We all know how easy it is to explore a library's contents online—it's quick, easy, and usually very reliable. But, there is also a huge benefit to actually physically visiting the library other than to take the orientation workshop we mentioned earlier in the book. Here's the thing: What you may find in the library, incidental to what you are looking for, you may never find online. For example, you're in the stocks exploring articles on charter schools and reading through journal articles organized by volume. Aren't you delightfully surprised to find that the article before the one you are looking for seems to contain some very relevant information to the question you are asking? And, you take out a few more volumes, find a nice easy chair, turn off your MP3 player, and find even more—treasures that were unanticipated, but nonetheless, very valuable. Make a visit—you'll be delightfully surprised.

> Both the computer as a tool and the library as a storehouse of information play different, but equally important and complementary, roles in the research process.

Searching Online

At the University of Kansas, students can walk into Watson Library (one of the main research libraries), sit down at a computer terminal, access ERIC documents, and search through them in seconds for the references of interest—not bad. They can access a network connection that can lead them to millions of other abstracts and full-length articles from hundreds of databases "leased" by the university each year. And they can, of course, do all this from the comfort of their dorm room, apartment, or home 10 or 1,000 miles away. In fact, if they have any difficulty during their online activity, they can even *Ask the Librarian*—that's right, open a new window in the **browser** and enter a question such as "Does the *New York Times* still have an index?" or "What is the leading journal on business education?" These reference librarians are not known as the original search engine for no good reason. They know lots, but most importantly, they know where to find the answers—the key to a good research foundation.

University, business, and government researchers are turning to online information providers more and more to find the key information they need, whether a specific reference or fact, such as the number of bicycles manufactured by Japan or the number of young adults who live in urban areas.

Your local public library, as well as the university's library system, has access to the Internet as well as guides to the information available electronically.

The Value of Online Searches

Doing online searches boils down to a savings of time and convenience and in some cases, thoroughness versus a visit to the library. You can do a search using one of the online services in a quarter of the time it takes to do it manually.

Another important advantage of online searches, if your search skills are anywhere near competent, is that you are not likely to miss very much. The information providers provide access to tens of thousands of documents, either in their own databases or in others they can access. Dedicated databases have millions of pieces (such as the APA's PsycINFO) of information. Most colleges and universities now allow access to their libraries from off campus, and an increasing number allow you access to the complete record of the article (as a PDF), not just an abstract.

Finally, and this may be the most attractive advantage, online searches are the way of the future. There is so much information out there that soon it will be close to impossible to search intelligently without the aid of a computer.

If there is any real downside (as we mentioned earlier), it's that when you use online services, you don't get a chance to browse among the thousands of books at the library and since books are organized by area of specialization you will very often find yourself opening books that you didn't even know existed and finding things that can be very valuable.

The Great Search Engines

Although there is no central listing of Web sites, there are **search engines** that can help you find what you are interested in. For example, the most popular search engine, by far, is Google (www.google.com), and more about that soon. Fill in the term you are looking for and click Google Search and you are bound to find material you can use. Better yet, combine words such as "résumé nursing" to find people who have entered that phrase on their résumé. Type in "www.yahoo.com," which takes you to an opening page with hundreds of links to topics in every area imaginable.

Search engines are tools that help you sift through the thousands of pages of information available on the Internet and identify the specifics of what you need.

For example, let's say you are interested in finding information on homelessness. As you can see in Figure 3A.7, almost 7,000,000 results came up in less than .3 of a second. Amazing. Figure 3A.7 shows the term entered in the search area of Google and the results of that search. We'll get to an analysis of a Google screen later in this section.

Figure 3A.7 A sample Google search.

Google™ is a registered trademark of Google, Inc.

After the search is completed, the results will show several suggested links which you then can click on to find out the contents of the home pages that were found.

Are all search engines created equally? No. And one of the ways in which they are not created equal is what they are best suited for. Table 3A.4 lists a variety of search engines by what they do. The URL don't have the ubiquitous http://www as the start of each one since browsers such as Firefox, Internet Explorer, Chrome, and Bing can search and locate with that additional information (and keystrokes on your part).

You can also consult a search engine that, in itself, searches many different search engines. For example, search engines such as SurfWax (www.surfwax.com) and Mamma (www.mamma.com and billed, of course, "The Mother of All Search Engines®"), are **meta-search engines**, or those search engines that return the results of exploring many search engines all at once. Let's say that your research involves looking at the history of baseball and you need to review various major league teams. In Figure 3A.8 you can see the results of a SurfWax search for information about the Washington Nationals where almost 70,000,000 pages were identified.

Here are some tips about using a search engine:

- Enter the narrowest search terms and then broaden your search from there. Entering "intelligence" will find lots of stuff, most of it irrelevant; however, if you enter "intelligence" and "children" and "school," the results will be much more manageable and closer to what you want. Remember that the fewer the words you enter, the more general the results will be.
- If you use more than one word, join them with the conjunction "AND," such as bilingual AND education, or use quotes, such as "bilingual education." This is the default for some search engines but not all.
- If a help file or function comes along with the search engine, open it and read it. It will have invaluable information that will save you time and effort.
- When you become more accustomed to using a search engine, look for the more advanced searching techniques and use them.
- Didn't you get what you wanted? The simplest solution is to check your typing. Simple typos spell disaster.

The original, and still the best, search engine is your reference librarian who never crashes, is always available, tends to be helpful, and is very knowledgeable.

If you need to do a general, all purpose search . . .	
Name	**URL**
Alltheweb	google.com
AltaVista	altavista.com
AOL	aol.com
ASK	ask.com
Cull	cull.com
Gigablast	gigablast.com
Google	google.com
Lycos	lycos.com
MSN	msn.com
Yahoo	Yahoo.com
If you want to search for blogs about a particular topic . . .	
Name	**URL**
Blogpulse	Blogpulse.com
Google blog search	blogsearch.google.com
LJSeek	Ljseek.com
Opinmind	Opinmind.com
Tecnhorati	Technorati.com
If you want to search for books . . .	
Name	**URL**
Your local library!	Easy to find at your school URL
Amazon	Amazon.com
BookFinder	Bookfinder.com
Google Scholar	scholar.google.com
Google Books	Books.google.com
ReadPrint	ReadPrint.com
If you want to search for images . . .	
Name	**URL**
Picsearch	Picsearch.com
PhotoBucket	photobucket.com
New York Public Library Digital Gallery	digitalgallery.nypl.org
Classroom Clipart	classroomclipart.com
stock .xchng	www.sxc.hu

Table 3A.4 Different types of search engines and what they search for

Courtesy of Google Inc.

- Try a synonym for the term or terms you're looking for. There's more than one way to eviscerate a feline (get it?).

And if you want to find out even more about search engines, go to websearch.about.com and Wendy Boswell's all-informative and useful About.com search engine site.

More About Google

Although Google is the most popular search engine and its share of searches continues, and you may use it regularly, it is still worth exploring what it does and how it does it. It regularly catalogues millions of web pages and returns results in very short order. Since it is so popular, here are some specific tips about using this search engine, including some special features you may not know about.

Not just Google, but every search engine has its own special tips and tricks you can learn (at their Web site) to facilitate your searching activities and increase your success rate.

Figure 3A.8   Searching for information about the Washington Nationals Baseball team.

Google™ is a registered trademark of Google Inc.

Google Search Results

Figure 3A.9 shows a search conducted on the term "grade retention." There's more to the search results than meets the eye (not only a listing of other Web sites), and here's a more detailed analysis on what's in that window and how it might help you.

1. Across the top of the Google search results is a listing of other "tabs" you can click on to find additional information about the topic (Web, Images, Videos, Maps, News, etc.). For example, if you want to find news about the topic on which you searched, click on News. In this case, you can find related news stories that can further your understanding of this topic.
2. To the right of the Google search area (where you enter the terms for which you want to search) are Advanced search and Preferences options. These basically allow you to refine your searches and are easy to learn on your own but surely not necessary as you are learning to use Google and even when you are a fairly competent Google user. As we said earlier, the more refined the words you identify as search terms, the better your results will be.
3. In this example, there are no sponsored links (really advertisements on which Google makes a ton of money), which are usually located on the right-hand side of the page. These advertisements are located away from the results listing so that you very clearly know they are to be treated separately.
4. Below (and to the right of) the Google search term (in this case "grade retention") is a tally of the results, showing that 1,460,000 "hits" accumulated in .23 second (fast!). Note that if you repeated the same search, you will get a different outcome (probably just slightly) since things change so fast.

Figure 3A.9 A Google search on the phrase "grade retention" and the results.

5. Right below the results line is the all-important results of the search. Most show the following:
   a. The title of the page (Grade Retention—The Great Debate). Notice how the words "grade retention" are highlighted since this is one of the original search words.
   b. Next is a brief abstract of the contents of that page, which should allow you to determine whether it is worth exploring.
   c. Next is the URL, or the Web address, for this particular page followed by the size of the page, the cache (any stored record of this page), and other pages that are similar to this one. As always, you can click on any underlined link.

Word Order and Repetition

You already know that word order matters (we talked about that earlier), but the repetition of words in the search box matters as well.

For example, you saw in Figure 3A.8 the result of a search on grade retention. However, if we enter the search terms "grade retention retention" (we entered it twice), then the weighting of the search leans more toward retention, less toward grade. Similarly, if we entered the terms "grade grade retention," the search would be weighted toward the topic of grades. Word repetition is not a science, but it does allow you to prompt Google to provide another set of results on the same topic.

Using the Phonebook

This may be the greatest nondocumented, and not generally known, tip and feature about using Google.

A great deal of what we all do as researchers is to find information and locate people. If you find a particularly interesting research article and want to know more about the topic, there's just nothing wrong with searching for more information about the author of that article and contacting him and her.

For example, let's say you want to contact this author. The first place to try is his home institution (the University for Kansas, which you can find at www.ku.edu). This should get you what you want. Let's say, however, that in spite of your efforts, you have no luck.

Using the Google phonebook feature, you can enter the terms *phonebook:salkind ks* (notice there is no space after the colon and you have to know the state in which the listing is located), and you'll get the contact information you need. You can reverse the process as well by entering the phone number and seeing the listing. For your information, *rphonebook* will search only for residential listing and *bphonebook* only for business listings.

Using Bibliographic Database Programs

Anyone who does research and writes about that research can tell you that one of the most tedious parts of writing a research manuscript is references, references, references—keeping track of them, entering them, and organizing them is just about the least fun anyone can have.

There are a welcome set of tools that can help you do these three things and more. Bibliographic database programs are tools that help you manage your set of references, and the best ones allow you to do things such as

- Enter the data for any one reference using a standard form
- Change the format to fit the manuscript requirements, such as the American Psychological Association (APA) or the Modern Language Association (MLA)
- Search the database of references using key words
- Add notes to any one reference which can also be searched
- Generate a final list of references for use in the manuscript

You can, of course, do all these by using $3'' \times 5''$ index cards, but entering the references only once and never having to retype them, track them, and organize them—we could go on and on, but we think you get the picture.

A bunch of such bibliographic database programs are available—some of them free and some of them commercially available. Let's take a look at EndNote (http://www.endnote.com), a commercially available product. All of these tend to offer the same features—you enter information about the reference, and the tool formats it according to the format you specify. They all accomplish this goal in different ways and also offer different bells and whistles, so you should take advantage of the free download and try them out. Other commercial products that work well are ProCite (www.procite.com) and Biblioscape (http://www.biblioscape.com). Be sure that the program works on your operating system because some only work for a Windows- or a Mac-based operating system.

As you can see in Figure 3A.10, EndNote works by your choice of the type of references (book, journal, web page) and then entering the pertinent information. The information then appears in your "library" (we created on named "term paper"). Once finished creating the library of references, EndNote (or another application) generates the bibliography for you with a few clicks, formatted as you want or even using a custom format.

As you can see, each element of the reference (author, date, etc.) is entered in its own space. You complete a separate form for each reference (be it a journal article, a book chapter, or a presentation at a convention) and you select the entry format.

Although one of the most tedious, time-consuming parts of creating a research document is tracking and dealing with bibliographic references, there are now several different software programs that can greatly reduce the necessary time and effort.

Figure 3A.10 Using Endnotes, one of many citation creation tools.

Courtesy of Google Inc.

Looking for Articles Online

This clever design from the Google People fits very well the needs of any researcher, from the most basic to the most advanced.

Researchers are in the business of finding information and using that information to lay the groundwork for their research. One might search specific sites such as the Washington Post, U.S. News & World Report, or the American Psychological Association, and one would surely find material about a particular topic. But Google is an excellent tool for finding information across many different sites since it will look not only for topics that may have appeared on a particular site, but also for topics that appear secondarily to that site. For example, a search on the NYT Web site for articles on day care would result in a bunch of productive hits. But, how about a search for articles on this topic that may have appeared originally in the *Times* but in other locations as well? Of course, this can be done for newspapers, periodicals, magazines, journals—anywhere material might appear. How to do it?

Here are the search terms for a simple search for articles about day care in the *New York Times:* day care site: www.nytimes.com.

Day care appears in quotes so Google will look for it as a set of terms and not just "day" and then "care." This search results in 28,100 hits.

Now, if we search for the magic words copyright * The New York Times Company day care, we find 851 hits, which includes all the articles on day care from the *Times*, as well as all the articles used by other publications from the *Times* (in which they may have cited the *Times*).

The * in the search terms acts as a wild card so any year of copyright is searched for, and we could get rid of the site: command since the New York Times Company (which is their copyright line) serves the same purpose. Pretty cool.

Finding Tons of Directories and Lists

This is the last Google tip, but another one that could prove invaluable. Much of our job as researchers is to find information, but also collections of information. The command intitle: can serve us quite well.

For example, the search terms intitle: directory day care would return listings of directories containing information about day care. If we changed the search terms to include a wild card, such as intitle: directory * day care, we then get a much more broadly defined list since it can include elderly day care, adult day care, Miami day care, and so on—and the number of returns is much, much higher than the simple direct search we first showed you.

More About Google Than You Can Imagine

Google has a set of help centers located at http://www.google.com/support/ where you should go if you need support about one of their products such as Gmail, Google Docs, or help on searching the Web.

Advanced Google Search Tools

Sure it's easy to find the phone number of a researcher who lives in Wyoming, but phonebook is only one of many search operators that Google allows to help you refine what you want to do and you can find about all of them at http://www.googleguide.com/advanced_operators.html.

For example, you can use the search operator "define:" to find the definition of a word. So, entering *define:mysticism* will give you huge lists of the definition of the term on various locations around the Web. If you typed in "definition of mysticism", you would get web pages that define mysticism, but not central directory of definition. Another really useful operator is "source", which provides a search on a particular topic limited to the source you identify. For example, if you want to search for information about iPads, but only which appeared in the *New York Times*, *iPad source:New York Times* would provide you with a nice collection of articles that have appeared. You can even search for the latest weather report (*weather:losangeles*) and yes, what time the movies are showing (*movie:title* such as *movie:Greenberg Lawrence, ks*) and it really works!

TEST YOURSELF

It's really easy—and maybe too easy—to conduct your background research online without regard to that massive building in the idle of campus called the library. Do you think it is adequate to conduct your literature review online? What advantages does this strategy offer? Disadvantages?

Using the Internet: Beyond Searches

Most of you who are reading this text are very savvy when it comes to using the Internet, but there are still some of you who are not. The following material is a refresher for those who can always learn something new and an introduction to those who are unfamiliar with the Internet, how it works, and what it can do for a new researcher.

In the most basic of terms, the Internet is a **network** of networks. A network is a collection of computers that are connected to one another and can communicate with each other. Imagine all these networks being connected to one another and imagine hundreds of networks and thousands of computers of all different types attached to one another and millions of people using those computers. Now you have some idea how large the Internet is. It is growing geometrically and millions of people connect every day for work, for fun, and of course, to pursue research activities.

Research Activities and the Internet

If you are talking about information in all shapes and sizes, there is not much that you cannot do on the Internet. Here is a brief overview of how the Internet can be used for research purposes:

- The Internet is often used for **electronic mail** or **e-mail.** You can exchange postal mail with a colleague across the United States or the world, but you can also do the same without ever putting pen to paper. You create a message and send it to your correspondent's electronic address with documents, images, and more attached. It is fast, easy, and fun. For example, if you would like a reprint of an article you find interesting, you could e-mail the author and ask for a copy and it may very well come back to you electronically. Virtually all faculty, staff, and students at educational institutions have access to e-mail. Also if you want further information about a particular person's work, you could probably find his or her résumé online.
- Thousands of **electronic newsgroups**, often called Usenet newsgroups, are available on the Internet. These are places where information can be posted and shared among Internet users, with topics that range from space exploration to the authenticity of a Civil War–era land deed. You can "drop in" and contribute to any of these **newsgroups**. For example, if you are interested in K–12 math curricula, try the k12.ed.math newsgroup. How about pathological behavior? Try the sci.psychology. psychotherapy newsgroup. We will return to them again later for a short demonstration.
- And finally, there is the world of social media including Facebook and Twitter and these lend themselves to entirely new ways of being used for research purposes. More about these later in this chapter.

More About E-Mail

Imagine it is 1925 and you are sitting at your desk at college, writing a letter to a friend in England. You stamp the letter, mail it, and three weeks later you receive an answer. You are amazed at how fast the mail is and sit down to answer your friend's new questions about how much you like college and what you will do after you graduate.

Now imagine it is 2012 and you are writing to a friend in England, only this time you use e-mail. From your home, you compose the message, press the send key, and your friend has it almost instantly. Not only does your friend have it, but you copied it to three other members of the research team, including your primary professor. The reply arrives within 20 minutes and "attached" to the message is well-written response to your message and a new paper on the topic of interest.

E-mail works much like conventional mail. You write a message and send it to an address. The big difference is that there is no paper involved. Rather, the messages you send travel from one computer to another in a matter of minutes or hours, rather than in days or weeks, as fast as your voice travels in a telephone conversation.

How should you use e-mail, which is the really big question here? It's fun for social and family reasons, but it's an indispensable part of the research process. Imagine having a question about a particular test you want to use in a research study. e-Mail the test's author. Imagine not being able to find a critical reference. e-Mail the author of that reference (and you should know how to find that author by now given the tips we discussed throughout other parts of this chapter). Imagine not being able to understand a point your professor made in class about a particular statistical technique. With permission, e-mail your professor. This stuff really works.

One note about e-mail. It works because there are servers to which the mail is sent and then distributed. Sometimes these servers break down and mail can be delayed, for an hour or, in some cases when perhaps they have been infected with a virus, for days.

Our advice is to have two e-mail addresses, one that you access from school and one of the other many free ones that are available such as those from Yahoo! (www.yahoo.com), Hotmail (www.hotmail.com), or GMail (from Google). You can always use these as a backup and receive or send mail from there. In many cases, you can even view your other mail account receipts (such as your school mail) within your secondary account.

A huge advantage of Web-based mail is that you can access your mail from any computer in the galaxy. It is always available as long as you have an Internet connection. In addition, as Web-based mailing programs become more sophisticated, they offer features that even fancy commercial mailers such as Outlook might not have, such as being able to (easily) enter a vacation message when you are away from your mail client and want people to automatically be notified. Or, you can send mail through GMail and make it appear as if it is being sent through any other account. Very handy. Many researchers create such new mail accounts for each research or writing project so they can segregate their mail and track it more effectively.

Another note: A host of roadblocks have been introduced along with the millions of e-mails that appear every day in mailboxes around the world in the form of spam, adware, viruses, and other nefarious mechanisms for unscrupulous people to gain access to your privacy. No matter how you do it, take advantage of some of the relatively inexpensive commercial products and install them on your home computer. For the most part, your college or university should be taking care of these concerns at some central location. But for you, it is critical (and almost inexcusable) to have some type of effective and current (and this is really important) way to keep your machine free of viruses and other junk.

And yet another note! In your electronic workings these days, you will see reference to the "cloud." Cloud-based computing is coming—it's where data, e-mail, and other information are stored on a remote computer (known as a server), so there is nothing locally available on your desktop. Everything, in other words, is Web based including applications (much like Google Docs is today).

The advantage? Clearly, you can do anything from any connected computer. No more new disk to install when applications change; rather, you would work on a subscription basis and every time a new version of Microsoft Office is released, the changes are right there the next time you open it up. It should be cheaper and more readily available (remember, *being connected is everything*) and, no more backing up (well, sort of). The cloud system you use stores your data in a safe place.

OK, so what's the drawback? Although we are told otherwise, oops!—there goes the server and there goes everything you created. While cloud computing enthusiasts speak to the reliability and safety of the system—and it is there—you and I both know that someday it will fail. The lesson? It's the future, but be sure to use whatever local backup system is available as well.

An Introduction to Usenet (News) Groups

Here's a topic that interestingly enough many people do not know much about. It's interesting since newsgroups are such an immense source of information and there are so many from which to select.

Imagine being able to find information on more than 100,000 topics, ranging from stereo systems to jokes (censored and otherwise) to the ethics of law to college football to astronomy. Where would you be able to find a collection of such diverse information that can be easily accessed? You guessed it—the Internet and the various newsgroup sites that ship news each day around the world. The news that fits in one category, such as college football or the ethics of law, forms a newsgroup (also called a group). A newsgroup is simply a collection of information about one topic. Once again, surprisingly, very few students are aware of and use newsgroups.

To help manage the flow of articles, news sites are managed, moderated, administered, and censored by system administrators who work for institutions such as universities and corporations. The newsgroups from which you can select news are those made available by the system administrator and more often than not, the system administrator has to give approval before you are allowed to join and contribute.

What's in the News?

Newsgroups are named and organized based on a set of rules. The most general of these rules has to do with the name of the group itself. There is a hierarchical structure to a newsgroup name, with the highest level of the hierarchy appearing in the left-most position. For example, the newsgroup name k12.ed.tech means that within k12 (the general name for the kindergarten through twelfth-grade newsgroup), there is a subset named ed (for education) and within that another subset named tech (for technology).

Table 3A.5 is a sample of some newsgroups: what these groups are named, the general area they cover, and examples of what is in each of these groups. Originally, all

> Newsgroups can be small or huge discussions of just about any topic.

Newsgroup	General Area	Examples
Alt	Everything that doesn't fit anywhere else and certainly lots of stuff out of the ordinary	• alt.actors.dustin-hoffman (welcome back to the graduate) • alt.amazon.women (xena, the warrior princess and more) • alt.anything (guess)
Comp	Information about computers, computer science, computer software, and general interest computer topics	• comp.ai (danger! will robinson!—all about artificial intelligence) • comp.compression (a discussion of ways to compress or reduce files) • comp.software engineering (so you want to design a new chip?)
Hum	Discussion of issues in the humanities	• humanities.classics (more about the classic texts) • humanities.language (discussion about languages and how they fit into the study of the humanities) • humanities.philosophy (all about the great masters and their ideas)
Misc	A catchall of topics and ideas	• misc.forsale (kind of like a garage sale online) • misc.books (discussions about books and writers) • misc.invest (how and where to invest your hard-earned money)
News	Information about news, newsgroups, and the newsgroup network	• news.admin.censorships (all about what should and shouldn't be on the Net) • news.admin.net-abuse.email (don't like all that junk e-mail? come here for advice) • news.accounce.conferences (where to go to be seen)

Table 3A.5 The Big newsgroups prefixes

Newsgroup	General Area	Examples
Rec	Information about recreation, hobbies, the performing arts, and fun stuff	• rec.sport.swimming (make a splash) • rec.bicycles.racing (what cool stuff to buy for your bike to go faster) • rec.skydiving (take an extra 'chute)
Sci	Information about science, scientific research and discoveries, engineering, and some social science stuff	• sci.astro (astronomy) • sci.cognitive (so that's what you're thinking!) • sci.skeptic (ufos do exist!)
Soc	Information about the social sciences	• soc.couples (people getting along) • soc.penpals (why people write to one another) • soc.misc (stuff that doesn't fit anywhere else)
Talk	Discussion of current affairs	• talk.atheism (about atheism) • talk.rumor (rumor central) • talk.radio (find out about Air America, Sean Hannity and more)

Table 3A.5   *(Continued)*

newsgroups started with the .net suffix. Then, a renaming of newsgroups occurred in 1986 and there were seven main groups; .comp, .news, .sci, .rec, .soc, .talk, and .misc. Humanities (.hum) was added so that the number of primary newsgroups was finalized (for now) at eight. The suffix .alt represents all other newsgroups that do not have a clear place in any other groups (and sometimes jokingly is meant to represent Anarchists, Lunatics, and Terrorists due to the subversive and anything goes nature of .alt newsgroups).

To see how a newsgroup works, let's follow an example of someone who is interested in educational technology. Almost every browser, such as Firefox, Chrome, or Internet Explorer, comes with its own reader built in and ready to go, but most browsers also come with a groups function that is even easier to use, as you can see in Figure 3A.11. These tools allow you to read existing news and to post new messages.

The first thing you need to do when you are ready to access a newsgroup is to subscribe to it. Your e-mail program or browser (such as Internet Explorer) can do this, or in some cases you may need a separate **news reader**. From the list of newsgroups, you can select the ones to which you want to subscribe. Each time you go to the newsgroup, you will get the updated version of those newsgroups, including all the news that has been added to that group since the last time you opened it.

The next step would be to open the k12.ed.tech newsgroup and examine the contents, as shown in Figure 3A.12 (we used Google as our reader). Within newsgroups, you will see a listing of topics open for discussion, each one started by an individual as a source for more information, a place to meet electronically, discuss issues, and so forth.

If someone wants to participate in a certain newsgroup, he or she can add a new topic at this level, or go into an existing newsgroup and make a contribution.

Figure 3A.11 The Opening screen for Google groups where you can search for groups, start one of your own or explore the most popular ones.

Google™ is a registered trademark of Google Inc.

Figure 3A.12 The newsgroup is a wide-open community where everyone is welcome to contribute and learn.

Google™ is a registered trademark of Google Inc.

Using Mailing Lists or ListServs

Another really neat way to use the Internet is a great source of information. You can sign up (subscribe) for a **listserv** discussion group, which is an automatic depository for information. If you subscribe, you receive everything that the list receives. A listserv is also known as a mailing list.

For example, if you belong to the K–12 educational technology mailing list, then each time someone sends mail to that list, you will receive it as well. There are more listservs than you can imagine, and it will take some exploration to find out which ones best fit your needs.

To subscribe to a mailing list, you need to send a message to the list's administrator. As soon as you do that, a constant stream of messages will come your way. Be careful— if a list is very active, you can receive hundreds of messages in any one day. If you go even a day without checking your mail, your electronic mailbox is likely to get so full of messages that you won't be able to read anything! Imagine your real mailbox outside your apartment or home. When it gets stuffed full, it is very difficult to pull out any one piece because the mail is packed so tightly. You would need a bigger box (more storage space), or you need to empty the box before it gets so full. Such is the case with an Internet mailing list: Either get a larger e-mail box (ask for more storage space from the system administrator) or check your mail more than once a day.

At Catalist (http://www.lsoft.com/catalist.html) you can find a guide to the always update list of over 500,000 lists(!), all available to you and me, and you can search by the number of subscribers, the country of origin, and, of course, the topic. Want to spend unending hours at your computer learning about everything from black holes to death rays, this is the place to start.

And, Just a Bit about Web Sites

In the last edition of *Exploring Research*, this section was filled with information about home pages or Web pages and what is contained on them that might be of use. There was a screen shot of the Library of Congress Web site's opening page (which is a portal to the entire site at http://www.loc.gov), but times have changed, as does the information we include here.

Web sites are of course portals to more information but should a researcher use them? The most obvious way is by seeking out information contained at various sites, perhaps including links to other sites and on and on. But, as an active researcher there's another entirely different function that Web sites can perform.

You can easily, and at little expense, create a Web site of your own, for your own research project. Unlike the early days of Web development and design, today you can create a home for your content easily, quickly, and relatively inexpensively. No need to hire the 10-year-old from down the block or some fancy firm that charges $25 per hour. And, no need to know programming languages such as HTML (Hypertext Markup Language). Today, companies such as GoDaddy (www.godaddy.com) and Homestead (www.homestead.com) are not free, but are often ridiculously cheap (such as $4.99 per month for Homestead). And best of all, these companies and many others provide a wide variety of tools to help you drag-and-drop, modify, spruce up, and generally make your Web site quite professional looking.

What do you do once you have created it? As the home for your research activities, you can conclude such information as

- The title of the project
- How to get in touch with the project's coordinator (probably you!)
- A history of what is being done, where and how
- Forms that may need to be completed
- Data that may have been collected that can be shared

- Links to similar studies, and
- Any information that educates the viewer and may encourage him or her to participate.

Using Social Media and Blogs

There's no end to the imagination of entrepreneurs when it comes to the use of technology to have an impact on our lives, and correspondingly, there is no end to the imagination of researchers to use that technology in their research as well.

What About Facebook and Twitter?

You know about *Facebook* and *Twitter,* but could you imagine using these tools in a research setting? There are many others, but we'll look at just these two. Here's how to use them.

Facebook is a social networking tool that allows users to form groups, communicate with each other, and even play games. With over 600,000,000 active users, it is an amazing way to get like-minded people together to discuss and participate in research where some common interest is maintained. You would be well suited to begin a Facebook group based on your own research interests and reach out for others who have interests that are similar to your's.

And, of course, Facebook participants can very well become participants in a study as well. Facebook is a magnificent naturally occurring laboratory to study (mostly) young people's ideas and actions as they exist in virtual and real-time groups. Researchers from Harvard, Indiana, and Carnegie-Melon are all using online subject samples to collect data and test hypothesis.

Twitter is another social networking tool that allows users to create 140-character messages and then allows those messages to be sent out to anyone who is following the author. Sometimes small potatoes and only 10-20 followers. But sometimes, followers number in the hundreds of thousands.

Among other ideas, you can of course follow a researcher in whose work you are interested by simply signing up to follow him on Twitter (you need a Twitter account to do any of these things). Then, each time he or she creates one of those 140 character messages, it comes to you and the hundreds or thousands of other people who signed up on his or her list.

Another way to use Twitter is to find out what is being written as people are being followed by searching on this huge and vast electronic archives that are available. For example, if you wanted to know what people were saying (or Tweeting) about nursing education, you can use Twitter's simple search box on the main page and enter the words "nursing education" (using quotes since you would want the search to return for both terms together, not each one separately). Or, if you want to dig even deeper, go to the advanced search form (look for it under Help or at http://search.twitter.com/advanced) as you see in Figure 3A.13. And, it's simple enough to find people—just click the Find People button on the main page.

Writing the Literature Review

It is now time to take all the information you have collected using all the tools you have learned about in this chapter and somehow organize it so it begins to make sense. This is your review of literature, and now you actually need to write it (horrors!). Here are some writing hints.

First, *read other literature reviews*. There is no arguing with success. Ask a student who has already been through this course or your adviser for a successful proposal. Look carefully at the format as well as the content of the literature review. Also, look at some of the sources mentioned earlier in this chapter, especially sources that are reviews of the literature, journal articles, and other review papers.

Figure 3A.13   Using Twitter help.

Second, *create a unified theme,* or a line of thought, throughout the review. Your review of literature is not supposed to be a novel, but most good literature reviews build from a very general argument to a more specific one and set the stage for the purpose of the research. You should bring the reader "into the fold" and create some interest in where you will be going with this research that other people have not gone.

Third, *use a system to organize your materials.* Most reviews of the literature will be organized chronologically within topics. For example, if you are studying gender differences in anxiety and verbal ability among adults, you would organize all the references by topic area (anxiety and verbal ability), and then within each of these topics, begin your review with the earliest dated reference. In this way you move from the earliest to the latest and provide some historical perspective.

Fourth, *work from an outline* even if you are an accomplished and skilled writer. It is a good idea to use this tool to help organize the main thought in your proposal before you begin the actual writing process.

Fifth, *build bridges between the different areas you review.* For example, if you are conducting a cross-cultural study comparing the ways in which East Indian and American parents discipline their children, you might not find a great deal of literature on that specific topic. But there is certainly voluminous literature on child rearing in America and in India and tons of references on discipline. Part of the creative effort in writing a proposal is being able to show where these two come together in an interesting and potentially fruitful way.

Sixth, *practice may not always make perfect but it certainly doesn't hurt.* For some reason, most people believe that a person is born with or without a talent for writing. Any successful writer would admit that to be a class-A basketball player or an accomplished violinist, one has to practice. Should it be any different for a writer? Should you have any doubts about this question, ask a serious writer how many hours a day or week he or she practices that craft. More often than not, you will see it is the equivalent of the ballplayer or the musician. In fact, a writer friend of mine gives this advice to people who want to write but don't have a good idea about the level of involvement it requires: "Just sit down at your typewriter or word processor, and open a vein." That is how easy it is.

So the last (but really the first) hint is to *practice your writing.* As you work at it and find out where you need to improve (get feedback from other students and professors), you will indeed see a change for the better.

Summary

There's a lot to know about this selecting a problem topic and doing the necessary background research and it just begins when you have some familiarity with your field and some experience using both online and offline resources. Finding a topic and a question that works for you (in every sense of the word) is a real challenge and often an obstacle for beginning students and beginning scientists. Take your time, talk to your colleagues and your faculty, and make it into an exploration looking for the gold that represents a topic that will carry you to a new level of intellectual growth.

Exercises

1. Make a list of 10 research topics that you would find interesting to pursue. These can be any topics dealing with education or psychology which you might glean from newspapers, radio and television news, magazines, research journals, and even overheard conversations. Rank these various ideas by level of interest, and for each of the top five write one sentence explaining why it appeals to you.

2. Take the idea that you ranked no.1 in exercise 1 and do the following:
   (a) Write a one-paragraph description of a study that incorporates that idea.
   (b) List the steps you could take in reviewing the specific literature relevant to this topic.
   (c) From this idea, generate three more questions derived from the original question or idea.

3. Use the idea that you ranked no. 2 in exercise 1 and do the following:
   (a) Locate a related reference from a journal and write out the complete citation.
   (b) Locate an abstract from a study that focuses on the topic.

4. Find ten other sources of information about any of the topics you ranked in exercise 1 and write out the complete citation for each. Try to complete a set of other sources that is as diverse as possible.

5. Go to your library and find five journals in your field of study. After you have located the journals, examine them to determine:
   (a) What type of articles are published (reviews of literature, empirical studies, etc.).
   (b) Whether the journal is published by a professional organization (such as the American Psychological Association) or by a private group (such as Sage Press).

    (c) The number of articles in each journal and if there is any similarity in the topic areas covered within each issue of the journal.

    (d) How often the journal is published and other information about its editorial policies (e.g., guidelines, features).

6. Select any topic that you are interested in and use three different search engines to obtain on-line information. How do the results differ? Which one gave you the most interesting and useful information? How might you revise your search terms to get the same degree of usefulness from other search engines?

7. Visit Google Groups at http://groups.google.com. Type in a topic of interest for you next to the "Search for a group" link and click on the link. Write down the title of the group or the group e-mail address.

8. Find three abstracts from recent research journals. For each abstract identify the following:
    (a) The purpose
    (b) The hypothesis
    (c) The type of study (e.g., correlational, experimental)
    (d) The conclusion

9. You have been assigned the topic of gender differences in adolescent development for a research study. Formulate five research questions that address this topic.

10. What are some helpful things you can do to help you figure out if your first idea for a research study is the best one?

11. Use the Internet to find five references on any of the topics in which you have an interest (as you defined in earlier questions).

12. What purpose do the following search commands serve?
    (a) phonebook:
    (b) *
    (c) "blended families families" (entering one word twice)

13. What are some potential advantages to reading peer-reviewed journal articles instead of relying on information obtained through other online sources such as Wikipedia? What are some potential advantages to using Wikipedia?

14. Indicate which of the following are general, which are primary, and which are secondary sources:
    (a) *Encyclopedia of Psychology*
    (b) *Time* Magazine
    (c) *Statistics for People Who (Think They) Hate Statistics* (textbook)
    (d) *Journal of Sport Health*
    (e) Facts on File
    (f) A review of Freud's dream interpretations
    (g) Dissertation Abstracts Online

15. A recent study found that college freshmen who participated in an occupational engagement intervention wherein they e-mailed professors, learned ways to increase their information about careers, and wrote about their experiences of learning more about careers scored significantly higher on a measure of career decision-making efficacy than students in a control group. How might you work from or replicate this study without being redundant?

16. Look up the keyword phrase "test anxiety" in Google Scholar. What are the first three titles that appear?

17. Wang and Amato found in their 2000 study that divorce adjustment was significantly related to income levels, age, remarriage status, and previous attitude toward marital dissolution, among other variables. What are three more variables you could examine in relation to divorce adjustment?

18. Why is it helpful to review literature before finalizing your hypothesis?

Online. . .

The Gale Directory of Online, Portable, and Internet Databases

The Gale Database Directory at http://library.dialog.com/bluesheets/html/bl0230.html provides detailed information on publicly available databases and database products that are accessible through an on-line vendor or the Internet.

The GPO Database List

Want to see how a huge amount of data can be organized and made easily accessible to the online user? Check the U.S. Government Printing Office (GPO) database online at http://www.gpoaccess.gov/databases.html. You can find out about everything referred to in a specific House or Senate session through the Congressional Quarterly or what bills have been passed. Best of all, this whole collection illustrates what power is possible when the Web and databases come together.

The National Library of Medicine Databases

The National Library of Medicine provides a wide variety of past and present resources related to the biomedical and health sciences at http://www.nlm.nih.gov/databases/index.html. The format of databases varies, including being searchable to just bibliographic citations to full text. You'll find tons of stuff for the social and behavioral sciences researcher as well as the aspiring nuclear scientist.

Choosing the Best Search Engine for your Information Need

Noodle Tools compares different search engines and recommends the best ones based on your need (identifying a topic, narrowing a topic, finding primary sources, by topic, historical or current, etc.) at http://www.noodletools.com/debbie/literacies/information/5locate/adviceengine.html.

Ready 'Net Go!

On this Web site, available at http://www.tulane.edu/~lmiller/ArchivesResources.html, Tulane University exhibits a "meta index" with links to nearly every archival resource available. The site contains general search tools as well.

❖ ❖ ❖ Chapter 3B ❖ ❖ ❖

The Importance of Practicing Ethics in Research

This is a short chapter on a very big and very important topic. Why short? Well, it does not take much room to present the important guidelines that all scientists who deal with participants (be they human or animal) should adhere to. And, it's all you need to get started ensuring participants well being as a part of your research activities.

Why important? Without exaggeration, not following these guidelines can result in consequences that are extremely serious including the loss of funding from federal and other agencies, censure by professional organizations, and even losing employment. As a student, this is just the right time for you to begin thinking about these ideas. Even if you never do research, you'll be informed and be able to make judgments about the appropriateness of the behavior of the researchers around you.

WHAT YOU'LL LEARN ABOUT IN THIS CHAPTER:

- Why practicing ethical behavior is important

- The most important and basic principles of ethical behavior

- The different ethical guidelines presented by professional organizations

A Bit of History

David Resnick from the National Institute of Environmental Health Sciences (NIEHS) has assembled a very informative timeline of this history and issues within the general sphere of ethical research since the 1930s. What follows is an abbreviated version and you can find the entire timeline at http://www.niehs.nih.gov/research/resources/bioethics/timeline.cfm.

What is so interesting about these dates and events is that they sometimes repeat each other, different minorities are clearly taken advantage of, and at times little was done to prevent such abuses. It was not until the 1960s that much attention was paid to these issues.

1932–1972 The Tuskegee Syphilis Study, sponsored by the U.S. Department of Health, studies the effects of untreated syphilis in 400 African American men. Researchers withheld treatment even when penicillin became widely available and researchers did not tell the subjects that they were in an experiment.

1939–1945 German scientists conduct research on concentration camp prisoners.

1944–1980s The U.S. government sponsors secret research on the effects of radiation on human beings. Subjects were not told that they were participating in the experiments, which were conducted on cancer patients, pregnant women, and military personnel.

1947 The Nuremberg Code for research on human subjects is adopted. The Allies use the document in the Nuremberg Trials to convict Nazi scientists of war crimes.

1953 James Watson and Francis Crick discover the structure of DNA, for which they eventually would share the Nobel Prize in 1962. They secretly obtained key x-ray diffraction data from Rosalind Franklin without her permission. She was not awarded a Nobel Prize because she died in 1953 from ovarian cancer (at age 37), and the prize is not awarded posthumously.

1956–1980 Saul Krugman, Joan Giles, and other researchers conduct hepatitis experiments on mentally disabled children at the Willowbrook State School, where they intentionally infected children with the disease and observed its natural progression.

1950s–1963 The CIA administers LSD to unknowing participants.

1961–1962 Stanley Milgram proves that many people are willing to do things that they consider to be morally wrong.

1964 Ethical principles for research on human participants presented at the World Medical Association, Helsinki Declaration.

1966 Henry Beecher publishes an article in *the New England Journal of Medicine* exposing 22 unethical studies in biomedicine, including the Tuskegee syphilis study and the Willowbrook hepatitis study.

1960s / 1970s The beginning of the animal rights movement with the adoption of the Animal Welfare Act.

1972 The national media and Congress focus on unethical research practices with human subjects, including the Tuskegee study.

1974 Congress passes the National Research Act, which authorizes federal agencies to develop human research regulations.

1979 The National Commission releases the Belmont Report, principles of ethical research on human subjects. The report becomes a key document in human research ethics regulations in the United States.

1981 The Department of Health, Education, and Welfare conducts major revisions of the federal human research regulations on human subjects research.

1989 The Public Health Service forms two agencies, the Office of Scientific Integrity and the Office of Scientific Integrity Review, to investigate scientific misconduct and provide information and support for universities.

1989 The NIH requires that all graduate students on training grants receive education in responsible conduct of research.

1989 The National Academy of Sciences publishes *On Being A Scientist* (revised in 1995), which is a free, short book on research ethics for scientists in training.

1992 The National Academy of Sciences publishes *Responsible Science: Ensuring the Integrity of the Research Process*.

1994–1995 The Ryan Commission holds meetings on scientific misconduct.

1994 The Clinton Administration declassifies information about secret human radiation experiments conducted from the 1940s to the 1980s and issues an apology.

1995–2003 Dozens of studies are published in biomedical journals which provide data on the relationship between the source of research funding and the outcomes of research studies, the financial interests of researchers in the biomedical sciences, and the close relationship between academic researchers and the pharmaceutical and biotechnology industries.

1997 The International Committee of Medical Journal Editors, of over 400 biomedical journals, revises its authorship guidelines.

1999 The NIH and the OHRP require all people conducting or overseeing human subjects research have some training in research ethics.

2001 Journals such as *Nature* and the *Journal of the American Medical Association* experiment with requiring authors to describe their responsibilities when publishing research.

2002 The NAS publishes *Integrity in Scientific Research*, which recommends that universities develop programs for education in responsible conduct of research, as well as policies and procedures to deal with research ethics.

Basic Principles of Ethical Research

Although researchers should be excited and enthusiastic about their work (and about publishing that work), the most important thing to remember is that human beings are serving as participants in the research. These individuals must be treated so that their dignity is maintained in spite of the research or the outcomes. Is this easier said than done? You bet.

The challenges presented by ethical behavioral research have created a whole field of study called ethics. As long as researchers continue to use humans and animals as participants, the way in which these people and animals are treated and how they benefit, even indirectly, from participation are critical issues that must be kept in the forefront of all our considerations.

Later in this chapter, specific guidelines published by professional groups for their members are listed. But first, let's address the general issues arising in any discussion of ethical behavior.

Protection from Harm

Above all, participants (who used to be referred to as subjects) must be prevented from physical or psychological harm. If there is any doubt at the outset that there is a significant risk involved (relative to the payoffs), then the experiment should not be approved. Notice that risks and benefits are the focus. In the case of a terminally ill child, the most dramatic and even unconfirmed techniques that may save the child's life (but may also hasten the child's death) may have a high risk, but the potential benefits may be just as important to consider.

The journals in the social and behavioral sciences are filled with egregious reports about unethical behavior. Here's just a sample of the events you would learn about if you studied more about this interesting and important topic:

- The Tuskegee syphilis study is always cited as a horrific example of how things can go wrong when ethical considerations are not taken into account. During the later 1930s, a study was launched in several southern counties to examine the effects of syphilis. However, several of the participants were never told they had the illness nor were they treated. This activity went on for decades until it was stopped in the early 1970s.
- In the early 1960s, Stanley Milgram, then of Harvard University, conducted an experiment that focused on the "just following orders" claims of Nazi collaborators and sympathizers during World War II as a defense for their actions. Milgram looked at how much "pain" an individual was willing to inflict on another individual (who was part of the study and the pain reaction was faked). The primary concern here is one of deception and how the participants (the ones giving the shock) were debriefed

or informed about their role. Deception can be an effective component of an experiment, but one has to be very, very careful in using it.

- And, the Willowbrook State School (Staten Island, New York) is one of the most interesting examples in lapses of ethical behavior. Here, children were intentionally infected with hepatitis but also provided with medical treatment in an attempt to prevent the infection, which indeed worked. But, a huge outcry resulted from the fact that parents had to sign a letter of informed consent for their children to be admitted to the hospital to begin with to say nothing of the fact that the children had no say in their own participation. The results of the research proved to shed a great deal of light on hepatitis as a disease. The way the knowledge was generated continues to raise questions about ethical behavior.

Maintenance of Privacy

Maintenance of privacy speaks to several concerns, but most directly to anonymity. Being anonymous within a research context means that there is no way that anyone other than the principal investigator (usually the director) can match the results of an experiment with the participant associated with these results.

Anonymity is most often maintained through the use of a single master sheet which contains both the names of the participants and their participant number. Only the number is placed on scoring sheets, code sheets, or other testing materials. The list of corresponding names and numbers is kept in a secure place out of the public eye and often under lock and key.

A second concern regarding privacy is that one does not invade another's private space to observe behavior and collect data. For example, it would be unethical secretly to record the verbal interaction between therapists and their clients. Although this might be a rich source of information, it would not be legitimate unless the client and therapist agreed to it.

Coercion

People should not be forced, for whatever reason, into participation in a study. College students, especially those in introductory classes, are the most commonly used population for many different research studies. Is it ethical to require these students to participate in an experiment? Probably not, yet many students must participate as a course requirement. Similarly, people in the workplace are often required to complete surveys, answer questionnaires, and provide other types of information for research purposes as a part of their job-related duties.

The key here is never to force people to participate. If they do not want to participate, then an alternative way to fulfill a course or job requirement should be provided.

Informed Consent

Many colleges and universities require students to obtain informed consent even when simple classroom projects are involved.

This may be the most important requirement. The informed consent form or letter might be the one tool that ensures ethical behavior. Without question, every research project that uses human participants should have an informed consent form that is read and signed by each participant or the person granting participation (in the case of a minor child with the parent signing).

What does such a consent form look like? As you can see in Figure 3B.1, these forms are not just invitations to participate (although they may be that as well) but a description of what will happen throughout the course of the research.

Such a letter contains at least the following information for *participants:*

- The purpose of the research
- Who you are
- What you are doing
- How long you will be involved
- An offer to withdraw from the experiment at any time for any reason
- Potential benefits to you as well as to society
- Potential harm or risks for discomfort to you
- An assurance that the results will be kept in strictest confidence
- How you can get a copy of the results
- How you can be reached should anyone have questions

University of Kansas

Department of Psychology and Research in Education
610 JRPHall
University of Kansas
Lawrence, KS 66045

July 12, 2007

Dear Mr. and Mrs. Shafer:

The Department of Psychology and Research in Education supports the practice of informed consent and protection for human subjects participating in research. The following information is for you to decide whether you will allow Noah to participate in the present study. You are free to withdraw his participation at any time.

Noah will be asked to play a game with a child with a disability in a room that has toys and books and your child's behavior will be recorded on videotape. One session will last approximately 25 minutes. We are interested in studying the interaction between children who have a disability and children who do not. This information is important because it will help us develop methods for increasing the effectiveness of efforts to integrate children with disabilities into the regular education classroom.

Your child's participation is solicited but is strictly voluntary. I assure you that your child's name will not in any way be associated with the research findings. The information will be identified only through a code number.

If you would like additional information concerning this study before or after it is completed, please contact me by phone or mail. Thank you very much for your time and I appreciate your interest and cooperation.

Sincerely,

Bruce Saxon, Assistant Professor
Bsaxon23@ukans.edu
(785) 555-3931

We give permission for Noah to participate in the above described research study.

_____   _____
Parent Signature   Date

_____   _____
Parent Signature   Date

Figure 3B.1   A sample human participants informed consent form.

A place for the prospective subjects (or their parents) to sign, indicating that they agree to participate and that they understand the purpose of the research, also appears on the form.

The letter in Figure 3B.1, printed on official (letterhead) stationery, illustrates all of these points. It is not written in scientific mumbo-jumbo, but it is as straightforward as possible. The goal here is to inform, not to coerce or cajole people into participating.

Informed Consent with Children

There is an obvious problem when it comes to ensuring informed consent with children in any investigation in which the child is too young to give consent of any kind. In this case, the parents must determine whether they will allow their child to participate.

There are issues galore when it comes to ethics and children, far beyond the difficult process of ensuring that children will not be placed in any danger, either physical or psychological. For example, are 6-year-old children old enough to make a decision about withdrawing, as the consent form should clearly state is an option for them? Can they understand the long-range implications or the potential risks of the research in which they are participating?

This is where the good judgment and personal ethics of the researcher come into play. If a child feels strongly about not participating, you may lose that participant and those data, but the child's wishes must be respected just as those of any adult would be. Additionally, forcing participation may result in an unhappy or angry child and, thus, untrustworthy data.

As children mature, however, the issue becomes more complex. For example, what about the 12-year-old who is old enough to understand the purpose of the experiment? Should this child sign the consent form as well as the parent(s)? No researcher would not first obtain permission from the parent(s). Additionally, when school-age children are used in research, more and more school districts require that the proposal be reviewed by a school-wide research committee. More researchers than ever now have liability insurance to cover themselves if an angry parent sues or some unintended injury occurs.

The best advice is to make any experimental session or treatment with children as pleasant as possible. Encourage them, make the activities pleasant, and reward them when you have finished (as long as the promise of a reward does not interfere with what you are studying). Above all, remember that children are physically, emotionally, and socially different from adults, and those differences must be taken into account when they are used as subjects. Finally, get all the institutional clearances you need to proceed. Make sure your adviser or professor knows what you are doing.

Confidentiality

Whereas anonymity means that records cannot be linked with names, confidentiality is maintained when anything that is learned about the participant is held in the strictest of confidence. This means that information is disguised when necessary (which touches on anonymity as well) but, more important, all the data are kept in a controlled situation.

The best way to maintain confidentiality is to minimize the number of people who see or handle the data. There is no better example of this than recent concerns about AIDS and the results of screening tests. People are reluctant to be tested for human immunodeficiency virus (HIV) (the virus associated with AIDS) because they are concerned that potential employers and insurance companies will have access to the test results and use the data against them when they apply for a job or for health or life insurance. Even with possible changes in health and insurance practices and policies, this is still a concern.

Debriefing

Another component of sharing the results of an experiment occurs when a particular group of subjects needs to be debriefed. For example, you design an experiment in which one group of participants is asked to do something for a reason other than which they are told. A famous experiment (and there have been many on the same theme of coercion) involving deception asked individuals to apply electric shock (or so the participants thought) to their counterpart in the experiment (who was not really being shocked) to see how far the participants would go before stopping. Once the experiment is completed, it is your responsibility to inform them that they have been deceived to some extent for the purposes of the experiment. Most people will take that just fine (as do the contestants on *Candid Camera*), but some will get upset when they learn that they have been manipulated. If they remain angry, it is difficult to do anything other than apologize and try to set the record straight. The easiest way to debrief participants is to talk with them immediately following the session or to send a newsletter telling participants the general intent and results of the study but leaving out specifics such as names.

Sharing Benefits

This last principle may be the one that is least often observed. Here is the scenario: In an experiment, a treatment was used to increase the memory of older people with early-stage Alzheimer's disease, a devastating and almost always fatal illness. Let's say that the researcher uses two groups, one that receives the treatment (the experimental group) and one that does not (the control group). Much to the researcher's pleasure, the treatment group learns faster and remembers much more for much longer. Success!

What is the concern? Simply that the group that did not receive the treatment should now be exposed to it. It is the right thing to do. When one group benefits from participation in a study, any other group that participated in the study should benefit as well. This does not mean that it is possible that all people with the disease can be helped. That may not be feasible. But all direct participants in the experiment should benefit equally.

All these ethical issues apply to the different types of research methods described in Chapters 9–12, with differing degrees of importance. For example, one need not be concerned about debriefings when conducting a case study because no treatment and no deception is involved, nor would one be concerned with sharing benefits.

TEST YOURSELF

Select any of the principles you just read through and create a scenario where it is violated. What might the violations of the principle mean for the participants in the study as well as for the value of the study itself?

Ensuring High Ethical Standards

There are several steps that even the beginning researcher can take to ensure that ethical principles are maintained. Here are some of the most important:

1. Do a computer simulation in which data are constructed and subjected to the effects of various treatments. For example, mathematical psychologists and statisticians often use Monte Carlo studies to examine the effects of a change in one variable (such as sample size) on another (such as accuracy of measurement). Elaborate models of

human behavior can be constructed and different assumptions can be tested and conclusions drawn about human behavior. Although this is somewhat advanced work, it does give you an idea of how certain experiments can be conducted with the "participants" being nothing more than values generated by a computer.

2. When the treatment is deemed harmful, do not give up. Rather, try to locate a population that has already been exposed to the harmful effects of some variable. For example, the thousands of children and pregnant women who were malnourished during World War II provided an invaluable sample for estimating the effects of malnourishment on fetal and neonatal development as well as the long-range effects of malnourishment on young children. Although it is not pleasant, this is about the only way that such research can be conducted. This type of research, called quasi-experimental, will be covered in greater detail in Chapter 12.

3. Always secure informed consent. If the treatment includes risk, be absolutely sure that the risks are clear to the participant and other interested parties (e.g., parents, other family members).

4. When possible, publish all reports using group data rather than individual data. This measure maintains confidentiality.

5. If you suspect that the treatment may have adverse effects, use a small, well-informed sample until you can expand the sample size and the ambitiousness of the project. Also, be sure to check with your institutional review board (more about that below).

6. Ask your colleagues to review your proposal, especially your experimental procedures, before you begin. Ask them the question, "Would you participate without any fear of being harmed?" If they say "No," go back to the drawing board.

7. Almost every public institution (such as public universities) and every private agency (such as some hospitals and private universities) has what is called an **institutional review board**. Such boards consist of a group of people from several disciplines (including representatives from the community) who render a judgment as to whether participation in an experiment is free from risk. At the University of Kansas, the group is called the Institutional Review Board; there is a separate review board for experiments using animals. The groups usually meet and then approve or disapprove the procedure (but not necessarily the content of research) and take into consideration the issues already discussed. These committees usually meet about once per month, and if a proposal that they review is not acceptable, they invite the researcher to resubmit according to their recommendations.

The Role of Professional Organizations

It is unquestionably the role of the researcher to ensure that ethical standards are always kept in mind when conducting any type of research. Formalized sets of guidelines are published by professional organizations such as the American Psychological Association (APA), the Society for Research in Child Development (SRCD), the American Sociological Association (ASA), the American Educational Research Association (AERA), and just about every other social or behavioral science professional group. To illustrate just what these guidelines suggest, the following is a summary of these various sets. You can find the exact guidelines at the Internet locations listed.

A Summary of Ethical Guidelines

Instead of having you to go through each of the guidelines given, here's a summary that cuts across these various organizations. What follows should give you a general idea of what kinds of topics and principles are important. Should you undertake your own

Professional Organization	Internet URL
American Psychological Association	http://www.apa.org/ethics/index.aspx
Society for Research in Child Development	http://www.srcd.org/index.php?option=com_content&task=view&id=68&Itemid=110
American Educational Research Association	This is a PDF document from AERA that can be found by searching for "Ethical Standards of the American Educational Research Association"
American Sociological Association (last updated 1997)	http://www2.asanet.org/members/ecostand2.html
American Medical Association	http://www.ama-assn.org/ama/pub/physician-resources/medical-ethics/code-medical-ethics.shtml

research, be sure to consult the organization that most closely represents your work and review their ethical guidelines in detail.

1. The person conducting the research is the one who is the first and most important judge of its ethical acceptability.
2. Every effort should be made to minimize risk to the participants.
3. The researcher is responsible for ensuring ethical practices, including the behavior of assistants, students, employees, collaborators, and anyone else involved in the process.
4. A fair and reasonable agreement must be reached between the researcher and the subjects prior to the beginning of the research.
5. If deception is necessary, the researcher must be sure it is justified and a mechanism must be built in to ensure that subjects (or their representatives in the case of children or people who cannot make such decisions) are debriefed when the research is concluded.
6. Researchers must respect a subject's choice to withdraw and must not coerce the subject to return to the study.
7. Whenever possible, participants should be shielded from physical and psychological harm.
8. Once the research is complete, results of the work should be made available, and the participant should be given a chance to clarify any discrepancies of which she or he might be aware.
9. If the research activity results in harm of any kind, the researcher has the responsibility of correcting the harm.
10. All the information about the participants of a study, and any related results, are confidential.

Ethics and Children

Children are a special group and need to be treated as such. The Society for Research in Child Development, perhaps the premier international group of researchers about children, has developed a special set of guidelines. Here's a summary. Keep in mind that the general principles we identified in the preceding list apply as well, and the two sets in combination should provide you with all the guidance you need.

1. The rights of the child supersede the rights of the investigator no matter what the age of the child.
2. If there are changes in approved procedures that might affect the ethical conduct of the research, consultation with colleagues or experts should be undertaken.
3. The child should be fully informed as to the research process, and all questions should be answered in a way that can be understood. If the child is too young, then the child's representative (parent or guardian) should be closely involved in all discussions.
4. Informed consent from parents, teachers, or whoever is legally responsible for the child's welfare must be obtained in writing.
5. Informed consent must also be obtained from others who are involved in the experiment (such as parents) besides the individual child.
6. The responsibilities of the child and of the investigator must be made clear.
7. When deception is necessary, a committee of the investigator's peers should approve the planned methods.
8. The findings from any study should be reported to the participants in a way that is comprehensible to them.
9. Investigators should be especially careful about the way in which they report results to children and should not present the results in the form of advice.
10. If treatments are effective, control groups should be offered similar opportunities to receive the treatment.
11. These ethical standards should be presented to students in the course of their training.
12. Editors of journals that report investigations of children should provide authors space to summarize the steps they took to ensure these standards. If it is not clear such standards were followed, editors should request additional information.

Do the ethical standards of the APA and the SRCD work? In general, the answer is probably "yes," but if they do work, it's because of the individuals who make up the research community and follow these rules.

Ethics Regarding Online Research

More and more often, researchers are using the Internet and associated electronic tools to conduct research. For example, let's say that you are interested in studying the interactions between adolescent girls and you select a chat room to observe their verbal behavior and you intend to categorize the behavior into different categories.

Professor Amy Bruckman from Georgia Institute of Technology has developed an extensive and very useful set of guidelines (you can find them at http://www.cc. gatech.edu/~asb/ethics/) that are unique to this type of research. Keep in mind that almost all of what we have already talked about earlier in this section on ethical practices applies here as well—these are just some special guidelines.

1. You can quote and analyze online information without asking for permission as long as the information is officially and publicly archived, no password is required to access the information, and there is nothing stated on the site that prohibits the use of the information.
2. Requesting consent, in and of itself, should not disrupt the very process that is being examined. The process of requesting consent must not disrupt normal group activity. For example, if you are observing chat room statements, you have to gain permission

to then use that information, but you need to do it in such a way as not to change the nature of the interaction by asking for such.

3. You can obtain consent electronically if participants are 18 years of age or older, and the risk is judged to be relatively low. If you cannot obtain informed consent electronically, you need to mail, fax, or e-mail the proper form and ask the participant (or his or her representative) to sign it and return it. There must be a hardcopy.

4. As best as possible, the confidentiality of the participants and their identity must be assured. This can be difficult in a public forum such as a chat group, but every effort should be made to do such when the results are reported.

Test Yourself

For each of the principles mentioned in this chapter, how might they differ for children versus adults?

Summary

Under no circumstances should you take this material lightly or not try and follow the ethical guidelines of your own professional organization. The little bit of extra attention you pay to adhering to these will have significant payoffs later on when you are involved as a participant or as a researcher in some project. There's no better place to apply the saying that an ounce of prevention is worth a pond of cure.

Exercises

1. What precautions should you take when considering completing a study involving deception?

2. Having approval from your school's research review board is a crucial step in completing your research. Visit your school's home page online and search, either in a search box or an A to Z index, for information on your school's institutional review board. You may need to search for the Center for Research or the Human Subjects Committee. Find the e-mail address or phone number for contacting the review board and report it here.

3. Visit Professor Amy Bruckman's Web page of guidelines for online research at http://www.cc.gatech.edu/~asb/ethics/. Read it and answer the following question: Under what three conditions may consent be obtained electronically rather than on paper?

4. What do you believe should be the penalty for a researcher who violates one or more of the principles of ethical research that we discussed in this chapter?

5. What are some of the similarities between the ethical guidelines that some organizations offer and those of others? Compare any two (beyond those shown in this chapter if you want).

Online . . .

Research Methods Knowledge Base

You can find an interesting and useful summary of ethics in research at http://
www.socialresearchmethods.net/kb/ethics.php. Here's the complete reference where
you can find it and more about the research process all online.
Trochim, William M. *The Research Methods Knowledge Base,* 2nd ed. Internet WWW
page, at http://www.socialresearchmethods.net/kb/.Ethical practices is a topic that
simply cannot be ignored either in your education or in practice.

Ethics: Why So Important?

You can find out more about why ethics are important at http://www.niehs.nih.gov/
research/resources/bioethics/whatis.cfm where you can read What is Ethics in
Research & Why is It Important? by David B. Resnik, J.D., Ph.D. This comes to us
from the National Institute of Environmental Sciences and focuses on a summary of
general codes and practices practiced at federal, professional, and other groups.

❖ ❖ ❖ Chapter 4 ❖ ❖ ❖
Sampling and Generalizability

Imagine that you are assigned the task of measuring the general attitude of high school students toward unrestricted searches of their lockers for drugs. You are already enough of a research expert to know you will have to develop some kind of questionnaire and be sure it covers the important content areas and is easy to administer and score. After all that preliminary work has been done, you are faced with the most important question: Whom will you ask to complete the questionnaire: all 4,500 students in all the high schools throughout the district? You cannot do that because it would be too expensive. Will you ask students at only those schools where there is reportedly a drug problem? You cannot do that either. It is too likely that there also are drugs in schools that have not been identified as problem schools. How about asking only seniors because they are supposed to know what is going on about town? You cannot do that because freshmen, sophomores, and juniors use drugs as well. What do you do?

These are decisions that cannot be taken lightly. The success of any research project depends on the way in which you select the people who will participate in your study—whether you will be distributing a questionnaire or administering a treatment you think will facilitate interoffice communications. This chapter discusses various ways of selecting people to participate in research projects and the importance of the selection process to the research outcomes. It is all about populations, samples, and sampling.

Populations and Samples

In several places throughout the early chapters of this volume, you read about the importance of inferring the results of an experiment from a sample to a population. This is the basis of the inferential method. If everyone in the population cannot be tested, then the only other choice is to select a sample, or a subset of that population. Good sampling techniques include maximizing the degree to which this selected group will represent the population.

A **population** is a group of potential participants to whom you want to generalize the results of a study. A **sample** is a subset of that population. And generalizability is the name of the game; only when the results can be generalized from a sample to a population do the results of research have meaning beyond the limited setting in which they were originally obtained. When results are generalizable, they can be applied to different populations with the same characteristics in different settings. When results are not generalizable

WHAT YOU'LL LEARN ABOUT IN THIS CHAPTER:

- Why good sampling may be the most important step in any research project

- The importance of generalizability

- The difference between a sample and a population

- What the word "random" means

- How to use a table of random numbers in selecting a sample

- The difference between simple random sampling and stratified sampling

- How probability and nonprobability sampling strategies differ

- What sampling error is and why it is important

- How to reduce sampling error

- How to estimate the sample size you need

A sample is a subset of a population.

Generalization can often be the key to a successful study.

(when the sample selected is not an accurate representation of the population), the results are applicable only to the people in the same sample who participated in the original research, not to any others.

For example, if you want to find out about high school students' attitudes toward locker searches, one class of senior honors chemistry students could be given the questionnaire. But how much are they like the general population of students who attend all the high schools in the district? Probably not much. Or 10% of the female freshman and sophomore girls from all the high schools could be asked the same questions. This selection encompasses a far larger group than just the 30 or so students in the chemistry class, but how representative are they? Once again, not very.

Our task is to devise a plan to ensure that the sample of students selected is representative of all students throughout the district. If this goal is reached, then the results can be generalized to the entire population with a high degree of confidence, even when using a small percentage of the 4,500 high school students. In other words, if you select your sample correctly, the results can be generalized. How will you know if you are doing the job right?

Some guidelines are discussed in this chapter, but one way to do a self-check is to ask yourself this question: Does the sample I selected from the population appear to have all the characteristics of the population, in the same proportion? Is the sample, in effect, a mini population?

To understand sampling, you first need to distinguish between two general sampling strategies: probability and nonprobability sampling. With **probability sampling**, the likelihood of any one member of the population being selected is known. If there are 4,500 students in all the high schools, and if there are 1,000 seniors, then the odds of selecting one senior as part of the sample is 1,000/,4,500, or 0.22.

In **nonprobability sampling**, the likelihood of selecting any one member from the population is not known. For example, if you do not know how many children are enrolled in the district's high schools, then the likelihood of any one being selected cannot be computed.

TEST YOURSELF

Why is sampling important to the success of research in the social and behavioral sciences?

Probability Sampling Strategies

Probability sampling strategies are the most commonly used because the selection of participants is determined by chance. Because the determination of who will end up in the sample is determined by nonsystematic and random rules, the chance that the sample will truly represent the population is increased.

Simple Random Sampling

The most common type of probability sampling procedure is **simple random sampling**. Here, each member of the population has an *equal* and *independent* chance of being selected to be part of the sample. *Equal* and *independent* are the key words here: equal because there is no bias that one person will be chosen rather than another, and independent because the choice of one person does not bias the researcher for or against the choice of another. When sampling randomly, the characteristics of the sample should be very close to that of the population.

For example, would it be simple random sampling if you were to choose every fifth name from the phone book? No, because both the criteria of equal and independent are

1. Jane	11. Susie	21. Ed T.	31. Dana	41. Nathan
2. Bill	12. Nona	22. Jerry	32. Bruce	42. Peggy
3. Harriet	13. Doug	23. Chitra	33. Daphne	43. Heather
4. Leni	14. John S.	24. Glenna	34. Phil	44. Debbie
5. Micah	15. Bruce	25. Misty	35. Fred	45. Cheryl
6. Sara	16. Larry	26. Cindy	36. Mike	46. Wes
7. Terri	17. Bob	27. Sy	37. Doug	47. Genna
8. Joan	18. Steve	28. Phyllis	38. Ed M.	48. Ellie
9. Jim	19. Sam	29. Jerry	39. Tom	49. Alex
10. Terrill	20. Marvin	30. Harry	40. Mike G.	50. John D.

Table 4.1 Group of 50 names constituting a population for our purposes. Notice that each one is numbered and is ready to be selected (also, realize that populations are often much larger)

being violated. If you begin with name 5 on page 234 of the phone book, then names 1, 2, 3, and 233 never had an equal chance of being selected, so this example fails the test of independence. Second, if you chose name 5 on the list and then every fifth name from there on, only names 10, 15, 20, and so on have any chance of being selected. Once again, it is a failure of independence that does not make this a truly random process.

The process of simple random sampling consists of the following four steps:

1. The definition of the population from which you want to select the sample.
2. The listing of all the members of the population.
3. The assignment of numbers to each member of the population.
4. The use of a criterion to select the sample you want.

Table 4.1 shows a list of 50 names with numbers already assigned (steps 1, 2, and 3 above). It is not a very large population but it is fine for illustrative purposes. From this population, a sample of 10 individuals will be selected using what is called a **table of random numbers**.

> A table of random numbers is the most unbiased tool you can use to select participants from a population.

Using a Table of Random Numbers

A table of random numbers is a terrific criterion because the basis on which the numbers in the table are generated is totally unbiased. For example, in Table 4.2 there are nearly equal numbers of 1s, 2s, 3s, 4s, 5s, and so on. As a result, the likelihood of selecting a number ending in a 1 or a 2 or a 3 or a 4 or a 5 is equal. This means that when names are attached to the numbers, the likelihood of selecting any particular name is equal as well.

23157	48559	01837	25993
05545	50430	10537	43508
14871	03650	32404	36223
38976	49751	94051	75853
97312	17618	99755	30870
11742	69183	44339	47512
43361	82859	11016	45623
93806	04338	38268	04491
49540	31181	08429	84187
36768	76233	37948	21569

Table 4.2 Partial table of random numbers. In such a table, you can expect there to be an equal number of single digits which are randomly distributed throughout all the numbers

23157	48 55 9	01837	25993
05545	50 43 0	10537	43508
14871	03 65 0	32404	36223
38976	49 75 1	94051	75853
97312	17 61 8	99755	30870
11742	69 18 3	44339	47512
43361	82 85 9	11016	45623
93806	04 33 8	38268	04491
49540	31 18 1	08429	84187
36**68**	76 23 3	37948	21569

Randomly determined starting point

Table 4.3 Starting point in selecting 10 cases using the table of random numbers. You can begin anywhere, as long as the place you begin is determined by chance and is not intentionally chosen

With that fact in mind, we will select one group of 10 names using the table of random numbers in Table 4.2. Follow these steps:

1. Select a starting point somewhere in the table by closing your eyes and placing your finger (or a pencil point) anywhere in the table. Selecting your starting point in this way ensures that no particular starting point (or name) is selected.

    For this example, the starting point was the first column of numbers, last row (36,768), with the pencil point falling on the fourth digit, the number 6.

2. The first two-digit number, then, is 68 (in boldface type in Table 4.3). Because the population goes up to 50, and there is no number 68, this number is skipped and the next two-digit number is considered. Because you cannot go down in the table (no place to go), go to the top of the next column and read down, once again selecting the first two digits. For your convenience, each pair of two-digit numbers in the second column of Table 4.3 is separated.

3. The next number available is 48. Success! Person 48 on the list is Ellie, and she becomes the first of the 10-member sample.

4. If you continue to select two-digit numbers until 10 values between 01 and 50 are found, the names of the people that correspond in Table 4.1 with the numbers in boldface type in Table 4.4 are selected. Here is a breakdown of which numbers worked and which did not for the purposes of selecting a random sample of 10 people from the population of 50.

Reading down the first column of two-digit numbers, 48, 50, 03, 49, and 17 are fine because they fall within the range of 50 (the size of the population) and they have not been selected before:

23157	**48** 55 9	01837	25993
05545	**50 43** 0	10537	43508
14871	**03** 65 0	32404	36223
38976	**49** 75 1	94051	75853
97312	**17** 61 8	99755	30870
11742	69 **18** 3	44339	47512
43361	82 85 9	11016	45623
93806	**04 33** 8	38268	04491
49540	31 18 1	08429	84187
36768	76 23 3	37948	21569

Table 4.4 Ten two-digit numbers (each one appearing in bold) selected from the population

- 69 and 82 are out of the range
- 04 and 31 are fine
- 76 is out of the range

Because you cannot read farther down the column, it is time to go up to the next set of two digits (in the same five-digit column) at the top of the column, which begins with the number 55.

- 55 is not within the range
- 43 is fine
- 65, 75, and 61 are not acceptable
- 18 is
- 85 is not
- 33 is

And there you have the 10 people:

Number	Name
48	Ellie
50	John D.
03	Harriet
49	Alex
17	Bob
04	Leni
31	Dana
43	Heather
18	Steve
33	Daphne

Now you have a sample of 10 names from a population of 50 selected entirely by chance. Remember, the probability of any one of these people being selected from the population is the same as the probability of any other person from the population being selected.

Your sample is selected by chance because the distribution of the numbers in the partial table of random numbers in Table 4.2 was generated by chance. Is it just a coincidence that three of the first five numbers (48, 50, 03, 49, 17) in the partial table of random numbers are grouped together? Absolutely yes. This group of five is the best approximation and the most representative of any sample of five from the entire population, given that each member of the population has an equal and independent likelihood of being chosen (1/50 or .02 or 2% in this case).

A further assumption is that the names in the population (Table 4.1) were listed in a random fashion. In other words, names 01–20 were not listed as the first 20 of 50 because they come from a different neighborhood, are very wealthy, or have no siblings, or some other characteristic that might get in the way of an unbiased selection.

The general rule (and this may be the most important point in the entire chapter) is to *use a criterion that is unrelated to that which you are studying*. For example, if you are doing a study on volunteering, you do not want to ask for volunteers!

Using the Computer to Generate Random Samples

You should always do new things at least once manually so you understand how a process works, such as selecting a random sample from a population as you were shown earlier. After you are comfortable with the technique, it is time to turn to the computer.

	id_stud	id_prof	sex_stud	teacher1	teacher2	teacher3	teacher4	teacher5	filter_$
1	80761	1	Male	4.00	4.00	2.00	1.00	3.00	0
2	22920	1	Male	5.00	4.00	2.00	1.00	3.00	0
3	84768	2	Male	4.00	3.00	3.00	2.00	3.00	1
4	89225	2	Male	3.00	3.00	3.00	1.00	4.00	0
5	94354	3	Male	3.00	5.00	1.00	2.00	3.00	0
6	40351	4	Male	2.00	4.00	2.00	2.00	2.00	1
7	62034	4	Male	2.00	4.00	2.00	2.00	4.00	0
8	26841	5	Male	2.00	4.00	2.00	1.00	3.00	0
9	13691	5	Male	2.00	3.00	1.00	3.00	2.00	0
10	70386	6	Male	3.00	4.00	2.00	3.00	5.00	1
11	45176	6	Male	5.00	4.00	1.00	1.00	4.00	1
12	29627	6	Male	2.00	4.00	2.00	1.00	4.00	0
13	24824	6	Male	1.00	5.00	2.00	2.00	4.00	0
14	39986	7	Male	5.00	5.00	2.00	1.00	5.00	0
15	77974	7	Male	5.00	4.00	2.00	1.00	4.00	1
16	38396	7	Male	5.00	5.00	2.00	1.00	5.00	1
17	78665	7	Male	4.00	3.00	2.00	1.00	3.00	0
18	20227	7	Male	4.00	5.00	1.00	1.00	5.00	0
19	66298	8	Male	5.00	5.00	1.00	1.00	3.00	0
20	27423	8	Male	5.00	5.00	1.00	1.00	4.00	1
21	79359	8	Male	5.00	5.00	1.00	1.00	5.00	0
22	66513	8	Male	5.00	5.00	1.00	1.00	5.00	1
23	28796	9	Male	2.00	4.00	4.00	3.00	1.00	1
24	67564	9	Male	3.00	3.00	4.00	4.00	1.00	0
25	35598	9	Male	3.00	3.00	2.00	1.00	2.00	0
26	77823	10	Male	5.00	5.00	2.00	1.00	5.00	0
27	34850	10	Male	5.00	5.00	1.00	2.00	5.00	0
28	54217	10	Male	3.00	5.00	1.00	1.00	4.00	0

Figure 4.1   Selecting a sample.

SPSS, Inc.

As you can see in Figure 4.1, ten participants have been selected. Those who have not been selected have a diagonal line (for example case) through the cell, and subsequent analyses will only use the selected cases. This figure shows how SPSS works, but any capable data analysis tool can do the same.

Systematic Sampling

Systematic sampling reduces the chances of certain participants being selected; therefore, it is less unbiased than simple random sampling.

In another type of sampling, called **systematic sampling**, every kth name on the list is chosen. The term "kth" stands for a number between 0 and the size of the sample that you want to select. For example, here is how to use systematic sampling to select 10 names from the list of 50 (although these steps apply to any size population and sample) shown in Table 4.1. To do this, follow these steps:

1. Divide the size of the population by the size of the desired sample. In this case, 50 divided by 10 is 5. Therefore, you will select every fifth name from the list. In other words,

$$\text{Size of population} \longrightarrow \frac{50}{10} = 5 \longleftarrow \text{Size of step} \longleftarrow \text{Size of sample}$$

2. As the starting point, choose one name from the list at random. Do this by the "eyes closed, pointing method" or, if the names are numbered, use any one or two digits from the serial number on a dollar bill. The dollar bill used in this example has as its first two digits 43, which will be the starting point.
3. Once the starting point has been determined, select every fifth name. In this example, using the names in Table 4.1 and starting with Heather (#43), the sample will consist of Ellie (#48), Harriet (#3), Joan (#8), Doug (#13), Steve (#18), Chitra (#23), Phyllis (#28), Daphne (#33), and Ed M. (#38).

Because systematic sampling is easier and less trouble than random sampling, it is often the preferred technique. It is also, however, less precise. Clearly, the assumption of each member of the population having an equal chance to be selected is violated. For example, given that the starting point is Heather (#43), it would be impossible to select Debbie (#44).

Stratified Sampling

The two types of random sampling that were just discussed work fine if specific characteristics of the population (such as age, gender, ethnicity, and ability group) are of no concern. In other words, if another set of 10 names were selected, one would assume that because both groups were chosen at random, they are, in effect, equal. But what if the individuals in the population are not "equal" to begin with? In that case, you need to ensure that the profile of the sample matches the profile of the population, and this is done by creating what is referred to as **stratified sampling.**

The theory behind sampling (and the entire process of inference) goes something like this: If you can select a sample that is as close as possible to being representative of a population, then any observations you can make regarding that sample should also hold true for the population. So far so good. Sometimes, though, random sampling leaves too much to chance, especially if you have no assurance of equal distributions of population members throughout the sample and, most important, *if the factors that distinguish population members from one another (such as race, gender, social class, or degree of intelligence) are related to what you are studying*. This is a very important point. In that case, stratified sampling is used to ensure that the strata (or layers) in the population are fairly represented in the sample (which ends up being layered as well, right?).

For example, if the population is 82% Methodists, 14% Catholics, and 4% Jews, then the sample should have the same characteristics *if* religion is an important variable in the first place. Understanding the last part of the preceding sentence is critical. If a specified characteristic of the population is not related to what is being studied, then there is no reason to be concerned about creating a sample patterned after the population and stratifying on one of those variables.

Let's assume that the list of names in Table 4.1 represents a stratified population (females and males) and that attitudes toward legalizing abortion is the topic of study. Because gender differences may be important, you want a sample that reflects gender differences in the population. The list of 50 names consists of 20 females and 30 males, or 40% females and 60% males. The sample of 10 should mirror that distribution and contain four females and six males. Here is how you would select such a sample using **stratified random sampling**. Once again, the example is the population we created, but these steps apply to all circumstances.

1. All the males and all the females are listed separately.
2. Each member in each group receives a number. In this case, the males would be numbered 01–30 and the females 01–20.
3. From a table of random numbers, four females are selected at random from the list of 20 using the procedures outlined earlier.
4. From a table of random numbers, six males are selected at random from the list of 30 using the procedures outlined earlier.

Although simple examples (with only one stratum or layer) such as this often occur, you may have to stratify on more than one variable. For example, in Figure 4.2, a population of 10,000 children is stratified on the variables of grade (40% first grade, 40% third grade, and 20% fifth grade) and location of residence (30% rural and 70% urban).

Location	Grade			Total
	1	3	5	
Rural	1,200 [120]	1,200 [120]	600 [60]	3,000 [300]
Urban	2,800 [280]	2,800 [280]	1,400 [140]	7,000 [700]
Total	4,000 [400]	4,000 [400]	2,000 [200]	10,000 [1,000]

Figure 4.2 Selecting a sample from a population that is stratified on two factors or layers: grade and location. Here the sample size is shown in brackets below the population size.

The same strategy is used: Select 10% (1,000 is 10% of 10,000) of each of the stratified layers to produce the sample size shown in Figure 4.1. For example, of the 1,200 rural children in the first grade, 10% (or 120) were randomly selected. Likewise, 140 urban children in fifth grade were selected.

Cluster Sampling

Clusters are groups of occurrences that occur together.

The last type of probability sampling is **cluster sampling**, in which units of individuals are selected rather than individuals themselves. For example, you might be doing a survey of parents' attitudes toward immunization. Rather than randomly assigning individual parents to two groups (say, for example, those who will be sent informational material and those who will not), you could just identify 30 pediatricians' offices in the city and then, using a table of random numbers, select 15 for one group and designate 15 for the second group. Another example can be found in large cities where police stations are divided into districts, and each district becomes one entry, as a cluster of stations.

Cluster sampling is a great time saver, but you must be sure that the units (in this case, the people who visit each pediatrician) are homogeneous enough such that any differences in the unit itself might not contribute to a bias. For example, if one pediatrician refuses to immunize children before a certain age, that would introduce a bias you would want to avoid.

TEST YOURSELF

Why is it critically important that the criterion used to assign people to groups not be related to the focus of the study or to the topic of interest?

Nonprobability Sampling Strategies

In the second general category of sampling strategies, nonprobability sampling, the probability of selecting a single individual is not known. Because this is the case, you must assume that potential members of the sample do not have an equal and independent chance of being selected. Some of these sampling methods are discussed in the following.

Convenience Sampling

Convenience sampling is just what it says. A football coach gives each team member a questionnaire. The audience (the team) is a captive one, and it is a very convenient way to generate a sample. Easy? Yes. Random? No. Representative? Perhaps, but to a limited extent.

You might recognize this method of sampling as the reason why so many experiments in psychology are based on results using college sophomores; these students are a captive audience and often must participate for credit.

Quota Sampling

You might be in a situation where you need to create a sample that is stratified on certain variables, yet for some reason proportional stratified sampling is not possible. In this case, quota sampling might be what you want.

Quota sampling selects people with the characteristics you want (such as first-grade, rural children) but does not randomly select from the population a subset of all such children, as would occur in **proportional stratified sampling**. Rather, the researcher would continue to enlist children until the quota of 120 is reached. The 176th rural kid in first grade never has a chance, and that is primarily why this is a nonprobability sampling technique.

Here is another example of a quota system. You have to interview 20 freshmen of both genders. First, you might interview 10 men and, knowing that the distribution of males and females is approximately a 50/50 split, you interview the next 10 women who come along, and then you call it quits. Whereas quota sampling is far easier than stratified sampling, it is also less precise. Imagine how much easier it is to find any 10 men, rather than a specific 10 men, which is what you would have to do in the case of stratified sampling.

Table 4.5 provides a summary of probability and nonprobability sampling methods.

Samples, Sample Size, and Sampling Error

No matter how hard a researcher tries, it is impossible to select a sample that perfectly represents the population. The researcher could, of course, select the entire population as the sample, but that defeats the purpose of sampling—making an inference to a population based on a smaller sample.

One way that the lack of fit between the sample and the population is expressed is as **sampling error**, which is the difference between a measure of the characteristics of the sample and a measure of the characteristics of the population from which the sample was selected. For example, the average height of 10,000 fifth graders is 40 inches. If you take 25 samples of 100 fifth graders and compute the average height for each set of 100 children, you will end up with an average height for each group, or 25 averages. If all those averages are exactly 40 inches, there is no sampling error at all. This result, however, is surely not likely to be the case. Life is not that easy nor is the selection of samples that perfect. Instead, you will find the values to be something like 40.3 inches, 41.2 inches, 39.7 inches, 38.9 inches, and so on. The amount of variability or the spread of these values gives you some idea of the amount of sampling error. The larger the diversity of sample values, the larger the error and the less precise and representative your sample.

> Reducing sampling error is the goal of any sampling technique.

Type of Sampling	When to Use It	Advantages	Disadvantages
Probability Strategies			
Simple random sampling	When the population members are similar to one another on important variables	Ensures a high degree of representatives	Time consuming and tedious
Systematic sampling	When the population members are similar to one another on important variables	Ensures a high degree of representatives and no need to use a table of random numbers	Less random than simple random sampling
Stratified random sampling	When the population is heterogeneous and contains several different groups, some of which are related to the topic of study	Ensures a high degree of representatives of all the strata or layers in the population	Time consuming and tedious
Cluster sampling	When the population consists of units rather than individuals.	Easy and convenient	Possibly members of units are different from one another, decreasing the technique's effectiveness
Nonprobability Sampling Strategies			
Convenience sampling	When the members of the population are convenient to sample	Convenient and inexpensive	Degree of generalizability is questionable
Quota sampling	When strata are present and stratified sampling is not possible	Ensures some degree of representativeness of all the strata in the population	Degree of generalizability is questionable

Table 4.5   Summary of the different types of probability and nonprobability strategies

Think for a moment what would happen if the entire population of 10,000 fifth graders were the sample. You would find the average height to be 40! Perfect! No error! The lesson? The larger the sample, the smaller the sampling error, because larger samples approach the size of the population and thus are more representative of the population. But, as you already know, studying too large a sample is expensive and inefficient, and often not necessary.

The exact process for computing the sampling error, which is expressed as a numerical value, is beyond the scope of this book, but you should recognize that your purpose in selecting a good sample is to minimize that value. The smaller the value, the less discrepancy there is between the sample and the population.

But there's more. You already know that the larger a sample is, the more representative the sample is of the population. And, in general, the better that the samples represent their respective populations, the more accurate any test of differences (for example) will be. In other words, better sampling leads to more accurate, more valid tests of population differences.

How do you minimize sampling error? Use good selection procedures as described earlier in this chapter and increase the sample size as much as possible and reasonable. The next question you are ready to ask (I hope) is, "How big should the sample size be?" Glad you asked. Let's look at the last section in this chapter for more insight into the answer to that question.

How Big Is Big?

Now that you know something about sampling, just how many of those high school students do you need to select from the population of 4,500? If 50 is good, is not 500 better? And why not 1,500, if you have the time and resources to commit to the project?

You already know that too small a sample is not representative of the population and too large is overkill. Sampling too many high school students would be self-defeating because you are no longer taking advantage of the power of inference. Some people believe that the larger the sample the better, but this strategy does not make economic or scientific sense. Too big a sample does not increase the precision of testing your question beyond the costs and trouble incurred in getting that size sample.

Remember, the less representative the sample is of the population, the more sampling error is present. In addition, the larger the sampling error, the less generalizable the results will be to the population and the less precise your test of the null hypothesis.

A more advanced way of dealing with sample size is through a consideration of effect size. This concept was made popular with the pioneering work of Jacob Cohen (1988) and the notion that the stronger the effects of a treatment (such as the larger the expected difference between samples, for example), then the smaller the sample size need be. Now this is pretty advanced stuff, but you can use a set of tables and, given the expected effect (or the magnitude of the difference you expect between two groups, for example), you can get a pretty clear estimate of the number of participants you need in each group.

Estimating Sample Size

Every situation is different. Let's assume that you are examining the difference between two groups. How would you go about determining what the "correct" sample size might be? There are several numerical formulas for this, but you should at least be aware of what the important factors are that figure into your decision. Keep in mind that 30 is the general magic number of how many participants should be in each group.

In general, you need a larger sample to represent the population, acccurately when

- The amount of variability within groups is greater and
- The difference between the two groups gets smaller.

Why is this the case? First, as variability increases within groups, it means that the data points (perhaps representing test scores) are more diverse, and you need a larger number of data points to represent all of them. For example, if you test two groups of college sophomores to determine whether their grade point averages differ and each group is highly variable, then it is likely that you will need a larger number of data points to represent the population fairly and show any difference between the groups (if a difference exists).

Second, as the difference between groups gets smaller, you need a larger number of participants to reach the critical mass where the groups can differ. For example, if you were to compare a first grader and a sixth grader on height, you would need only one participant in each group to say fairly confidently that there is a difference in height. In fact, there are very few (if any) short sixth graders who are shorter than the tallest first grader. But, if you examined a first grader and a third grader, the differences become much less noticeable, and a larger number of participants would be necessary to reveal those differences (if they are even there).

Do you want the real scoop on sample size? Keep the following in mind:

- In general, the larger the sample is (within reason), the smaller the sampling error will be and the better job you can do.
- If you are going to use several subgroups in your work (such as males and females who are 10 years of age, and healthy and unhealthy rural residents), be sure that your initial selection of subjects is large enough to account for the eventual breaking down of subject groups.
- If you are mailing out surveys or questionnaires (and you know what can happen to many of them), count on increasing your sample size by 40% to 50% to account for lost mail and nonresponders.
- Finally, remember that big is good, but accurate and appropriate are better. Do not waste your hard-earned money or valuable time generating samples that are larger than you need.

TEST YOURSELF

Why is it so important to get the size of a sample as close as possible to what is "correct" or most useful?

Summary

Although some people might not agree with you on your selection of topics to study, what you choose is your business as long as you can provide a reasonable rationale to support what you are doing. Your selection of a sample, however, is another story entirely. There are many right ways, and then there is the wrong way. If you choose the wrong way (where you are arbitrary and follow no plan), you could very well sabotage your entire research effort because your results might have no generalizability and, therefore, no usefulness to the scientific community.

Exercises

1. You are the head researcher on a study that is tracking vocational preferences from high school through middle adulthood. List the steps you would take in selecting the sample to be used in the study.

2. A researcher decides to give a questionnaire on television watching behaviors to every student in a large freshman college orientation course in her university. What sampling method is she using?

3. Why is a table of random numbers so useful as a tool for assigning people to different groups?

4. What's wrong with this scenario? An experimenter is interested in better understanding why some people love fast food and some do not. He stands in the fast-food isle of the market and asks buyers their opinion.

5. What is the difference between a probability and a nonprobability sampling strategy? Provide an example of each. Also, what are the advantages and disadvantages of each type of sample?

6. What is the easiest way to reduce sampling error? What is the relationship between sampling error and the generalizability of the results of a study? Finally, what happens to sampling error as the size of the sample increases? Why?

7. With a population of 10,000 children (50% boys and 50% girls, 70% white and 30% nonwhite, and 57% single-parent family and 43% dual-parent family), what steps would you use to select a representative sample size of 150?

8. You have identified that you need a sample size of 100 for your study. If you decide to mail your surveys instead of administering them in person, what would your new ideal sample size be?

9. How should a greater amount of variability within groups and a smaller difference between groups affect sample size?

10. Using a table of random numbers, select six names from the following list of 10:
    Michael
    Susan
    Sara
    Kent
    Selma
    Harriet
    Annette
    David
    Sharon
    Ed

    How many of the six would you expect to be males, and how many would you expect to be females? Why?

11. What are the implications of using a sample that is too big or a sample that is too small?

12. How big is big enough?

13. What are the risks of increasing a sample size too much?

14. When should cluster sampling and simple random sampling be used?

15. When would it be important to use a stratified sampling method in a population of 58% Democrats, 38% Republicans, and 4% Independents?

16. What is an advantage to using systematic sampling? What is a disadvantage to this method?

17. An employee at a supermarket is giving out samples of cake, and his boss asks him to get opinions from 20 males and 20 females on the quality of the cake. The

employee does not want to bother shoppers, so he only gives the cake sample and requests participation from the first 20 males and 20 females who make eye contact with him. What type of sampling method is this employee using?

18. What is sampling error and what factors contribute to how big a sample you should use?

Online. . .

The Research Randomizer

The *Research Randomizer* (http://www.randomizer.org/) is a cool little tool that assists you in performing a simple random sampling and assigning participants to experimental conditions.

Doug's Random Sampling Applet

If you don't find the above fun, try *Doug's Random Sampling Applet* at http://www.dougshaw.com/sampling/. You enter the population size and the size of the sample, and Doug computes which participants you need to select (by number).

How to Calculate Sample Size

At http://www.ehow.com/how 5262463 calculate-sample-size-formula.html, eHow provides a formula for calculating the appropriate sample size for your research. You will need a calculator and a z-score conversion table (the site provides a link to one).

Random Number Generator

At http://www.graphpad.com/quickcalcs/randomn1.cfm, GraphPad Software created this tool for generating random numbers. Simply enter the number of columns and rows you would like in addition to the range of possible integers, and voila!

❖ ❖ ❖ Chapter 5 ❖ ❖ ❖

Measurement, Reliability, and Validity

The Measurement Process

Even without knowing it, you probably spend a good deal of time making judgments about the things that go on around you. In many cases, these judgments are informal ("I really like the way he presented that material"), but at times they are as formal as possible ("Eighty-five percent of her responses are correct").

In both these examples, a judgment is being made about a particular outcome. That is what the process of measurement is all about, and its importance in the research process cannot be overestimated. All your hard work and efforts at trying to answer this or that interesting question are for naught if what you are interested in cannot be assessed, measured, gauged, appraised, evaluated, classified, ranked, graded, ordered, sorted, arranged, estimated, rated, surveyed, or weighed (get the idea?).

The classic definition of measurement was offered more than 45 years ago by an experimental psychologist, S. S. Stevens (1951), as the "assignment of numerals to objects or events according to rules." With all due respect to Professor Stevens, this definition can be broadened such that measurement is the assignment of values to outcomes. Numbers (such as 34.89 and $54,980) are values, but so are outcomes, such as hair color (red or black) and social class (low or high). In fact, any variable, by its very definition, can take on more than one value and can be measured. It is these values that you will want to examine as part of the measurement process.

This chapter introduces you to some of the important concepts in the measurement process, including levels of measurement, a classification system to help assess what is measured, and the two primary qualities that any assessment tool must possess: reliability and validity.

> **WHAT YOU'LL LEARN ABOUT IN THIS CHAPTER:**
>
> - Why measurement is an important part of the research process
> - What the process of measurement includes
> - What the different levels of measurement are and how they are applied
> - What reliability means
> - The different types of reliability and how they are used
> - How to increase the reliability of a test
> - What validity means
> - The different types of validity and how they are used
> - How to increase the validity of a test
> - The relationship between reliability and validity

Levels of Measurement

Stevens (1951) is owed credit, not only for the definition of measurement on which much of the content of this chapter is based, but also for a method of classifying different outcomes into what he called levels of measurement. A **nominal level of measurement** is the scale that represents a hierarchy of precision on which a variable might be assessed. For example, the variable

> The nominal level of measurement used reflects how an outcome is measured.

109

Level of Measurement	For example ...	Quality of Level
Ratio	Rachael is 5 feet 10 inches and Gregory is 5 feet 5 inches	Absolute zero
Interval	Rachael is 5 inches taller than Gregory	An inch is an inch is an inch
Ordinal	Rachael is taller than Gregory	Greater than
Nominal	Rachael is tall and Gregory is short	Different from

Table 5.1 Different levels of measurement used when measuring the same variable. The advantage (and maximum precision) occurs when you use the highest level possible

"height" can be defined in a variety of ways, with each definition corresponding to a particular level of measurement as shown in Table 5.1.

One way to measure height is simply to place people in categories such as A and B, without any reference to their actual size in inches, meters, or feet. Here, the level of measurement is called nominal because people are assigned to groups based on the category to which they belong.

A second strategy would be to place people in groups that are labeled along some dimension, such as Tall and Short. People are still placed in groups, but at least there is some distinction beyond a simple categorical label. In other words, the labels Tall and Short have some meaning in the context they are used, whereas Category A and Category B tell us only that the groups are different, but the nature of the difference is not known. In the second strategy, the level of measurement is called ordinal.

A third strategy is one in which Rachael is found to be 5 inches taller than Gregory. Now we know that there is a difference between the two measurements and we also know the precise extent of that difference (5 inches). Here, the level of measurement is called interval.

Finally, the height of an object or a person could even be measured on a scale that can have a true zero. Although there can be problems in the social and behavioral sciences with this ratio level of measurement, it has its advantages, as you shall read later in this chapter. This level of measurement is called ratio.

Keep in mind three things about this whole idea of level of measurement:

1. In any research project, an outcome variable belongs to one of these four levels of measurement. The key, of course, is how the variable is measured.
2. The qualities of one level of measurement (such as nominal) are also characteristic of the next level up. In other words, variables measured at the ordinal level also contain the qualities of variables measured at the nominal level. Likewise, variables measured at the interval level contain the qualities of variables measured at both the nominal and ordinal levels. For example, if you know that Lew is 60 inches tall and Linda is 54 inches tall (interval or possibly ratio level of measurement), then Lew is taller than Linda (ordinal level of measurement) and Lew and Linda differ in height (nominal level of measurement).
3. The more precise (and higher) the level of measurement, the more accurate the measurement process will be and the closer you will come to measuring the true outcome of interest.

What follows is a more detailed discussion of each of these different levels of measurement, with examples and applications. Table 5.2 summarizes these four levels and what you can and cannot say about them.

Level	Qualities	Example	What You Can Say	What You Can't Say
Nominal (categories)	Assignment of labels	• Gender (male or female) • Preference (like or dislike) • Voting record (for or against)	Each observation belongs to its own category	An observation represents "more" or "less" than another observation
Ordinal (category and order)	Assignment of values along some underlying dimension	• Rank in college • Order of finishing a race	One observation is ranked above or below another	The amount that one variable is more or less than another
Interval (category, order, and spacing of equal intervals)	Equal distances between points	• Number of words spelled correctly • Intelligence test scores • Temperature	One score differs from another on some measure that has equally appearing intervals	The amount of difference is an exact representation of differences on the variable being studied
Ratio (category, order, and spacing of equal intervals and a zero point)	Meaningful and nonarbitrary zero	• Age • Weight • Time	One value is twice as much as another or no quantity of that variable can exist	Not much!

Table 5.2   Different levels of measurement and some of their qualities

Nominal

The **nominal** (from the Latin word *nomin* [name]) level of measurement describes variables that are categorical in nature and that differ in quality rather than quantity; that is, the variable you are examining characterizes your observations such that they can be placed into one (and only one) category. These categories can be labeled as you see fit. All nominal levels of measurement are solely *qualitative*.

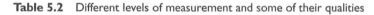

Nominal level variables are categorical in nature.

For example, hair color (blond, red, or black) and political affiliation (Republican, Democrat, or Independent) are examples of nominal level variables. Even numbers can be used in the measurement of nominal level variables, although the numbers have no intrinsic value. Assigning males as Group 1 and females as Group 2 and giving all offensive linemen on a football team jerseys with the numbers 40–50 are examples of nominal or categorical measurement. There is no intrinsic meaning to the number, but it is a label that identifies the items being measured.

An example of a study using a nominal level variable is one that examined the merits of two school-based programs which attempted to facilitate the integration of children with severe mental disabilities with children without disabilities (Cole et al., 1987). The nominal or categorical variable here is the type of arrangement in which the children participated: the Special Friend or the Peer Tutor program. They could participate in one program or the other but not both. The researchers examined how interaction between children with disabilities and children without disabilities differed as a function of the type of program in which they participated. Differences in social interaction during the program, during free play, and during a tutorial session were examined.

There are several things to remember about the nominal level of measurement. First, the categories are mutually exclusive. One cannot be in more than one category at the same time. You cannot be categorized as both Jewish and Catholic (even if you do celebrate both Hanukkah and Christmas). Second, if numbers are used as values, they are meaningless beyond simple classification. You simply cannot tell if someone in Category Blue is less or more intelligent than someone in Category Red.

Ordinal

Ordinal level variables reflect rankings.

The **ordinal level of measurement** describes variables that can be ordered along some type of continuum. Not only can these values be placed in categories, but they can be ordered as well. For this reason, the ordinal level of measurement often refers to variables as rankings of various outcomes, even if only two categories are involved, such as big and little.

For example, you already saw that Tall and Short are two possible outcomes when height is measured. These are ordinal because they reflect ranking along the continuum of height. Your rank in your high school graduating class was based (probably) on grade point average (GPA). You can be 1st of 300 or 150th of 300. You will notice that you cannot tell anything about the absolute GPA score from that ranking but only the position relative to others. You could be ranked 1st of 300 and have a GPA of 3.75 or be ranked 150th of 300 and have a GPA of 3.90.

From the variables Tall and Short or 1st and 150th, you cannot tell anything about how tall or how short or how smart a student is because ordinal levels of measurement do not include this information. But you can tell that if Donna is shorter than Joan, and Joan is shorter than Leni, then Donna is also shorter than Leni. So although absolute judgments (such as how much taller Leni is than Donna) cannot be made, relative ones can. You can assign the value "graduate with honors" as well as "honors with distinction" and "highest honors with distinction" to further distinguish among those graduating with honors. This scale is ordinal in nature.

Interval

Interval level variables have equidistant points along some underlying continuum.

The **interval level of measurement**, from the Latin *intervalum* (meaning spaces between walls), describes variables that have equal intervals between them (just as did the walls built by Roman soldiers). Interval level variables allow us to determine the difference between points along the same type of continuum that we mentioned in the description of ordinal information.

For example, the difference between 30° and 40° is the same as the difference between 70° and 80°. There is a 10° difference. Similarly, if you get 20 words correct on a spelling test and someone else gets 10 words correct, you can accurately say that you got 10 more words correct than the other person. In other words, a degree is a degree is a degree, and a correct spelling word is a correct spelling word is a correct spelling word.

A review conducted by A. Wigfield and J. Eccles (1989) of test anxiety in elementary and secondary school units illustrates how a construct such as anxiety can be measured by interval level variables. For example, the Test Anxiety Scale for Children (Sarasm, 1959) is a 30-item scale that assesses various aspects of anxiety and yields an overall measure. Items such as

If you are absent from school and miss an assignment, how much do you worry that you will be behind the other students when you come back to school?

provide an accurate measure of the child's anxiety level in this widely used measure of this fascinating construct.

To contrast interval with ordinal levels of measurement, consider the variable age where the ranking in age is as follows:

Oldest ————|————|————|————|————|———— Youngest
        Bill   Harriet   Joshua   Rachael   Jessica

We know that Bill is older than Harriet, but not by how much. He could be 2 years older than Harriet, and Harriet could be 20 years older than Joshua. Interval level variables give us that difference, whereas ordinal scales cannot. Put simply, using an interval scale, we can tell the difference between points along a continuum (and the exact difference between the ages of Bill, Harriet, Joshua, Rachael, and Jessica), but with ordinal scales we cannot.

Although an interval level scale is more precise and conveys more information than a nominal or ordinal level scale, you must be cautious about how you interpret the actual values along the scale. Eighty degrees might be 10° more than 70°, and 40° might be the same distance from 30°, but what a difference those 10° can make. The 10° between 80° and 70° might make water a bit cooler, but in the 10° between 40° and 30° water freezes. Similarly, just because you got 10 more words correct than a classmate does not mean you can spell twice as well (2 times 10) because we have no idea about the difficulty of the words or whether those 20 words sample the entire universe of all spelling words. More important, if you get no words correct, does that mean you have no spelling ability? Of course not. It does mean, however, that on this test, you did not do very well.

Ratio

The **ratio level of measurement**, from the Latin *ratio* (meaning calculation), describes variables that have equal intervals between them but also have an absolute zero. In its simplest terms, this means they are variables for which one possible value is zero, or the actual absence of the variable or trait.

Ratio level variables have a true zero

For example, a study on techniques to enhance prosocial behavior in the classroom (Solomon et al., 1988) measured prosocial behavior with behavior tallies. The five categories of behavior that were measured over a 5-year period, a long time, were cooperative activities, developmental discipline, activities promoting social understanding, highlighting prosocial values, and helping activities. These researchers spent a great deal of time developing systems that could consistently (or reliably, as we will call it later) measure these types of behaviors. The scales they designed are ratio in nature because they have a true zero point. For example, it is easily conceivable that a child could demonstrate no prosocial behaviors (as defined in the study).

This is indeed an interesting level of measurement. It is by far the most precise. To be able to say that Scott (who is 8 years old) is twice as old as Erin (who is four) is a very accurate, if not the most accurate, way to talk about differences on a specific variable. Imagine being able to say that the response rate using Method A is one-half that using Method B, rather than just saying that the response rate is "faster" (which is ordinal) or is "faster by 10 seconds" (which is interval).

This is the most interesting scale of the four levels discussed for other reasons as well. First, the zero value is not an arbitrary one. For example, you might think that because temperature (in Celsius units) has a zero point, it is ratio in nature. True, it does have a zero point, but that zero is arbitrary. A temperature of 0°C does not represent the absence of molecules bumping off one another creating heat (the nontechnical definition of temperature, and my apologies to Lord Kelvin). But the Kelvin scale of temperature does have a theoretical absolute zero (about −275°C), where there is no molecular activity, and here is a true zero or an absence of whatever is being measured (molecular activity).

Continuous Versus Discrete Variables

There is one more distinction we need to make before we move on to hypotheses and their importance in the research process.

Variables, as you well know by now, can take many different forms and can differ from each other in many ways. One of these ways can be whether they are continuous, or whether they are categorical (or discrete).

A **continuous variable** is one that can assume any value along some underlying continuum. For example, height is a continuous variable in that one can measure height as 64.3 inches or 64.31 inches or 67.000324 inches.

A **discrete** or **categorical variable** is one with values that can be placed only into categories that have definite boundaries. For example, gender is a discrete variable consisting of the categories of male and female; type of car driven is a discrete variable as well—consisting of such possibilities as Volvo, Chevrolet, or Saturn. As you may have already noticed, discrete variables can take on only values that are mutually exclusive. For example, each participant in your study is either female or male.

What's important to remember about the continuous–discrete distinction is that it is the "real" occurrence of the variable that determines its type—not the artificial system we might impose. We can say that there are tall and short people, but it is the actual nature of the variable of height, which ranges from 0 (no height) to an infinite height, which counts.

What Is All the Fuss?

Let's be practical. In a research study, you want to measure the variable of interest as precisely as possible. There is just no advantage in saying that Group A is weaker than Group B when you can say that Group A averaged 75 sit-ups and Group B averaged 100. More information increases the power and general usefulness of your conclusions.

Sometimes you will be limited to the amount of information that is available. For example, what if you wanted to study the relationship between age in adulthood and strength, and all you know is which group an adult belongs to (strong or not strong), not that person's strength score? Such limitations are one of the constraints of doing research in the real world—you have to make do with what you have. Those limitations also provide one of the creative sides of research: defining your variables in such a way that the definition maximizes the usefulness of the information.

At what level of measurement do we find most variables in the behavioral and social sciences? Probably nominal or ordinal, with most test scores (such as achievement) yielding interval level data. It is highly questionable, however, whether scores from measures such as intelligence and personality tests provide anything more than ordinal levels of measurement. A child with an IQ of 110 is not 10 points smarter than a child with an IQ of 100 but might have only scored 10 points more. Likewise, Chris might prefer the chocolate chips from package A to the chocolate chips from package B twice as often, but he might not necessarily like them twice as much.

Therein lies an important point: How you choose to measure an outcome defines the outcome's level of measurement. "Twice as often" is a ratio level variable; how much Chris likes package A chips can be attitudinal and ordinal in nature.

Most researchers take some liberty in treating ordinal variables (such as scores on a personality test) as interval level variables, and that is fine as long as they remember that the intervals may not be (and probably are not) equal. Their interpretation of the data must consider that lack of equivalency.

Also, you should keep in mind that Stevens' typology of measurement levels has not gone unchallenged. In the 50 years that this methodology has been around, various questions have been raised about the utility of this system and how well it actually reflects the real-world variables that researchers have to assess (Vellman & Wilkinson, 1993).

These criticisms focus primarily on the fact that a variable may not conveniently fit into any one of the four classifications but may be valuable nonetheless. For example, although intelligence may not be ratio level in nature (no one has none), it is certainly beyond interval in its real-life applications. In other words, the taxonomy might be too strict to apply to real-world data. As with so many things in the world of research, this four-level taxonomy is a starting point to be worked with but not to be followed as law.

TEST YOURSELF

What is the relationship between the levels of measurement and the amount or precision of information available from some test score or other outcome?

Reliability and Validity: Why They Are Very, Very Important

You can have the sexiest-looking car on the road, but if the tires are out of balance, you can forget good handling and a comfortable ride. The tires, or where "the rubber meets the road," are crucial.

> Respected levels of reliability and validity are the hallmarks of good measurement practices.

In the same way, you can have the most imaginative research question with a well-defined, clearly articulated hypothesis, but if the tools you use to measure the behavior you want to study are faulty, you can forget your plans for success. The reliability (or the consistency) and validity (or the does-what-it-should qualities) of a measurement instrument are essential because the absence of these qualities could explain why you act incorrectly in accepting or rejecting your research hypothesis.

For example, you are studying the effect of a particular training program and you are using a test of questionable reliability and validity. Let's assume for the moment that the treatment truly works well and could be the reason for making significant differences in the groups you are comparing. Because the instrument you are using to assess skills is not consistently sensitive enough to pick up changes in the behavior you are examining, you can forget seeing any differences in your results, no matter how effective the treatment (and how sound your hypothesis).

With that in mind, remember: Assessment tools must be reliable and valid; otherwise, the research hypothesis you reject may be correct but you will never know it!

Reliability and validity are your first lines of defense against spurious and incorrect conclusions. If the instrument fails, then everything else down the line fails as well. Now we can go on to a more detailed discussion of reliability and validity, what they are, and how they work.

A Conceptual Definition of Reliability

Here we go again with another set of synonyms. How about dependable, consistent, stable, trustworthy, predictable, and faithful? Get the picture? Something that is reliable will perform in the future as it has in the past. **Reliability** occurs when a test measures the same thing more than once and results in the same outcomes.

> Reliability consists of both an observed score and a true score component.

You can use any of the synonyms for reliability listed earlier as a starting definition, but it is important to first understand the theory behind reliability. So, let's begin at the beginning.

When we talk of reliability, we talk of scores. Performance for any one person on any variable consists of one score composed of three clearly defined components, as shown in Figure 5.1.

Method Error

Observed Score = True Score + Error Score

Trait Error

Figure 5.1   The components of reliability.

The **observed score** is the score you actually record or observe. It is the number of correct words on a test, the number of memorized syllables, the time it takes to read four paragraphs of prose, or the speed with which a response is given. It can be the dependent variable in your study or any other variable being measured. Any observed score consists of the two other components: true score and error score (see Figure 5.1).

The **true score** is a perfect reflection of the true value of that variable, given no other internal or external influences. In other words, for any person there is only one true score on a particular variable. After repeated measurements, there may be several values for a particular measurement (due to error in the measurement process which we will get to in a minute), but there is only one true one. However, one can never ascertain what that true value is. Why? First, because most variables, such as memory, intelligence, and aggression, cannot be directly measured and, second, because the process of measurement is imperfect.

Yet, the measurement process and the theory of reliability always *assume* a true score is there. For example, on a variable such as intelligence, each person has a true score that accurately (and theoretically) reflects that person's level of intelligence. Suppose that, by some magic, your true intelligence score is 110. If you are then given a test of intelligence and your observed score comes out to be 113, then the test overestimates your IQ. But because the true score is a theoretical concept, there is no way to know that.

The **error score** is all of those factors that cause the true score and the observed score to differ. For example, Mike might get 85 of 100 words correct on a spelling test. Does this mean that Mike is an "85% correct speller" on all days on all tests of spelling? Not quite. It means that on *this* day, for *this* test, Mike got 85 of 100 words correct. Perhaps tomorrow, on a different set of 100 words, Mike would get 87 or 90 or even 100 correct. Perhaps, if his true spelling ability could be measured, it would be 88. Why are there differences between his true score (88) and his observed score (85)? In a word, error. Whose or what error? You'll find out about that in a moment.

Perhaps Mike did not study as much as he should have, or perhaps he did not feel well. Perhaps he could not hear the teacher's reading of each word. Perhaps the directions telling him where he was supposed to write the words on the test form were unclear. Perhaps his pencil broke. Perhaps, perhaps, perhaps . . . . All of these factors are sources of error.

Repeated scores on almost any variable are nearly always different from one another because the trait being assessed changes from moment to moment, and the way in which the trait is assessed also changes (albeit ever so slightly) and is not perfect (which no measurement device is).

What Makes Up Error Scores?

Let's go beyond the catchall of error scores. You can see in Figure 5.1 that error scores are made up of two elements that help to explain why true and observed scores differ.

The first component of error scores is called **method error**, which is the difference between true and observed scores resulting from the testing situation. For example, you are about to take an exam in your introductory psychology class. You have studied well,

Try as we might, we can never design a test that reflects the true score on any variable or characteristic.

Both trait and method errors contribute to the unreliability of tests.

attended reviews, and feel confident that you know the material. When you sit down to take the test, however, there are matching items (which one in Column A goes with Column B?) and crossword puzzle–like items, and you were expecting multiple choice. In addition, the directions as to how to do the matching are unclear. Instead of reaching your full potential on the test (or achieving as close to your true score as possible), you score lower. The error between the two results from the method error—unclear instructions and so on.

The second component is **trait error**. Here, the reason for the difference between the true and observed scores is characteristic of the person taking the test. For example, if you forgot your glasses and cannot read the problems, or if you did not study, or if you just do not understand the material, then the source of the difference between the true score (what you really know if nothing else interferes) and the score you get on the test (the observed score) is a result of trait errors.

Table 5.3 lists some examples of major sources of error which can affect test scores from one testing situation to the next. The more influential these various factors are, the less accurate the measurement will be; that is, the more influential these factors, the less likely the obtained score will be as close as possible to the true score, the ultimate goal.

What do the components of error have to do with reliability? Quite simply, the closer a test or measurement instrument can get to the true score, the more reliable that instrument is. How do you get closer? By reducing the error portions of the equation you see illustrated in Figure 5.1. So conceptually, reliability is a ratio as shown in Figure 5.2.

If you look at the structure of the equation, you can see that as the error score gets smaller, the degree of reliability increases and approaches 1. In a perfect world, there would be no error, and the reliability would be 1 because the true score would equal the observed score. Similarly, as error increases, the reliability decreases because more of what you observe is caused by something that cannot be predicted very accurately: the changing contributions of trait and method error.

The question of what the components of an observed score are and which one is amenable to change leads us to our next discussion of how to increase reliability.

Source of Error	Example
General characteristics of the individual	• Level of ability • Test-taking skills • Ability to understand instructions
Lasting characteristics of the individual	• Level of ability related to the trait being measured • Test-taking skills specific to the type of items on the test
Temporary individual factors	• Health • Fatigue • Motivation ("Yuck, another test") • Emotional strain • Testing environment
Factors affecting test administration	• Conditions of test administration • Interaction between examiner and test taker • Bias in grading
Other factors	• Luck (no kidding!) • Superstition

Table 5.3   Sources of error in reliability. Error can be part of the method used to assess behavior or the person or trait being assessed

$$\text{Reliability} = \frac{\text{True Score}}{\text{True Score} + \text{Error Score}}$$

Figure 5.2 The ratio of true score to true score plus error score forms the conceptual basis for reliability.

Increasing Reliability

Given all that we have discussed so far, it should be almost crystal clear that reliability is closely related to both true and error scores. Given a fixed true score (which is always the case, right?), reliability decreases as the error component increases. Thus, if you want a reliable instrument, you must decrease error. You cannot affect true score directly, so you must minimize those external sources of error (be sure there are clear and standardized instructions, bring more than one pencil in case one breaks, make sure the room is comfortable) that you can control. Strive to minimize trait sources as well (ask participants to get a good night's sleep, put off the assessment if someone does not feel well, and on). Some important ways to increase reliability include the following:

1. Increase the number of items or observations. The larger the sample from the universe of behaviors you are investigating, the more likely that the sample will be representative and reliable.
2. Eliminate items that are unclear. An item that is unclear (for whatever reason) is unreliable regardless of knowledge or ability level or individual traits; people may respond to it differently at different times.
3. Standardize the conditions under which the test is taken. If the fourth grade class in Pickney Elementary School has to take its achievement test with snowblowers operating right outside the window or the heat turned up too high, you can certainly expect these conditions to affect performance (compared to Sunset Elementary where it is nice and quiet) and, therefore, reliability.
4. Moderate the degree of difficulty of the tests. Any test that is too difficult or too easy does not reflect an accurate picture of one's performance.
5. Minimize the effects of external events. If a particularly important event—spring vacation, the signing of a peace treaty, or the retirement of a major faculty member, for example—occurs near the time of testing, postpone any assessment. These events are too likely to take center stage at the expense of true performance.
6. Standardize instructions. Bill in one class and Kelly in another should be reading identical instructions and should take the test under the exact same conditions.
7. Maintain consistent scoring procedures. Anyone who has graded a stack of tests containing essay questions will tell you that grading the first one is much different from grading the last. Strive for consistency in grading, even if it means using a sheet with scores in one column and criteria in the other.

How Reliability Is Measured

Reliability is most often reflected in the value of the correlation coefficient.

You know scientists—they love numbers. It is no surprise, then, that a very useful and easy-to-understand statistical concept called correlation (and the measure of correlation, the **correlation coefficient**) is used in the measurement of reliability. You will learn more about the correlation coefficient in Chapter 9. Correlations are expressed as a numerical value, represented by a lowercase r. For example, the correlation between test 1 and test 2 would be represented as

$$r_{\text{test1} . \text{test2}}$$

where the scores on test 1 and test 2 are being correlated with one another.

For now, all you need to know about correlations and reliability is that the more similar the scores in terms of change from one time to another (that is, from one test to another), the higher the correlation and the higher the reliability. Keep in mind that reliability is a concern of the instrument, not of the individual.

For example, as you will soon see, one way to measure the reliability of a test is to give the test to a group of people at one point in time and then give the same test to the same group of people at a second point in time, say 4 months later. You end up with two scores for each person.

Now, several things can happen when you have these two sets of scores. Everyone's score can go down from time 1 to time 2, or everyone's score can go up from time 1 to time 2. In both these cases, when the scores tend to change similarly and in the same direction, the correlation tends to be positive and the reliability high.

However, what if the people who score high at time 1 score low at time 2, or the people who score low at time 1 score high at time 2? Then the reliability would not be as high. Instead it might be low or none at all because there is no consistency in performance between time 1 and time 2. In general, when the scores on the first administration remain in the same *relative* (a really important word here) position on the second (high on test 1 and high on test 2, for example), the reliability of the test will be substantial.

Reliability coefficients (which are roughly the same as correlation coefficients) range in value from 21.00 to 11.00. A value of 1.00 would be perfect reliability, where there is no error whatsoever in the measurement process. A value of 0.00 or less indicates no reliability. The standardized tests used in most research projects, which you will learn about in Chapter 6, usually have reliability coefficients in the 0.80 to 0.90 range—about what you need to be able to say a test is reliable.

Types of Reliability

Reliability is a concept, but it is also a practical measure of how consistent and stable a measurement instrument or a test might be. There are several types of reliability, each one used for a different purpose. A discussion of what these types are and how they are used follows. A comparison and a summary of the information are shown in Table 5.4.

TEST YOURSELF

In the simplest of terms, what is reliability and why is it important?

Test–Retest Reliability

Two synonyms for reliability used earlier in this section were consistency and stability. **Test–retest reliability** is a measure of how stable a test is over time. Here, the same test is given to the same group of people at two different points in time. In other words, if you administer a test at time 1 and then administer it again at time 2, will the test scores be stable over time? Will Jack's score at time 1 change or be the same as his score at time 2, relative to the rest of the group?

Test–retest reliability examines consistency over time.

An important factor in the establishment of test–retest reliability is the length of the time period between testings. The answer depends on how you intend to use the results of the test, as well as the purpose of your study. For example, let's say you are measuring changes in social interaction in young adults during their first year in college. You want to take a measure of social interaction in September and then another in May, and you would like to know whether the test you use has test–retest reliability. To determine this, you would have to test the same students at time 1 (September) and

Type of Reliability	What It Is	How You Do It	What the Reliability Coefficient Looks Like
Test–retest	A measure of stability	Administer the same test/measure at two different times to the same group of participants	$r_{test1 \cdot test2}$
Parallel-forms	A measure of equivalence	Administer two different forms of the same test to the same group of participants	$r_{form1 \cdot form2}$
Inter-rater	A measure of agreement	Have two raters rate behaviors and then determine the amount of agreement between them	Percentage of agreements
Internal consistency	A measure of how consistently each item measures the same underlying construct	Correlate performance on each item with overall performance across participants	• Cronbach's alpha • Kuder–Richardson

Table 5.4 Different types of reliability used for different purposes. However, no matter what type of assessment device you use, reliability is an essential quality that must be established before you test your hypothesis

time 2 (May) and then correlate the set of scores. Because you are not interested in change in social interaction over a 2-week period, establishing test–retest reliability over such a short period of time, given your intent, is not useful.

Parallel-Forms Reliability

Parallel-forms reliability examines consistency between forms.

A second common form of reliability is **parallel-forms reliability** or equivalence. Here, different forms of the same test are given to the same group of participants. Then the two sets of scores are correlated with each other. The tests are said to be equivalent if the correlation is statistically significant, meaning that it is large enough that the relationship is due to something shared between the two forms, not some chance occurrence.

When would you want to use parallel-forms reliability, assuming you have created (or have) two forms of the same test? The most common example is when you need to administer two tests of the same construct within a relatively short time and you want to eliminate the influence of practice effects on participants' scores.

For example, you are studying short-term memory. You read a list of words to people, and you ask them to recite what they can remember 2 minutes later. You might need to repeat this type of test every day for 7 days, but you certainly could not use the same list of 10 words each day. Otherwise, by the last day, the subjects surely would have a good deal of the list memorized as a result of repetition, and the test would provide little information about short-term memory. Instead, you could design several sets of words which you believe are equivalent to one another. Then, if you can establish that they are parallel forms of the same test, you can use them on any day and expect the results from day 1 to be equivalent to the results from day 2.

Inter-Rater Reliability

Test–retest reliability and parallel-forms reliability are measures of how consistent a test is *over time* (test–retest) and how consistent it is from *form to form* (parallel forms). Another type of reliability is inter-rater reliability.

Inter-rater reliability is a measure of the consistency from rater to rater, rather than from time to time or even from test to test. For example, let's say you are conducting a study that measures aggression in preschool children. As part of the study, you are training several of your colleagues to collect data accurately. You have developed a rating scale consisting of a list of different behaviors preschool children participate in, numbered 1–5, each representing a different type of behavior, as shown in Table 5.5.

> Inter-rater reliability examines consistency across raters.

As you can see, the behavior coded number 1 on the list is labeled Talking and is defined as verbal interaction with another child. The behavior coded number 4 on the list, labeled Hitting 1, is defined as physically striking another child without provocation. There is nothing complicated about these definitions, right? They seem to be fairly operational and objective. But who is to say that, even with these definitions, Steven and Andrea (the two raters) will identically categorize the behaviors they observe?

What if Steven sees Jill hit Elizabeth and categorizes it as a behavior 4, but Steven categorizes it as a behavior 5 because Andrea saw Elizabeth hit Jill first? You could be in trouble. Raters need to be able to rate and place events in the same category.

To be sure that all raters are in agreement with one another, inter-rater reliability must be established. This is done by having raters rate behavior and then examine the percentage of agreement between them. Let's say you have Andrea and Steven rate the behaviors of one child every 10 seconds as you train them on the use of the rating scale. Their pattern of choices could look something like what is shown in Table 5.6. To compute their inter-rater reliability, take the number of agreements and divide it by the number of total periods of time rated (20 in this example). In their pretraining rating, the inter-rater reliability comes out to 15 (the number of agreements) divided by 20 (the number of possible agreements), which is 0.75 (75%). After training, as you can see, the value has increased to 18 ÷ 20 or 0.90 (90%), which is quite respectable.

What elements were included in the training? The head of the project probably examined the problems in misclassification and reviewed the definition of behaviors and discussed examples with the raters. In Table 5.6, you can see how the most frequent problems were disagreements between ratings of behavior 4 and behavior 5, which are types of hitting behaviors. Here is where any differences between raters' judgments would be clarified.

The consequences of low inter-rater reliability can be serious. If one of your raters misclassified 20% of the occurrences, it means that 20% of your data might be wrong.

Behavior	Code	Definition
Talking	1	Verbal interaction with another child
Solitary play	2	Playing alone and no interaction with other children
Parallel play	3	Playing alongside other children in the same or different activity
Hitting 1	4	Physically striking other children without provocation
Hitting 2	5	Physically striking another child with provocation

Table 5.5 Categorizing behaviors. Categories can then be used to record their frequency objectively, but reliability is as important here as with any other kind of measure

Period	Before Training																			
	1	2	3	4	5	6	7	8	9	10	11	12	13	14	15	16	17	18	19	20
Andrea	5	5	4	5	5	3	4	2	3	2	2	3	3	3	5	3	3	4	3	4
Steven	4	5	4	4	5	3	5	2	3	2	2	3	3	3	4	3	3	5	3	4
Period	After Training																			
	1	2	3	4	5	6	7	8	9	10	11	12	13	14	15	16	17	18	19	20
Andrea	5	5	4	5	5	3	5	2	3	2	2	3	3	3	5	3	3	5	3	4
Steven	4	5	4	4	5	3	5	2	3	2	2	3	3	3	5	3	3	5	3	4

Table 5.6 Inter-rater reliability before and after training

Internal Consistency

> Internal consistency examines the unidimensional nature of a set of items.

Although internal consistency is a less commonly established form of reliability, you need to know about it as a beginning researcher. **Internal consistency** examines how unified the items are in a test or assessment.

For example, if you are administering a personality test that contains 100 different items, you want each of these items to be related to one another as long as the model or theory upon which the test is based considers each of the 100 items to reflect the same basic personality construct.

Likewise, if you were to give a test of 100 items broken down into five different subscales consisting of 20 items each, then you would expect that test to have internal consistency for each of the subscales if the 20 items within each subscale relate more to one another than they do to the items within any of the other four subscales. If they do, each of the scales has internal consistency.

Internal consistency is evaluated by correlating performance on each of the items in a test or a scale with total performance on the test or scale and takes the form of a correlation coefficient. The most commonly used statistical tools are Cronbach's alpha and Kuder–Richardson correlation coefficients.

Establishing Reliability: An Example

One of the best places to look for reliability studies is in the Buros Institute's *Buros Mental Measurements Yearbook* (you can find complete information about this book in your library or at http://www.unl.edu/buros/), a compendium of summaries and reviews of tests that are currently available. As part of these reviews, the way in which reliability was established is often described and discussed.

For example, Multidimensional Aptitude Battery II is an objectively scored general aptitude or intelligence test for adults in the form of five verbal and five performance subtest scores. The authors of the test computed several types of reliability, including test–retest correlation coefficients which ranged from .83 to .97 for the verbal scale of the test and .87 to .94 for the performance scale. They also computed other reliability indices that provide some indication of how homogeneous or unidimensional the various tests are (as measures of internal consistency) to assess consistently only one dimension of aptitude or intelligence. Although the results of these reliability studies are not terribly exciting for us (but they certainly were for the authors of the test), they provide crucial information that a potential user needs to know and that the author of any test needs to establish for the test to be useful.

Reliability is a hallmark of a good test. Why is it important and describe one way by which it is established?

Validity

Earlier in this chapter, we mentioned two essential characteristics of a good test. The first is that it be reliable, which was just discussed. The second is that it be valid—the test does what it is supposed to do.

A Conceptual Definition of Validity

Remember consistency, stability, and predictability (among other synonyms for reliability)? How about truthfulness, accuracy, authenticity, genuineness, and soundness as synonyms for validity? These terms describe what **validity** is all about: that the test or instrument you are using actually measures what you need to have measured.

When you see the term "validity," one or more of three things should come to mind about the definition and the use of the term. Keep in mind that the validity of an instrument is often defined within the context of how the test is being used. Here are the three aspects of validity:

1. Validity refers to the results of a test, not to the test itself. So if we have the ABC test of social skills, the results of the test may be valid for measuring social interaction in adolescents. We talk about validity only in light of the outcomes of a test.
2. Just as with reliability (although validity is not as easily quantified), validity is never a question of all or none. The results of a test are not just valid or invalid. This progression occurs in degrees from low validity to high validity.
3. The validity of the results of a test must be interpreted within the context in which the test occurs. If this were not the case, everything could be deemed to be valid just by changing its name. For example, here is item number 1 from a 100-item test:

$$2 + 2 = ?$$

Most of you would recognize this question to have validity as a measure of addition skills. If we use the question in an experiment focusing on multiplication skills, however, the item loses its validity immediately.

The way the validity of a test should be examined, then, is whether the test focuses on the results of a study and whether the results are understood within the context of the purpose of the research.

Just as with reliability, there are several types of validity which you will come across in your research activities. And you will, of course, have to consider validity when it comes time to select the instruments you intend to use to measure the dependent variable of your interest.

A summary of different types of validity, what they mean, and how they are established is shown in Table 5.7.

Type of Validity	What Is It?	How Do You Establish It?
Content	A measure of how well the items represent the entire universe of items	Ask an expert if the items assess what you want them to assess
Criterion		
Concurrent	A measure of how well a test estimates a criterion	Select a criterion and correlate scores on the test with scores on the criterion in the present
Predictive	A measure of how well a test predicts a criterion	Select a criterion and correlate scores on the test with scores on the criterion in the future
Construct	A measure of how well a test assesses some underlying construct	Assess the underlying construct on which the test is based and correlate these scores with the test scores

Table 5.7 Types of validity

Types of Validity

There are three types of validity, each of which is used to establish the trustworthiness of results from a test or an assessment tool.

Content Validity

Expert opinion is often used to establish the content validity of a test.

The simplest, most straightforward type of validity is content validity. **Content validity** indicates the extent to which a test represents the universe of items from which it is drawn, and it is especially helpful when evaluating the usefulness of achievement tests or tests that sample a particular area of knowledge.

Why just a sample? Because it is impossible to create all the possible items that could be written. Just think of the magnitude of the task. Imagine writing all the possible multiple-choice items you could on the material covered (not necessarily contained) in an introductory psychology book. There must be 1 million items that conceivably could be written on the domains of personality, perception, or personality alone. You could get tired just thinking about it. That is why you sample from all the possible items that could be written.

But back to the real world. Let's say you are dealing with eighth-grade history, and the unit deals with the discovery of North America and the travels and travails of several great European explorers. If you were to develop a history test that asks questions about this period and wanted to establish the validity of the questions, you could show it to an expert in early American history and ask, "Do these questions fairly represent the universe or domain of early American history?" You don't have to use such 25-cent words as universe and domain, but you need to know whether you have covered what you need to cover.

If your questions do the job, then the sample of questions you selected to test an eighth grader's knowledge of early American history, for example, was done as well. Congratulations. That is content validity.

Criterion Validity

Criterion validity is concerned with either how well a test estimates present performance (called **concurrent validity**) or how well it predicts (future) performance (called

predictive validity). Criterion validity is a measure of the extent to which a test is related to some criterion. An assumption of this method is that the criterion with which the test is being compared has some intrinsic value as a measure of some trait or characteristic. Criterion validity is most often used to evaluate the validity of ability tests (current skills) and aptitude tests (potential skills). And, if you have not already guessed, the important thing about criterion validity is the use of a criterion.

In both types of criterion validity, a criterion is used as a confirmatory measure. For example, let's say you want to investigate the use of graduate school grades in predicting which people in the clinical psychology program will become especially successful researchers. To that end, you locate a sample of "good" researchers (as defined by the number of journal articles they have published in the past 20 years). Then, you would find out how well those researchers did as graduate students and how well their school performance (or grades) *predicted* membership in the "good" group. You might also want to locate a group of "not good" researchers (or those who did not publish at all) and compare how well their graduate school grades predicted membership in the "good" or "not good" group. In this case, graduate school grades would have predictive validity (of success as a researcher) if grades (the test) predicted performance as a researcher (the criterion).

This sounds nice and neat and clean, but who is to judge the nature and the value of the criterion? Does the number of articles published constitute good research? What if 90% of one researcher's articles are published in journals that have a rejection rate of 50%, whereas someone else has published only one article in one journal where the rejection rate is 90%? And what if that one article has a significant and profound effect on the direction of future research in the discipline? As with any other building block in the research process, the criterion that you use to establish validity must be selected with some rationale. In this case, you would have to provide the rationale for assuming that the number of articles published, regardless of their quality, is what is important (if that is what you believe).

Another problem that occurs with both concurrent and predictive validity is the serious concern for what the tests actually measure. One assumes that if the tests correlate with the criterion, then the relationship must be meaningful. So, if the results of your intelligence test correlate with eye color or nose size or the shape of the bumps on your head, does that mean the test has criterion validity? The answer is "Yes," if you think that eye color and nose size and study of bumps on the head (the study of which is called phrenology, by the way) are good indicators of intelligence. Don't laugh—the history of science is filled with such well-meaning (and some not so well-meaning), but mistaken, assumptions and conclusions.

Construct Validity

Construct validity is the big one. It is a time-consuming and often difficult type of validity to establish, yet it is also the most desirable. Why? First a definition: **Construct validity** is the extent to which the results of a test are related to an underlying set of related variables. It links the practical components of a test score to some underlying theory or model of behavior.

For example, construct validity allows one to say that a test labeled as an "intelligence test" actually measures intelligence. How is this validity established? Let's say that, based on a theory of intelligence (which has undergone some scrutiny and testing and stands the test of time), intelligence consists of such behaviors as memory, comprehension, logical thinking, spatial skills, and reasoning; that is, intelligence is a construct represented by a group of related variables. If you develop a set of test items based on the construct and if you can show that the items reflect the contents of the construct, then you are on your way to establishing the construct validity of the test.

Therefore, the first step in the development of a test that has construct validity is establishing the validity (in the most general scientific terms) of the underlying

> Construct validity examines whether test performance reflects an underlying construct or set of related variables.

construct on which the test will be based. This step might require many studies and many years of research. Once the evidence for the validity of the construct is there, you then could move on to the design of a test that reflects the construct.

There is a variety of ways in which construct validity can be established.

First, as with criterion validity, you can look for the correlation between the test you are developing and some established test which has already been shown to possess construct validity. This is a bit of a "chicken-and-egg" problem because there is always the question of how construct validity was first established.

Second, you can show that the scores on the newly designed test will differ between groups of people with and without certain traits or characteristics. For example, if you are developing a test for aggression, you might want to compare the results for people known to be aggressive with the results of those who are not.

Third, you can analyze the task requirements of the items and determine whether these requirements are consistent with the theory underlying the development of the test. If your theory of intelligence says that memory is important, then you would expect to have items that tap this ability on your test.

Establishing Validity: An Example

Speaking of intelligence, here is how three researchers (Krohn et al., 1988) went about exploring the construct validity of the Kaufman Assessment Battery for Children (K-ABC).

The issue these researchers attacked is a familiar one: Is a test that is valid for one group of people (white preschoolers) also valid for another group (black preschoolers)? To answer this question, the researchers used perhaps the most common strategy for establishing construct validity: They examined the correlation between the test in question and some other established and valid measure of intelligence, in this case the Stanford–Binet Intelligence Scale, the most widely used intelligence test for young children.

I hope you are asking yourself, "If a widely used, presumably good test of intelligence exists, why go through the trouble to create another?" A very good question. The answer is that the developers of K-ABC (Kaufman & Kaufman, 1983) believe that intelligence should tap cognitive abilities more than previous tests have allowed. K-ABC measures both intelligence and achievement and is based on a theoretical orientation that is tied less to culture than tests such as the Stanford–Binet and the Wechsler Intelligence Scale for Children (WISC).

In one study, Krohn, Lamp, and Phelps (1988) tested the same children using both K-ABC and Stanford–Binet and found that K-ABC had substantial support as a measure of intelligence in the population of black preschool children from which the sample was selected.

Another way in which the construct validity of a test is established is through the use of the **multitrait-multimethod matrix**—quite a mouthful but quite a technique, and very demanding as well.

This technique measures various traits using various methods. What you would expect to happen is that, regardless of how you measure the trait, the scores are related. Thus, if you measure the same trait using different methods, the scores should be related, and if you measure different traits using the same methods, the scores should not be related.

For example, if we are trying to establish the construct validity of a test of children's impulsivity using a paper-and-pencil format, we might measure it two ways: by using a pencil-and-paper instrument (the one we're trying to develop) and by attaching an activity meter to the child's wrist. At the same time, we'll also measure another variable, such as movement or activity level. So each trait—impulsivity and activity level—is measured using each method, the paper-and-pencil test as well as the wrist-attached activity level meter. The matrix might look like that shown in Figure 5.3.

| | | Trait I Impulsivity | | Trait 2 Activity Level | |
		Method I Paper-and-Pencil	*Method 2* Activity Meter	*Method I* Paper-and-Pencil	*Method 2* Activity Meter
Trait I Impulsivity	*Method I* Paper-and-Pencil	High	Moderate	Low	Low
	Method 2 Activity Meter	Moderate	High	Low	Low
Trait 2 Activity Level	*Method I* Paper-and-Pencil	Low	Low	High	Moderate
	Method 2 Activity Meter	Low	Low	Moderate	High

▢ Evidence of convergent validity   ▢ Evidence of discriminant validity

Figure 5.3 Using a matrix of more than one method to measure more than one trait allows for the use of the multitrait-multimethod matrix method of testing for construct validity.

If the paper-and-pencil test measure of impulsivity does what it should, then the cells indicating low, medium, and high (for the strength of the relationship) should turn out as shown in Figure 5.3.

For example, the relationship between impulsivity measured using a paper-and-pencil test and that measured using an activity meter should be moderate. Because these methods are so different from one another, any relationship we observe has to be the result of what they share in common in the analysis of the construct (which is impulsivity). This is called **convergent validity** because the methods converge upon one another.

Similarly, you would expect there to be no relationship between the different methods being used to assess different variables or traits, and that's what the "lows" are for in Figure 5.3. For example, you would expect that the relationship between measuring impulsivity using paper and pencil and activity level using an activity monitor to be low—they share nothing (not method or trait) in common. This is called **discriminant validity** because method and trait variance are distinct from one another.

What's good about the multitrait-multimethod procedure? It really works fine in establishing the validity of a test because it places it in direct contrast to existing tests and ties it to the methods that are to be used in the assessment process.

What's not good? It requires lots of time, and time means money. But, if this is where you have to go to get the proof, what's a few thousand more lost dollars when school has cost so much already.

TEST YOURSELF

List at least one advantage and one disadvantage of the multitrait-multimethod technique for establishing construct validity. Then, name one other way to establish construct validity.

The Relationship Between Reliability and Validity

Yes, it's true! A test can be reliable without being valid. Do you know why?

The relationship between reliability and validity is straightforward and easy to understand: A test can be reliable but not valid, but a test cannot be valid without first being reliable. In other words, reliability is a necessary, but not sufficient, condition of validity.

For example, let's go back to that 100-item test. Here is the same example we used before:

$$2 + 2 = ?$$

Now, we can almost guarantee that this is a reliable item because it is likely to result in a consistent assessment of whether the person taking the test knows simple addition. But what if we named it a spelling test? It is obviously not a test of spelling and would certainly be invalid as such. This lack of validity, however, does not affect the test's reliability.

This might be an extreme example, but it holds true throughout the assessment of behavior. A test may be reliable and consistently assess some outcome, but unless that outcome addresses the issue being studied, it is not valid. End of argument!

Closing (and Very Important) Thoughts

The measurement process is incredibly important and, like so many of the other things that guide researchers' work, is not simple. It is an area of endeavor filled with its share of controversies and new ideas. Let me plant one idea in your thinking that illustrates how generative and filled with potential the study of measuring human behavior is.

In an article in the prestigious scientific journal *Science*, M. Lampl, M. L. Veldhuis, and M. L. Johnson (1992) undertook a study that was implicitly suggested by a friend's comment on how fast the friend's young baby was growing (as in your mother's report to your grandmother, "He shot up overnight!"). Doctors usually check infants' height and weight every other month in the beginning and then every few months as they get older. These researchers decided to see if babies really do grow in particularly fast spurts, so they measured babies' growth over an extended period of time. What did they find?

You will be amazed to learn that some infants grew as much as one whole inch in a 24-hour period! What is the big deal? Well, the average length of infants of that age is about 20 inches, and the change represents about a 5% increase. If you are an average male adult (about 5 feet, 10 inches) and you grew 5% in 1 day, you would be about 6 feet, 2 inches, and if you are an average female (about 5 feet, 4 inches), you would be about 5 feet, 7 inches. Now about those new pants you need . . . . That's the big deal.

The lesson is that there are undoubtedly thousands of things going on in the social and behavioral sciences that we don't notice either because we don't measure them appropriately (not intentionally, but because that is the way X or Y has been measured before) or because we might be making the wrong assumptions (such as that an infant's growth rate increases smoothly with no abrupt changes). Most important, what researchers know about human behavior ultimately depends on *how* they measure what they are interested in studying. In other words, the measurement technique used and the questions asked go hand and hand and are very closely related, both in substance and in method.

Do you want to cut corners in your research? Don't—but if you have to, don't ignore anything about the measurement process.

Now, a last thought.

Many students set out to answer interesting questions about this or that research question without having defined a reliable and valid dependent variable. The message here is that if the test is not reliable or valid and the null hypothesis is rejected (or not accepted), then how does one know that "truly" there is no difference between groups rather than the test just not doing its job? All the months of work and effort that would go into a project might be for naught (that is, you don't get a true reading of what you are examining) if an unreliable or invalid instrument is used.

The moral of this story is: Use a test with established and acceptable levels of reliability and validity. If you cannot find one, do one of two things. Develop one for your thesis or dissertation (which in itself is a huge undertaking) and do no more than that, or change what you are measuring so you are sure that what you ask can be answered in a fair and unbiased fashion.

TEST YOURSELF

A researcher tests the hypothesis that an intervention targeted at malnourished senior citizens works but uses unreliable tests to assess outcomes. What's wrong with the conclusion that the intervention worked?

Summary

There are no two ways about it—the measurement process is a critical part of putting together a research project and seeing it to fruition. This part of the research project is especially important because a test without the appropriate levels of reliability or validity is of no use to you or anybody else. Using poorly designed measurement tools leads you down the path of never knowing whether you are on the right track or never really accurately measuring what you want. Use your good sense and look around for instruments that have already been shown to have respectable levels of reliability and validity. It will save you time, trouble, and endless headaches.

Exercises

1. Identify the level of measurement associated with each of the variables listed below: *P. 110*
   (a) Number of words correct as a spelling test score *interval*
   (b) The name of the neighborhood you live in *nominal*
   (c) Age in years *interval*
   (d) Color expressed as wavelength *Ratio*
   (e) Grade point average from 1.0 to 4.0 in increments of 0.1 *interval*
   (f) Name of color of stimulus objects *nominal*
   (g) Time to run 100-yard dash in seconds *ratio*
   (h) After-school club choice *nominal*
   (i) IQ score in points *Interval*
   (j) Grade level in years *ordinal*

2. Indicate which of the sources of error in reliability are trait (t) and which are method (m).
   (a) Not enough sleep on the night before the test *t*
   (b) Poor test instructions *m*
   (c) A test proctor who walks around too much *m*
   (d) Instructions that are poorly printed and difficult to read *m*
   (e) Age of test taker *t*

3. Describe two ways in which the reliability of a test can be established and explain the purpose of each.

4. Consider the following example. Your car engine stalls three times every time you drive the car, regardless of how you drive it. According to the definition of reliability in this chapter, is your car reliable? Why or why not?

5. Review the following sets of test items. Which set is more internally consistent? Why?

   Set A –
   1. The death penalty is immoral.
   2. The death penalty is necessary in some cases.
   3. The existence of the death penalty helps keep society safer.
   4. No state should enforce the death penalty.

   Set B –
   1. The death penalty is immoral.
   2. Crime in big cities is out of control.
   3. People should not steal.
   4. Laws are in place for a reason.

6. You have just developed the ABC Test of History, which contains 100 items and tests a student's knowledge of history. What kind of validity would you need for a test like this and how would you establish it?

7. Among easy, difficult, or moderate, which type of test most accurately reflects the picture of an individual's performance?

8. What are some tests you have taken that were assumed to have predictive validity?

9. You have decided to enlist the help of two high school science teachers in administering the test you are using for your research. When administering the test, Mr. Barnes instructs his students to "choose the correct answer" and Mrs. Fletcher instructs her students to "choose the best answer." How might their differences in administration be a threat to your research?

10. As part of his research evaluating a short-term intervention to develop Calculus skills, Professor Lee administers a Calculus test to participants and 2 weeks later administers another version of the test, with different but comparable items, to the same participants. What type of reliability is Professor Lee demonstrating for his test results? If Professor Lee gave the same version of the Calculus test to participants at both time points, with a greater period of time in between the tests, what type of reliability would he be demonstrating for his test results then?

11. Define level of measurement.

12. Name the four levels of measurement and provide an example of each.

13. What is the relationship between reliability and validity?

14. You are interested in developing a hyperactivity scale, and you ask an expert on Attention Deficit Hyperactivity Disorder whether the items you have created accurately assess hyperactivity. In asking the expert, what type of validity are you trying to establish?

15. You have developed a scale of altruism and you want to demonstrate your items truly reflect altruism and not another concept, such as social desirability. You compare results from your test with results from a test of social desirability and find significant differences between the results of the two tests. What type of validity have you established for your scale?

Online. . .

The Buros Institute

The Buros Center for Testing (http://www.unl.edu/buros/) is in the business of advancing the field of measurement by providing professional assistance, expertise, and information to users of commercially published tests. The institute accomplishes this by publishing such invaluable books as *Mental Measurements Yearbook* and *Tests in Print,* as well as by sponsoring meetings and other professional activities. You may be able to access the more than 4,000 reviews of test online through your library as well as directly from the Buros Institute.

The ERIC Test Locator

The Eric Test Locator (http://ericae.net/testcol.htm) is a joint project of the ERIC Clearinghouse on Assessment and Evaluation, the Library and Reference Services Division of the Educational Testing Service, the Buros Institute of Mental Measurements at the University of Nebraska in Lincoln, the Region III Comprehensive Center at George Washington University, and Pro-Ed Test Publishers. You can search through the Educational Testing Service (ETS) Test Collection database, which contains descriptions of more than 10,000 tests and research instruments.

The ETS Test Collection

The ETS Test Collection at http://www.ets.org/testcoll/index.html includes 20,000 tests and other measurement devices from the early 1900s to the present. The largest in the world, it is full of great resources.

Tests and Test Reviews

The University of Southern Maine, at http://usm.maine.libguides.com/content.php?pid=15724, provides descriptions of some of the most comprehensive test review sites, including the Mental Measurements Yearbook, Tests in Print, and a host of other comprehensive testing handbooks and resources.

Screening Tools and Rating Scales

This site (http://www2.massgeneral.org/schoolpsychiatry/schoolpsychiatry_screeningtools.asp) from the Massachusetts General Hospital psychiatry program lists different screening tools for assessing mental health concerns in young individuals.

❖ ❖ ❖ Chapter 6 ❖ ❖ ❖

Methods of Measuring Behavior

In Chapter 5, you got a healthy dose of the theoretical issues that provide the foundation for the science of measurement, why measurement is crucial to the research process, how reliability and validity are defined, and how each of these can be established.

In this chapter, you will begin learning about the application of some of these principles as you read about different methods that can be used to measure behavior, including the ubiquitous test, the questionnaire, the interview, and other techniques.

As you read this chapter, keep several things in mind. Your foremost concern in deciding what method you will use to measure the behavior of interest should be whether the tool you intend to use is a reliable and valid one. This is equally true for the best-designed test and for the most informal-appearing interview. If your test does not "work," then virtually nothing else will.

Second, the way in which you ask your question will determine the way in which you go about measuring the variables that interest you. If you want to know about how people feel toward a particular issue, then you are talking about attitudinal scales. If you want to know how much information people have about a particular subject, then you are talking about an achievement test or some other measure of knowledge. The focus of a study (such as the effects of unemployment on self-esteem) might be the same, whether you measure attitude or achievement, but what you use to assess your outcome variable depends on the question you ask. You need to decide the intent of your research activity, which in turn reflects your original research question and hypothesis.

Third, really efficient researchers are fully onboard for using whatever method helps them answer the questions that are being asked. This might include a mixed-methods model where one aspect of a research program might include qualitative methods while another might include qualitative methods (see Chapter 10). As research questions and their associated hypotheses become more intricate and complex, the creative side of using a particular research method correctly becomes more important.

Finally, keep in mind that methods vary widely in the time it takes to learn how to use them, in the measurement process itself, and in what you can do with the information once you have collected it. For example, an interview might be appropriate to determine how teachers feel about changes in the school administration, but interviewing would not be very useful if you were interested in assessing physical strength.

So, here is an overview of a variety of measurement tools. Like any other tool, use the one you choose well and you will be handsomely rewarded. Likewise, if you use the tool incorrectly, the job may not get done at all, and even if it does, the quality and value of your finished report will be less than what you expected.

WHAT YOU'LL LEARN ABOUT IN THIS CHAPTER:

- The use of different methods of measuring behavior and collecting data

- What a test is

- How different types of tests are designed to assess different types of behavior

- The use of achievement tests in the behavioral and social sciences

- The design of multiple-choice items

- How to do an item analysis

- The application of attitude scales

- The difference between Thurstone and Likert attitude scales

The way in which you ask your research question will determine the method you use to assess the variables you are studying.

133

What better place to start than with the measurement method that all of us have been exposed to time and again: the good ol' test?

Tests and Their Development

In the most general terms, the purpose of a test is to measure the nature and the extent of individual differences. For example, you might want to assess teenagers' knowledge of how AIDS is transmitted. Or you may be interested in differences that exist on some measure of personality such as the Myers–Briggs Type Indicator or an intelligence test such as the Wechsler Intelligence Scales. Tests also are instruments that distinguish among people on such measures as reaction time, physical strength, agility, or the strategy someone selects to solve a problem. Not all tests use paper and pencil, and as we just mentioned, the technique that a researcher uses to assess a behavior often reflects that researcher's creativity.

A good test should be able to differentiate people from one another reliably based on their true scores. Before continuing, here are just a few words of clarification. The word "test" is being used throughout this chapter to indicate a tool or technique to assess behavior but should not be used synonymously with the term "dependent variable." Although you may use a test to assess some outcome, you may also use it for categorization or classification purposes. For example, if you want to investigate the effectiveness of two treatments (behavior therapy and medication, for example) on obsessive-compulsive disorders, you would first use the results of a test to categorize subjects into severe or mild categories and then use another assessment to evaluate the effectiveness of each treatment.

Why Use Tests?

Tests are highly popular in the assessment of social and behavioral outcomes because they serve a very specific purpose. They yield a score that reflects performance on some variable (such as intelligence, affection, emotional involvement, and activity level), and they can fill a variety of the researcher's needs (summarized in Table 6.1).

First and foremost, *tests help researchers determine the outcome of an experiment*. Quite simply, tests are the measuring stick by which the effectiveness of a treatment is judged or the status of a variable such as height or voting preference in a sample is assessed. Because test results help us determine the value of an experiment, they can also be used to help us build and test hypotheses.

Second, *tests can be used as diagnostic and screening tools, where they provide insight into an individual's strengths and weaknesses*. For example, the Denver Developmental Screening Test (DDST) assesses young children's language, social, physical, and personal development. Although the DDST is a general screening test at best, it does provide important information about a child's developmental status and areas that might need attention.

Third, *tests assist in placement*. For example, children who missed the date for kindergarten entrance in their school district could take a battery of tests to determine whether they have the skills and maturity to enter public school early. High school students often take advanced placement courses and then "test out" of basic required college courses. In these two cases, test scores assist when a recommendation is made as to where someone should be placed in a program.

Fourth, *tests assist in selection*. Who will get into graduate school is determined, at least in part, by an applicant's score on tests such as the Graduate Record Examination (GRE) or the Miller's Analogy Test (MAT). Businesses often conduct tests to screen individuals before they are hired to ensure that they have the basic skills necessary to complete training and perform competently.

What Tests Do	How Tests Do It	Examples
Help researchers determine the outcome of a study	Tests are used as dependent variables	A researcher wants to know which of two training programs is more effective
Provide diagnostic and screening information	Tests are usually administered at the beginning of a program to get some idea of the participant's status	A teacher needs to know what type of reading program in which a particular child should be placed
Help in the placement process	Tests are used to place people in different settings based on specified characteristics	A mental health worker needs to place a client into a drug rehabilitation program
Assist in selection	Tests are used to distinguish between people who are admitted to certain programs	A graduate school committee uses test scores to make decisions about admitting undergraduates
Help evaluate outcomes	Tests are used to determine whether the goals of a program were met	A school superintendent uses a survey to measure whether the in-service programs had an impact on teachers' attitudes

Table 6.1   What tests do and how they do it

Finally, *tests are used to evaluate the outcomes of a program*. Until you collect information that relates to the question you asked and then act on that information, you never really know whether the program you are assessing had, for example, the impact you sought. If you are interested in evaluating the effectiveness of a training program on returning war veterans, it is unlikely that you can judge the program's efficacy without conducting some type of formal evaluation.

However, whether you use a test for selection or evaluation, *it is not the test score that is in and of itself important, but rather the interpretation of that score*. A score of 10 on an exam wherein all the items are simple is much different than a score of 10 where everyone else in the group received scores between 3 and 5.

Learning to design, create, administer, and score any test is important, but it is very important—and almost essential—to be able to know how to interpret that score.

What Tests Look Like

You may be most familiar with achievement-type tests, which often include multiple-choice items such as the following:

The cube root of 8 is

a.   2
b.   4
c.   6
d.   8

Multiple-choice questions are common items on many of the tests you will take throughout your college career. But tests can take on a variety of appearances, especially when you have to meet the needs of the people being tested and to sample the behavior you are interested in learning more about.

For example, you would not expect people with a severe visual impairment to take a pencil-and-paper test requiring them to darken small, closely placed circles. Similarly, if you want to know about children's social interactions with their peers, you would probably be better served by observing them at play than by asking them about playing.

With such considerations in mind, you need to decide on the form a test might take. Some of the questions that will arise in deciding how a test should appear and be administered are as follows:

- Is the test administered using paper and pencil, or is it administered some other way?
- What is the nature of the behavior being assessed (cognitive, social, physical)?
- Do people report their own behavior (self-report), or is their behavior observed?
- Is the test timed, or is there no time limit?
- Are the responses to the items subjective in nature (where the scoring is somewhat arbitrary) or objective (where there are clearly defined rules for scoring)?
- Is the test given in a group or individually?
- Are the test takers required to recognize the correct response (such as in a multiple-choice test) or to provide one (such as in a fill-in item or an open-ended question)?

TEST YOURSELF

Why test? Provide at least two reasons and an example of each.

Types of Tests

Tests are designed for a particular purpose: to assess an outcome whose value distinguishes different individuals from one another. Because many different types of outcome might be measured, there are different types of tests to do the job. For example, if you want to know how well a group of high school seniors understood a recent physics lesson, an achievement test would be appropriate.

On the other hand, if you are interested in better understanding the structure of an individual's personality, a test such as the Minnesota Multiphasic Personality Inventory or the Thematic Apperception Test, two popular yet quite different tests of personality, would be more appropriate.

What follows is a discussion of some of the main types of tests you will run into in your research work, how they differ from one another, and how they can best be utilized.

Achievement Tests

Achievement tests are
used to assess expertise
in a content area.

Achievement tests are used to measure knowledge of a specific area. They are the most commonly used tests when learning is the outcome that is being measured. They are also used to measure the effectiveness of the instruction that accompanied the learning. For example, school districts sometimes use students' scores on achievement tests to evaluate teacher effectiveness.

The spelling test you took every Friday in fourth grade, your final exam in freshman English, and your midterm exam in chemistry all were achievement tests administered for the same reason: they were designed to evaluate how well you understood specific information. Achievement tests come in all flavors, from the common multiple-choice test to true–false and essay examinations. All have their strengths and weaknesses.

There are basically two types of achievement tests: standardized tests and researcher-generated tests. **Standardized tests**, usually produced by commercial publishers, have broad application across a variety of different settings. What distinguishes a standardized test from others is that it comes with a standard set of instructions and scoring procedures.

For example, the Kansas Minimum Competency Test is a standardized test that has been administered to more than 2 million children across the state of Kansas in rural and urban settings, from very different social classes, school sizes, and backgrounds. Another example is the California Achievement Test (CAT), a nationally standardized test of achievement in the areas of reading, language, and arithmetic.

Researcher/Teacher-made tests, on the other hand, are designed for a much more specific purpose and are limited in their application to a much smaller number of people. For example, the test that you might take in this course would most likely be researcher or teacher made and designed specifically for the content of this course. Another example would be a test designed by a researcher to determine whether the use of teaching machines versus traditional teaching makes a difference in the learning of a foreign language.

Achievement tests can also be broken down into two other categories. Both standardized and researcher-made tests can be norm-referenced or criterion-referenced tests.

Norm-referenced tests allow you to compare an individual's test performance to the test performance of other individuals. For example, if an 8-year-old student receives a score of 56 on a mathematics test, you can use the norms that are supplied with the test to determine that child's placement relative to other 8-year-olds. Standardized tests are usually accompanied by norms, but this is usually not the case for teacher-made tests nor is the existence of norms a necessary condition for a test to be considered standardized. Remember, a test is standardized only if it has a standard or common set of administration and scoring procedures.

Criterion-referenced tests (a term coined by psychologist Robert Glaser in 1963) define a specific criterion or level of performance, and the only thing of importance is the individual's performance, regardless of where that performance might stand in comparison with others. In this case, performance is defined as a function of mastery of some content domain. For example, if you were to specify a set of objectives for 12th-grade history and specify that students must show command of 90% of those objectives to pass, then you would be implying that the criterion is 90% mastery. Because this type of test actually focuses on the mastery of content at a specific level, it is also referred to as content-referenced testing.

When should you use which test? First, you must make this decision before you begin designing a test or searching for one to use in your research. The basic question you want to answer is whether you are interested in knowing how well an individual performs relative to others (for which norms are needed to make the comparison) or how well the individual has mastered a particular area of content (for which the mastery is reflected in the criterion you use).

Second, any achievement test, regardless of its content, can fall into one of the four cells shown in Table 6.2, which illustrates the two dimensions just described: Does the test compare results with those of other individuals or to some criterion, and who designed or authored the test?

Multiple-Choice Achievement Items

Remember those endless hours filling in bubbles on optical-scanner scoring sheets or circling the A's, B's, C's, and D's, guessing which answer might be correct or not, and being told not to guess if you have no idea what the correct answer is? All these

Type of Test		Comparison Group Used in Scoring	
		Norm-referenced	**Criterion-referenced**
	Standardized		
	Researcher/Teacher Made		

Table 6.2 Classifying achievement tests as norm- or criterion-referenced and as standardized or researcher designed

experiences are part of the multiple-choice question test, by far the most widely used type of question on achievement tests, and it is a type of test that deserves special attention.

The Anatomy of a Multiple-Choice Item

A multiple-choice question has its own special anatomy (see Figure 6.1). First, there is the **stem**, which has the purpose of setting the question or posing the problem. Second, there is the set of **alternatives** or options. One of these options must be the correct answer (alternative A in this example); the other three (in this example) should act as **distracters**.

A good distracter should be attractive enough that a person who does not know the right answer might find it plausible. Distracters that are far removed from reality (such as alternative d in Figure 6.1) are easily ruled out by the test taker and contribute to the lack of validity and reliability of the test. Why? Because the presence of poor distracters makes it even more difficult for the test to be an accurate estimator of a test taker's true score.

What makes a great multiple-choice item? Any item that discriminates positively (where more people in the high group get it correct than people in the low group) is a potential keeper. Also we'd like that item to be relatively difficult, moving toward 50%. In sum, we want positively discriminating items with difficulty levels as close to 50% as possible.

To Use or Not to Use?

Multiple-choice questions are ideal for assessing the level of knowledge an individual has about a specific content domain, such as home economics, child development, geology, chemistry, Latin, fiber optics, sewing, or volleyball. But whatever the content of the test, the items must be written with the original objectives in mind of the lessons, chapters, papers, lectures, and other instruction to which the test takers were exposed.

If your Geology I professor did not have as an objective the distinction between different types of landforms, then items on distinguishing landforms should not be on the test. In other words, the content of a multiple-choice test should unequivocally reflect the content and objectives from which the items are drawn, and the number of items for each content area should reflect the amount of time spent on that content area during the teaching session.

> The stem of a multiple-choice item should be written as clearly as possible to reduce method error.

> Multiple-choice items have clear advantages and disadvantages.

> Tests can take many different forms depending on their design and intended purpose.

12. Intelligence tests that are given to preschool children   ← **stem**

alternatives {
a. favor middle-class children.
b. have questionable construct validity.   } **distracters**
c. are based on motor skills.
d. are no fun at all.

Figure 6.1 The anatomy of a multiple-choice item.

In fact, many test creators use what is called a table of specifications which reflects the amount of teaching time as a function of topics so that if, for example, 20% of teaching time is spent on the basics of physical chemistry, the midterm should reflect that and have about 20% of the items on the basics.

There are several advantages and disadvantages to using multiple-choice items on an achievement test. These pros and cons should be taken into consideration if you intend to use such a test to assess a knowledge-based outcome. Here are some advantages of multiple-choice items:

- They can be used to assess almost any content domain.
- They are relatively easy to score and can be easily scored by machine.
- Test takers do not have to write out elaborate answers but just select one of the test item's alternatives.
- Because multiple-choice items focus on knowledge and not on writing, people who are not good writers are not necessarily penalized for being unable to show what they know.
- Good items are an investment in the future because they can be used over again, thus saving you preparation time.
- Similarly, crummy items (you'll find out what that is in a minute) can be discarded and no longer contribute to the unreliability of a test.
- Good distracters can help a teacher diagnose the nature of the test taker's failure to get the answer correct.
- It is difficult to fake getting the answer correct, because the odds (such as .25 with four alternatives, including one correct answer) are stacked against it.

There are also some liabilities to multiple-choice items:

- They may limit students' options to generate creative answers.
- There is no opportunity to evaluate writing skills.
- Some people just do not like them and do not do well on them.
- A multiple-choice type of question limits the kind of content that can be assessed.
- Items must be very well written because bright students will detect poorly written alternatives and eliminate those as viable distracters.

Item Analysis: How to Tell If Your Items Work

A good multiple-choice item does one thing very well: It discriminates between those who know the information on the test and those who do not. For example, an item that everyone gets correct is of no use because it does not tell the examiner who knows the material and who does not. Similarly, an item that everyone gets wrong provides little information about the test takers' understanding of the material. In other words, and in both cases, the item does not discriminate.

Wouldn't it be nice if there were some numerical indices of how good a multiple-choice item really is? Wait no longer! **Item analysis** generates two such indices: difficulty level and discrimination level, which are two independent but complementary measures of an individual item's effectiveness. Using these powerful tools, you can easily assess the value of an item and decide whether it should be kept in the item pool (the collection of multiple-choice items in a specific content area), revised, or tossed out!

Item analysis results in a difficulty and discrimination index for each item on a test, not for the test as a whole.

Before either of these indices is computed, the total number of test scores has to be divided into a "high" group and a "low" group. To create these two groups, follow these steps:

1. Rank all the test scores from the highest to the lowest, so that the highest score is at the top of the list.
2. Define the high group as the top 27% of the test scores.

3. Define the low group as the bottom 27% of the test scores. For example, if you have 150 adults in your sample, then the top 41 scores (or 27% of 150) would be in the high group, and the bottom 41 scores would be in the low group. Why is 27% the magic number? It is the amount that maximizes the discrimination between the two groups. If you recall, you want to compute the difficulty and discrimination indices to contrast groups of people who perform well with those who do not perform well.

4. For each item, examine the number of alternatives that were chosen by constructing the type of table you see in Table 6.3. For example, 23 people in the high group selected alternative item A (which is the correct response) and 6 people in the low group selected alternative D.

The **difficulty index** is simply the proportion of test takers who got the item correct. The formula is

$$D = \frac{NC_h + NC_l}{T}$$

where D = difficulty level

NC_h = number of people in the high group who got the item correct

NC_l = number of people in the low group who got the item correct

T = total number of people in the low and high groups

In this example, the difficulty level is

$$D = \frac{23 + 11}{82} = .41$$

meaning that the difficulty level for that item is .41 or 41%, a moderately difficult item. (If everyone got the item wrong, the difficulty level would be 0%, and if everyone got the item correct, the difficulty level would be 100%.)

The **discrimination index** is a bit more complicated. It is the proportion of test takers in the upper group who got the item correct minus the proportion of test takers in the lower group who got the item correct. This value can range from 21.00 to 11.00. A discrimination index of 11.00 means that the item discriminates perfectly, and all the people in the high group got the item correct, whereas all the people in the low group got the item incorrect. Likewise, if the index is 21.00, this means that everyone in the low group got the item correct, whereas none of the high-scoring people got the item correct (not really the way it should be!).

To compute the discrimination index, use this formula:

$$d = \frac{NC_h - NC_l}{(.5)T}$$

12. Intelligence tests that are given to preschool children

    a. favor middle-class children.
    b. have questionable construct validity.
    c. are based on motor skills.
    d. are no fun at all.

Item Alternative	A	B	C	D	Total
High group ($n = 41$)	23	12	4	2	41
Low group ($n = 41$)	11	9	15	6	41
Total	34	21	19	8	82

Table 6.3 Data for computing the difficulty and discrimination indices of a multiple-choice item

where d = discrimination level

$\quad$ NC$_h$ = number of people in the high group who got the item correct

$\quad$ NC$_l$ = number of people in the low group who got the item correct

$\quad\quad T$ = total number of people in the low and high groups

In this example, the discrimination level is

$$d = \frac{23 - 11}{(.5)82} = .29$$

or 29%. You want items that discriminate between those who know and those who do not know but are not too easy or too hard.

$\quad$ Figure 6.2 shows the relationship between item discrimination and item difficulty. You can see that the only time an item can discriminate perfectly (1.00 or 100%) is when the item difficulty is 50%. Why? Because an item can discriminate perfectly only when two conditions are met. First, one-half of the group gets it right, and one-half of the group gets it wrong; second, the half that gets it right is in the upper half of those who took the test. As difficulty increases or decreases, discrimination is constrained.

$\quad$ You can work on the discrimination level as well as on the difficulty level in an effort to make your items better.

$\quad$ To change the difficulty level, try increasing or decreasing the attractiveness of the alternatives. If you change the attractiveness of the alternatives, you will find that the value of the discrimination will also change. For example, if an incorrect alternative becomes more attractive, it is likely that it will discriminate more effectively because it will fool those folks who almost—but not quite—know the right answer.

$\quad$ Computing these indices (by hand) can be a painstaking job, but using them is just about the only way you can tell whether an item is doing the job that it should. Many people who regularly use multiple-choice items suggest that you do the following to help track your items.

$\quad$ Each time you create an item, place it on a 3 inch × 5 inch index card. On the back of the card, enter the date of the test administration (and any other information you might deem important). Under the date, add any comments you might have and record the difficulty and discrimination indices for that particular test item. Then, as you work with these test items in the future, you will develop a file of test items with varying degrees of difficulty and discrimination levels. These items can be reused or altered as needed.

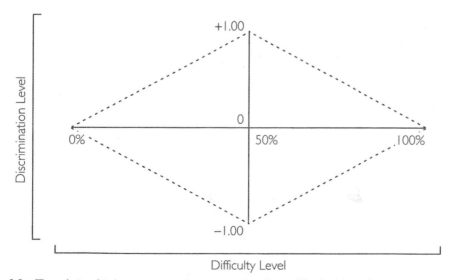

Figure 6.2 The relationship between item discrimination and item difficulty. Notice how item discrimination can be maximized only when item difficulty is 50%.

Item #12		A*	B	C	D	Total		D=	0.41
	High Group	23	12	4	2	41		d=	0.29
	Low Group	11	9	15	6	41			
		34	21	19	8	82			
Item #12		A*	B	C	D	Total		D=	=(C9+C10)/G11
	High Group	23	12	4	2	=SUM(C9:F9)		d=	=(C9-C10)/G10
	Low Group	11	9	15	6	=SUM(C10:F10)			
		=SUM(C9:C10)	=SUM(D9:D10)	=SUM(E9:E10)	=SUM(F9:F10)	=SUM(G9:G10)			

Figure 6.3   Data for computing the difficulty and discrimination indices of a multiple-choice item.

In order for you to discriminate between groups maximally, try to adjust the difficulty level of the item (which, to a large extent, is under the control of the researcher) so that it comes as close as possible to the 50% mark.

And instead of using index cards, create a spreadsheet for each test, where you can easily compute difficulty and discrimination indices for each item using simple formulas you create as shown in Figure 6.3 where the values of D and d are shown in the top of the example, and the actual formulas used to compute the values are shown in the bottom of the example.

If you chose to use a spreadsheet and formulas, just adjust the example in the table to fit your particular situation, such as the number of alternatives, the correct alternative, etc.

TEST YOURSELF

Achievement tests are ubiquitous in our society. Why do you think that's the case?

Attitude Tests

Whereas achievement tests are probably the most commonly used type of test in our society (think of all those Friday afternoon spelling tests), other types are used in a variety of research applications. Among these are **attitude tests**, which assess an individual's feelings about an object, person, or event. Attitude tests (sometimes called scales) are used when you are interested in knowing how someone feels about a particular thing, whether it be preference for a brand of microwave popcorn or feelings about euthanasia legislation.

For example, Figure 6.4 illustrates the basic format of a simple attitude scale. A statement is presented and then the individual indicates his or her attitude along some scale such as "Agree," "No Strong Feeling," and "Disagree." The selection of items to be included and the design of the scale are tricky tasks that should not be undertaken lightly. Let's look at two of the standard methodologies used for creating two types of scales, Thurstone and Likert, and see how they were developed.

Item	Agree	No Strong Feeling	Disagree
The day before Thanksgiving should be a holiday.	——	——	——
Final exams should be elective.	——	——	——
The dining room should serve gourmet food.	——	——	——
My parents don't appreciate how smart I am.	——	——	——
My professors don't appreciate how smart I am either.	——	——	——

Figure 6.4   A simple attitude scale.

Thurstone Scales

L. L. Thurstone was a famous psychometrician who developed the **Thurstone scale**, a method of measuring attitudes. He reasoned that if you could find out what value experts placed on a set of statements, then these statements could be scaled. People's responses to these statements would indicate their attitude about the item in question. Here are the steps involved in the development of such a scale:

1. As many statements as possible are written as potential test items. For example, if one were looking at parents' attitudes toward their child's school, some of these items might be
   a. I like the way my child's teacher greets him or her in the morning.
   b. The principal does not communicate effectively with the teachers.
   c. My child's education and potential are at risk.
   d. School lunches are healthy and nutritious.
2. Judges who are knowledgeable about the area of interest place the statements into 11 (actual physically different) stacks, ranging from the least favorable statement to the most favorable statement. Stack 6 (being right in the middle) represents a neutral statement. For example, item C below might be rated 1, 2, 3, 4, or 5 because it appears to be somewhat unfavorable.
3. Those statements rated consistently (with low variability) by judges are given the average score according to their placement. For example, if item A were rated as being 9 or 10 (somewhere around very favorable), it could receive a scale value of 9.5.
4. A group of statements then is selected that cover the entire range from unfavorable to favorable. That is your attitude scale.

> Thurstone scales come very close to measuring at the interval level.

One of the major advantages of Thurstone-like scales is that they are as close to the interval level of measurement (see Chapter 5 for a review of that idea) as one can get because the judges who rated the items placed them in stacks that have (presumably) equal distances between points which reflect psychological differences. It is for this reason that a Thurstone scale is also referred to as the **method of equal-appearing intervals**.

Respondents are asked to check off items on which they agree. Because the scale value assigned to the items that were checked off is known, an attitude score can be easily computed. If a person checks off many different items with scale values that are not approximately the same, then the individual's attitude is not consistent or not well formed, or the scale has not been developed properly.

For example, here are some items on attitudes toward church from Thurstone and Chave's classic work on attitude measurement, *The Measurement of Attitudes* (1929). Accompanying each item is its scale value.

I believe the church is the greatest institution in America today (11)

I believe in religion, but I seldom go to church (9.6)

I believe in sincerity and goodness without any church ceremonies (6.7)

I believe the church is a hindrance to religion for it still depends upon magic, superstition, and myth (5.4)

I think the church is a parasite on society (.2)

It should be clear that the item with a scale value of 5.4 is more neutral in content relative (and that's the really important term here) to any of the others.

Likert Scales

> Likert scales are the most popular type of attitude assessment scale.

The **Likert scale** (Likert, 1932) is simple to develop and widely used. Although its construction is similar to a Thurstone scale, its development is less time consuming.

Here are the steps involved in the development of a Likert scale:

1. Statements are written that express an opinion or feeling about an event, object, or person. For example, if one were examining attitude toward federal support for child care, items might look like this:
    a. The federal government has no business supporting child care.
    b. Child care is an issue that the federal government should fully support.
2. Items that have clear positive and negative values (in the developer's judgment) are selected.
3. The statements are listed, and to the right of each statement is a space for the respondent to indicate degree of agreement or disagreement, using a five-point scale such as:

SA Strongly agree

A   Agree

U   Undecided

D   Disagree

SD Strongly disagree

Respondents are asked to circle or check their level of agreement with each item, as shown in Figure 6.5.

Likert scales are scored by assigning a weight to each point along the scale, and an individual's score is the average across all items. But it is not that simple. Because items can be reversed (such as where some are stated in the negative; for example, *Government has no business funding child care programs*), you must be consistent and reverse the scale when you score these items. The rule is that favorable items (such as *Child care should be supported by federal, state, and local tax dollars*) are rated 1–5, with 5 representing Strongly Agree. Unfavorable items are reversed in their scoring so that 1 represents Strongly Agree.

In the example in Figure 6.5, the first item is written in the negative and the second one is written as a positive expression. Given the choices you see in Figure 6.5, the scoring for these two items would be:

Item	Racing	Score
1	A	2 (which was a 4 but was reversed)
2	SD	1

Directions: Indicate to what extent you agree or disagree with the statements listed below by circling one of the following:				
SA means that you strongly agree with the statement. (value = 5)				
A means that you agree with the statement. (value = 4)				
U means that you are undecided about the statement. (value = 3)				
D means that you disagree with the statement. (value = 2)				
SD means that you strongly disagree with the statement. (value = 1)				
Item	**Rating**			
1. Government has no business funding child care programs.	SD	D	U	(A)	SA
2. Child care should be supported by federal, state, and local tax dollars.	(SD)	D	U	A	SA

Figure 6.5 A set of Likert items.

producing a score of (2 + 1)/2 or 1.5, indicating a relatively strong level of general disagreement. Remember, item 1 was scored in reverse fashion because it is stated in the negative. And, remember that this is an abbreviated example using only two items. Because you sum ratings, the development of a Likert scale is often referred to as the **method of summated ratings**.

Personality Tests

Personality tests assess stable individual behavior patterns and are the most common type of test listed in the *Buros Mental Measurement Yearbook* (see http://www.unl.edu/buros). Although personality tests can be very valuable assessment tools, they are extremely time consuming to develop and require training for the administration, scoring, and interpretation of the scores.

There are basically two types of personality tests: projective and structured tests. **Projective tests** present the respondent a somewhat ambiguous stimulus and then ask the person to formulate some type of response. The assumption underlying these types of tests is that the person being tested will project (or impose) his or her own view of the world on the stimuli and that these responses will form a pattern that can be evaluated by the trained person who is administering the test. These tests are unstructured.

Scoring these kinds of tests and reaching conclusions about personality patterns and behavior are not pie-in-the-sky stuff. Psychologists know that certain types of personalities respond in characteristic patterns; however, being able to recognize those patterns takes a great deal of time, training, and practice. Examples of these tests are the Thematic Apperception Test and the Rorschach Test.

Structured tests use a format that you might be familiar with, such as true–false, multiple choice, or yes–no. In these tests, people are asked to agree or disagree with an item that describes their feelings toward themselves (such as, "I like myself"). Examples of these tests are the Sixteen Personality Factor Questionnaire and the Minnesota Multiphasic Personality Inventory. One of the major advantages of the structured test over the projective test is that the structured test is objective in its item design and is easy to score. In fact, the publishers of these (and many other types of tests for that matter) offer scoring services. However, ease of scoring has nothing to do with interpreting the results of the test. Have no doubts, interpreting personality tests is best left to the experts who have the skills and the training. In fact, most publishers of personality tests will not sell you the materials until you can show proof of training (such as a Ph.D.) or have a trained person (such as your adviser) vouch for you.

There are all kinds of tests to test all kinds of things. What factors determine what kind of test you should use?

Observational Techniques

You may be most familiar with the type of test results that include an individual taking a test. That kind of test makes the respondent the active agent in the measurement process. In an entirely different class of behavior-assessment methods, the researcher (such as yourself) becomes the active agent. These are known as observational methods or observational techniques. In this technique, the researcher stands outside of the behavior being observed and creates a log, notes, or an audio or video record of the behavior.

Many terms are used to describe observational activity (several of which have been taken from the work done by anthropologists and ethnologists), such as fieldwork or naturalistic observation. The most important point to remember about observational methods is why they have been so useful to scientists in other disciplines; their primary goal is to record behavior without interference. As an observer, you should make every effort to stay clear of the behavior you are observing so that you are unobtrusive and do not interfere.

For the most part, observers want to remove themselves from the action so that their presence does not affect the phenomena under observation.

For example, if you are interested in studying play behavior among children with disabilities and those without disabilities, you will be well served to observe these children from afar rather than to become a part of their setting. Your presence while they play would undoubtedly have an impact upon their behavior.

You can find a great deal of additional information on observational techniques in Chapter 10, which covers qualitative methods and discusses such techniques as ethnographic research and case studies.

Techniques for Recording Behavior

Several different techniques can be used to observe and record behavior in the field. They fall into four general categories: duration recording, frequency recording, interval recording, and continuous recording.

In the first category, **duration recording**, the researcher uses a device to keep track of time and measures the length of time that a behavior occurs. For example, the researcher might be interested in knowing how much physical activity occurs during kindergarteners' morning recess. The researcher might use a stopwatch to record the length of time that physical activity takes place for one child, then go on to another child, and so forth. The researcher is recording the duration of a particular event.

The second major technique category for observing behavior is **frequency recording**, in which the incidence or frequency of the occurrence of a particular behavior is charted. For example, a researcher might want to record the number of times that a shopper picks up and feels the fabric of which clothes are made or the number of comments made about a particular brand of soap.

A third category is **interval recording or time sampling**, in which a particular subject is observed during a particular interval of time. For example, the researcher might observe each child in a play group for 15 seconds, record the target behaviors, and then move on to the next child for 15 seconds. Here, the interval deals with the time the observer focuses on a particular subject, regardless of what the subject might be doing.

Finally, in **continuous recording**, all of the behavior of the target subject is recorded, with little concern as to the specificity of its content. Often, people who complete case studies observe a child for a particular length of time and have no previously designated set of behaviors for which to look. Rather, the behaviors that are recorded are those that occur in the natural stream of events. This is a rich and fruitful way of collecting information, but it has a major disadvantage: The little planning that goes into recording the information necessitates intensive sifting through of the records at analysis time.

Table 6.4 provides a summary and gives an example of these four different kinds of techniques—and what each kind does.

There are a few potentially unattractive things about the use of these techniques. Primarily (you've just read this but it's important enough to repeat), the very act of observing some behaviors interferes with the actual behavior that researchers may want to study. For example, have you ever walked into an elementary school classroom and noticed that all the children look at you? Some children may even put on a bit of a show for you. Sooner or later that type of behavior on the part of the children would settle down, but you certainly are not going to get an uninfluenced view of what occurs there.

The key word, then, is "unobtrusive"—observing behavior without changing the nature of what is being observed.

The use of these four different techniques has been eased greatly by the introduction and availability of easy-to-use technology. For example, you need not sit and continuously observe a group of adults making a decision when you can videotape the group and then go back to do an in-depth analysis of their behaviors. Similarly, rather than using a pencil and paper to record behavior every 10 seconds, you can use your iPhone or other smartphone (appropriately programmed) to beep every 10 seconds and then press a key to enter the category of the behavior.

Remember that any such collection of data needs to be done with particular attention given to such concerns as anonymity and respect for the person being observed (addressed

Technique	How It Works	Example
Duration recording	The researcher records the length of time that a behavior occurs	How much time is spent in verbal interaction between two children?
Frequency recording	The researcher records the number of times a behavior occurs	How often are questions asked?
Interval recording	The researcher observes a subject for a fixed amount of time	Within a 60-second period, how many times do members of the group talk to another person?
Continuous recording	The researcher records everything that happens	During a 1-hour period, all the behavior of a 6-year-old boy is recorded

Table 6.4 Four ways to observe and record behaviour

in Chapter 3B). For example, you have to pick and choose where and how you do your observing. Although it might be very interesting to listen in on the private talk of adolescents in the restroom, it also might be a violation of their right to privacy. Recording phone conversations might be an effective way to assure anonymity, because you might not know the caller's name (if you solicit callers), but people need to be notified when conversations are being recorded (remember Watergate, Linda Tripp, and other famous folks).

Observational Techniques? Be Careful!

No technique for assessing behavior is perfect, and all are fraught with potential problems that can sink your best efforts. Some particular problems that you should consider if you want to use observational techniques are as follows:

- Your very presence may affect the behavior being observed.
- Your own bias or viewpoints might affect the way in which you record behavior, from what you select to record to the way you do the recording.
- You may become fatigued or bored and miss important aspects of the behavior being recorded or miss the behavior itself.
- You may change the definition of those behaviors you want to observe such that what was defined as aggression at time 1 (touching without permission) is redefined at time 2 because you realize that all touching (even without permission) is not necessarily aggressive.

There are a few good reasons why one should be very careful when using observational techniques mostly having to do with contamination by the observer.

TEST YOURSELF

Provide an example of where the person doing the examining might interfere with the measurement itself.

Questionnaires

Questionnaires are (most often) a paper-and-pencil set of structured and focused questions. Questionnaires save time because individuals can complete them without any direct assistance or intervention from the researcher (many are self-administered).

In fact, when you cannot be with participants personally, a mailed questionnaire can produce the data you need.

There are other advantages to questionnaires besides their being self-administered:

- By using snail mail or e-mail, you can survey a broad geographical area. Also relatively new to the world of doing survey research are online, Web-based survey tools such as SurveyMonkey (at surveymonkey.com), Zoomerang (at zoomerang.com), and SurveyGizmo (at surveygizmo.com). These are all free in the limited version. For example, SurveyMonkey allows for 100 responses and no customization or downloading, but for $20 per month, there are no limits. For a large-scale research project, where data is only collected for a few months, this can be a huge help and savings of time and effort.
- They are cheaper (even with increased postage costs) than one-on-one interviews.
- People may be more willing to be truthful because their anonymity is virtually guaranteed.

The objectivity of the data also makes it easy to share with other researchers and to use for additional analysis. Although the time that the data were collected may have passed, answers to new questions beyond those originally posed might just be waiting to be answered.

For example, in one study, S. L. Hanson and A. L. Ginsburg (1988) used the results of the High School and Beyond surveys originally collected in the spring of 1980 from more than 30,000 sophomore students. These researchers were interested in examining the relationships among high school students' values, test scores, grades, discipline problems, and dropout status. With an original 84% response rate, these surveys provide a large, comprehensive database. The response rate may have been unusually high because the students were probably part of a captive audience. In other words, they were given the questionnaires as part of regular school activities.

Keep in mind, however, that all these advantages are not necessarily a recommendation to go out and start collecting all your data using this method. One of the big disadvantages of questionnaires is that the completion and return rates are much lower than if you personally asked the questions of each potential respondent through an interview, a technique you will get to shortly. Although you would expect a high participation rate (up to 100%) if you were to visit people's homes and ask them questions, you can expect about a 35% return rate on a mailed questionnaire.

What Makes Questionnaires Work

What's a good questionnaire? Several factors make a questionnaire successful, or result in a high number of returns with all the items (or as many as possible) completed. You have completed questionnaires at one time or another, whether they were about your attitude toward the 2004 Green Grass Party ticket or what you want in a stereo receiver. Whether or not the questionnaires work depends on a variety of factors under your control. Let's look at a brief discussion of each of these factors, which are summarized in Table 6.5 and broken down into three general parts: the basic assumptions on which the questionnaire is based, the questions themselves, and the format in which the items are presented.

Basic Assumptions of the Questionnaire

There are five important points regarding the basic assumptions that one makes when designing a questionnaire. Possible respondents are probably quite willing to help you, but you must help them to be the kind of respondent you want.

1. You would not ask respondents to complete a 40-page questionnaire or to take 3 hours on Saturday to do it. Your questionnaire must be designed in such a way

> Questionnaires are very useful, but they take a lot of time and effort to develop.

The Basic Assumptions
• The questionnaire does not make unreasonable demands upon the respondent • The questionnaire does not have a hidden purpose • The questionnaire requests information that respondents presumably have
The Questions
• The questionnaire contains questions that can be answered • The questionnaire contains questions that are straightforward
The Format
• The items and the questionnaire are presented in an attractive, professional, and easy-to-understand format • All questions and pages are clearly numbered • The questionnaire contains clear and explicit directions as to how it should be completed and how it should be returned • The questions are objective • The questions are ordered from easy to difficult and from easy to specific • Transitions are used from one topic to the next • Examples are given when necessary

Table 6.5 Some important things to remember about the design and use of questionnaires

that its demands of time, expense, and effort are reasonable. You also want to avoid asking questions that are inappropriate (too personal) or phrased in the wrong way. Anything that you would find offensive will probably offend your potential respondents as well.

2. Your questionnaire must be designed to accomplish your goal, not to collect information on a related but implicit topic. If you are interested in racial attitudes, then you should direct your questions to racial attitudes and not ask questions framed within a different context that is related, but not central, to your purpose.

3. If you want to find out about a respondent's knowledge of some area, you must assume that the person has the knowledge to share. Asking a first-semester freshman on the first day of classes about the benefits of college would probably not provide meaningful data. However, on a student's last day of college, you would probably get a gold mine of information.

4. Encourage respondents by designing a questionnaire that contains interesting questions, that engages respondents in answering all your questions, and that prompts them to return the questionnaire to you. If you cannot make your questions interesting, perhaps you do not have enough knowledge or enthusiasm about the topic and you should select another topic.

5. If you can get the same information through a source other than a questionnaire, by all means do so. If an interview gets you a better response and more accurate data, use an interview. If you can find out someone's GPA through another source, it's better to take the extra time necessary than to load the respondent with issues that really are secondary to your purpose.

What About the Questions?

Questions come in all shapes and sizes, and some are absolutely terrible. For example: *Do you often feel anxious about taking a test and getting a low grade?*

Can you see why this is not a good question? To begin with, the *and* makes it two questions rather than one, making it very difficult to know what the respondent was reacting to. Designing good questions takes some time and practice.

If you are using a questionnaire, be reasonable when planning the what, when, where, and how of your research plan.

First, be sure the questions you ask can be answered. Do not ask about a person's attitude toward political strife in some foreign country if they know nothing about the country's state of affairs.

Similarly, ask the question in a straightforward manner: for example, *Do you never not cheat on your exams?* This question is convoluted, uses a double negative, and is just as easily asked as, *Do you ever cheat on your exams?* This form is clearer and easier to answer accurately.

Finally, take into account the social desirability of questions. Will anyone graciously and positively answer the question, *Do you beat your children?* Of course not, and information from such direct questions may be of questionable value.

The Format of the Questionnaire

As you can see in Table 6.5, several criteria can be applied to the format of a questionnaire, and each one of them is so important that glossing over it could sink your entire project.

For example, let's say that you create this terrific questionnaire with well-designed questions, and you allow just the right amount of time for completion, and you even call all the participants to see if they have any questions. Unfortunately, you forget to give them detailed instructions on how to return it to you! Or perhaps you include clear return instructions but forget to tell them how to answer the questions.

- If your questionnaire does not consist of items or questions that are easy to read (clearly printed, not physically bunched together, etc.), you will get nowhere fast. The items must be neatly arranged, and the entire questionnaire must be clearly duplicated. Almost any word processing program contains templates that can help you with such considerations as white space, proportion, and balance, so you end up with a professional-looking document.
- All questions and pages should be plainly numbered (e.g., 1, 2, 3, 4 . . .). Do not use cumbersome or potentially confusing combinations such as I-1.2 or II.4.
- Good questionnaires contain directions that are complete and to the point. They tell the respondent exactly what to do ("complete this section") and how to do it ("circle one answer," "check all that apply"). These directions also offer explicit directions as to how the questionnaire should be returned, including preaddressed stamped envelopes and a phone number to call for more information if necessary.
- Your respondents are doing you a favor by completing the questionnaire. Your goal is to get as many as possible to do just that. One way to encourage responses is to show that your work is supported by a faculty member or your adviser, which you can do through a cover letter like the one you saw in Figure 3B.1.
- You want as honest an answer as possible from your respondents and, consequently, you must be careful that your questions are not leading them to answer in a particular direction. Questions must be objective and forthright. Once again, be careful of socially undesirable statements.
- Initial questions should warm up the respondent. In the beginning, relatively simple, nonthreatening, and easy-to-answer questions ("How old were you on your last birthday?") should be presented to help the respondent feel comfortable. Then as the questions progress, more complicated (and personal) questions might be asked. For example, many questionnaires begin with questions about demographics such as age, gender, race, and so on, all information that most people find relatively nonintimidating to provide. Subsequent questions might deal with issues such as feelings toward prejudice, questions about religion, and the like.

> Don't underestimate the appearance of the instruments you use. Neat and tidy helps increase reliability.

- When your questionnaire changes gears (or topics), you have to let the respondent know. If there is a group of questions about demographics followed by a set of questions about race relations, you need a transition from one to the other; for example: *"Thank you for answering these questions about yourself. Now we would like to ask you some questions about your experiences with people who are from the same ethnic group as you as well as from other groups."*
- Finally, make every effort to design a questionnaire that is easy to score. When possible, provide answer options that are objective and close ended, such as
  27. What is your annual income?
  a. Below $20,000
  b. $20,000 to $24,999
  c. $25,000 to $29,999
  rather than
  27. Please enter your annual income: $———.

In the first example, you can enter a code representing the letter as the response to be used for later analysis. In the second, you must first record the number entered and then place it in some category, adding an extra step.

The Cover Letter

An essential part of any questionnaire is the accompanying cover letter. This message is important because it helps set the scene for what is to come. A good cover letter is especially important for questionnaires that are mailed (snail mail or e-mail) to respondents so that the sense of authority is established and the importance of the project is conveyed. Here are some tips on what a good cover letter should contain:

> A good cover letter can make or break the success of a project.

- It is written on official letterhead, which helps favorably to impress respondents and increases the likelihood that they will respond.
- It is dated recently, thus indicating that there is some urgency to the request.
- It is personalized; it opens by stating "Dear Mr. and Mrs. Margolis," not "Dear Participant."
- It clearly states the purpose of the questionnaire and the importance of the study.
- It gives a time estimate so respondents know when to return it.
- It clearly promises confidentiality and indicates how confidentiality will be ensured.
- It makes respondents feel that they are part of the project in that a copy of the results will be sent to them when the study is complete.
- It includes a clear, physically separate expression of thanks.
- It is signed by the "big boss" and by you. Although you would like to stand on your own name and work, at this early point in your career this little bit of help from the boss can make an important difference.

Summary

In our society, tests for everything from selection to screening are everywhere, and their use has become one of the most controversial topics facing social and behavioral scientists. Tests definitely have their place, and in this chapter different kinds of measurement tools and how they can be used to reliably and validly assess behavior has been discussed. Remember, however, that careful formulation of hypotheses and attention to detail throughout the research project are also required for your measurement method to yield an accurate result.

Exercises

1. Before beginning the test, individuals taking one of the Wechsler Intelligence Scales are informed that some questions will be easy, some questions will be difficult, and test takers are not expected to be able to answer every question. Why is this information a sign of a good test?

2. What is a standardized test? How does it differ from a researcher- or teacher-made test?

3. A psychology licensing examination requires individuals to answer 70% of questions correctly in order to receive a passing score. (a) Is this exam norm-referenced or criterion-referenced? (b) What if the test required individuals to perform better than 70% of individuals who took the test in order to receive a passing score?

4. How can you change the difficulty level of your multiple-choice test items?

5. For the following set of information about two achievement test scores, compute the difficulty and the discrimination indices. The asterisk corresponds to the correct answer.

Item 1

Alternatives	A*	B	C	D
Upper 27%	28	6	7	20
Lower 27%	6	12	21	22

Item 2

Alternatives	A*	B	C	D
Upper 27%	10	7	28	15
Lower 27%	15	0	15	30

6. Write a 10-item questionnaire (using Likert-type items) that measures attitude toward stealing. Be sure to use both positive and negative statements and state all of the items simply enough so that they can be easily answered. Also, be sure to include a set of instructions. Give your work a day or two rest and then have a classmate check it over.

7. Consult the latest edition of *Buros Mental Measurements Yearbook* (online or in the library) and summarize a review of any test that is mentioned. What was the purpose of the test? Is the review positive or negative? How can the test be improved?

8. Interpret the following discrimination and difficulty scores:
   (a) $D = .50$
        $d = -.90$
   (b) $D = .90$
        $d = .25$

9. Describe three basic characteristics of a questionnaire.

10. What are three advantages of using a questionnaire?

11. Consider the following response set on a Likert scale with 1 representing Strongly Disagree and 5 representing Strongly Agree. What total score would you give this respondent (responses are in bold)?
    1. The actors in the movie performed well.   1 **2** 3 4 5
    2. The plot was interesting.   1 2 3 **4** 5
    3. Most of the scenes in the movie were boring.   1 2 3 **4** 5
    4. Overall, the movie was enjoyable.   1 2 3 **4** 5

Online. . .

Educational Testing Service

The Educational Testing Service (http://www.ets.org/) is the home page for the mother of all commercial test services. These are the people who bring you the SATs, GREs, APs, and more. They score the tests, send the results where you want, and even help you understand why you didn't get that perfect 800 on the math portion. This is a good site for general information about testing, financial aid, and other college-related topics.

FairTest: The National Center for Fair & Open Testing

FairTest (http://www.fairtest.org/) is an advocacy organization that works to end the misuses and flaws they claim are inherent in standardized testing and make sure that the testing process is fair. This entire area of tests and their fairness is very controversial and well worth learning about.

Rethinking Schools

Why the testing craze won't fix our schools. See Rethinking Schools Online at http://www.rethinkingschools.org/, for a collection of articles on testing and assessment, from the perspective of the classroom teacher and students.

Personality Tests

Play around on this site (http://www.similarminds.com/personality_tests.html) by SimilarMinds to learn about different personality types and personality research. The site also has personality tests available for taking, but keep in mind that personality tests are best administered by a professional with the appropriate credentials.

❖ ❖ ❖ Chapter 7 ❖ ❖ ❖

Data Collection and Descriptive Statistics

In every type of research endeavor, whether it is a historical examination of the role of medication in treating mental illness or the effects of using a computer mouse on children's eye–hand coordination, data about the topic need to be collected and analyzed to test the viability of the hypotheses. You can speculate all you want on the relationship between certain variables or about why and how one might affect another, but until there is objective evidence to support your assertions, your work is no more accurate than if you randomly drew 1 of 10 possible answers out of a hat.

In the main part of this chapter, you will learn about data collection, beginning with the design of data collection forms and ending with a discussion of the actual process itself. Once you are familiar with these important first steps, you will move on to an introduction to the use of descriptive statistics—sets of tools to make sense out of the data you collect. (You will continue learning about data analysis in Chapter 8.) Then you can learn about how to use your personal computer and software applications such as SPSS to conduct data analysis.

On to the beginning of data collection and descriptive analysis.

Getting Ready for Data Collection

After all that very hard thinking, going to the library, and formulating what you and your adviser feel is an important and (don't forget) interesting question and hypothesis, it is now time to begin the process of collecting your data.

The data collection process involves four steps:

1. The construction of a data collection form used to organize the data you collect,
2. The designation of the coding strategy used to represent data on a data collection form,
3. The collection of the actual data,
4. Entry onto the data collection form.

Once you have completed these steps, you will be ready to begin analyzing your data. Throughout this chapter, we will use a sample data set representing 200 sets of scores collected during the testing of elementary and secondary school children as part of the Kansas Minimum Competency Testing Program.

WHAT YOU'LL LEARN ABOUT IN THIS CHAPTER:

- How to get started collecting your data

- How to begin coding your data

- All about constructing a data collection form

- The use and importance of descriptive statistics

- The difference between descriptive and inferential statistics

- What a distribution of scores is and how distributions can differ among themselves

- How to use measures of central tendency and variability to describe a set of scores

- How to compute the mean, median, and mode, and what these numbers are used for

- How to compute the range, standard deviation, and variance, and what these numbers are used for

- What the normal curve is and why it is important to the research process

---

Count

		GRADE					
		2.00	4.00	6.00	8.00	10.00	Total
gender	male	20	16	17	23	19	95
	female	19	21	31	18	16	105
Total		39	37	48	41	35	200

Figure 7.1   Grade and gender frequencies for the data sample in Appendix B.

> The more systematic you are in the collection of your data, the easier every subsequent step will be.

These tests in reading and mathematics are given to children in grades 2, 4, 6, 8, and 10 throughout the state. About 200,000 children are tested each year. This particular sample consists of 200 children, 95 boys and 105 girls. These data are shown in Appendix B, and you or your professor can get the data set (titled "Appendix B.doc") directly from the amazing *Exploring Research* Website (www.prenhall.com/salkind) or by e-mail at njs@ku.edu. As we go through specific, simple statistical procedures, use some of these data and follow along. Try it, you'll like it.

Here is a list of the information collected in this data set for each child:

- Identification number
- Gender
- Grade
- Building
- Reading score
- Mathematics score

Six **data points** were gathered for each child. Figure 7.1 shows one way to organize the data using some basic demographic information (grade and gender). The information in Figure 7.1 was generated using SPSS, which you can learn about in Appendix A.

The Data Collection Process

Now that you have your idea well in hand (and your professor or committee has approved your plans), it is time to start thinking about the process of collecting data. This involves everything from contacting possible sources and arranging data collection trips to the actual recording of the data on some type of form that will help you organize this information and facilitate the data analysis process.

Constructing Data Collection Forms

> Ask your colleagues to help you test your data form to be sure that it is easy to understand and easy to use.

Once you know what information to collect and where you are going to get it (a critical part of your research), the next step is to develop an organizational scheme for collecting it so you can easily apply some techniques to analyze and make sense of your findings.

Think of your **raw data** (unorganized data) as the pieces to a jigsaw puzzle and the results of your data analysis as the strategy you use to put the pieces together. When you first open the box, the pieces look like a jumble of colors and shapes, which is just what they are. These are the raw data. The strategy you use to assemble them is just like the tools you use to analyze data.

When researchers collect data, their first step is to develop a **data collection form**. Table 7.1 is an example of a data collection form that could be used to record scores and

ID	Gender	Grade	Building	Reading Score	Mathematics Score
1	2	8	1	55	60
2	2	2	6	41	44
3	1	8	6	46	37
4	2	4	6	56	59
5	2	10	6	45	32

Table 7.1 The first 5 of 200 cases from the data set in Appendix B (each case is represented by a row, and each variable is represented by a column)

other information after the tests have been scored. Notice that the possible values (when known) for all the variables are included on the data collection form to make the recording easier. For example, boys are to be coded as 1 and girls as 2, and so on. Coding is discussed in more detail later in this chapter.

One criterion to use in judging whether a data collection form is clear and easy to use is to show it to someone (such as a fellow student in your class) who is unfamiliar with your project. Then ask that person to take data from the primary data source (such as the reading test itself) and enter it onto the data collection form. Would the individual know what to do and how to do it? Is it clear what goes where? What do the entries mean? These questions should all be answered with a definite "yes."

The key to the design of an effective data collection form is the amount of planning invested in the process. You could use the test form itself as a data collection form if all the information you need is recorded in such a way that it is easily accessible for data analysis. Perhaps at the top of the test booklet or questionnaire, you have spaces to record all the relevant information other than the test results—you won't have to hunt to find all the data because they are right at the top of the first page. Such a plan reduces the possibility of an error in the transfer from the original data to entry into the statistical program you use to analyze your data.

Table 7.1 shows the first five cases recorded on the completed data form. The columns are organized by variables, and the information on each student is entered as an individual row. These five cases are the first of the 200 cases (in Appendix B) that will be used in later sections of this chapter to demonstrate various data analysis techniques.

Remember, the data form you construct should be easy to understand and easy to work with, because it is your main link between the original data and the first step in data analysis. Many researchers have two people work on the transfer of data from the original sheet to the data form to ensure minimization of the number of errors. That is one reason why it is helpful to use graph paper or some other form that includes vertical and horizontal lines, as shown in Table 7.1. Perhaps best is to use a spreadsheet program such as Excel and create the data collection form as a spreadsheet file and then print the document. The form then matches what's on the screen, and data collection and entry become much easier tasks and you have an easily available appendix (the raw data) available for your final report.

Here are some general hints about constructing a data collection form such as the one shown in Table 7.1:

- Use one line (or row) for each subject. If your data form needs lots of space, you may need to use one page per subject.
- Use one column for each variable.
- Use paper that has columns or grids (like graph paper).
- Record the subjects' ID numbers as rows and scores or other variables as columns.
- Include enough space for all the information that you want to record as well as information that you anticipate recording in the future. For example, if you are doing

Make a copy of your data (or even two copies) and keep it (or each one) in a safe, off-site location.

a study for which there will be a follow-up, leave room for the set of scores that will be entered later.
- As data collection forms are completed, make a copy of each form and keep it in another location just in case the original data or your other data collection record is damaged or lost. If you use a spreadsheet, backup your data in at least two places! You'll read this again later, but there are two types of people: those who have lost data and those who will. Be extra careful!
- Date each form and initial it as it is completed.

Collecting Data Using Optical Scanners

If you are collecting data where the subject's responses are recorded as one of several options (such as in multiple-choice tests), you might want to consider scoring the results using an **optical scoring sheet** which is scored on an **optical scanner**. You have probably taken tests using these (such as the College Boards or the SATs).

The responses on special scoring sheets are read by an optical scanner, and each response is compared with a key (another sheet which you have prepared). The scanner then records correct and incorrect responses, providing a total score at the top of the sheet. What are the benefits?

- The process is very fast. Hand scoring 50 subjects' data, each with 100 items, can easily take hours.
- These scanners are more accurate than people. They (usually) do not make mistakes. Interestingly, in recent years, there has been an increase (or it has just been shared with the public and going on for years) where huge testing companies have reported inaccurate results due to optical scanning failures (such as when the scoring sheets were damp).
- Scanned responses can provide additional analysis of individual items, such as the difficulty and discrimination indices discussed in Chapter 6 in the case of a test. Even in the case of no-test items, you can often program the software used for scoring to give you certain configurations of results.

Are these machines expensive? Yes—they'll put a little dent in a budget, but the amount of time and money they save will more than cover the cost. Imagine having your data scored the day you finish collecting it.

So, when you can, use optical scoring sheets or, if appropriate, transfer the original data onto one of these sheets to make your work easier and more accurate. Optical scanning equipment is usually available at all major universities. Several companies also publish tests designed to use special answer sheets which are then returned to the company for scoring.

One word of caution, however. Just because this is an attractive methodology and may save you some time, do not fall victim to the trap of believing that an optical scoring sheet is the only way to collect and score data. If you do, you will end up trying to manipulate your objectives into a framework of assessment that may not actually fit the question you are asking.

Using Newer Technologies

There is no question that technologies such as optical scanners are reliable and efficient and work quite well, but there has also been a host of new technologies that allow data collection (and analysis) to be facilitated as well.

As you very well know, cell phones are ubiquitous in their everyday presence and the design and use of **smartphones** is exactly the focus here. These mini computers, using such operating systems as the iPhone OS (in the case of Apple) or Android (in the case of Google), are becoming increasingly easy to program and customize for exactly the purpose that we are discussing here—the collection and analysis of data. In fact, the limits that these tools place on the researcher's activities are only bound by the creativity and resourcefulness of the people involved in the research endeavor. Look to these tools for assistance when it comes time to begin the data collection phase.

Coding Data

Data are coded when they are transferred from the original collection form (such as a test booklet) into a format that lends itself to data analysis. And this coding activity is important whether you are using plain old pencil and paper or a fancy smartphone that automatically enters data and then analyzes it. The important thing to remember is that you should be able to look at a data coding sheet and know exactly the nature of what's entered.

> When coding data, the simpler the system of codes the better.

For example, the gender of a child may be male or female. The actual letters that represent the labels male or female would not be entered into the actual data form. Instead, the gender of the child will be coded, with value 1 representing male and value 2 representing female (see Table 7.1). In this example, gender is coded as a 1 or a 2. Likewise, ethnicity or any other categorical variable can be entered as a single-digit number (as long as there are fewer than 10 categories using the numerals 0–9). In Table 7.2, you can see several different types of data and how they could be coded for the sample mathematics and reading scores.

The use of digits (rather than words) not only saves space and entry time, but when it comes time for data analysis, it is also much more precise. Remember levels of measurement—the higher the level, the more information that is communicated.

The one rule for **coding** data is to use codes that are as reduced in clutter and as unambiguous in meaning as possible, without losing the true meaning of the data themselves. For example, it is perfectly fine to code a fourth-grade boy as a 4 for grade and 1 for gender, but you would not be well served to use letters (such as Fs and Ms) because they are harder to work with. Also, do not combine categories, such as using 41 (for 4 and 1) for being in fourth grade (4) and male (1). The problem here is that later on you will not be able to separate grade and gender as factors and thus your data lose much of their value.

The rule here is always to record your data in elements that are as *explicit* and as *discrete* as possible. You can always combine data criteria during the analysis process. Do it right from the beginning. However, also realize that all data are not as "clean" as a simple "1" or a "2". Those values are OK for defining gender, but what if the response falls into less clear categories, and perhaps no categories at all (such as the transcription and coding of interview data)? Tough decisions have to be made in these cases as to how data will be coded and often it is best to do that along with the input or advice of advisers or colleagues.

Variable	Range of Data Possible	Example
ID	001–200	138
Gender	1 or 2	2
Grade	1, 2, 4, 6, 8, or 10	4
Building	1–6	1
Reading Score	1–100	78
Mathematics Score	1–100	69

Table 7.2   Coding data and using codes that provide the most information possible

The Ten Commandments of Data Collection

Do not let anyone tell you otherwise: The data collection process can be a long and rigorous one, even if it involves only a simple, one-page questionnaire given to a group of parents. The data collection process is probably the most time-consuming part of your project. If you are doing historical research, you will probably find yourself spending most of your time in the library searching through books and journals, or perhaps interviewing people about events that are relevant to your thesis. If you are actually collecting empirical data, other arrangements must be made.

The ten commandments for making sure your data are collected are not carved in stone like the original Ten Commandments, but if you follow them, you can avoid potentially fatal errors.

First, and we will talk more about this later, *go through the tedious process of getting permission from your institutional review board that grants permission for you to collect data*. The members on this board will assure you that your data collection forms and permission documents are suitable and that your institution blesses your efforts. No kidding—this is very important.

Second, as you begin thinking about a research process, *begin thinking about the type of data you will have to collect* to answer your question.

Third, as you think about the type of data you will be collecting, *think about where you will be obtaining the data*. If you are using the library for historical data or accessing data files that have already been collected (a great way to go!), you will have few logistical problems. But what if you want to assess the interaction between newborns and their parents? The attitude of teachers toward unionizing? The age at which people over 50 think they are old? All these questions require people to provide the answers, and finding these people can be tough. Start now.

Fourth, *make sure that the data collection form you are using is clear and easy to use*. Practice on a set of pilot or artificial data so you can make sure it is easy to go from the original scoring sheets to the data collection form.

Fifth, once you transfer scores to your data collection form, *make a duplicate copy of the data file and keep it in a separate location*. This rule does not mean that you should duplicate the original data collection instrument for each participant, be it a competency test booklet or a set of figure drawings. Instead, once you have finished scoring and have transferred the information to the data collection sheets, keep a copy of those data collection sheets in a separate location. If you are recording your data as a computer file, such as a spreadsheet (more about this later), be sure to make a backup copy! Remember (again!), there are two types of people: those who have lost their data and those who will lose their data.

Sixth, *do not rely on other people to collect or transfer your data unless you personally have trained them and are confident that they understand the data collection process as well as you do*. It is great to have people help you, and it helps keep morale up during long data collection sessions; however, unless your helpers are competent beyond question, all your hard work and planning could be compromised.

Seventh, *plan a detailed schedule of when and where you will be collecting your data*. If you need to visit three schools and each of 50 children needs to be tested for a total of 10 minutes at each school, that adds up to 25 hours of testing. That does not mean you can allot only 25 hours from your schedule for this activity. What about travel from one school to another? What about the child who is in the bathroom when it is his turn, and you have to wait 10 minutes until he comes back to the classroom? What about the day you show up and Cowboy Bob is the featured guest? Be prepared for anything, and allocate from 25% to 50% more time in your schedule for unforeseen happenings. Think you're so well organized you don't have to allocate this extra time? Wait and see—better safe than sorry.

Eighth, as soon as possible, *cultivate possible sources for your participant pool*. Because you already have some knowledge in your own discipline, you probably also know of people who work with the type of population you want or who might be able to help you gain access

Be sure to supervise the collection and coding of data if other people help you and be sure that these people are adequately trained.

to these samples. If you are in a university community, there are probably hundreds of other people competing for the same subject sample that you need. Instead of competing, why not try a more out-of-the-way (maybe 30 minutes away) school district, social group, civic organization, or hospital where you might be able to obtain a sample with less competition?

Ninth, *try to follow up on subjects who missed their testing session or interview*. Call them back and try to reschedule. Once you get in the habit of skipping possible participants, it becomes too easy to cut the sample down to too small a size. Interestingly, some research has shown that participants who drop out of studies may be different from those who stay on (on a variety of variables), so that the dropout is not random and so the remaining set of data may indeed be biased.

Tenth, *never discard original data*, such as test booklets, interview notes, and so forth. Other researchers might want to use the same database, or you may have to return to the original materials for further information.

TEST YOURSELF

What's the big deal about these 10 commandments of data collection? Identify any three and detail about the consequences of not following them.

Getting Ready for Data Analysis

You have spent many long, hard hours preparing a worthwhile proposal and a useful data collection form, and you have just spent 6 months collecting your data and entering it into a format that can be analyzed. What is next on the list?

First, through the use of **descriptive statistics**, you can describe some of the characteristics of the distribution of scores you have collected, such as the average score on one variable or the degree that one score varies from another. Finally, once the data are organized in such a way that they can be closely examined, you will apply the set of tools called **inferential statistics** to help you make decisions about how the data you collected relate to your original hypotheses and how they might be generalizable to a larger number of subjects than those who were tested.

The remainder of this chapter deals with descriptive statistics. Chapter 8 deals with inferential statistics.

Who would have ever thought that you would be enrolled in a class where that dreaded word "statistics" (sometimes called *sadistics*) comes up again and again? Well, here you will be learning about this intriguing part of the research process, and you may even gain some affection for the set of powerful tools that will be described. Because there is often so much anxiety and concern about this area of the research process, here are some pointers to make sure that you do not become a member of the group that suffers from the "I can't do it" complex before you even try:

- Read through the rest of this chapter without paying much attention to the examples. Just try to get a general feel for the organization and what material is covered.
- Start from the beginning of this section and carefully follow each of the examples as they are presented, step by step. If you run into trouble, begin again with step 1.
- If things become particularly difficult for you, take a short break and then come back to the part of the chapter or exercise that you clearly understood. Then, go on from there.
- Keep in mind that most of statistics is understanding and applying some simple and basic assumptions. Statistics is not high-powered, advanced mathematics. Rather, it is a step-by-step process that helps you to think about solving particular problems in a particular way. It's a very cool way of approaching problems and can give you insight that you might not have had before.

Work through the exercises both by hand and with a calculator to be sure you understand the basic operations involved. When you learn about SPSS (Appendix A), work through the exercises again. The more you practice these techniques, the better you will be at using them as tools to understand your data.

Descriptive Statistics

The first step in the analysis of data is to describe them. Describing data usually means computing a set of descriptive statistics, so-called because they describe the general characteristics of a set or **distribution of scores**. In effect, they allow the researcher (or the reader of the research report) to get an accurate first impression of "what the data look like" (that's research talk!).

Before discussing different descriptive statistics, let's first turn to what a distribution of scores actually is and how it can help you better understand the data.

Distributions of Scores

If you were to ask your best friend his or her age, you would have collected one piece of information or one data point for that individual. If you collect one piece of information for more than one individual, such as the ages of all the people in your class, you then have a set of scores and several data points. Two or more data points make up a distribution of scores. For example, Figure 7.2 illustrates one way of representing a distribution of scores, using a special type of graph (called a histogram) of the distribution of math scores for 200 children (once again, you can find these scores in Appendix B) and at http://www.pearsonhighered.com/salkind/

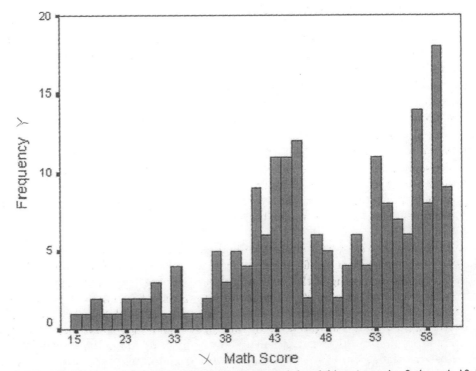

Figure 7.2 Distribution of data points (mathematics scores) for children in grades 2 through 10. Each score in a distribution represents one data point.

under link *Exploring Research (7th Edition) Data Sets* in the lower right-hand corner. By the way, this graph was created using SPSS.

The vertical (Y) axis corresponds to the frequency at which a particular score occurs. The horizontal (X) axis corresponds to the value of the score. In this figure, each band represents about 5 scores along the scale. For example, approximately 20 children scored between 15 and 33. Judging from the shape of the distribution, you can make several judgments about this set of 200 scores just by visually examining the histogram, including,

- Most children scored in the upper half of the distribution.
- Most children scored around 59.

Comparing Distributions of Scores

One of the most useful things researchers can do is to compare different distributions of scores; this chapter will discuss several ways to do so, including measures of central tendency, measures of dispersion or variability, and comparing standard scores. Each way adds information to our understanding of how distributions differ from one another.

Measures of Central Tendency

One property of a distribution of scores is an **average**, or an individual value that is most representative of that distribution or set of scores. There are three types of averages or **measures of central tendency**: the mean, the median, and the mode.

The Mean

The **mean** is the sum of a set of scores divided by the number of scores. You probably have computed several means over the years but referred to them as averages, such as the average amount of money you need to cover your expenses or to fill your car's gas tank or your average GPA for the past three semesters.

> Mean, median, and mode are all averages or measures of central tendency.

There are several types of averages. The one explored here is the arithmetic mean, which is the most commonly used measure of central tendency. The formula for the mean is as follows:

$$\overline{X} = \frac{\Sigma X}{n}$$

where

$\overline{X}$ = (or $X\ bar$) the mean value of the group of scores or the mean

Σ = the summation sign, which tells you to add together whatever follows it

X = each individual score in the group of scores

n = the size of the sample for which you are computing the mean.

To compute the mean, follow these steps:

1. Add all the scores in the group to obtain a total.
2. Divide the total of all the scores by the number of observations.

For example, the mean reading test score for the first 10 students is 47.3. The first 10 scores are 55, 41, 46, 56, 45, 46, 58, 41, 50, and 35. Their total is 473, which is divided by 10 (the number of observations) to get 47.3.

In this example, 47.3 is the value that best represents the most central location in the set of ten scores. For the 200 reading test scores in Appendix B, the mean for reading is 48.6; for math, 47.4. These values were computed the same way, by summing all 200 scores and dividing by the number of scores in the set (200).

The mean for any variable can be computed using the same method. As you learned in Chapter 5, however, it makes no sense to add nominal level values (such as those representing ID or gender) because the result is meaningless. (What do you get when you add a boy and a girl and divide by 2?)

The Median

The median is often used to compute an average when extreme scores are included in a data set.

The **median** is the score or the point in a distribution above which one-half of the scores lie. For example, in a simple set of scores such as 1, 3, and 5, the median is 3. If another score, say, 7, were added, the median would be the value that lies between 3 and 5, or 4. Here, 50% of the scores fall above the value 4 (and, of course, 50% fall below).

To compute the median when the number of scores in the set is odd, follow these steps:

1. Order the scores from lowest to highest.
2. Count the number of scores.
3. Select the middle score as the median.

For example, here is a set of reading scores for 15 second graders which were ordered from lowest in value to highest in value. The eighth score (the score occupying the eighth position in the group) is the median. In this case, that value is 43:

31 33 35 38 40 41 42 43 44 46 47 48 49 50 51

To compute the median when the number (not the sum) of scores in the set is even, follow these steps:

1. Order the scores from lowest to highest.
2. Count the number of scores.
3. Find the mean of the two middle scores; that's the median.

For example, the following 14 scores were ordered from lowest to highest in value. The median was computed by adding the seventh and eighth scores (or the scores occupying the seventh and eighth positions in the group, 42 and 43) and dividing by 2 to get 42.5.

31 33 35 38 40 41 42 43 44 46 47 48 49 50

The Mode

The **mode** is the score that occurs most frequently. Caution! It is not the number of times that the score occurs but the score itself. If you have the following numbers:

58 27 24 41 27 26 41 53 14 29 41 53 47 28 56

the mode is 41. The most common mistake made by students who are new to this material is identifying the mode as the number of times a value occurs (3 in this example for the value of 41) and not the value itself (41).

The mode is best used with nominal data such as gender. In the set of competency data, the mode for gender is female because there are 105 females and 95 males. Again, the mode is not how frequently the value female (which is 105) occurs. The mode is an excellent choice if you want a general overview of which class or category occurs most frequently.

Measure of Central Tendency	Level of Measurement	Examples
Mode	Nominal	Eye color, party affiliation
Median	Ordinal	Rank in class, birth order
Mean	Interval and Ratio	Speed of response, age in years

Most often
middle
Sum / Total # of scores

Table 7.3   Measures of central tendency and the corresponding level of measurement

When to Use Which Measure

The mean, the median, and the mode provide different types of information and should be used in different ways. Table 7.3 summarizes when each of these measures should be used. As you can see, the use of one or the other measure of central tendency depends on the type of data you are describing. And as you remember, the higher the level of measurement, the greater the precision with which you will be assessing the outcome.

For example, describing data that are interval or ratio in nature (such as speed of response) calls for the use of the mean, which provides relatively more information than the mode or the median. The rule of thumb is that when the data fit, and when you can, use the mean.

The median is best suited to data that are ordinal or ranked. For example, the set of scores 7, 22, 24, 50, 66, 76, and 100 have the same median (50) as does the set of scores 49, 50, and 51, yet the distributions are quite different from each other.

The median is also the appropriate choice when *extreme* scores are included in the sample. For example, here are the salaries for five people: $21,500, $27,600, $32,000, $18,750, and $82,000. The median is the middle-most (or the third-ranked) score, which is $27,600. The mean, however, is $36,370. Look at the large difference between these two values. Which measure do you think better represents the set of five scores and why? If you said the median, you are right. You certainly would not want an average ($36,370) to be larger than the second largest value in the set ($32,000). This number would not be very representative, which is the primary purpose of any measure of central tendency. From this example, you might conclude that the median works best when a set of scores is asymmetrical or unbalanced in the extreme. It is the $82,000 data point that throws off everything.

The mode should be your choice when the data are qualitative in nature (nominal or categorical), such as gender, hair color, ethnicity, school, or group membership. You will not see the mode commonly reported in the research literature (because it may not be meaningful to average the values of nominal variables), but it is the only measure of central tendency that can be used with nominal level information.

Clearly, the mean allows us to take advantage of the most information (when available), and thus it usually becomes the most informative measure of central tendency. When researchers can, they select variables on which this type of average can be computed.

TEST YOURSELF

As you have learned in this section, there are at least three different types of averages. Name each and provide an example of which you would use to collect different types of data. (Hint: You can think of "types" as those that are at different levels of measurement.)

Measures of Variability

You have just learned how a set of scores can be represented by different types of averages. But the average is not enough to describe a set of scores fully. There is another important quality or characteristic that describes the amount of variability or dispersion in a set of scores.

Variability is the degree of spread or dispersion that characterizes a group of scores, and it is the degree to which a set of scores differs from some measure of central tendency, most often the mean. For example, the set of scores 1, 3, 5, 7, and 9 (which has a mean of 5) has a higher amount of variability than the set of scores 3, 4, 5, 6, and 7, which also has a mean of 5—same mean, different scores, different distributions. The first set of scores is simply more spread out than the second.

There are several measures of variability, each of which will be covered in turn.

The Range

Quick and relatively inaccurate, but convenient—that's the range.

The **range** is the difference between the highest and the lowest scores in a distribution. It is the simplest, most direct measure of how dispersed a set of scores is.

For example, for the following set of scores,

31 33 35 38 40 40 41 41 41 42 43 44 46 47 48 48 49 49 50 51

the range is 20 (or 51–31). In reading the data being used as an example of a large data set (too large to list in order here), the range for mathematics scores is 45, or 60–15. The range is a rough measure which indicates the general spread or size of the difference between extremes.

The Standard Deviation

The standard deviation is the most commonly used measure of variability (and the most commonly appearing value in computer output when you ask for a general measure of variability). The **standard deviation** (abbreviated as s) is the average amount that each of the individual scores varies from the mean of the set of scores. The larger the standard deviation, the more variable the set of scores. If all the scores in a sample are identical, such as 10, 10, 10, and 10, then there is no variability, and the standard deviation is 0.

The formula for computing the standard deviation is

$$s = \sqrt{\frac{\Sigma(X - \overline{X})^2}{n - 1}}$$

where

s = the standard deviation

Σ = the summation of a set of scores

X = an individual score

$\overline{X}$ = the mean of all the scores

n = the number of observations

To compute the standard deviation, follow the steps shown in Table 7.4. You will be computing the standard deviation for the following set of 10 scores:

13 14 15 12 13 14 13 16 15 9.

1. List all the original scores and compute the mean (which is 13.4).
2. Subtract the mean (13.4) from each individual score and place these values in the column titled Deviations from the Mean. Notice that the sum of all these deviations (about the mean) is 0.

Raw Score (X)	Deviations from the Mean $(X - \bar{X})$	Squared Deviations $(X - \bar{X})^2$
13	−0.4 (13 − 13.4) =	0.16
14	0.6	0.36
15	1.6	2.56
12	−1.4	1.96
13	−0.4	0.16
14	0.6	0.36
13	−0.4	0.16
16	2.6	6.76
15	1.6	2.56
9	−4.4	19.36
mean $\bar{X} = 13.4$	sum $\Sigma(X - \bar{X}) = 0$	$\Sigma(X - \bar{X})^2 = 34.4$

Table 7.4 Individual scores, deviations of those scores from the mean, and the deviations squared (all you need to know to compute the standard deviation for a set of scores)

Remember when the standard deviation was defined as the average amount of deviation? You might want to know why you just do not stop here because an average has been computed. It is because this average is always 0 (more about this in a moment). To get rid of the zero value, each deviation is squared.

3. Square each of the deviations and place them in the column labeled Squared Deviations.
4. Sum the squared deviations (the total should be 34.4).
5. Divide the sum of the squared deviations (34.4) by the number of observations minus 1 (which is 9 in the example) to get 3.82.

You divide by 9 rather than 10 because you want to err on the conservative side and artificially increase the value of this descriptive statistic. You may notice that, as the sample size increases (say, from 10 to 100), the adjustment of subtracting 1 from the denominator makes increasingly little difference between the *biased* (with the full sample size as the denominator) and the *unbiased* (with the sample size minus 1 in the denominator) values.

6. Take the square root of 3.82, which is 1.95 and that's the standard deviation. Not as painful as a root canal, which is what you expected, right?

Are you wondering why the square root is used? Because you want to get back to the values as originally listed, and you had to square them back in step 3 (to get rid of the negative deviations; otherwise, they would add up to 0, and every standard deviation would be 0!).

Some of the numbers you get on the way to computing the standard deviation are very interesting. Look at the sum of the deviation about the mean. Do you know why it is (and always is) 0? Because the mean (from which each of the scores is subtracted) represents the point about which the sum of the deviations always equals 0. If the sum of this column is not 0, then either the mean is incorrectly computed, or the subtracted values are incorrect.

Another measure of variability you often see in research reports is the **variance**, which is the square of the standard deviation. The variance is everything in the formula for the standard deviation except the square root. Just as the variance is the square of the standard deviation, the square root of the variance is the standard deviation. The symbol for variance is s^2.

For the set of 200 reading and math competency scores in our example, the standard deviation is 7.22 for reading and 10.02 for math. The variance is 52.13 for reading and 100.40 for math.

Variability is the spice of life. What's important about understanding the variability in a distribution of scores?

Understanding Distributions

Several measures of central tendency and variability have been covered, but you need only two to get a very good picture of a distribution's qualities: mean and standard deviation. With these two descriptive statistics, you can fully understand the distribution and what it means.

The Normal (Bell-Shaped) Curve

> The two halves of the normal curve always mirror one another.

Note the shape in Figure 7.3. It is most commonly referred to as a **normal curve** or a bell-shaped curve. It is the shape that represents how variables (such as height and weight) are distributed, and it has some very interesting characteristics:

- The mean, the median, and the mode are all the same value (represented by the point at which the vertical line crosses the X-axis).
- It is symmetrical about its midpoint, which means that the left and right halves of the curve are mirror images.
- The tails of the curve get closer and closer to the X-axis but never touch it; that is, the curve is asymptotic.

In fact, many inferential statistics (which you will learn about in Chapter 8) are based on the assumption that population distributions of variables from which samples are selected are normal in shape.

Here is this nicely shaped theoretical curve (no curve is quite as pretty in reality)—now how can it be used to help you understand what individual scores mean?

Let's begin with the role that the mean and the standard deviation play in defining the characteristics of the normal curve and then move on to the concept of standard scores.

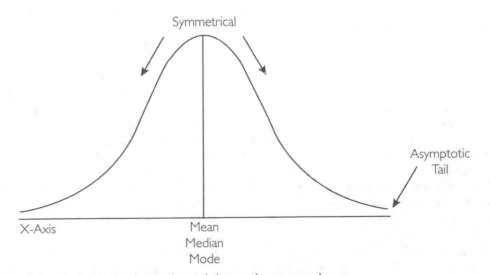

Figure 7.3 The impressive, interesting, and always relevant normal curve.

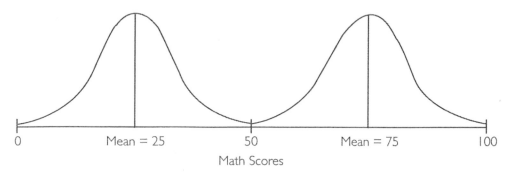

Figure 7.4 Distributions of scores can be equal in their variability but very different in their mean.

The Mean and the Standard Deviation

To begin with, curves can differ markedly in their appearance. For example, you can see how the two curves in Figure 7.4 differ in their mean scores but not in their variability. On the other hand, the two curves in Figure 7.5 differ in their variability but have the same mean.

Regardless of their shape or the location of the mean along the X-axis, some things (besides those three qualities listed earlier) hold true for all normal distributions (and they are very important, so pay attention!). These are as follows:

The distance between the mean of the distribution and one unit of standard deviation to the left or the right of the mean (no matter what the value of the standard deviation) always takes into account approximately 34% (really 34.12%) of the area beneath the normal curve as shown in Figure 7.6. If the mean for math for all 200 students is 47.37 and the standard deviation (s in this figure) is 10.02, then 34% of all the scores in the distribution fall between the values of 47.37 and 57.39 (the mean plus 1 standard deviation or $+1s$), and another 34% fall between the values of 37.35 (the mean minus 1 standard deviation or $-1s$) and 47.37.

This is pretty neat once you consider that the 34% number is independent of the actual value of the mean or the standard deviation. This 34% is such because of the shape of the curve, not because of the value of any of its members or measures of central tendency or variability. If you actually drew a normal curve on a piece of cardboard and cut

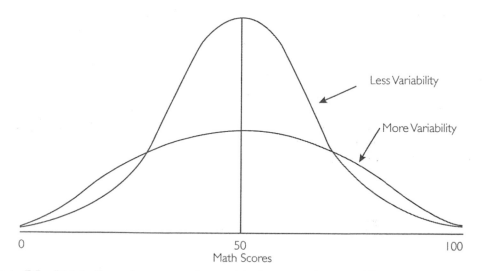

Figure 7.5 Distributions of scores can be equal in their mean but very different in their variability. Regardless of the value of the mean or the standard deviation, if a distribution is normal, you know exactly what percentage of cases in the distribution you can expect to fall where.

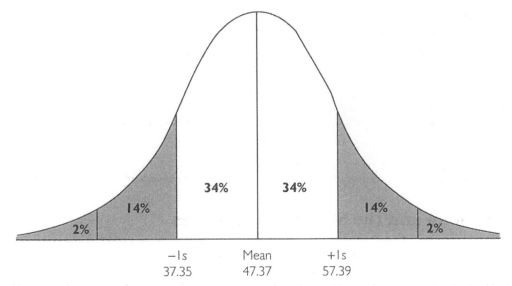

34% 34%

14% 14%

2% 2%

−1s   Mean   +1s
37.35   47.37   57.39

Figure 7.6 When you know the mean and the standard deviation, you can very accurately determine what percentage of cases falls under certain defined areas beneath the normal, or bell-shaped, curve.

out the area between the mean and +1 or −1 standard deviation and weighed it, it would tip the scale at exactly 34% of the weight of the entire piece of cardboard you cut out.

You can see that the curve is symmetrical. Thus, in a normal distribution, 68% of all the scores fall between the values represented by 1 standard deviation below the mean and 1 standard deviation above the mean.

In our example, this means that 68% of the scores fall between the values of 37.35 and 57.39 (shown in Figure 7.6). What about the other 32%? Good question. Those scores fall 1 standard deviation above (to the right of) the mean and 1 standard deviation below (to the left of) the mean in the shaded part of the curve shown in Figure 7.6. More precisely, you can see how different percentages of scores fall within different boundaries. Because the curve slopes and the amount of area decreases as you move farther away from the mean, it is no surprise that the likelihood that a score will fall more toward the extremes of the distribution is less than the likelihood that it will fall toward the middle.

Standard Scores: Computing and Using *z* Scores

You have seen in several places in this chapter how distributions differ from one another primarily as a function of the values of the mean and the standard deviation. To make sense of information obtained from different distributions, a method needs to be used that takes these differences into account. Welcome to standard scores.

Standard scores are scores that have the same reference point and the same standard deviation. The type of standard score that you will see most frequently in the literature, called a **z score**, is the result of dividing the amount that an individual score deviates from the mean by the standard deviation, using the following formula:

$$z = \frac{(X - \overline{X})}{s}$$

where

z = the standard score
X = the individual score
$\overline{X}$ = the mean of the group of scores to which X belongs
s = the standard deviation of the group of scores to which X belongs

Standard scores allow for the comparison of scores from different distributions, which enables accurate and straightforward comparisons.

Raw Scores	$(X-\bar{X})$	z score
13	−.4	−.20
14	.6	.31
15	1.6	.82
12	−1.4	−.71
13	−.4	−.20
14	.6	.31
13	−.4	−.20
16	2.6	1.33
15	1.6	.82
9	−4.4	−2.26

Table 7.5 Raw scores and their z score counterparts. (Notice how the scores get larger in absolute value as they deviate further from the mean)

For example, if the standard deviation is 10, and the raw score is 110, and the mean of the distribution of scores is 100, then the z score is

$$z = \frac{(110 - 100)}{10}$$

Table 7.5 shows the original raw scores plus the z scores for the set of the 10 mathematics test scores that appear in Table 7.4. Any raw score above the mean will have a positive z score, and any raw score below the mean will have a negative z score.

For example, a raw score of 13 has the equivalent z score of −0.20, which would be located slightly below the mean of 13.4. A raw score equal to the mean has a z score equal to 0. A score that is one standard deviation above the mean (15.35) has a z score equal to 1, and so forth.

The most valuable use of these standard scores is to compare scores from distributions that are different from one another. A simple example is shown in Table 7.6.

The average math score in Sara's class was 90 and the standard deviation was 2. She received a score of 92, for a z score of 1. In Micah's class, the average score was the same and he received the same absolute score as Sara, but the standard deviation was twofold that in Sara's class (4), making his z score .5. You can see that, although they received the same raw score, Sara's z score is located *above* Micah's score, indicating that she outperformed him when the same standard was used. Why did she outperform him?

Relative to the rest of the members of the class, Sara scored higher. There was less spread in her class, indicating that the same absolute score (which both kids received) situated them in a different place within each distribution. Thus, there was more variability in Micah's class, and the same raw score appears less extreme (than Sara's).

Student	Class Mean	Class Standard Deviation	Raw Score	z score
Sara	90	2	92	1
Micah	90	4	92	.5

Table 7.6 Comparing z scores that represent raw scores from different distributions illustrates the value of using standard scores for understanding your data

This is why raw scores should not just be added together and the averages compared. Instead, *z* scores (or some other type of standard score—and there are others, so go take a measurement class) should be used as the basis for comparison when scores from different distributions are being considered.

What *z* Scores Really, Really Mean

You already know that a *z* score represents a particular location along the X-axis. For example, in a distribution with a mean of 100 and a standard deviation of 10, a *z* score of 1 represents the raw score 110. Likewise, different *z* scores correspond to different locations along the X-axis of the normal curve. Because you already know the percent of area that falls between certain points along the X-axis (see Figure 7.6), such statements as the following are true:

- 84% of all the scores fall *below* a *z* score of +1.0 (the 50% that fall below the mean, plus the 34% that fall between the mean, plus 1 *z* score).
- 16% of all the scores fall *above* a *z* score of +1.0 (because the total area must equal 100%, and 84% fall below a *z* score of 1.0).

These types of statements can be made about the relationship between *z* scores at any point along the distribution, given knowledge of the corresponding area that is incorporated between points along the axis. For example, using special tables, one could determine that in any normal distribution of 50 scores, the number of scores that would fall between 1.5 and 2.5 standard deviations above the mean is about 3 scores, or 6% of the total. But because you have been reading along closely and paying attention to your instructor's lecture, you know all this, right? OK, so here's the new stuff—and it's very powerful, indeed.

These numbers are expressed as percentages, which can be considered a statement of *probability* as well. In other words, the likelihood that someone will score between 1.5 and 2.5 standard deviations above the mean is 3 of 50, or 6 of 100, or .06, or 6%. Likewise, the probability that someone will score above the mean is .50, or 50%.

In Chapter 8, this idea of assigning a value (in this case a percent or a probability) to an outcome (in this case a score) is discussed as part of the role of inference in the research process, and it is incredibly important. If we can assign probabilities to outcomes, we are on our way to understanding how likely certain outcomes are (and are not). And with that information, we can then develop a set of rules to help us make decisions about whether outcomes are unlikely enough for us to accept as owing to chance or to some other factor. Want to know what those other factors are? See you in Chapter 8.

What is the one most important reason for using standard, rather than raw, scores when comparing scores in one distribution to scores in another?

Summary

Some people really like to collect data, whereas others find it tedious and boring. Everyone, however, agrees that it is hard work. All the work pays off, though, when you begin to assemble the data into a body of information that makes sense. You collect the data, organize them, then apply some of the fundamental descriptive tools discussed in this chapter to begin to make sense of them. You are not finished by any means, but at least you have some idea of which direction your data are going.

> Z scores not only are essential for comparing raw scores from different distributions but they are also associated with a particular likelihood that a raw score will appear in a distribution.

Exercises

1. What are the advantages and disadvantages of using optical scanners to score the results of a test? *correct but a*

2. What is the advantage of using digits to enter categorical data rather than using words or letters? *quick view*

3. When is the best time in the research process to start searching for participants? *right away*

4. You have figured out that, for your research, you will need 20 classes of Biology 101 students to complete your questionnaire. You estimate that the average student will complete the questionnaire in 30 minutes.
   (a) How much time should you allot overall for data collection?
   (b) What factors should you take into account when estimating how much time data collection will require? *20 x 30 +*

5. Why is following up important with participants who did not show up for their scheduled participation in your research? *sample becomes small*

6. You are in charge of a project that is investigating the effects of gender differences on the reading scores of first, third, and fifth graders in three different school districts. Design a data collection form that takes into account the following independent and dependent variables:
   - Gender *m/f*
   - School district *(1 3 5 / 1 3 5 / 1 3 5)*

   Be sure you provide space on the form for important information, such as the initials of the person who collected the data, the date of data collection, an identification number for each participant, and any other necessary comments.

7. Using a spreadsheet such as Excel, create a data form with four variables of your choice. Two of them have to be gender (1 or 2) and group membership (1 = belong, 2 = does not belong). Then create a dependent variable and fill in all the class for 20 participants. You are going to use this data in later exercises in this and the next chapter.

8. For what data is the median best suited? *ranked data*

9. The mean of a sample of 10 scores is 100, and the standard deviation is 5. For the following raw scores, compute the z score:
   (a) 101   *.2*
   (b) 112
   (c) 97

   For the following z scores, work backward to compute the corresponding raw score:
   (a) −0.5
   (b) 1.1
   (c) 2.12

   Why would you want to work with z scores rather than raw scores? What is the primary purpose of standard scores? *compare   fall on curve*

10. For the following set of 10 scores, compute the range, the standard deviation, and the variance. 2.9

$$5, 7, 3, 4, 5, 6, 7, 2, 5, 3$$

11. Claire and Noah are wonderful students. The results of their math and science tests were as follows:

Student	Math Test Score	Science Test Score
Claire	87	92
Noah	78	95
Class $\bar{X}$	68	84
Class s	8.5	11.5

(a) What are the standard scores (z scores) for Claire and Noah in math?
(b) If a larger z score means a "better score," who received the higher grade and on which test?
(c) Who is the overall better student?

12. Why is it best to use standard scores to compare raw scores from different distributions?

13. If a student receives a z score of 0, how well did that student do in comparison with other students in the group?

14. When the average income of Americans is reported in the media, do you think that the mean, median, or mode is used?

15. One test has a mean of 100 and a standard deviation of 15. What percentage of children would have a test score of 115 or more when given this test?

16. What are the three types of measures of central tendency? Define each measure.

17. Which measure of central tendency should you use with categorical data?

18. What are the two most important measures of central tendency for fully understanding the distribution of data and the distribution's meaning?

19. The variance of a set of test scores is 64. What is the value of the standard deviation?

20. Determine the mean, the median, and the mode for the following groups:

Group 1	Group 2
1	3
1	2
1	10
4	3
3	7
5	5

21. Extra credit and a bit difficult but you can do it. . . . Use the data form and the data you created in #5 above and use Excel to compute the average score for the variables named text 1 and text 2. (Hint: You can create a formula or use the = average function. Hand in a printout of your spreadsheet as proof of your genius.

Online. . .

Introduction to Descriptive Statistics

Don't know enough about descriptive statistics? Or think that they are not fun? Try http://www.mste.uiuc.edu/hill/dstat/dstat.html for an introduction and even see how they can be applied to the results of a football game. No kidding!

Z score Convertor

Use the p to z convertor and convert normally distributed scores into z scores on http://wise.cgu.edu/sdtmod/reviewz.asp.

❖ ❖ ❖ Chapter 8 ❖ ❖ ❖

Introducing Inferential Statistics

Understanding measures of central tendency, variability, and the workings of the normal curve provides the tools to describe the characteristics of a sample. These tools are also an excellent foundation to help you make informed decisions about how accurately the data you collect reflect the validity of the hypothesis you are testing.

Once you have described a sample of data, as you learned to do in Chapter 7, the next step is to learn how this descriptive information can be used to infer from the smaller sample on which the data were collected to the larger population from which the data were originally selected.

Say Hello to Inferential Statistics!

Whereas descriptive statistics are used to describe a sample's characteristics, inferential statistics are used to infer something about the population from which the sample was drawn based on the characteristics (often expressed using descriptive statistics) of the sample. At several points throughout the first half of this book, we have emphasized that one hallmark of good scientific research is choosing a sample in such a way that it is representative of the population from which it was selected. The more representative the sample is, the more trusting one can be of the results based on information gleaned from the sample. The whole notion of inference is based on the assumption that you can accurately select a sample in such a way as to maximize this representativeness. The process then becomes an inferential one, wherein you infer from the smaller sample to the larger population based on the results of tests (and experiments) conducted using the sample.

How Inference Works

Let's go through the steps of a research project and see how the process of inference might work.

For example, a researcher wants to examine whether a significant difference exists between adolescent boys and girls in the way they solve

WHAT YOU'LL LEARN ABOUT IN THIS CHAPTER:

- Why the inferential process is important to research

- The role that chance plays in any scientific endeavor

- What statistical significance is and why it is important

- What Type I and Type II errors are and their importance

- The steps in completing a test of statistical significance

- Some of the basic types of statistical tests and how they are used

- A bit about multivariate statistics and their application

- A bit more about factor analysis and its application

- The difference between significance and meaningfulness

- The use of meta-analysis in behavioral and social science research

Inference is the key to the power of most inferential techniques.

moral dilemmas. Reviewing the general steps of the research process discussed in Chapter 1, here is a sequence of how things might happen:

1. The researcher selects representative samples of adolescent boys and girls in such a way that the samples represent the populations from which they are drawn.
2. Each participant is administered a test to assess his or her level of moral development.
3. The mean score for the group of boys is compared with the mean score for the group of girls using some statistical test.
4. A conclusion is reached as to whether the difference between the scores is the result of chance (meaning that some factor other than gender is responsible for the difference) or the result of true differences between the two groups as a function of gender.
5. A conclusion is reached as to the role that gender plays in moral development in the population from which the sample was originally drawn. In other words, an inference, based on the results of an analysis of the sample data, is made about the population.

The key to making an inference that works is selecting a sample that is very much like the population from which it came.

TEST YOURSELF

What is the primary difference between inferential and descriptive statistics?

The Role of Chance

Chance is initially the most attractive explanation for any outcome.

If nothing else is known about the relationship between the variables involved, chance is always the most attractive explanation for any relationship that might exist. Why? Because, given no other information, it is the most reasonable.

For example, before you eliminate all the possible causes for any differences in moral development between the two groups of adolescents, the one explanation that is most attractive is that if the groups do differ, it is because of **chance**. What is chance? It is the occurrence of variability which cannot be accounted for by any of the variables that you are studying. That is why you cannot begin with the assumption that any difference you observe between males and females is owing to gender differences. At that beginning point, no evidence exists to support such an assumption.

Your primary role as a scientist is to reduce the degree that chance might play in understanding the relationship between variables. This is done primarily by controlling the various sources of variance (causes of differences such as previous experience, age, etc.) that might exist.

You will learn more about how to control for various sources of error (or competing explanations for your outcomes) in Chapter 11. For now, let's move on to understanding the rationale behind how one can look at a relatively small sample of observations and make an inference to a much larger population. The technique (and the underlying rationale) is truly fascinating, and it is the basis for much of the everyday reporting of scientific results.

The Central Limit Theorem

The central limit theorem is in many ways the basis for inferential statistics.

The critical link between obtaining the results from the sample and being able to generalize these results to the population is the assumption that repeated sampling from the population will result in a set of scores that are representative of the population. If this is not the case, then many (if not all) tests of inferential statistics cannot be applied.

Remember this question posed earlier: How do you know if the population distribution from which a sample is selected is normal? The answer is that you don't know because you can never actually examine or evaluate the characteristics of the entire population. What is more, in a sense, you should not even care (horrors!) because of the **central limit theorem**, which dictates that regardless of the shape of the distribution (be it normal or not), the means of all the samples selected from the population will be normally distributed. This means that even if a population of scores is U shaped (the exact opposite of a bell-shaped curve) and if you select a number of samples of size 30 or larger from that population, then the means of those samples will be normally distributed. You will see this in a moment, but sit back for a second and ponder what this observation really means in the application of these principles to the real research world, where the true shape of the distribution of population scores is not normal, or bell shaped.

Most important, it means that nothing about the distribution of scores within the population needs be known to generalize results from a sample to the population. That's pretty heavy duty, but you can see that if this were not the case, it would be very difficult, if not impossible, to infer from a sample to the population from which it was drawn.

One of the keys to the successful operation of this theorem is that the sample size be greater than 30. If the sample size is less than 30, you may need to apply nonparametric or distribution-free meaning statistics which are not tied to a normal distribution.

An Example of the Central Limit Theorem

Table 8.1 shows a population of 100 values ranging from one to five, and Figure 8.1 shows a graph of their distribution (score by frequency). The mean of the entire population is 3.0. As you can see, the distribution is U shaped. Of course, in the real world, the entire population can never be directly observed (otherwise why be interested in inference?), but for illustrative purposes let's have some faith and assume it is possible.

A sample of 10 scores from this population is selected at random, and the mean is computed. Its value (mean #1) is 4. Now another sample is selected (mean #2) and so on, until the means of 30 different samples of size 10 are selected. The graph of these 30

1	5	2	5	5
2	3	5	2	1
1	5	1	2	1
4	4	1	5	1
1	5	5	5	1
1	3	1	5	1
4	5	1	4	4
1	3	4	1	5
5	2	5	5	5
1	1	3	5	5
2	5	2	2	1
5	2	4	5	1
5	5	4	5	1
2	4	2	2	1
1	1	1	1	2
4	4	4	3	5
1	1	5	4	1
5	4	5	1	4
3	4	1	4	5
1	1	2	2	5

Table 8.1   A population of 100 scores with a U-shaped distribution

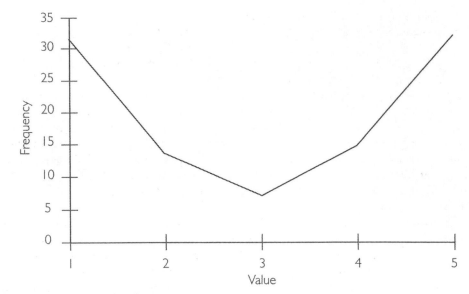

Figure 8.1 A U-shaped distribution.

means is shown in Table 8.2. Once these means are plotted (as if they were a distribution of scores) the distribution approaches normality, as shown in Figure 8.2. Thus, from a population whose scores were distributed in a way opposite (that is, U-shaped as shown in Figure 8.1) to what normal curves usually look like, a normal distribution of values can be generated. And the mean of all the means (the average of the 30 different sample means) is quite close (2.76) to the mean of the original population (it was 3.0) from which they were drawn. A coincidence? Nope. *X-Files*? Nope. Supernatural? Nope. A miracle? Nope. Amazing! Nope. It's just the power of the central limit theorem.

This theorem is important stuff. It illustrates how powerful inferential statistics can be in allowing decisions to be based on the characteristics of a normal curve when indeed the population from which the sample was drawn is not normal. This fact alone provides enormous flexibility and in many ways is the cornerstone of the experimental method. Without the power to infer, the entire population would have to be tested—an unreasonable and impractical task.

TEST YOURSELF

Why is the central limit theorem so powerful and so central to our discussion of inferential statistics?

4	3	3
1	2	5
3	3	3
2	3	3
3	2	4
3	2	2
1	3	4
3	1	3
4	3	3
3	2	2

Table 8.2 A collection of 30 means, each generated from samples (using the values in Table 8.1)

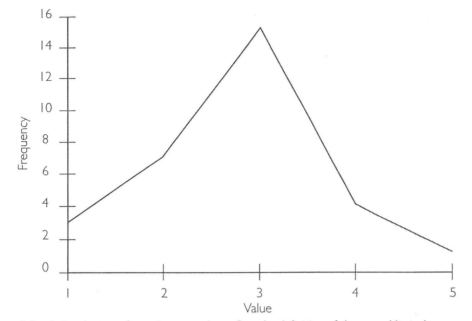

Figure 8.2 A distribution of sample means that reflect the definition of the central limit theorem.

The Idea of Statistical Significance

Because sampling is imperfect (in that you can never select a sample of subjects that exactly matches the profile of those in the population), some error (sampling error) is introduced into the sampling process. In addition, because hypotheses cannot be directly tested on populations (because that is simply impractical; populations are too big), inferences may not be perfect either. Also, inferences just might be plain old wrong in concluding that two groups are different from each other (which the sample data might show), when in reality (which is the condition that really exists in the population) they are not.

For example, let's say a researcher is interested in determining whether there is a difference in the academic achievement of children who participated in a preschool program compared with children who did not participate. The null hypothesis is that the two groups are equal to each other on some measure of achievement. The research hypothesis is that the mean score for the group of children who participated in the program is higher than the mean score for the group of children who did not participate in the program. Okay so far?

As a good researcher, your job is to show (as best you can) that any differences that exist between the two groups are due only to the effects of the preschool experience and no other factor or combination of factors. Using a variety of techniques described in Chapter 11, you control or eliminate all the possible sources of difference, such as the influence of the parents' education, the number of children in the family, and so on. Once these other potential explanatory variables are removed, the only remaining alternative explanation for differences is the effect of the preschool experience itself. But can you be absolutely sure? No, you cannot. Why? Because you are not sure that you are testing a sample that ideally fits the profile of the population. And if that is not the case, perhaps there is some room for error, and "error," sometimes, is another word for chance.

By concluding that the differences in test scores are due to differences in treatment (but considering that you are basing these conclusions on an examination of a sample, not the population itself), you accept some risk. This degree of risk is, in effect, the level of (drumroll, please) statistical significance at which you are willing to operate.

If You . . .	When the Null Hypothesis Is Actually . . .	Then You Have . . .
Reject the null hypothesis	True (there really are no differences)	Made a Type I error (don't worry and remember: Everyone makes this at one level or another)
Reject the null hypothesis	False (there really are differences)	No error
Accept the null hypothesis	False (there really are differences)	Made a Type II error (worry a little, but not too much)
Accept the null hypothesis	True (there really are no differences)	No error

Table 8.3   Types of errors that can be made when testing hypotheses

Type I error and level of statistical significance are the same things.

Statistical significance is the degree of risk that you are willing to take that you will reject a null hypothesis when it is actually true (see Table 8.3 for a preview). For our earlier example, the null hypothesis says that there is no difference between the two groups (remember, the null hypothesis is always a statement of equality). In your data, however, you did find a difference; that is, given the evidence you have so far, group membership seems to have an effect on achievement scores. In reality, however, perhaps there is no difference and, if you reject the null hypothesis you stated, you make an error. The risk you take in making this kind of error (or the level of significance) is also known as a **Type I error**.

The **level of significance** (also called alpha or α) has certain conventional values associated with it, such as .01 and .05. For example, if the level of significance is .01, it means that on any one test of the null hypothesis, there is a 1% chance you will reject the null hypothesis when it is true (and conclude that there is a group difference), when there really is no group difference. If the level of significance is .05, it means that on any one test of the null hypothesis, there is a 5% chance you will reject it when the null is true (and conclude that there is a group difference), when really there is no group difference. Notice that the level of significance is associated with each *independent* test of the null hypothesis, and it is not appropriate to say that "on 100 tests of the null hypothesis, I will make an error on only five."

In a research report, statistical significance is usually represented as $p < .05$, which reads as *the probability of observing that outcome is less than .05* and is often expressed in a report or journal article simply as "significant at the .05 level."

There is another kind of error you can make which, along with the Type I error, is shown in Table 8.3. A **Type II error** occurs when you inadvertently accept a false null hypothesis. For example, what if there really are differences between the populations represented by the sample groups, but you mistakenly conclude there are not?

Type II errors can be decreased by increasing the sample size.

Ideally, you want to minimize both Type I and Type II errors, but to do so is not always easy or under your control. You have complete control over the Type I error level or the amount of risk that you are willing to take because you actually set the level itself. Type II errors are not as directly controlled but instead are related to factors such as sample size. Type II errors are particularly sensitive to the number of subjects in a sample and, as that number increases, Type II error decreases. In other words, as the sample characteristics more closely match that of the population (achieved by increasing the sample size), the likelihood that you will accept a false null hypothesis also decreases.

Why do you think that as the sample size increases, the likelihood of a Type II error decreases?

Tests of Significance

What inferential statistics does best is allow decisions to be made about populations based on the information about samples. One of the most useful tools for doing this is a **test of statistical significance** which can be applied to different types of situations, depending on the nature of the question being asked and the form of the null hypothesis.

For example, do you want to look at the difference between two groups, such as whether employed men score significantly differently than employed women on a given test, or the relationship between two variables, such as number of weeks unemployed and level of self-confidence? The two cases call for the different approaches, but both will result in a test of the null hypothesis using a specific test of statistical significance.

> Tests of significance use the associated null hypothesis as the starting point.

How a Test of Significance Works

Tests of significance are based on the fact that each type of null hypothesis (such as $H_o : \mu_1 = \mu_2$, representing no difference between the means of two samples) has associated with it a particular type of test statistic. The statistic has associated with it a distribution of values which is used to compare what your sample data reveal and what you would expect to obtain by chance. Once again, chance is the most plausible of all explanations if you have no evidence to indicate otherwise.

Here are the general steps one takes in the application of a statistical test to any null hypothesis. Read and review these steps carefully because they will be used again as guidelines for testing various hypotheses:

1. *Statement of the null hypothesis.* Do you remember that the null hypothesis is a statement of equality? The null hypothesis is the true state of affairs given no other information on which to make a judgment. For example, if you know nothing about the relationship between long-term memory and daily practice of memory-building skills, then you assume they are unrelated. That might not be what you want to test as a hypothesis, but it is always the starting point.
2. *Establishing the level of risk (or the level of significance or Type I error) associated with the null hypothesis.* With any research hypothesis comes a certain degree of risk for Type I error. The smaller this error is (such as .01 compared with .05), the less risk you are willing to take. No test of a hypothesis is completely risk free because you never really know the true relationship between variables. You find that out only when you also find how much you really have in your checking account (that is, never).
3. *Selection of the appropriate test statistic.* Each null hypothesis has associated with it a particular test statistic. You can learn what test is related to what type of question in more detail in the Statistics 1 and Statistics 2 classes offered at your school. You can also use our cheat sheet which shows up later in this chapter!
4. *Computation of the test statistic value* (called the obtained value). The **obtained value** is the result of a specific statistical test. For example, there are test statistics for the significance of the difference between the averages of two groups, for the significance of the difference of a correlation coefficient from 0, and for the significance of the difference between two proportions.

> The proof of the pudding in the test of any hypothesis is the comparison of the critical and obtained values.

5. *Determination of the value needed for rejection of the null hypothesis using the appropriate table of critical values for the particular statistic.* Each test statistic (along with group size and the risk you are willing to take) has a **critical value** associated with it. This is the minimum value you would expect the test statistic to yield if the null hypothesis is indeed false.

6. *Comparison of the obtained value to the critical value.* This is the crucial step. Here the value you obtained from the test statistic (the one you computed) is compared with the value (the critical value) you would expect to find by chance alone.

7. If the obtained value is more extreme than the critical value, the null hypothesis cannot be accepted; that is, the null hypothesis as a statement of equality (reflecting chance) is not the most attractive explanation for differences that were found. Here is where the real beauty of the inferential method shines through. Only if your obtained value is more extreme than chance (meaning that the result of the test statistic is not a result of some chance fluctuation) can you say that any differences you obtained are not owing to chance and that the equality stated by the null hypothesis is not the most attractive explanation for any differences you might have found. Instead, the differences must be the result of the treatment.

8. If the obtained value does not exceed the critical value, then the null hypothesis is the most attractive explanation. If you cannot show that the difference you obtained is caused by something other than chance (such as the treatment), then the difference must be caused by chance or something over which you have no control. In other words, the null hypothesis is the best explanation.

Let's go through these steps in the context of an example of how one test of significance can be applied.

t-Test for Independent Means

There are many different types of statistcial tests; the *t*-test for independent means is just one of them.

The *t*-test for independent means is a commonly used inferential test of the significance of the difference between two means based on two independent, unrelated groups. These are two different groups, such as males and females or those who received a treatment and those who did not.

Chen and Stevenson (1989) examined cultural differences among 3,500 elementary school children and their parents and teachers in Beijing, Chicago, Minneapolis, Sendai (Japan), and Taipei. One of the research hypotheses associated with this large set of studies was that the amount of homework done (as estimated by the mothers of the children) changed (was either more or less) over the 4-year period of the study (1980–1984).

Here are the same eight steps just described using this study as an example.

1. *Statement of the null hypothesis.* In this case, the null hypothesis is as follows: There is no difference between the average amount of time spent on homework in 1980 and the amount of time spent on homework in 1984. Using symbols, the hypothesis is stated as

$$H_0 : \mu_{1980} = \mu_{1984}$$

where
  H_0 = the null hypothesis
  μ_{1980} = the population average for 1980 homework levels
  μ_{1984} = the population average for 1984 homework levels

Remember that because null hypotheses always refer to populations, parameters like μ are used to represent the mean rather than $\overline{X}$.

Degrees of Freedom	.05 Level of Significance	.01 Level of Significance
40	2.021	2.704
60	2.000	2.660
120	1.980	2.617

Table 8.4 A partial list of critical values used to determine the likelihood that an obtained value is due to chance or some other factor

2. *Establishing the level of risk (or the level of significance or Type I error) associated with the null hypothesis.* It is conventional to assign a value of .05 or .01. In this case, the value of .05 was used.
3. *Selection of the appropriate test statistic.* The appropriate test statistic for this null hypothesis is the *t*-test between independent means. The means are independent because they are averages computed from different groups.
4. *Computation of the test statistic (or the obtained value).* In this study, the value of the test statistic for the comparison of 320 mothers' estimates of the amount of time spent on homework in 1980 and 1984 was 2.00. This was the result of applying the formula mentioned in step 3. This value was taken directly from the journal article.
5. *Determination of the value (called the critical value) needed for rejection of the null hypothesis using the appropriate table of critical values for the particular statistic.* To determine the critical value, a table for that particular statistic has to be consulted (see Table 8.4).

    To determine the critical value that a test statistic needs to reach significance, you need to know two things: the level of significance at which the research hypothesis is being tested (.05 in this case) and the **degrees of freedom**, a reflection of the size of the sample (320 in this case). You need to know the sample size because the critical value changes as sample size changes. Can you figure out why? It is because as the sample size increases it becomes more like the population, and the difference you need between the obtained value and the critical value for rejection of the null hypothesis decreases.

    Use the information in Table 8.4 to determine the critical value. Read down the column labeled Degrees of Freedom until you get as close to 320 as possible (which is 120). Now read over to the column for the .05 Level of Significance. Because you did not hypothesize any direction to the difference, this is a two-tailed, or nondirectional, test. At the juncture of 120 degrees of freedom and the .05 level, you can see that the critical value of 1.980 is needed for rejection of the null hypothesis.
6. *Comparison of the obtained and critical values.* Here, the two values of interest are the obtained value (2.00) and the critical value (1.980).
7. If the obtained value is more extreme than the critical value, the null hypothesis cannot be accepted; that is, this statement of equality (reflecting chance) is not the most attractive explanation for any differences that were found. In this case, the obtained value is greater than the critical value. In other words, the likelihood that this *t*-value would result from chance alone is less than .05 (or 5 of 100) on any one test of the null hypothesis. Thus, based on the sample data, one concludes that there is a difference in the average number of minutes spent on homework between 1980 and 1984. What is the nature of the difference? An examination of the means (252 minutes per week in 1980 compared with 305 minutes per week in 1984) shows that time spent on homework increased.
8. If the obtained value does not exceed the critical value, the null hypothesis is the most attractive explanation. In this case, the obtained value exceeded the critical value. The null is not the most attractive or tenable explanation for differences.

What Does ($t_{120} = 2.00$, $p < .05$) Really Mean?

As you become more familiar with journal articles and how they are written, you will soon recognize a statement that goes something like this:

The results were significant at the .05 level ($t_{120} = 2.00$, $p < .05$).

The words are clear enough, but what do the parts mean?

- The t represents the type of statistical test, which in this case is a t-test. Remember, there are hundreds of other types of statistical tests.
- The 120 represents the number of degrees of freedom.
- The 2.00 is the obtained value, or the value which resulted from applying the t-test to the results of the study.
- The p represents probability.
- The .05 represents the level of significance or Type I error rate.

Once you have some experience reading these expressions through your exposure to completed studies and journal articles, you will find it very easy to glance quickly at the numbers and recognize what they mean. For the most part, you will find that this format is standard, with the value of these elements changing (such as F for an F-test, or .05 for a different level of significance) but not their meaning.

A New Twist to $p < .05$

For decades, statisticians and the like have been expressing the statistical significance of an outcome by using code such as $p < .05$ or $p < .01$ for example. And as you have just learned, something like $p < .05$ tells you only that the probability is less than .05, not what exact probability is. It actually could be anything from .0 to .0499999, right?

With the introduction of data analysis packages such as SPSS (and a host of others), the *exact* probability of an outcome is usually part of the results. For example, instead of $p < .05$ (which you must admit is fairly imprecise), the probability associated with the obtained value could be $p = .0375$! There's no guessing how strong the probability is of rejecting a null hypothesis when it is true—you have it right there.

Does this mean you don't need an understanding of how to use tables of critical value or what those values mean? No. It means that it is easier than ever to find out the *exact* probability associated with an outcome. You still need plenty of practice understanding what that particular value means in light of the question being asked and how the results should be interpreted. The technology has improved, but the ideas remain the same and to be a good beginning (or advanced) researcher, understanding the basic ideas is most important.

TEST YOURSELF

Why do you compare the obtained value with the critical value when making a decision about some observed outcome?

How to Select the Appropriate Test

Any null hypothesis has an associated test which you can use to test the viability of that hypothesis.

Now comes the big (but general) question: "How do I select the appropriate statistical test to use?" As mentioned previously, you need to take more statistics classes to master this skill fully. After all, experience is still the greatest teacher. In fact, there's no way you can really learn what to use and when to use it unless you've had the real-life opportunity to use these tools.

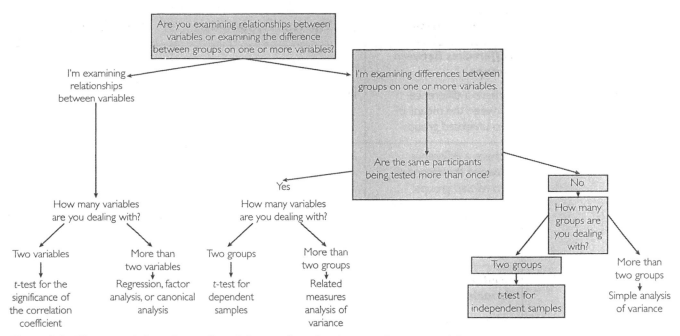

Figure 8.3 This general cheat sheet will work for now, but when it comes time to start doing your own research, you have to start learning which test should be used and when.

For our purposes, and to get started, we've created the nice little cheat sheet shown in Figure 8.3. You have to have some idea what you're doing so that selecting the correct statistical test is not entirely autopilot; however, it certainly is a good place to get started.

Don't think for a second that Figure 8.3 takes the place of the need to learn about when these different tests are appropriate. The flowchart is designed only to help you get started.

Here's How to Use the Chart

1. Assume that you're very new to this statistics stuff and that you have some idea what these tests of significance do, but you're pretty lost as far as deciding which one to use when.
2. Answer the question at the top of the flowchart and proceed down the chart by answering each of the questions until you get to the end of the chart. That's the statistical test you should use. In Figure 8.3, we highlighted the steps for the *t*-test for independent means, the one we just used as an example.

Some Other Tests of Significance

As you have already learned, different tests of significance can be applied to different types of questions. In the previous example, the appropriate test of significance examined the difference between the averages of two groups that were unrelated, or independent of each other. Let's look at other common tests of statistical significance. Keep in mind that there are well over 100 different tests that can be applied. Table 8.5 shows you a sample of some of these with the associated research question, the null hypothesis, and the appropriate statistical test.

The purpose of the following examples is to acquaint you with some of the most frequently used tests which you are likely to encounter in the literature. Once again, if you want to know more about these tests, you should consider taking the first- and second-level statistics courses offered by your department. The Greek letter "ρ" (rho) represents the population parameter for the correlation between two variables.

The Question	The Null Hypothesis	The Statistical Test
Differences Between Groups Is there a difference between the means of two *unrelated* groups?	$H_0 : \mu_{group1} = \mu_{group1}$	*t-test for independent means*
Is there a difference between the means of two *related* groups?	$H_0 : \mu_{group1a} = \mu_{group1b}$	*t-test for dependent means*
Is there an overall difference between the means of three groups?	$H_0 : \mu_{group1} = \mu_{group1} = \mu_{group3}$	Analysis of variance
Relationships Between Variables Is there a relationship between two variables?	$H_0 : \rho_{xy} = 0$	*t-test for the significance of the correlation coefficient*
Is there a difference between two correlation coefficients?	$H_0 : \rho_{ab} = \rho_{cd}$	*t-test for the significance of the difference between correlation coefficients*

Table 8.5 A very broad survey of some other tests of statistical significance and what they do

Looking at Differences Between Dependent Groups

You have just seen an example of applying a statistical test to examine the difference between the average of two groups when the measurements in each of the groups are unrelated; that is, the measurements are independent, such as two different groups of people, with each person in each group being tested once.

Another common situation is the one in which the groups are not independent. For example, what if you are interested in seeing the changes, if any, that occurred throughout the school year on reading competency scores for the same group of children? You could administer the competency test in September and then again in June. The null hypothesis would be that there is no difference in the scores between the two testings.

Because the scores are related (the same pupils are taking both tests), the *t*-test for independent means is not appropriate. Instead, the *t*-test for dependent means is the appropriate statistical test. The primary difference between these two procedures is that the test for dependent means takes into account the degree that the two sets of scores are related. Check out the cheat sheet in Figure 8.3 and see if you can work your way down to the *t*-test for dependent means. (Hint: The critical decision point is whether the same participants are being tested more than once whether two groups of different participants are being tested.)

For example, the mean score for the group of 28 boys on the fall reading test was 76.8, with a standard deviation of 6.5. The mean score for the same group on the spring reading test was 82.4, with a standard deviation of 7.8. Is there a significant difference between the two testings? Let's follow the same set of steps that we identified earlier and the same procedure.

1. *Statement of the null hypothesis.*

$$H_0 : \mu_{\text{group 1a}} = \mu_{\text{group 1b}}$$

2. *Establishing the level of risk (or the level of significance or Type I error) associated with the null hypothesis.* The value of .01 will be used.
3. *Selection of the appropriate test statistic.* The appropriate test statistic for this null hypothesis is the *t*-test between dependent means. The means are dependent because they are based on the performance of the same group.
4. *Computation of the test statistic value,* which is $t = 2.581$.
5. *Determination of the value needed for rejection of the null hypothesis.* Using the values given in Table 8.6, the critical value is determined just as was done for a test of independent means. The number of degrees of freedom is $n - 1$, or 27, where n equals the number of pairs of observations which, in this case, is 28. Here, $n - 1$, not n, is used because we want a conservative estimate of the population value. We intentionally underestimate the size of the sample (27 versus 28).

    You can see that the same type of information is contained in this table as that shown in Table 8.4, but now it applies to pairs of observations. The number of critical values in the table has also increased.

    Here's the important information: The level of significance at which the hypothesis is being tested is .01, and the critical value needed for rejection of the null hypothesis for a two-tailed test is 2.771.

6. If the obtained value is more extreme than the critical value, the null hypothesis cannot be accepted; that is, this statement of equality (reflecting chance) is not the most attractive explanation for any differences that were found. In this case, the obtained value of 2.581 (from the results of the analysis) does not exceed the critical value of 2.771.
7. If the obtained value does not exceed the critical value, then the null hypothesis is the most attractive explanation. The observation based on the sample data is not extreme enough to reject the null hypothesis and conclude that there is a significant difference between the two testings. The null hypothesis that there is no difference between the two groups is the most attractive explanation. Any difference that was observed (76.8 versus 82.4) is attributed to sampling error.

Looking at Relationships Between Groups

Chapter 9 discusses a descriptive statistic called the correlation coefficient (also mentioned in Chapter 5), which is a numerical index of the relationship between two variables. If you know nothing about two variables, say you call them X and Y, what would you expect the relationship between them to be by chance alone? Because you

	Level of Significance for a One-Tailed Test			
	.05	.025	.01	.005
	Level of Significance for a Two-Tailed Test			
Degrees of Freedom	.10	.05	.02	.01
26	1.706	2.056	2.479	2.779
27	1.703	2.052	2.473	2.771
28	1.701	2.048	2.467	2.763
29	1.699	2.045	2.462	2.756
30	1.697	2.042	2.457	2.750

Table 8.6 Another set of critical values used to make decisions about the tenability of the null hypothesis

have no reason to believe they are related, you have to assume that the relationship is 0. That is exactly what you would expect if chance were the only factor operating and if these two variables shared nothing in common.

The test of significance of a correlation is whether the value of the coefficient (ρ *or rho*), and hence the relationship between the variables, is significantly different from a value of 0. The null hypothesis is

$$\rho_{xy} = 0$$

For example, let's assume that you want to test the research hypothesis (at the .01 level) that the relationship between math and reading scores (where the correlation coefficient equals .13, or $r_{xy} = .13$) is different from 0.

The value for this test statistic is part of a distribution of *t*-scores. Once that *t*-value is computed, you go to the same table that was consulted for the various statistical tests where other *t*-scores are involved.

If the null hypothesis cannot be rejected, you are essentially saying that there is no relationship between the two variables. If there is no significant relationship (or real relationship between X and Y), then how can any correlation at all (such as .13) be different from 0? Simple. It is sampling error. Indeed, the value of .13 is not the true value that you would find in the population from which the sample was drawn, but rather only a function of inaccurate or less-than-precise sampling. Sampling error is that ever-present threat, and one of your jobs is to separate differences owing to sampling error from those caused by true differences or relationships in the sample being examined.

TEST YOURSELF

Provide an example of a situation where an independent test of the difference between means is appropriate versus a dependent test of the difference between means.

Working with More Than One Dependent Variable

Techniques such as multivariate analysis of variance (MANOVA) may be sophisticated, but they are easily learned and, with practice, applied to make your research even more interesting.

The research question you are asking may require you to assess more than one dependent variable. In this case, there are at least two advanced techniques with which you should be familiar.

Multivariate analysis of variance (or MANOVA) is an advanced technique that examines whether group differences occur on more than one dependent variable. In many ways, MANOVA resembles a series of simple *t*-tests between groups. The major difference between the two techniques is that MANOVA takes into account the relationship between the dependent variables. In other words, if the dependent variables are closely related, it would be difficult to tell whether a difference on dependent variable 1 is less than the result of differences on dependent variable 2. MANOVA separates the unique contribution that each dependent variable makes to understanding group differences so that if a difference exists on dependent variable 1, it is not mingled with any difference on variable 2.

The fact that dependent variables can be related makes several pairwise *t*-tests a serious threat to a sound study. For example, let's say that you are testing the differences between the experimental group and the control group on variables named comprehension, memory, recall, and speed of reading. As you might suspect, these variables are all related. Thus, a *t*-test between differences on speed of reading between groups may appear to be significant, but the real reason behind the difference is that speed of reading is very closely linked to comprehension, and that is where the real difference lies.

Because of the interrelated nature of these variables, the true Type I (or alpha error) is not .01 or .05 or whatever. Instead, it is

$$1 - (1 - \alpha)^k$$

where

α = the Type I error rate

k = the number of pairwise comparisons

For example, in the case of three variables, you can have three comparisons (variable 1 and variable 2, variable 1 and variable 3, variable 2 and variable 3). So, rather than .05, the true Type I error rate is $1 - (1 - .05)^3$, or .14, which is certainly different from the assumed .05. Rather than taking a 5% risk of rejecting the null hypothesis when it is actually true, it's now up to 14%! In other words, using multiple *t*-tests is risky because you would artificially inflate the level of the Type I error with which you think you are dealing.

The solution? Use some type of technique, such as MANOVA, which controls for these relationships between dependent variables followed by some type of post-hoc (after the fact) procedures that compare means with one another and control the level of Type I error.

Factor analysis is another advanced technique that allows the researcher to reduce the number of variables that represent a particular construct and then use factor scores as dependent variables. The more closely related the variables are, the fewer the factors needed to represent the entire matrix of variables.

For example, let's say you are studying the effects of the knowledge that expectant parents have of their child's gender on the parents' perceptions of the child's personality. A factor analysis groups similar variables together so that several variables can represent a particular construct. Each of these groups, or factors, are then named by the researchers. The greatest strength of factor analysis is that it allows researchers to examine sets of variables and see how closely they are related, rather than deal with individual variables. For example, rather than dealing with the variables eye contact, touching, and verbalizing (all of which are somewhat related), you can deal with the one construct called Attachment.

Significance Versus Meaningfulness

What an interesting situation for researchers when they discover that the results of an experiment are, indeed, statistically significant. Even though you may be at the start of your career, you probably have heard scuttlebutt around your department and from other students that the absolutely most desirable outcome of any research is that "the results are significant."

What your colleagues mean by this and what statistical significance really means may be two different things. What your colleagues mean is that the research was a technical success because the null hypothesis is not a reasonable explanation for what was observed, and, in theory, the research hypothesis that was being tested was supported. Now if your experimental design and other considerations were well taken care of, statistically significant results are unquestionably the first step toward making a contribution to the literature in your field. However, the presence and importance of statistical significance must be kept in perspective.

For example, let's take a case in which a very large sample of illiterate adults (say, 10,000) are divided into two groups. One group receives intensive literacy training using classroom teaching, and the other group receives intensive literacy training using computers. The average score for group 1 (who learned in the classroom) is 75.6 on a reading test, the dependent variable. The average score on the reading test for group 2 (who learned using computers) is 75.7. The amount of variance in both groups is about equal. It doesn't take a genius to see that the difference in score between the two groups is only .1 (75.6 versus 75.7). Yet when a *t*-test for the significance between independent means is applied, the results are significant at the .01 level, indicating that computers work better than classroom teaching. In other words, the role of chance is minimized.

The difference of .1 is indeed statistically significant, but is it meaningful? Does the improvement in test scores (by such a small margin) provide sufficient rationale for the $300,000 it costs to equip the program with computers? Or is the difference negligible enough that it can be ignored, even if it is statistically significant?

Here is another example. Because the larger the sample the more closely it approximates the characteristics of the population, often only a very small correlation is needed between two variables for statistical significance when the size of the sample is substantial. For 100 pairs of scores, a correlation between X and Y of .20 is significant at the .05 level. The square of this correlation coefficient (or the coefficient of determination as an indicator of how powerful the correlation is—more about this in Chapter 9) explains only 4% (or $.2^2$) of the variance! That means that 96% of the variance is unexplained or unaccounted for. Given a statistically significant relationship and one that is not occurring by chance alone, that is a lot of explaining to do. In fact, if samples are large enough, any difference between them will be significant.

From these two examples, the following conclusions can be made about the importance of statistical significance:

1. Statistical significance in and of itself is not very meaningful unless the study has a sound conceptual base that lends some meaning to the significance of the outcome.
2. Statistical significance cannot be interpreted independently of the context within which it occurs. If you are the superintendent in a school system, are you willing to retain children in first grade if the retention program significantly raises their standardized test scores by one-half point?
3. Statistical significance is important as a concept, but it is not the end-all and certainly should not be the only goal of scientific research. That is why we set out to test hypotheses rather than prove them. If your study is designed correctly, even null results tell you something very important. If a particular treatment does not work, it is important information about which others need to know. If your study is well designed, then you should know why the treatment does not work, and subsequent researchers can design their studies to take into account the valuable information you have provided.

Even more important are alternative theoretical designs for doing research. Some scientists use a case study or another qualitative method in which observations, interviewing, and other techniques look at the quality and naturalness of the experience rather than focusing on numbers and the results of statistical tests. It's a good thing to keep in mind.

TEST YOURSELF

Significance and meaningfulness are two very different properties that can result from an experiment and the appropriate analysis. Can you have one and not the other? Why and how?

Meta-Analysis

You may have heard this term before. One of the most important characteristics of good science is that results can be replicated. For example, if you successfully used a certain technique to teach illiterate adults how to read, you would like to think that the same technique can be used in similar circumstances with a similar population, with the same results.

But what about the case in which there are 10, 50, or even 100 studies on the same phenomenon where different numbers of subjects are used, in different settings, and even different treatments or programs? The only thing these studies have in common is the use of the same outcome or dependent variable, be it reading, cognitive ability, age at onset of dementia, or any one of thousands of dependent variables. How does one make sense of this collection of findings? Can they be combined, even though the studies that produced them differed from one another on many important factors, such as sample size and selection, treatment variables, and so forth?

The answer is a qualified "yes." Through the use of **meta-analysis**, the findings from a variety of studies with the same dependent variable can be compared. Before you see an example of how meta-analysis works, be sure you understand that the same dependent variable does not necessarily mean that the identical instrument is used across studies. Rather, the same conceptual variable is measured, such as intelligence, aggression, or achievement. If one were interested in studying a particular component of personality, a variety of instruments, such as the 16 Personality Factor Questionnaire or the Minnesota Multiphasic Personality Inventory, could be used and the results from these studies combined in a meta-analysis.

The term "meta-analysis" was coined by Gene Glass in 1976. He meant for it to represent an approach toward summarizing the results of individual experiments. It is an attempt to integrate a wide and diverse body of information about a particular phenomenon. Keep in mind that the data for a meta-analytic study and analysis come from experiments that have already been conducted, not new data that have yet to be collected and then analyzed. In effect, a good part of the work has already been done.

> Meta-analysis is a very effective technique for combining the outcomes from several different studies on the same topic that use the same dependent variable.

How Meta-Analyses Are Done

Here is an example of a meta-analysis conducted on the efficacy of early intervention programs (Castro & Mastropieri, 1988). There are basically four steps in a conventional meta-analysis, with lots of variation as to how these steps are conducted.

First, as many studies as possible, or as representative a group of studies as possible, on a particular phenomenon are collected. G. Castro and M. A. Mastropieri used many of the techniques and sources described in Chapter 3 to find what studies had been done, including Dissertation Abstracts, ERIC, and Psychological Abstracts. They also sent letters to every researcher they recognized as having published in this area or participated in some type of early intervention program. Castro and Mastropieri settled on 74 studies, each of which investigated the effectiveness of early intervention programs on preschoolers (ages birth through 5 years) with disabilities.

Second, the results of the studies need to be converted to some common metric so that they can be compared to one another. This makes sense because it would be a waste of time to compare unlike things. The metric used in many meta-analyses is called the **effect size**. This value is derived by comparing the observed differences between the results for the experimental group (or the one that received the intervention) and the control group (the group that did not receive the intervention) as measured in some standard unit. The larger the effect size, the larger the difference between the two groups. The use of the standard unit allows comparisons between different groups and outcomes, which is the heart of meta-analysis.

In a meta-analysis, the effect size reflects the influence of the dependent variable. The independent variable is the factor that was manipulated, such as type of intervention, age of children, and so forth. In the Castro and Mastropieri study, there were 215 experimental-control group comparisons and 215 effect sizes from the 74 studies that were reviewed.

Third, the researchers developed a system to code the various dimensions of the study, including a description of the subjects, type of intervention used, research design selected, type of outcome measured, and conclusions reached by the authors of the original study. These factors were then used in an examination of the effect sizes computed in step 2.

Finally, a variety of descriptive and correlational techniques are used to examine the outcomes of the studies as a whole. The researcher looks for a trend or a substantial commonality in the direction of the outcomes across the factors that were identified and coded as described in the previous two steps. Castro and Mastropieri concluded that early intervention programs do result in moderately large, immediate benefits for populations with disabilities. These benefits seem to apply to outcomes such as IQ scores, motor skills, language skills, and academic achievement. Efficacy of treatment was not found for other variables such as social competence, self-concept, and family relationships.

Here is another example to demonstrate the scope of these kinds of studies. In a classic study, M. Smith and G. Glass (1977) examined a classic question: Does psychotherapy work? They studied it as a meta-analytic problem.

These researchers conducted a meta-analysis of more than 375 studies, which yielded a total of 833 effects. These 833 effects represented more than 25,000 cases of experimental and control subjects (those who did and did not receive psychotherapy). An examination of the effects sizes yielded evidence of strong and convincing differences between the subjects who participated in psychotherapy and those who did not. On the other hand, there were no differences between types of therapy (such as behavioral or psychoanalytic).

What is so great about this meta-analytic technique? One thing: Meta-analyses do what good science does—they organize data and help us understand what they mean. Imagine a list of 375 studies with the results of each study listed in an adjacent column and imagine how difficult it would be to reach any generalizable and valid conclusion about the outcomes of these studies. To make matters even more confusing, let's say that some of the studies involved very young children, others studied infants, some examined social skills, others intelligence, and so on. It could be a mishmash of outcomes. Meta-analysis reduces the mishmash to something understandable.

TEST YOURSELF

What kinds of topics are usually the focus of a meta-analysis and why?

Summary

This chapter was a brief introduction to the world of inferential statistics and how the concept of inference provides some very powerful decision-making tools. In the last two chapters, you learned a great deal about collecting data and then examining them for patterns, differences, and relationships. Now you are ready to explore the first of several models of design used in research methods: nonexperimental research methods.

Exercises

1. What is chance and what role does it play in the use of inferential statistics?

2. Why is chance initially the most attractive explanation for the differences observed between two groups?

3. What is one implication of a sample size less than 30, with regard to the central limit theorem?

4. A researcher analyzed the results of an experiment and found that the obtained t-value (on a t-test of independent means) was 1.29, with a total of 25 children in group 1 and 30 children in group 2. Use a table of critical values and discuss whether the null hypothesis can or cannot be rejected.

5. How can the results of a study be statistically significant but not meaningful?

6. What is the relationship between a Type I error and level of statistical significance?

7. How does the central limit theorem work and why is it so important to the use of inferential statistics?

8. From the following set of scores, select a random sample of 10 scores. Now do this four more times until you have a total of five separate samples of size 10.
   (a) What is the mean of the entire population?
   (b) What is the mean of the means?
   (c) How can the central limit theorem be used to explain why the answers to (a) and (b) are so close?
   (d) How does this example illustrate the power of the central limit theorem?

9. What does the term "statistically significant mean"?

10. Provide an example of a statistically significant result that is relatively meaningless.

11. Explain why a research scientist does not set out to prove a hypothesis.

12. As a researcher, what is one way to reduce your chances of making a Type II error?

13. As a researcher, you are interested in the effect of child care on the security of attachment which develops between infant and caregiver. You suspect that infants in child care will be insecurely attached at 11 months after being in child care from 2 months of age, compared with infants who are cared for at home by their principal caregiver. What general steps would you take to test your hypothesis?

14. What is the difference between a Type I and a Type II error?

15. What does $p < .01$ mean in a results section of a research report?

16. In research, establishing a level of significance before testing for a relationship between variables is preferable, rather than running the statistical test and then making a decision about the accepted level of significance. Why do you think this is the case?

17. What relationship would need to occur between the obtained value and critical value in a significance test in order for you to appropriately reject the null hypothesis?

18. Why does the critical value change as the sample size changes?

19. What statistical test described in this chapter is most appropriate in evaluating group differences when more than one dependent variable is involved in your research?

20. As a researcher, you are interested in investigating the effects of a new reading curriculum on average reading scores. You plan to do this by quarterly monitoring the progress in reading of four groups of tenth graders using the curriculum. Which statistical test would be most appropriate to use and why?
    (a) *t*-test for independent means
    (b) *t*-test for dependent means
    (c) Analysis of variance

21. What is a meta-analysis and when is it most likely to be used? What is the meaning of the effect size in meta-analytic research?

Online. . .

The Web Center for Social Research Methods

Do you want to know more about research methods and have the Internet at hand? Go to http://www.socialresearchmethods.net/ for lots of really good links to everything from a random dice generator to a tool for helping you select a statistical test like our cheat sheet.

Choosing an Appropriate Level of Significance for Hypothesis Testing

Ever wonder why some researchers choose an alpha level of .01 while others choose .05? Professor Christine Case from Skyline College answers this and similar questions about hypothesis testing at http://www.smccd.edu/accounts/case/biol690/hypothesis.html.

❖ ❖ ❖ Chapter 9 ❖ ❖ ❖

Nonexperimental Research: Descriptive and Correlational Methods

In some ways, your work on the first eight chapters of *Exploring Research* has been done to prepare you for the next four, all of which deal with particular types of research designs or research methods. In this chapter, you will learn about nonexperimental research methods, which are ways of looking at research questions without the direct manipulation of a variable. Chapter 10 discusses another nonexperimental approach: qualitative methods. Why a separate chapter? Because the whole area of qualitative methods stands alone as a somewhat unique approach to asking and answering social and behavioral science research questions.

So, let's turn our attention to the techniques we will deal with here.

For example, if you wanted to understand the factors that may be related to why certain undergraduates smoke and why others do not, you might want to complete some type of survey, one of the descriptive techniques that will be covered in this chapter. Or, if you were interested in better understanding the relationship between risk-taking behavior and drug abuse, perhaps the first (but not the last) step would be to conduct a correlational study in which you would learn about questions of a correlational nature. You would be examining the association between variables and learning about the important distinction between association (two things being related since they share something in common) and causality (one thing causing another).

This chapter focuses on descriptive research questions, how they are asked and how they are answered. It's the first chapter on methods before we move on to qualitative, true experimental, and quasi-experimental methods.

Descriptive Research

Although several factors distinguish different types of research from one another, probably the most important factor is the type of question that you want to answer (see the summary chart on page 00 in Chapter 1). If you are conducting descriptive research, you are trying to understand events that are occurring in the present and how they might relate to other factors. You generate questions and hypotheses, collect data, and continue as if you were conducting any type of research.

The purpose of descriptive research is to describe the current state of affairs at the time of the study. For example, if you want to know how many teachers use a particular teaching method, you could ask a group of students to complete a questionnaire, thereby measuring the outcome as it occurs. If you wanted to know whether there were differences in the frequency of use

> **WHAT YOU'LL LEARN ABOUT IN THIS CHAPTER:**
>
> - What survey research is as well as some of its advantages and disadvantages
>
> - The development and use of surveys
>
> - The value and validity of survey research
>
> - The importance and use of follow-up studies
>
> - The purpose and use of correlational research
>
> - How correlational studies are used
>
> - How to compute and interpret a correlation coefficient

Descriptive research describes the current state of some phenomenon.

of particular types of words among 3-, 5-, and 7-year-olds, you would describe those differences within a descriptive or developmental framework.

The most significant difference between descriptive research and causal comparative or experimental research (discussed in detail in Chapter 11) is that descriptive research does not include a treatment or a control group. You are not trying to test the influence of any variable upon another. In other words, all you are doing for readers of your research is painting a picture. When people read a report that includes one of the several descriptive methods that will be discussed, they should be able to envision the larger picture of what occurred. There may be room to discuss why it occurred, but that question is usually left to a more experimental approach.

Although there are many different types of descriptive research, the focus of this discussion will be on survey research, and correlational studies in which relationships between variables are described.

Survey Research

The best application of sampling in theory and practice can probably be found in survey research. Survey researchers attempt to study directly the characteristics of populations through the use of surveys. You may be most familiar with the types of surveys done around election time, wherein relatively small samples of potential voters (about 1,200) are questioned about their voting intentions. To the credit of the survey designers, the results are often very close to the actual outcomes following the election.

Survey research, also called sample surveys, examines the frequency and relationships between psychological and sociological variables and taps into constructs such as attitudes, beliefs, prejudices, preferences, and opinions. For example, a sample survey could be used to assess the following:

- Parents' attitudes toward the use of punishment in schools
- Voting preferences
- Neighborhood residents' attitudes toward new parking restrictions
- Adolescents' perceptions of curfew enforcement
- Use of drugs in high schools
- A legislator's views on capital punishment

The Interview

Interviews are much more challenging and difficult to do well than just discussing a topic with someone.

The basic tool used in survey research is the **interview**. Interviews (or oral questionnaires) can take the form of the most informal question-and-answer session on the street to a highly structured, detailed interaction between interviewer and interviewee. In fact, many of the points that were listed for questionnaires also apply to interviews. For example, although you need not be concerned about the physical format of the questions in an interview (because the respondent never sees them), you do need to address such issues as transitioning between sections, being sensitive to the type of information you are requesting, and being objective and straightforward.

Most interviews begin with what is called **face-sheet information**, or neutral information, about the respondent such as age, living arrangements, number of children, income, gender, and educational level. Such information helps the interviewer accomplish several things.

First, it helps establish a rapport between the interviewer and the interviewee. Such questions as "Where did you go to college?" or "How many children do you have?" are relatively nonthreatening.

Second, it establishes a set of data that characterizes the person being interviewed. These data can prove invaluable in the analysis of the main focus of the interview which comes later on in the survey.

Interviews contain two general types of questions: structured and unstructured questions. **Structured** or **closed-ended** questions have a clear and apparent focus and call for an explicit answer. They are comprehensible to the interviewer as to the interviewee. Such questions as "At what age did you start smoking?" and "How many times have you visited this store?" call for explicit answers. On the other hand, **unstructured** or **open-ended** questions allow the interviewee to elaborate upon responses. Such questions as "Why were you opposed to the first Persian Gulf War?" or "How would you address the issue of teenage pregnancy?" allow for a more broad response by the interviewee. In both cases, the interviewer can follow up with additional questions.

Interviews can be especially helpful if you want to obtain information that might otherwise be difficult to come by, including firsthand knowledge of people's feelings and perceptions. For example, in a study conducted by M. L. Smith and L. A. Shepard (1988), interviews with teachers and parents were part of a multifaceted approach to understanding kindergarten readiness and retention. In this study, interviewing was combined with other techniques such as in-class observations and the analysis of important documents. These researchers put the interview results to good use when they examined these outcomes in light of other information they collected throughout the study.

On the positive side, interviews offer great flexibility by letting you pursue any direction (within the scope of the project) with the questions. You could also note the interviewee's nonverbal behavior, the setting, and other information that might provide valuable information. Another advantage of interviews is that you can set the general tone and agenda at your own convenience (to a point, of course).

There is also a downside to interviews. They take time, and time is expensive. Interviewing 10 people could take 20–30 hours including travel time and such. Also, because interviews have less anonymity than, for example, a questionnaire, respondents might be reluctant to come forward as honestly as they might otherwise. Other disadvantages are your own biases and the lack of a standardized set of questions. A good interviewer will probe deeply for additional information, perhaps of a different type, than would another interviewer who started with the same questions. Asking follow-up questions is an excellent practice, but what do you do about the interview where probing did not lead to the same information and thus produced different results?

TEST YOURSELF

What do you think a primary advantage of an interview is over a more structured tool such as a questionnaire, and when might you want to use the interview technique?

Developing an Interview

The development of an interview begins much like that for any proposal for a research project. Your first step is to state the purpose of the interview by taking into account your goals for the project. Then, as before, you review the relevant literature to find out what has been done in the past and whether other interview studies have been conducted. You may even find an actual interview that was previously used and be able to use parts of that in your own research. This is a very common practice when researchers use the same interview, say, 10 years later to look for changes in trends.

Second, select a sample that is appropriate for your study, both in characteristics and in size. If you want to know about feelings regarding racial unrest, you cannot question only white citizens—you need to address all minorities. Similarly, even if interviews take lots of time and effort, you cannot skimp on sample size with the thought that what is lost in sample size can be made up in richness and detail. It does not work that way.

Next, the interview questions need to be developed. As you know by now, questions, whether structured or unstructured, need to be clear and concise without any hidden agenda, double negatives, 75-cent words that cannot be understood, and so forth. One of the best ways to determine the appropriateness of your interview is by field-testing it. Use it with people who have the same characteristics as the intended audience. Listen to their feedback and make whatever changes you find necessary.

After the interview form is (more or less) finished, it is time to train the interviewers. Most of the traits you want in an interviewer are obvious: They should be polite, neatly dressed, uncontroversial in appearance, and responsible enough to get to the interview site on time. These qualities, however, are not enough. Interviewers must learn how to go beyond the question should the need arise. For example, if you are asking questions about racial discrimination, the respondent might mention, "Yes, I sometimes feel as if I am being discriminated against." For you not to ask "Why?" and to follow up on the respondent's answer would result in the loss of potentially valuable and interesting information. The best way to train is to have an experienced interviewer watch the trainees interview a practice respondent and then provide feedback.

Finally, it is time to conduct the actual interviews. Allow plenty of time, and go to it. Do not be shy, but do not be too aggressive either.

The Ten Commandments of Interviewing

If you have worked hard at getting ready for the interview, you should not encounter any major problems. Nonetheless, there are certain things you should keep in mind to make your interview run a bit more smoothly and be more useful later, when it comes time to examine the results of your efforts.

With that in mind, here are the 10 commandments of interviewing (drumroll, please). Keep in mind that many, if not all of these, could also be classified as interviewer effects, in which the behavior of the interviewer can significantly affect the outcome.

> No one is perfect, but you should strive to adhere to these 10 guidelines about interviewing as well as you can.

1. *Do not begin the interview cold.* Warm up with some conversation about everything from the weather to the World Series (especially if there is a game that night and you know that the interviewee is a fan). Use anything you can to break the ice and warm up the interaction. If you are offered coffee, accept (and then do not drink all of it if you don't want to). If you do not like coffee, politely refuse or ask for a substitute.

2. *Remember that you are there to get information.* Stay on task and use a printed set of questions to help you.

3. *Be direct.* Know your questions well enough so that you do not have to refer constantly to your sheet, but do not give the appearance that you are being too casual or uninterested.

4. *Dress appropriately.* Remove five of your six earrings if you feel wearing six would put off respondents. No shorts, no shirt, no interview, got it?

5. *Find a quiet place where you and the interviewee will not be distracted.* When you make the appointment for the interview, decide where this place will be. If a proposed location is not acceptable (such as "in the snack bar"), then suggest another (such as the lounge in the library). Call the day before your interview to confirm your visit. You will be amazed at how many interviewees forget.

6. *If your interviewee does not give you a satisfactory answer the first time you ask a question, rephrase it.* Continue to rephrase it in part or in whole until you get closer and closer to what you believe you need.

7. *If possible, use a tape or digital recorder.* If you do, you should be aware of several things. First, ask permission to tape the session before you begin. Second, the tape

recorder should not be used as a crutch. Do not let the tape run without your taking notes and getting all the information you can while the interview is underway.

8. *Make the interviewee feel like an important part of an important project, not just someone who is taking a test.* Most people like to talk about things if given the chance. Tell interviewees you recognize how valuable their time is and how much you appreciate their participation. Be sure to promise them a copy of the results!

9. *You become a good interviewer the same way you get to Carnegie Hall: practice, practice, practice.* Your first interview, like everyone else's, can be full of apprehension and doubt. As you do more of these, your increased confidence and mastery of the questions will produce a smoother process which will result in more useful information.

10. *Thank the interviewee and ask if he or she has any questions.* Offer to send (or call) the interviewee a summary of the results of your work.

Other Types of Surveys

Have you ever been at home during the dinner hour and the phone rings, and the person on the other end of the line wants to know how often you ride the bus, recycle your newspaper, use a computer, or rent a car?

Those calls represent one of several types of survey research, all of which are descriptive in nature. In addition to interviews—the primary survey research method—and telephone surveys, surveys include panels or focus groups (in which a small group of respondents is interviewed and reinterviewed) and mail questionnaires.

How to Conduct Survey Research

Survey research starts out with a general plan (a **flow plan**) of what activities will occur when. The plan begins with the objective of the study, leads into the various methods that may be used to collect the data, and finishes with a final report and a summary of the findings.

1. Clarifying the objectives. The first step is to clarify the objectives of the survey research. For example, let's say that a researcher is asked by a small school system to study attitudes toward the use of punishment in public schools. As part of the research plan, the researcher needs to consider the nature of the question being asked. Is the concern over the effectiveness of punishment? The way punishment is administered? The type of punishment (physical or other)?

   Defining the nature of the objectives may require some preliminary interviewing of respondents who might be interviewed in depth later in the project. One of the primary goals in this step of the project is to define the variables, such as punishment and attitudes, which are to be studied. Both of these terms, which are fairly vague by themselves, need further clarification and definition if the questions that are eventually asked by the researcher are to yield information of any importance.

2. *Identifying a sample.* After the objectives have been specified, the next step is to define a sampling plan and obtain a sample of individuals who will participate in the study. Will all teachers and parents be included? Probably not, because they would be too large a sample, and it would be inefficient to survey such a large group. But how can one fairly represent the community?

   Back to Chapter 4—how about taking a stratified random sample of three parents from each grade from four schools in the district, and a random sample of administrators from each of two administrative levels, building and central administration? If children are involved, the researcher may want to devise a plan that takes into account how frequently these children have been punished themselves and for what reason. Including only children who are rarely punished or only children who are always punished would skew the characteristics of the sample and, thus, the results.

3. *Defining a method*. Now that the objectives and the sampling plan are clear, exactly what will happen during the interview or panel study? Here are some of the questions about which a researcher may be concerned:

   - Will the questions be primarily open-ended, closed-ended, or a combination of both? How will each question sample content, opinions, or attitudes?
   - How will the sample of respondents be defined? Will it include parents, teachers, administrators, or all three? What about students?
   - How will the data be collected? Will interviews be used? Mail surveys?
   - What types of questions will be asked? What factual information will be included?

   These questions will be answered, in part, by the types of information the researcher needs to meet the objectives that were defined early in the project.

4. *Coding and scoring*. Survey research can result in anything from lengthy responses that have to be analyzed to a simple yes–no response, depending on the format and the content of the question. After the data have been collected, the researcher needs to code them (1 for male; 2 for female, for example) and then score the responses in an organized fashion that lends itself to easy tabulation.

   A simple example is shown in Table 9.1, which shows a breakdown of parents who regularly use physical punishment and those who do not and the judgments of both groups as to effectiveness of physical punishment.

Some type of analysis of the frequencies of these responses can be performed to answer the question about parents' attitudes toward punishment.

The Validity of Survey Data

Collecting survey data is hard work. It means constantly seeking subjects and dealing with lots of extraneous sources of variance that are difficult to control. It is somewhat of a surprise, however, how relatively easy it is to establish the validity of such data. For example, one way to establish the validity of the data gained from an interview is to seek an alternative source for confirmation. Public records are easy to check to confirm such facts as age and party affiliation. Respondents can even be interviewed again to confirm the veracity of what they said the first time. There is no reason why people could not lie twice, but a good researcher is aware of that possibility and tries to confirm factual information that might be important to the study's purpose.

	Physical Punishment Is Cruel and Ineffective	Physical Punishment Is Harsh and Unnecessary	Physical Punishment Can Work Under Certain Conditions	Physical Punishment Is a Useful Deterrent for Poor Behavior	Physical Punishment Is the Most Effective Method for Dealing with Poor Behavior
Parents Who Use Punishment	12	14	15	23	32
Parents Who Don't Use Punishment	46	13	14	7	6

Table 9.1 An example of how data can be collected and scored in a survey setting

Evaluating Survey Research

Like all other research methods, survey research has its ups and downs. Here are some ups. First, survey research allows the researcher to get a very broad picture of whatever is being studied. If sampling is done properly, it is not hard to generalize to millions of people, as is done on a regular basis with campaign polling and such. Along with such powers to generalize comes a big savings in money and time.

Second, survey research is efficient in that the data collection part of the study is finished after one contact is made with respondents and the information is collected. Also, minimal facilities are required. In some cases, just a clipboard and a questionnaire is enough to collect data.

Third, if done properly and with minimal sampling error, surveys can yield remarkably accurate results.

The downs can be serious. Most important are sources of bias which can arise during interviews and questionnaires. **Interviewer bias** occurs when the interviewer subtly biases the respondent to respond in one way or another. This bias might take place, for example, if the interviewer encourages (even in the most inadvertent fashion) approval or disapproval of a response by a smile, a frown, looking away, or some other action.

On the other hand, the interviewee might respond with a bias because he or she may not want to give anything other than socially acceptable responses. After all, how many people would respond with a definite "yes!" to the question, "Do you beat your spouse?"

These threats of bias must be guarded against by carefully training interviewers to be objective and by ensuring that the questions neither lead nor put respondents in a position where few alternatives are open.

Another problem with survey research is that people may not respond, as in the case of a mail survey. Is this a big deal? It sure can be. Nonresponders might constitute a qualitatively distinct group from responders. Therefore, findings based on nonresponders will be different than if the entire group had been considered. The rule? Go back and try to get those who didn't respond the first time.

TEST YOURSELF

You read about ethics and some guidelines in Chapter 3B. What might be some conflicts that can arise with those ethical principles and the use of the various survey methods we discussed earlier?

Correlational Research

Correlational research describes the linear relationship between two or more variables without any hint of attributing the effect of one variable on another. As a descriptive technique, it is very powerful because this method indicates whether variables (such as number of hours of studying and test score) share something in common with each other. If they do, the two are correlated (or co-related) with one another.

In Chapter 5, the correlation coefficient was used to estimate the reliability of a test. The same statistic is used here, again in a descriptive role. For example, correlations are used as the standard measure to assess the relationship between degree of family relatedness (e.g., twins, cousins, unrelated) and similarity of intelligence test scores. The higher the correlation, the higher the degree of relatedness. In such a case, you would expect that twins who are raised in the same home would have more similar IQ scores (they share more in common) than twins raised in different homes. And they do! Twins reared apart share only the same genetic endowment, whereas twins (whether monozygotic [one egg] or dizygotic [two eggs]) reared in the same home share both hereditary and environmental backgrounds.

The Relationship Between Variables

The most frequent measure used to assess degree of relatedness is the correlation coefficient, which is a numerical index that reflects the relationship between two variables. It is expressed as a number between 21.00 and 11.00, and it increases in strength as the amount of variance that one variable shares with another increases. That is, the more two things have in common (like identical twins), the more strongly related they will be to each other (which only makes sense). If you share common interests with someone, it is more likely that your activities will be related than if you compared yourself with someone with whom you have nothing in common.

For example, you are more likely to find a stronger relationship between scores on a manual dexterity test and a test of eye–hand coordination than between a manual dexterity test and a person's height. Similarly, you would expect the correlation between reading and mathematics scores to be stronger than that between reading and physical strength. This is because performances on reading and math tests share something in common with each other (intellectual and problem-solving skills, for example) than a reading test and, say, weight-lifting performance.

> Positive correlations are not "good" and negative ones are not "bad." Positive and negative have to do with the direction of the relationship and nothing else.

Correlations can be direct or positive, meaning that as one variable changes in value, the other changes in the same direction, such as the relationship between the number of hours you study and your grade on an exam. Generally, the more you study, the better your grade will be. Likewise, the less you study, the worse your grade will be. Notice that the word "positive" is sometimes interpreted as being synonymous with "good." Not so here. For example, there is a negative correlation between the amount of time parents spend with their children and the child's level of involvement with juvenile authorities. Bad? Not at all.

Correlations can also reflect an indirect or negative relationship, meaning that as one variable changes in value in one direction, the other changes in the opposite direction, such as the relationship between the speed at which you go through multiple-choice items and your score on the test. Generally, the faster you go, the lower your score; the slower you go, the higher your score. Do not interpret this to mean that if you slow down, you will be smarter. Things do not work like that, which further exemplifies why correlations are not causal. What it means is that, for a specific set of students, there is a negative correlation between test-taking time and total score. Because it is a group statistic, it is difficult to conclude anything about individual performance and impossible to attribute causality.

The two types of correlations we just discussed are summarized in Table 9.2.

Interestingly, the important quality of a correlation coefficient is not its sign, but its *absolute value*. A correlation of 2.78 is stronger than a correlation of 1.68, just as a correlation of 1.56 is weaker than a correlation of 2.60.

What Correlation Coefficients Look Like

> The absolute value of the correlation coefficient, not the sign, is what's important.

The most frequently used measure of relationships is the **Pearson product moment correlation**, represented by letter r followed by symbols representing the variables being correlated. The symbol r_{xy} represents a correlation between the variables X and Y.

To compute a correlation, you must have a pair of scores (such as a reading score and a math score) for each subject in the group with which you are working. For example, if you want to compute the correlation between the number of hours spent studying and test score, then you need to have a measure of the number of hours spent and a test score for each individual.

As you just read, correlations can range between -1.00 and $+1.00$ and can take on any value between those two extremes. For example, look at Figure 9.1, which shows

If X . . .	and Y . . .	The Correlation Is	Example
Increases in value	Increases in value	Positive or direct	The taller one gets (X), the more one weighs (Y)
Decreases in value	Decreases in value	Positive or direct	The fewer mistakes one makes (X), the fewer hours of remedial work (Y) one participates in
Increases in value	Decreases in value	Negative or indirect	The better one behaves (X), the fewer in-class suspensions (Y) one has
Decreases in value	Increases in value	Negative or indirect	The less time one spends studying (X), the more errors one makes on the test (Y)

Table 9.2   Two types of correlations: positive or direct, and negative or indirect

four sets of data (A, B, C, and D) represented by an accompanying scattergram for each of the sets.

A **scattergram** is a plot of the scores in pairs. In set A, the correlation is +1.70. (You will see how to compute that value in a moment.)

To draw a scattergram, follow these steps:

1. Using graph paper, set up an X-axis (horizontal) and a Y-axis (vertical).
2. Indicate which variable from the pair will be X and which will be Y. The first in a pair is usually designated as the X value.
3. For participant 1, enter the coordinates for the X and Y values. In this example (data set A in Figure 9.1), the X score is 3 and the Y score is 3, so a data point corresponding to (3, 3) was entered.
4. Repeat step 3 for all the data points, and you will see the scattergram as shown in Figure 9.1 for data set A.

Now look at data set B, where the correlation is only .32, which is substantially weaker than .70. You can see that the stronger correlation (set A) is characterized in the following ways:

* The data points group themselves closer and closer along a straight line as the correlation increases in strength.
* As the slope of this grouping approaches a 45° angle, the correlation becomes stronger.

The data in set A show a high positive correlation (.70), whereas the data in set B show a much lower one (.32). The data in set C show a high negative correlation (−.82) and, just as with a high positive correlation, the coordinates that represent the intersection of two data points align themselves along a diagonal (in this case, from the upper left-hand corner to the lower right, approaching a 45° angle). The last data set, set D, shows very little relationship (−.15) between the X and the Y variables, and the accompanying plot of the coordinates reveals a weak pattern. In other words, a line drawn through these points would be almost flat or horizontal.

The scattergram is a visual representation of the correlation coefficient of the relationship between two variables.

Data Set A

X	Y
3	3
5	6
4	7
6	8
7	7
8	6
6	7
7	9
8	8
9	9

Data Set B

X	Y
3	3
5	6
4	7
6	5
7	7
8	3
6	7
7	9
8	5
9	9

Data Set C

X	Y
3	9
5	8
4	7
6	7
7	6
8	3
6	3
7	4
4	9
5	8

Data Set D

X	Y
3	2
5	4
4	5
6	4
7	3
8	4
6	5
7	4
8	2
9	3

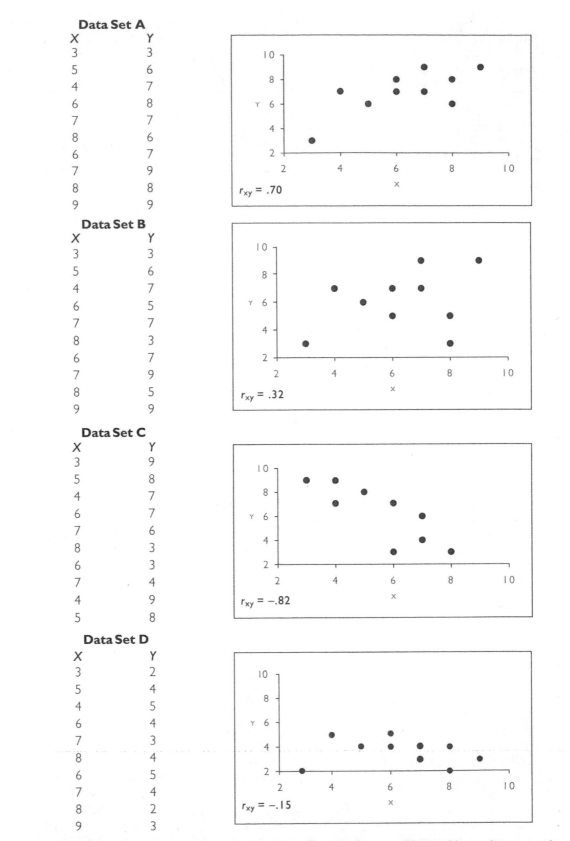

Figure 9.1 Four scattergrams and their corresponding correlation coefficients. Notice that as correlations become stronger, the data points seem to align themselves on a 45° angle with either a positive or negative slope.

In summary, the stronger the formation of a pattern and the more the pattern aligns itself in a 45° angle (either from the lower left-hand corner of the graph to the upper right-hand for positive correlations, or from the upper left-hand corner of the graph to the lower right-hand corner for negative correlations), the stronger the visual evidence of the existence of a relationship between two variables.

TEST YOURSELF

Correlations can be negative or positive, but give an example of how *negative* does not carry a pejorative meaning and *positive* outcomes are not always good.

Computing the Pearson Correlation Coefficient

The easiest manual way to compute the correlation between two variables is through the use of the raw score method. The formula for r_{xy} (where xy represents the correlation between X and Y) is as follows:

The Pearson correlation coefficient is the most frequently computed type of correlation.

$$r_{xy} = \frac{n\Sigma XY - \Sigma X \Sigma Y}{\sqrt{[n\Sigma X^2 - (\Sigma X)^2][n\Sigma Y^2 - (\Sigma Y)^2]}}$$

where r_{xy} = the correlation coefficient between X and Y
   Σ = the summation sign
   n = the size of the sample
   X = the individual's score on the X variable
   Y = the individual's score on the Y variable
   XY = the product of each X score times its corresponding Y score
   X^2 = the individual X score, squared
   Y^2 = the individual Y score, squared.

Let's look at a simple example where the correlation coefficient is computed from data set C shown in Figure 9.1. The mean for variable X is 6.3, and the mean for variable Y is 4.6. Here is what the finished equation looks like:

$$r_{xy} = \frac{-.37}{3 \ [32.1][62.4]} = -.82$$

Try it yourself and see if you can get the same result ($r_{xy} = -.82$). You can also use SPSS or Excel to get the answer.

The correlation is the expression of the relationship between the variables of X and Y, represented as r_{xy}. What happens if you have more than two variables? Then you have more than one correlation coefficient. In general, if you have n variables, then you will have "n taken two at a time" pairs of relationships. In Table 9.3, you can see a correlation

	Grade	Reading	Math
Grade	1.00	.321	.039
Reading	.321	1.00	.605
Math	.039	.605	1.00

Table 9.3 An example of more than two variables and the possible correlations between them

matrix, or a table revealing the pairwise correlations between three variables (grade, reading score, and mathematics score). Each of the three correlation coefficients was computed by using the formula described earlier.

You may notice that the diagonal of the matrix is filled with 1.00s because the correlation of anything with itself is always 1. Also, the coefficients to the right of the diagonal and to its left form a mirror image. The correlations for the other "half" of the matrix (above or below the diagonal of 1.00s in Table 9.3) are the same.

Interpreting the Pearson Correlation Coefficient

To interpret the meaning of the correlation coefficient, look to the correlation of determination.

The correlation coefficient is an interesting index. It reflects the degree of relationship between variables, but it is relatively difficult to interpret as it stands. However, there are two ways to interpret these general indicators of relationships.

The first method is the "eyeball" method, in which correlations of a certain value are associated with a certain nominal degree of relationship such that:

Correlations between	Are said to be
.8 and 1.0	Very strong
.6 and .8	Strong
.4 and .6	Moderate
.2 and .4	Weak
.0 and .2	Very weak

Remember: Do not be fooled by these numbers. Even the weakest correlation (such as .1) can be statistically significant if the sample upon which it is based is large enough and sufficiently approaches the size of the population. You read about the significance versus meaningfulness distinction in Chapter 8.

A sounder method for interpreting the correlation coefficient is to square its value and then compute the **coefficient of determination**. This value, r_{xy}^2, is the amount of variance that is accounted for in one variable by the other. In other words, it allows you to estimate the amount of variance that can be accounted for in one variable by examining the amount of variance in another variable. Thus, if the correlation between two variables is .40, then the coefficient of determination is .16. Sixteen percent (16%) of the variance in one variable can be *explained* by the variance in the other variable; 84% (or 100%−16%)

If r_{xy} is	and r_{xy}^2 is	then the change from . . .	accounts for this much more variance (%)
0.1	0.01		
0.2	0.04	.1 to .2	3
0.3	0.09	.2 to .3	5
0.4	0.16	.3 to .4	7
0.5	0.25	.4 to .5	9
0.6	0.36	.5 to .6	11
0.7	0.49	.6 to .7	13
0.8	0.64	.7 to .8	15
0.9	0.81	.8 to .9	17
1.0	1.00	.9 to 1.0	19

Table 9.4 Differences in the amount of variance accounted for as a function of different values of the correlation coefficient

Figure 9.2 How the amount of variance accounted for in a relationship changes as a function of the strength of the relationship.

of the variance is unexplained. This portion of *unexplained* variance is often referred to as the **coefficient of alienation**.

It is interesting to compare how the amount of variance explained in the relationship between two variables changes as the correlation gets stronger. The change isn't as predictable as you might think.

Table 9.4 shows the simple correlation coefficient (the first column) and the coefficient of determination (the second column). Notice the change in the amount of variance accounted for as the value of the correlation coefficient increases. For example, if the correlation is increased from .4 to .5, the increase in the amount of variance accounted for is 9%. But if the correlation is increased a similar amount (say, from .6 to .7, which is still .1), then the increase in the amount of variance accounted for is 13%. The increase in the variance explained is not linear; therefore, the higher the correlation is, the larger the "jump" in explained variances.

Figure 9.2 is a graphic illustration of what is shown in Table 9.4. As the correlation increases in value, an increasingly larger amount of variance is accounted for. That's why the line shown in Figure 9.2 curves—the amount of variance (Y) increases disproportionately as the value of the correlation coefficient (the X axis) increases and that's why the higher the value of the correlation, the more relative variance you can explain as a relationship between variance than for a lower correlation value.

TEST YOURSELF

Of the various research method tools you have learned about so far, what are some of the advantages and disadvantages of the correlational research methods?

Summary

Is a nonexperimental—descriptive or correlational—design right for you? This is not really the question that should be asked. Rather, you should ask if your subject of interest demands that you use the tools suggested by the descriptive method. As emphasized before, the question that is asked determines the way it is answered. If you want to investigate how the Oklahoma settlers of the 1930s raised their children or how child rearing has changed, historiography may be for you. And what does the descriptive method offer? It provides an account of an event, often in such detail that it serves as a springboard for other questions to be asked and answered. Case studies, **developmental research**, and correlational studies describe a particular phenomenon in a way that communicates the overall picture of whatever is being studied. Although these methods do not allow the luxury of implying any cause-and-effect relationship between variables, their use provides the tools needed to answer questions that are otherwise unanswerable.

Exercises

1. Write out several questions that would be interesting to study using survey research. Create a few questions of a survey nature for each of the studies.

2. Name two advantages and two disadvantages to interviews.

3. Write three potential follow-up questions to this initial interview question: What is your attitude toward eliminating score keeping in children's sports?

4. Briefly outline the five steps of developing an interview.

5. Rank the following correlation coefficients in order of their strength from strongest to weakest.
   (a)   .21
   (b)   −.67
   (c)   .53
   (d)   −.01
   (e)   .78

6. What is wrong with the following argument? The relationship between the number of hours you spend studying is directly related to how well you do on school tests. Therefore, if you do not do well on a test, it means that you did not study long enough.

7. Indicate the type of correlation each of the following relationships describes: positive, negative, or no relationship.
   (a)   As A increases, B increases in value.
   (b)   As A increases, B decreases in value.
   (c)   As A decreases, B increases in value.

8. For each of the three relationships in exercise #4, provide an example.

9. Tell whether the following hypotheses are correlational in nature.
   (a)   There are no differences in cognitive ability between preschoolers in child-care settings and preschoolers who are cared for at home.
   (b)   There is a relationship between parents' education, socioeconomic status, and children's achievement levels in math.
   (c)   There is no relationship between the rate of violent crime in New York and socioeconomic status.
   (d)   Parent education does not increase a child's performance on a math achievement test.
   (e)   Over time, there are differences in the discipline policies used in rural and urban schools.

10. Improve the following interview questions:
    (a) Do you think it is acceptable for teenagers to smoke cigarettes and drink alcohol?
    (b) What are the most common colloquialisms used at your junior high school?

11. What is the purpose of descriptive research?

12. Provide an example of when descriptive research might be the appropriate method to use to answer your research question. And while you are at it, what is your question?

13. Which of the following statements about correlation coefficients are true?
    (a) Correlations can be positive.
    (b) Correlations can be negative.
    (c) Correlations reflect causation.
    (d) Correlations measure the relationship between two variables.

14. What is an example of where a correlation might be significant but not meaningful?

15. Examine the relationship between consumption of milk during dinner and night-time bedwetting and find a significant correlation of .25. How would you interpret the meaningfulness of this finding?

16. What does the coefficient of determination mean? What would the value of the coefficient of determination be for two variables with a correlation of .60? What would be the value of the coefficient of alienation?

Online. . .

Educational Databases

A huge number of educational databases (as part of the main reading room of the Library of Congress) to start your own descriptive research can be found at http://www.loc.gov/rr/main/alcove9/education/database.html. You can find everything here from ERIC to a listing of universities worldwide.

Using Interviews in Research

Dr. John Suler at Rider University gives tips on how to conduct the interview and how appropriately to include information from interviews in your research paper at http://www-usr.rider.edu/~suler/interviews.html.

❖ ❖ ❖ Chapter 10 ❖ ❖ ❖
Nonexperimental Research: Qualitative Methods

Conducting Qualitative Research

Although quantitative research is an integral part of doing research in the social and behavioral sciences, there is another set of methods that may, at times, be a more appropriate tool for conducting research. **Qualitative research**, in the simplest terms, is social or behavioral science research that explores the processes that underlie human behavior using such exploratory techniques as interviews, surveys, case studies, and other relatively personal techniques.

Half-jokingly, some people consider qualitative research to be research without the numbers. In fact, many students choose to perform qualitative research because they believe it will be easier to perform because there is usually little statistical analysis involved. In many ways, however, the opposite is the case, in terms of complexity, level of effort required, and the increasingly sophisticated analytic methods that are becoming available (e.g., computer programs).

Qualitative research methods have been around for thousands of years, as long as people have shared ideas and traditions orally, interviewed others, and so on. Only in the past 25 or so years have these methods received any attention as a legitimate tool for understanding behavior and answering important social and behavioral science research questions. Much of what you read about in this chapter may have been mentioned elsewhere in this volume; however, these methods and techniques are particular to the qualitative method. For example, case studies are descriptive in nature, but they are also used as a qualitative tool.

In Chapter 8, you learned about specific statistical tests and how clear the process is through which these are applied. As it turns out, much of the process of qualitative research can be very demanding because all the discipline forced upon you by the use of statistics transfers itself to the researcher. You must describe your every move in great detail in a manner different from the more traditional approach. However, relatively few scholars are adequately trained in its use. There are ways to establish the legitimacy of qualitative research, as we will discuss later in this chapter, but for now, let's start with the distinction between the types of sources that are regularly used in qualitative research.

Research Sources

As you learned earlier in this volume, both primary and secondary resources are valuable assets. In this first section, different sources of information for qualitative research are discussed: documentation, archival records, physical artifacts, direct observation, participant observation, and focus groups. Most of the other sources that are used are the same as those discussed in the sections on secondary and general resources in Chapter 3.

Documentation

Documentation that is composed and released either internally or for public consumption can provide a wealth of information. For example, a new policy on requirements for child-care workers, meant for either internal use or a press release, provides a context to the official goals and policies of an organization. Documents also serve to confirm or contradict information gathered through other means.

An interesting bit of detective work that is sometimes done is comparing the official distribution list (who is supposed to get what) with any information you can gather as to who else was provided with informal copies of the document (who really got what). This can be important from the viewpoint of a person who, one would think, would be privy to certain issues but was not, as well as those who were included without having a readily apparent need to be included in direct distribution.

Archival Records

Archival records, when available, give the researcher descriptive data about the composition of an organization. Often of particular interest are such records as organizational charts and budgets which help track change in the organization being studied. For example, knowledge that two people who are now in more senior positions previously worked together could imply either a close relationship or one in which "familiarity bred contempt." Archival records can also show the researcher which employees have not been promoted in recent years, whether from refusing an offer or from a lack of confidence on the part of higher management.

Former employees of a hospital could hint about the current and future direction of the health care facility. For example, has the hospital or the former employee prospered more since they parted ways? Did the separation come about because of a change of direction by the hospital's executive committee or because the person was offered a promotion at a different hospital? If the employee left on friendly terms, there could be a potential for strategic collaborations in the future. If the parting was unfriendly, there could be the possibility of two hospitals competing for the same market or same intellectual space.

Physical Artifacts

Physical artifacts are physical objects or elements that are open to your interpretation. For example, what would a dark, somber physical space convey about organization morale or the individual's role in that organization? Or, for example, let's say you are conducting a study on the use of information technology policy in a school system company, but when you walk into the superintendent's office you notice that there is no computer in the office and the superintendent admits that he is computer illiterate and "does not know the first thing" about computers. One can reach the conclusion that the superintendent may be a good administrator, but what about his aspect of the organization's success?

Direct Observation

Direct observation occurs when the researcher is actually in or directly adjacent to the environment being studied but is not actually a participant in the environment itself. For this method, the surroundings, as well as the interactions of people, are viewed in order to confirm or disconfirm stated hypotheses or, alternatively, as a way to gain an understanding of the study setting and to help form hypotheses.

Direct observation is unobtrusive, meaning that the researcher allows the normal activity of the environment to proceed without interruption. Questions, if asked at all, are reserved for times when the normal flow of events will not be interrupted. This method of research is also used to study nonhuman subjects, such as animals in the wild. When used to observe humans, this method can be very helpful in sensing formal and informal relationships and networks of the research subjects.

Participant Observation

Participant observation is a difficult method of conducting research because it requires the researcher to be an active participant in the social network being studied while maintaining sufficient objectivity and detachment to be able to evaluate accurately the material being gathered. However, it can yield some terrific and very useful information. For example, being a gang member or a member of the Peace Corps and writing about those activities provides a personal perspective that would probably be impossible to derive through traditional quantitative methods.

One aspect of participant observation, which might make it undesirable to the casual researcher (if there is such a thing), is the time-consuming nature of the method. In order to be sufficiently accepted in a community to see its true character, the researcher must be there long enough for people to act naturally in his or her presence. If they don't, the information is useless, unless the research question being studied is how the community will react to an outsider.

Focus Groups

A **focus group** is a gathering of people who are being moderated by a member of a research team and perhaps observed, either openly or secretly, by other members of the research team. For example, parents could be called together to find out about their feelings and perceptions regarding the implementation of a new school day schedule or the elimination of busing for all students who live close to school.

The setting in which the focus group occurs should provide an encouraging environment for frank, open communication, and the moderator should take pains not to force his or her own opinions on the group members (after all, it's *their* opinions that count). Discussion is encouraged, and the moderator's job is to ensure that participation in the process isn't "hijacked" by one or several members of the group and that shy members are included in the discussion.

Focus groups have four main functions, which are summarized in Table 10.1. First, they are a great way to gather a lot of information from relatively large numbers of people in a relatively short period of time. For example, if one were studying the perceptions that people have of professional wrestling, one could interview preteens, adolescents, young adults, and parents to learn their thoughts about various social aspects of watching professional wrestling on television. It is critical to keep distinct groups separated, however. A 10-year-old is much less likely to speak freely with a parent present in the room than in a roomful of peers.

Function	Example
Gather information	Asked of parents of junior high students: "How effective do you think it would be if the last period in the school day were not used for instruction, but for community activities?"
Generate insight	Asked of preschool workers: "It seems that in the last few weeks, parents are forgetting to sign their children out. What do you think might be the cause of their forgetting?"
Determine how group members reach decisions	Asked of nurses: "How did you reach a decision as to how you will share information about your patients when shift changes occur?"
Encourage group interaction	Asked of police officers: "We'd like to know how you as a group feel about the new health benefits programs and how they might be an incentive to add new men and women to the force?"

Table 10.1   Functions of a focus group

Second, focus groups can help generate insight into topics that previously were not understood. Speaking of professional wrestling, some people cannot understand how more than 10 viewers a week watch it, when, in fact, it is a multibillion dollar industry. Indeed, it has a significant following of educated, professional men and women. An interesting focus group, some would conclude, would be to find educated, white-collar men who regularly watch wrestling and ask them to discuss why they find it so appealing. Sure, many would say, such a discussion has no meaning, but it could speak to something not obvious, which is perhaps the whole point of conducting qualitative research.

Third, focus groups help the researcher understand how members of the group arrive at their conclusions. Having participants "talk out" their thought processes can help the researcher dissect each individual's motivations and determine critical steps along the way toward deciding what is truly important to the members of the group.

Finally, focus groups encourage group interaction, which helps to bring various viewpoints together in a way that individual interviews do not. Sometimes a question requires more than one person's input to answer it. Other times there is a task involved that forces a team to work together to complete it in an allotted amount of time.

Focus groups can be a very productive way to research a question, but their success depends on the ability of the facilitator to keep the group on task.

TEST YOURSELF

In general, what kinds of questions would you want to answer using qualitative methods rather than quantitative methods?

Case Studies

Case studies are highly detailed, often personal descriptions.

There once was a child named Genie who was isolated from human companionship for the majority of her early years (Curtiss, 1977). When at last she was discovered and released at age 14, she provided psychologists with a bounty of information about the effects of delayed speech on language development.

Psychologists and linguists studied her language development through the use of a **case study**, which is a method used to study an individual or an institution in a unique setting or situation in as intense and as detailed a manner as possible. The word "unique" here is critical because the researcher is as interested in the existing conditions surrounding the person as much as the person himself or herself. It is the quality of uniqueness that sets this person (and this case) apart from others.

You may have heard the term "case study" used before. The case study idea represents a major part of the methodology used by physicians to collect and disseminate information. The *Journal of the American Medical Association* or *JAMA* (published weekly by the American Medical Association) regularly offers case studies of individuals whose conditions are so unusual that their symptoms and treatment demand special attention, and information about their cases needs to be disseminated.

Physician-turned-psychologist Sigmund Freud pioneered the use of the case study in the development of his psychoanalytic theory of personality development. His famous patient, Anna O., and his detailed observations about her condition led to the use of free association as a method in the treatment of hysteria and other conditions. Also notable is the work of Jean Marc Itard, one of the first "special educators," and his case study description of the wild boy of Aveyron, which was the basis for a popular movie, *The Wild Child*.

Case studies are not limited to people. The Harvard Business School makes a regular practice of including case studies of businesses that fail, as well as those that succeed, as a staple of its graduate students' diet of materials to study. Investigating one case, under the microscope so to speak, allows students to review the steps that were taken and better understand the mechanics of how a business might be affected by a variety of factors. Similarly, families, schools, gangs, and social organizations have all been the focus of the case study approach.

For example, the well-known description of an experimental school, Summerhill (Neill, 1960), is an elaborate and detailed case study of a unique English school based on the idea of an "open" education. A similar, more recent work is T. Kidder's (1989) *Among School Children*, a narrative case study of a fifth-grade teacher and her activities over the course of a school year. In part because of the skill of these writers and in part because of the case study nature of the books, the reader gets an intimate look into the life of the two different types of school. And we should not forget author Jonathan Kozol who, in his books *Rachel and Her Children*, *Savage Inequalities*, and *Amazing Grace*, let the larger social community know about how poor-quality schools, homelessness, and poverty affect individual children and families.

> Case studies take a long time to complete but can yield a great deal of detail and insight.

Some Advantages of the Case Study Method

Case studies are a unique way of capturing information about human behavior for a variety of reasons. First, case studies focus on only one individual or one thing (for example, a person or a school district), which enables a very close examination and scrutiny and the collection of a great deal of detailed data. It is for these reasons that case studies have always been a popular method in clinical settings.

Second, case studies encourage the use of several different techniques to get the necessary information ranging from personal observations, to interviews of others who might know the focus of the case study, to schools' or doctors' records regarding health and other matters.

Third, there is simply no way to get a richer account of what is occurring than through a case study. This was exactly what Freud did in his early work. He certainly could not have used a questionnaire to inquire about his patients' dreams, nor could he think to reach his level of analysis through the use of anything other than intensive scrutiny of the most seemingly minor details concerning the way the mind functions. These data helped contribute to his extraordinary insight into the functioning of the human mind and the first accepted stage theory of human development.

Fourth, while case studies do not necessarily result in hypotheses being tested, they suggest directions for further study.

Some Disadvantages of the Case Study Method

The case study method has provided some very important information (which probably could not have been revealed any other way), but it does have its shortcomings.

First, as with everything else, what you see is not always what you get. The case study might appear to be easy to do (you need to find only one subject, one school, one classroom, one office, and one family), but it is actually one of the most time-consuming research methods imaginable. You need to collect data in a wide variety of settings and sources, under a wide variety of conditions, and you rarely have the choice about these settings and conditions. If the child you are observing stays in the room and does not go out for recess, then so do you.

Second, the notes you record in your log or journal may accurately reflect "reality" (or what you observe), but it is only one reality. Everyone comes to a given situation with a bias, and researchers must try not to let that bias interfere with the data collection and interpretation processes. A step in the right direction here is recognizing that you are biased (as am I or as is your best friend), so you can be sure that the conclusions you draw are based on a biased view of what's happening.

Third, what case studies provide in depth, they lose in breadth. Although they are extremely focused, they are not nearly as comprehensive as other research methods. As a result, case studies are appropriate only if you want to complete an in-depth study of one type of phenomenon.

Fourth, do not even think about trying to establish any cause-and-effect links between what you see and what you think might be responsible for the outcomes. Although you might want to speculate, there is nothing in the case study approach that allows you to reach such conclusions. Not only are there insufficient data (an n of 1) to conclude that a cause–effect relationship exists but, most important, studying causal relationships is not the purpose of the method. If you want to study causal relationships, you will need to use tools that are popularly accepted to do so.

Finally, by their very nature, the generalizability of the findings from case studies is limited. Although you might be able to learn about another child or another institution like the one your case study is based on, it is not wise to conclude that because the focus of the study is similar, the findings might be as well.

Some scientists believe that case studies will never result in groundbreaking basic research (which is not their purpose anyway). Case studies do, however, reveal a diversity and richness of human behavior that is simply not accessible through any other method.

TEST YOURSELF

Case studies have specific advantages over other research methods. Illustrate each of these advantages with an example where the topic of interest is family mealtime.

Ethnographies

An **ethnography**, as the root word "ethnic" suggests, is geared toward exploring a culture. To picture in your mind what the stereotypical ethnography would be, imagine a person in khaki shirt and shorts with a pith helmet perched on her head wandering around the jungle, taking up residence with what by Western technological standards would be a primitive village and studying the village's culture firsthand. Dr. Livingston, I presume?

This example is, of course, not the only way to study culture. One could decide to take a job in a factory to study the organizational culture of the workers from the perspective of a blue-collar employee. Another way would be to volunteer at a homeless shelter to observe how people without homes conduct their lives inside and outside the shelter, or to move into a neighborhood with a high crime rate to learn how law-abiding citizens cope with their and their families' daily struggle to avoid the danger that is always just around the corner.

Ethnographies have many methods in common with case studies, including the use of interviews and documents where available, but these methods differ in several key characteristics (Goodwin & Goodwin, 1996).

First, there is the *holistic perspective*, wherein ethnographers view the group or phenomenon being studied in its entirety. It is considered a strength of ethnography that a researcher will take the less-structured route of looking at the system as a whole, rather than as the sum of its component parts.

Second, ethnographers take advantage of *naturalistic orientation* in that they actually take up residence in the culture being studied and become a participant-observer. Successful acceptance into the culture ensures the least disturbed view of it for the researcher.

Ethnographies are also characterized by *prolonged field activity* which generally requires the researcher to spend years within a culture, probably for a long time period just to gain the level of acceptance necessary for activity to return to normal.

Finally, ethnographers may incorporate into their research design *preconceived ideas* as to how the research will come out. In fact, ethnographers should use any information on the culture only to give themselves enough familiarity to be able to function. There should be no design of research questions, formulation of hypotheses, or identification of constructs until actual observation provides sufficient knowledge to be able to do so after being in place.

In many ways, more discipline is required of an ethnographer than of a researcher performing a case study; for example, the ethnographer must be able to formulate research questions and hypotheses "on the fly" instead of having them already prepared before entering the research environment.

Historical Research

Just by reading the preface of Thomas Jordan's *Victorian Childhood* (1987), you can get at least one clue about how different historical research is from the types of experimental research you usually see in the journals for the social and behavioral sciences. His thanks to libraries at the University of Missouri, the Church of Jesus Christ of Latter-day Saints, Washington University, the Library of Congress, the British Library, the Royal Society of Health, the Reform Club, and the Royal Statistical Society indicate their contribution of data in one form or another to his book, which focuses on the children of the Victorian era. These data, whether they are 150-year-old records of children's heights or the percentage of children under 15 years of age who worked in the textile mills (about 14%), were his "subjects," and how he used them exemplifies the focus of our discussion about historical research.

Victorian Childhood is organized into nine chapters, each focusing on a separate theme such as cities, work, life and death, learning and advocacy, and reform. Jordan consulted particularly interesting sources of data to support his conclusions about the way in which children were raised and treated during this period in England. The data are not just from this or that article from a journal by another scholar. Jordan often went

> Understanding the past can lend significant understanding to the future. Take that history course!

to primary sources (you will learn more about what they are in a moment) which you might not even have imagined existed, let alone have known they were accessible.

Some of the materials he used include the following:

- Data from the records of the ships that regularly transported boy "felons" from England to Australia
- Poems reflecting attitudes about children and the roles of parents, such as "The Baby"

> *If baby holds his hands,*
> *And asks by sounds and sign*
> *For what you're eating at your meals,*
> *Tho' mother's heart inclines*
> *To give him what he wants,*
> *Remember, he can't chew;*
> *And solid food is bad for him,*
> *Tho' very good for you.*

- Newspaper classified ads, such as the one from the September 14, 1817, *Morning Chronicle* advertising care and education for a governess for "Young Ladies," who will be "treated with the tenderest attention, be constantly under her immediate inspection and form in every respect . . . " and instructed in "History, Geography, Writing, Arithmetic, and Needle Works . . . " all for 30 guineas a year
- The number of Sunday schools open from 1801 through 1851, classified by denomination (there were at least 11).

It is clear that Jordan did his homework. He looked here, there, and everywhere to find what he needed to present as complete a picture as possible of what it was like to be a child during that period. Like any other good scientist, he collected data (of a wide variety from a wide variety of sources) and organized this information in a way that allows the reader to reach some conclusions that would go unnoticed without his efforts.

Conducting Historical Research

"Historiography" is another term for "historical research."

Historical research (or **historiography**) in the social and behavioral sciences is sometimes unfairly given second-class status. People often cannot decide whether such research should be placed in the social sciences or in the humanities, and it often ends up within each domain (history of education, history of physics, etc.), without a home of its own. It certainly is a social science because historians collect and analyze data as do social scientists. On the other hand, it is a humanity as well, because historians (or anyone doing historical research) also examine the roles played by individuals in social institutions such as the school and the family. Further, because few behavioral and social scientists are ever taught about historical research and its associated methodology, few actually do research in that area or are even familiar with the appropriate techniques. For the most part, "historians" who are interested in such topics as the history of child care or educational reform or the origins of psychoanalysis or one of hundreds of other interesting topics make the important contributions.

Understanding the historical nature of a phenomenon often is as important as understanding the phenomenon itself. Why? Because you cannot fully evaluate or appreciate the advances that are made in science (be it developmental psychology or particle physics) without some understanding of the context within which these developments occurred.

For example, the aging of the American population that has occurred over the past 50 years (and continues) is a historical event that has prompted increased interest in the field of gerontology. Similarly, understanding the customs and conditions of the

Victorian era and late nineteenth-century Vienna (when Freud began to develop his theory of psychoanalysis) provides insights that help us understand and appreciate more about Freud's theory than we otherwise would.

It is not just idle talk when you hear the quote, "Those who cannot remember the past are condemned to repeat it." It is true, and it is another reason why you should add an understanding of the historical method to your arsenal of research skills.

The Steps in Historical Research

Although you may have never thought it to be the case, conducting historical research is, in many ways, very similar to conducting any of the other types of research already mentioned in this volume.

Although the data or the basic information may differ markedly from that of other research, the historical researcher proceeds with many of the same steps as a researcher using any other method. Let's take a look at each of these six different steps.

First, *historical researchers define a topic or a problem that they wish to investigate.* Historical research is unlimited in scope because it consists of a constant interchange between current events and events of the past. All of the past is the historian's database, a vast collection of documents and ideas, many of which can be difficult to find and more difficult to verify their authenticity. Like detectives, historical researchers search through everything from ships' logs to church birth registers to find who is related to whom and what role this or that person might have played in the community. It is an inspection (which might be just simple reading or a discussion with a colleague) of this legacy of information that prompts ideas for further explorations.

This step is much like any other researcher's mental effort, which usually results from a personal interest in a particular area. For example, one might be interested in the history of educational reform and specifically in the notion of the origin of laws requiring children to go to school.

Second, to whatever extent possible, *the researcher formulates a hypothesis, which often is expressed as a question.* For example, the question might be, "When, how, and why did school become mandatory for children under the age of 16?" Although posing hypotheses in a nondeclarative form is something not usually done in scientific studies, historical research demands a different set of rules. Some of the criteria for a good hypothesis discussed in Chapter 2 are applicable to historical research (such as hypothesis being an educated guess), but others are not (such as looking for statistical relationships between variables).

Third, as with any other research endeavor, one has to *utilize a variety of sources to gather data.* As you will shortly see, these sources differ quite markedly from those with which you are acquainted. Interviewing can be a source of data in almost any type of research, but the analysis of written documents and the culling of records and such are usually the province of the historical researcher.

Fourth, *evidence needs to be evaluated for its authenticity as well as for its accuracy.* More about these characteristics later in this chapter.

Fifth, *data need to be synthesized or integrated to provide a coherent body of information.* This is similar to the steps you may have taken when you reviewed the literature in the preparation of a proposal, but here you are integrating outcomes and looking for trends and patterns that eventually might suggest further questions that would be worth asking.

Finally, as with any other research project, you will need to *interpret the results in light of the argument you originally made* about why this topic is worth pursuing and in light of the question that you asked when the research began. Your skill as an interpreter will have a great deal to do with how well prepared you are for understanding the results of your data collection. For example, the more you know about the economic, political, and social climate of the late nineteenth and early twentieth centuries, the more comprehensively you will be able to understand how, why, and when mandatory school attendance became the rule rather than the exception.

Historical research shows up in smart nonfiction books all the time such as Walter Isaccson's Pulitzer prize-winning biography of Benjamin Franklin. What is it about this type of research that lends itself to popular consumption?

Sources of Historical Data

Historians usually rely on two different sources of data: primary and secondary. Each plays a particular role in conducting historical research and each is equally valuable.

Primary Sources of Historical Data

Primary sources of historical data are original artifacts, documents, interviews and records of eyewitnesses, oral histories, diaries, and school records (Table 10.2).

Although the data for historical research may look different, many steps in the process are similar to those used in traditional research models.

Primary sources can yield otherwise unobtainable information.

Source	Examples
Documents	Minutes of meetings Contracts Deeds Wills Permits Photographs Lists Bills Films Catalogues Maps Newspaper accounts Diaries Graduation records
Oral histories	First-person spoken or recorded accounts of events Court transcripts
Remains, remnants, and relics	Tools Food Religious artifacts Clothing Buildings Equipment Books Notes Scrolls

Table 10.2   Some primary sources of historical data

For example, if you wanted to know how Japanese families adjusted to internment during World War II, the child you interview from such a family would be a primary source, as would a diary kept by an adult of the experience. In his award-winning book *Daddy's Gone to War* (1995), Bill Tuttle wrote about the feelings and experiences of children during World War II in regard to their absent fathers. As data for his account, he used more than 4,000 letters collected from these now adults. It was an intense effort that took hundreds of hours just to accumulate the data, but it resulted in a fascinating description of what life was like for millions of American children at that time.

Primary sources are the direct outcomes of an event or experience that are recorded without there necessarily being any intent for later use by a historian. Such sources might be a newsreel shown in a movie theater 50 years ago, or a record of the number of people who received psychotherapy in 1952, or the minutes from a school board meeting like those in *Daddy's Gone to War*. If you were a historian, the only thing that would prevent you from forming a very accurate picture of what it was like to be at that school board meeting is the fact that you are viewing someone else's perspective through the minutes. Still, you are as close to being there as it may be possible to get.

Secondary Sources of Historical Data

Whereas primary sources are firsthand accounts of events, **secondary sources of historical data** are secondhand or at least once removed from the original event, such as a summary of important statistics, a list of important primary sources, and a newspaper column based on an eyewitness account (the account itself would be a primary source). These sources give accounts witnessed by others, such as a bystander, but not witnessed directly by the source. And just like the children's game telephone, something often gets lost in the translation.

Secondary sources are often more readily available than primary sources, but they are not as rich in detail and possibly not as accurate.

The most important consideration when using secondary sources is the degree to which can you trust the original source of the data. For example, a reanalysis of Sir Cyril Burt's 100-year-old data on twins led several scientists to conclude (almost 100 years later) that the data had been falsified. A great deal of what was known (and was believed to be true) about the nature of intelligence, for example, had been based on that initial analysis.

Primary or Secondary Sources: Which Are Best?

It would be an ideal world for the historian if primary sources were always available, but that is often not the case. As with so many other situations in the research world, the ideal (such as the perfect sample) is simply unattainable. Instead, one must settle for the next best thing, which may be a secondary source.

Given that both types of sources may be equally useful (and trustworthy), researchers should not place any implicit value on one over the other, since they both provide important information. For example, you would have a difficult time interviewing the teachers who taught in the Victorian England described by Jordan, but you might very well get a good idea of what happened during the school day by reading a letter written by a parent and sent to the principal. Good historians do not bemoan the lack of primary sources or whether a potentially important letter is missing; instead, they make the best of what is available.

Here is another example. For those of you interested in child development, there is an incredible repository of manuscripts and visual materials at Antioch College in Yellow Springs, Ohio, where both types of sources can be found. There, the Society for Research in Child Development has stored (and continues to solicit) thousands of primary and secondary sources relating to children and their families, often contributed by the scientists who originally conducted the work. Some of the materials they have available include

- Correspondence between researchers about a particular topic
- Personal letters that include information about ideas and progress toward a particular goal
- Drafts of what would later be important research papers
- Original data that can be used and analyzed with new techniques by other people interested in the same area
- Films of research studies, such as those detailing the growth and development of young children compiled by "ages and stages" Dr. Arnold Gesell
- Programs and schedules from hundreds of meetings of professional societies that focus on children

The final, ultimate rule for the historian? Nobody should throw anything away! Archivists, the keepers of the past, encourage those who are participating in an activity to save everything and send it to them. They can then decide, based on their training, what's important to keep and what's disposable.

Authenticity and Accuracy

Nonetheless, just as researchers who use achievement tests as a source of data must ensure that the test is reliable and valid, so historians need to establish the value of the data from the primary and secondary sources that underlie their arguments. As do others, historiographers need to adopt a critical and evaluative attitude toward the information they collect; otherwise, the inaccurate primary document of today (perhaps a forgery) becomes another historian's source of misinformation tomorrow. The cycle repeats itself, with one's primary source becoming another's secondary source, and the whole database becomes increasingly contaminated with inauthentic information.

The evaluation of primary and secondary data is accomplished through the application of two separate criteria: authenticity (also known as external criticism) and accuracy (also known as internal criticism).

External Criticism as a Criterion

External criticism, as applied to historical data, is concerned with the authenticity of the data. Basically, this criterion asks whether the data are genuine and trustworthy. Were they written when claimed? By the person who signed them? And found where one might expect? These are only some of the questions that must be asked before the data can be trusted.

The **authenticity** of a document or some other primary source is sometimes easy to establish and other times next to impossible. The age and quality of particular inks can be examined to date a document. Types of writing styles, printing techniques, composition of paper, use of language, and general knowledge are all indicators of when (and even how) a document was prepared. The historiographer looks for consistency. Do all the pieces fit together as in a jigsaw puzzle, or are there important outliers that just do not fit in, thereby raising doubts? And of what value can any work be if the data upon which it is based are questionable?

For example, the presence of ancient coins in the same containers as the famous Dead Sea scrolls lent additional evidence that the scrolls were as old as suspected.

> "Authenticity" is another term for "validity."

The coins and some very sophisticated forensic tests, such as carbon dating, led to the conclusion that the scrolls were about 2,500 years old (at this writing).

As a beginning historian, you would have neither the training nor the techniques available to perform such sophisticated analyses, so you more or less have to base your decisions about authenticity on several pieces of evidence and make a judgment about the usefulness of the data. Even if you do not have the tools, you must ensure that you have exhausted every possibility to establish the authenticity of your data. Otherwise, your research efforts may be for naught.

Internal Criticism as a Criterion

A second evaluative criterion is **internal criticism**, which is concerned with **accuracy**, or how trustworthy the source is as a true reflection of what occurred. Do the numbers from the 1890 survey of how many children were enrolled in school seem plausible? Are parents' reports of adolescent mood swings during the 1950s an accurate reflection of the children's real behavior?

"Accuracy" is another term for "trustworthiness."

One way to determine the level of accuracy is to have an expert examine the documents or relics and give an opinion as to whether it is an accurate reflection of what events were like during the period under investigation.

TEST YOURSELF

Isn't it enough to just have an eyewitness for a source of information? Why bother with authenticity and accuracy as criteria?

The Limitations of Historical Research

There is no question that historical research comes with some significant shortcomings compared with other methods of doing research in the social and behavioral sciences.

Limitation in generalizability is one of the main drawbacks to the results gleaned from historical research.

First, because the availability of data is always limited by factors that are not under the control of the researcher, results will likely be limited in their generalizability. If all you have to go on is correspondence, with nothing to verify whether events really occurred, then you cannot take much from such findings and apply them to another time or setting. In fact, historians often have to settle for what they can get to study a particular topic, rather than the ideal.

Second, historical research data are often questioned because they are primarily derived from the observations of others, such as letters, books, or works of art. Those schooled in the belief that firsthand observation (e.g., tests, tasks) yields information that has the most potential for understanding behavior may be correct in part, but that is no reason to ignore other types of data presented by history.

Third, historical research is often a long and arduous task that can require hundreds, if not thousands, of hours of poring over documents (if you can locate them) as you look for clues and hints to support your hypotheses. For the historian, this is more of a fact of life than a limitation, but it certainly discourages some people from entering into this type of activity.

Fourth, because some of the criteria that would normally be applied to empirical research include such things as the reliability and validity of the instruments used, in historical research other less rigorous (but more comprehensive) criteria are used to evaluate measurement tools.

Qualitative Research Tools

Research tools to help qualitative researchers were slow in coming, but they have recently become very sophisticated tools that greatly assist the tasks associated with the magnitude and potential complexity of large, qualitative data sets. QSR International (http://echo.gmu.edu/toolcenter-wiki/index.php?title=QSR_International) sells various software packages such as Scrapbook. Among the most popular (and one of the first but constantly improved) is N6 (which used to be called NUD*IST). With this software, you can do such things as work in plain text and automate clerical tasks, such as importing and coding research data, searching for text or coding patterns, or generating reports. They also market NVivo (which comes in a student edition), which allows the user to import, create and edit documents, code and annotate text, link project documents to one another (such as video and audio files), search for relationships between text, and create models of the user's data.

Another program from ResearchWare (at http://www.researchware.com/) is Hyper-RESEARCH, which allows coding, analysis, and organization of data. HyperRESEARCH comes in a Mac version as well as a Windows version, and the company is considering generating a Linux version.

Summary

Qualitative research can be a powerful and appropriate nonexperimental way to explore an academic question rigorously, as when additional context is needed to explain phenomena missed by quantitative research methods. When properly performed, qualitative research projects add to the body of knowledge on their subjects and make the researcher even more well informed.

Exercises

1. Assume that it is your job to conduct a qualitative study on the usefulness of school vouchers. What research sources discussed in this chapter might you be able to find?

2. If you were going to study the impact of integration on small southern communities, what primary and secondary sources might you consult?

3. How do qualitative and quantitative methods differ from one another, and when would you use each one?

4. Create a research question for which a case study approach would be most appropriate. Be sure to consider the advantages and disadvantages as discussed in this chapter.

5. What are some of the most important differences in the methods used by historical researchers compared with those used by the more traditional (experimental) researchers in the social and behavioral sciences?

6. Write a one-paragraph description of a historical research study that you would like to complete. Answer the following questions:
    (a) How would you establish the authenticity of your sources?
    (b) How would you establish the accuracy of your sources?

7. List five research questions that would not be appropriate to study using qualitative methods.

8. In conducting focus groups on women's roles within marriage, would you be better off having women and their husbands in the same group or in separate groups? Why?

9. Find a journal article where the author uses a case study for research. Briefly summarize the case study.

10. Documentarian Morgan Spurlock's film *Supersize Me* exemplifies, by documenting his 30-day journey of eating only fast food at a popular chain, the case study method in a modern medium. What are some other examples, fact or fiction, of case studies in popular film, television, or books?

11. Consider the following potential conclusion from *Supersize Me*: Eating fast food and avoiding exercise for 30 days causes a 13% weight gain, bouts of depression, and a reduced sex drive. From a research standpoint, why would this conclusion be inappropriate?

12. An ethnographer spends 3 weeks in a new culture and then returns home to begin examining the data she collected. What is inappropriate about her method?

Online. . .

Qualitative Research

Want to know everything there is about qualitative research on the Internet? It's too much for any one person, but Judy Norris at http://www.qualitativeresearch.uga. edu/QualPage/ sure makes a good try. Take a look at the QualPage and see for yourself. Another source of wonderful tools and links is available at Qualitative Methods at http://www.communicationresearch.org/qualitative.htm.

❖ ❖ ❖ Chapter 11 ❖ ❖ ❖

Pre- and True Experimental Research Methods

What scientists do is try to find out why things happen. They go to great lengths trying to establish, for example, what the best way is to facilitate learning, why some adults are more successful than their peers, or where differences in attitudes come from. The methods and models described in this chapter can go a long way toward understanding such phenomena.

One tool that can assist in understanding the search for these differences is the **true experimental research method**. Unlike any of the other methods discussed thus far, the experimental method tests for the presence of a distinct cause and effect. This means that once this method is used, the judgment can be made that A does cause B to happen or that A does not cause B to happen. Other methods, such as historical and descriptive models, do not offer that luxury. Although they can be used to uncover relationships between variables, there is no way that a causal relationship can be established.

Why? It is by virtue of the experimental method itself, which allows for the control of potential sources of differences (or variance), that the following can be said: One factor is related to another in such a way that changes in that factor are causally related to changes in the other. So, it's not just a relationship where two variables share something in common (as is the case with a correlational relationship); it's much more. They share something, but one directly affects the other.

For example, the simplest experimental design would be one in which two groups of subjects are randomly selected from a population and one group (the **experimental group**) receives a treatment and the other group (the **control group**) receives no treatment. At the end of the experiment, both groups are tested to see if there is a difference on a specified test score. Assuming (and this is the big assumption) that the two groups were equivalent from the start of the experiment, any observed difference at the end of the experiment must be due to the treatment. That is what experimental design, in one form or another, is all about.

When done correctly, experimental designs can provide a tremendous amount of power and control over understanding the causal relationships between variables. Their use, to a significant extent, is responsible for a good deal of the understanding scientists have about behavior.

TEST YOURSELF

There are many famous discoveries in science, but one of the most important methodological ones is the scientific method where groups are compared to one another. Why has this method become so popular and taken on such importance?

Experimental Designs

There is a variety of types of experimental designs. In this section, you will find a description of the set made famous by Donald Campbell and Julian Stanley in their 1963 monograph "Experimental and Quasi-Experimental Design for Research on Teaching," which helped revolutionize the way in which research projects are planned and conducted.

Campbell and Stanley identified three general categories of research designs: pre-experimental, true experimental, and quasi-experimental. (Quasi-experimental designs are also referred to as **causal-comparative designs**.) This chapter will discuss the pre-experimental and true experimental designs; Chapter 12 covers quasi-experimental design.

The most significant difference among these types of experimental designs is the degree to which they impose control on the variables being studied. The pre-experimental method has the least amount of control, the true experimental method has the most, and the quasi-experimental method is somewhere in the middle. The more control a design allows, the easier it is to attribute a cause-and-effect sequence of events.

Another way in which these three designs differ from one another is the *degree of randomness* that enters into the design. You already know that the word "random" implies an equal and independent chance of being selected, but that definition and concept can be applied beyond the selection of a sample of subjects from a population to the concept's importance in experimental design.

Actually, different steps need to be taken to ensure the quality of true randomness in the best of all experimental designs.

The first step is one you know most about, *the random selection of subjects from a population to form a sample*. This is the first procedure you would undertake in an experiment. Now you have a sample.

Second, you want to *assign subjects randomly to different groups*. You want to make sure, for example, that subjects assigned to group 1 had an equal chance of being assigned to group 2.

Finally (if you followed steps 1 and 2), you have two groups you can assume are equivalent to each other. Now you need to *decide which of the two groups will receive the treatment* or, if you have five groups, which treatment each group will receive. In the same way that you used a table of random numbers in previous examples, you assign (at random) different treatments to the groups.

By following these steps, you can ensure that:

1. The subjects are randomly selected from a population and randomly assigned to groups.
2. Which group receives which treatment is decided randomly as well.

Table 11.1 summarizes some of the primary differences between pre-experimental, true experimental, and quasi-experimental designs. Even though quasi-experimental designs will be discussed in Chapter 12, it is included here so you can see a comparison of all design types. Notice that many of these differences focus on the process of randomization of selection procedures, subjects, and assignment.

Pre-Experimental Designs

Pre-experimental designs are not characterized by random selection of participants from a population, nor do they include a control group. Without either of these, the power of the research to uncover the causal nature of the relationship between independent and dependent variables is greatly reduced, if not entirely eliminated.

Condition	Pre-Experimental Design	True Experimental Design	Quasi-Experimental Design
Presence of a control group?	In some cases, but usually not	Always	Often
Random selection of subjects from a population?	No	Yes	No
Random assignment of subjects to groups?	No	Yes	No
Random assignment of treatment to groups?	No	Yes	No
Degree of control over extraneous variables?	None	Yes	Some

Table 11.1   Differences between pre-experimental, true experimental, and quasi-experimental designs

These designs allow little or no control over extraneous variables that might be responsible for outcomes other than what the researcher intended.

For example, a parent uses an old folk remedy (wearing garlic around the neck) to ward off the evil spirits associated with a child's cold. Lo and behold, it works! This is the weakest type of experimental conclusion to reach because there is virtually no comparison to show that the garlic worked better than anything else, or better than nothing at all for that matter. The child, of course, might have recovered on his or her own. There is simply no control over other factors that might cause the observed outcome (such as the cold virus running its course).

In research terms, this type of study is called a **one-shot case study design**, as shown in the following table. For this design and the rest that follow, we're showing you events that occur in a sequence such as a group for participants being assigned to a group *and then* some kind of treatment being administered *and then* some posttest is given (in this example).

Step 1	Step 2	Step 3
Participants are assigned to one group	A treatment is administered	A posttest is administered

A group is exposed to some type of treatment and then tested. What shortcomings might you notice about this one-shot case study type of pre-experimental design? First, no attempt at randomization has been made. How might this one-shot case study be used? It would not be very useful for experimental work or for establishing cause-and-effect relationships, but it would be acceptable if you were speculating about factors that occurred at an earlier time and the effect they had on later behavior.

Another pre-experimental design, called the **one-group pretest posttest design**, is represented by the following:

Step 1	Step 2	Step 3	Step 4
Participants are assigned to one group	A pretest is administered	A treatment is administered	A posttest is administered

For example, a researcher is interested in studying how effective method A is in increasing muscle strength. The researcher follows these steps in the completion of the experiment:

1. Advertises for volunteers for the experiment
2. Administers a pretest to measure each participant's muscle strength
3. Exposes the participants to the hypothesized strength-increasing treatment
4. Administers the posttest

The important comparisons are between the pretest and posttest scores for each participant. The primary problem with this type of design is that there is no control group. Without any control group, how can the researcher tell that any difference observed between the pretest and posttest scores is a function of the treatment or a function of some other factor? What if 50% of the sample did not get enough sleep the night before the posttest? Or what if they participated in another study that also was designed to increase strength? These factors, rather than the specific treatment, might be responsible for any differences in strength.

TEST YOURSELF

What does the "pre" in "pre-experimental design" represent?

True Experimental Designs

True experimental designs include all the steps in selecting and assigning subjects in a random fashion, *plus a control group*, thereby lending a stronger argument for a cause-and-effect relationship. One of the reasons these designs are so powerful is that they all have random selection of participants, random assignment of treatments, and random assignment to groups.

For example, let's look at one of the most popular of these designs, the **pretest posttest control group design**, which looks like this:

> True experimental designs control selection of subjects, assignment to groups, and assignment of treatments.

Step 1	Step 2	Step 3	Step 4
Random assignment of participants to a control group	A pretest is administered	No treatment is administered	A posttest is administered
Random assignment of participants to the experimental (or treatment) group(s)	A pretest is administered	A treatment is administered	A posttest is administered

For this design, the researcher would follow these steps:

1. Randomly assign the subjects to the experimental group or the control group
2. Pretest each group on the dependent variable
3. Apply the treatment to the experimental group (the control group does not receive the treatment)
4. Posttest both the experimental group and the control group on the dependent variable (in another form or format, if necessary)

The assumption here, and you are probably on to this, is that because the subjects are randomly assigned to either the control group or the experimental group, they are equivalent at the beginning of the experiment. Any differences observed at the end of the experiment must be due to the treatment because all other explanations have been taken into account.

Pretest and posttest control group designs are not limited to two groups. For example, let's say that a researcher wants to examine the effects of different literacy programs on how well adults learn to read. One treatment might involve instruction 5 days per week and another might involve instruction 3 days per week. The third group, the control group, would not receive any instruction.

An example of such an experimental design would look something like this:

Step 1	Step 2	Step 3	Step 4
Random assignment of participants to a control group	A pretest is administered	No treatment is administered	A posttest is administered
Random assignment of participants to experimental or treatment group 1	A pretest is administered	Treatment takes place three days a week	A posttest is administered
Random assignment of participants to experimental or treatment group 2	A pretest is administered	Treatment takes place three days a week	A posttest is Administered

The number of treatment groups (in this example, two) does not really make any difference so long as there is a control group. There is, however, an important difference as to the nature of the control group. In some cases, the control group might receive no treatment whatsoever; in others, the control group might receive a different type of treatment from the others. The difference in the role of a control group is a reflection of the type of question that was originally asked.

If the control group does not receive any treatment, then the obvious question is whether the treatment is effective, compared with no treatment at all. If the treatment group is compared with another group receiving treatment, then the question is: Which of the two is the more effective? Although it is a somewhat fine distinction, it is an important one to remember when you are thinking about how to structure your research.

Another popular true experimental design is the **posttest-only control group design**, which looks like this:

Step 1	Step 2	Step 3
Random assignment of participants to a control group	No treatment is administered	A posttest is administered
Random assignment of participants to the experimental or treatment group	Treatment takes place five days a week	A posttest is administered

The most apparent characteristic here is that there is no pretest for either the control group or the experimental group. The rationale for this approach is that if participants are randomly selected and assigned to groups, there is no need for a pretest. They are already equivalent anyway, right? The answer is "yes" when you have a sufficiently large sample (at least 30 or so in each group). Another reason to use the posttest-only design instead of the pretest posttest design is that sometimes it is not convenient or may even be impossible to administer a pretest. Under these conditions, you can use the posttest-only design.

There are basically two disadvantages to using a posttest-only design. First, if the randomization procedures were not effective, the groups might not be equivalent at the start. Second, you cannot use the pretest to assign people to other experimental groups, such as high or low on some variable. These disadvantages may be of little consequence, yet they deserve some consideration.

The last true experimental design is kind of the grandmommy and daddy of them all, the **Solomon four-group design**, as shown here:

> The Solomon four-group design is extremely useful, but it is also expensive and time consuming.

Step 1	Step 2	Step 3	Step 4
Random assignment of participants to a control group	A pretest is administered	Treatment is administered	A posttest is administered
Random assignment of participants to experimental or treatment group 1	A pretest is administered	No treatment is administered	A posttest is administered
Random assignment of participants to experimental or treatment group 2	No pretest	Treatment is administered	A posttest is administered
Random assignment of participants to experimental or treatment group 3	No pretest	No treatment is administered	A posttest is administered

There are four groups in this design: one experimental group (which receives the treatment) and three control groups, one of which actually receives the treatment as well.

The most interesting and most useful aspects of this design are the many types of comparisons that can be made to determine what factors might be responsible for certain types of outcomes. You might recognize that the relatively simple pretest posttest control group design compares the experimental group with control group 1. However, let's say, for example, that you are interested in determining the effects of the treatment, but you also want to know if the very act of taking a pretest also changes the final scores. You would then compare the results from the experimental group with those from control group 2. The only thing that differs between these groups is the inclusion of a pretest. To determine the influence of the pretest on posttest scores, compare control group 1 and control group 3 to derive the information you need. The only difference is that group 1 received the pretest, whereas group 3 did not.

You can make all kinds of other comparisons as well. For example, the effect of the treatment on groups that did not receive the pretest (but did receive the treatment) would result in a comparison of group 3 and group 4. This is the same comparison that occurs in the posttest-only control group design mentioned earlier.

Why doesn't everyone who conducts true experimental research use this particular type of design? One good reason: time. Although the Solomon four-group experimental design is very effective for separating out factors that are responsible for differences in the dependent variable, it is a time-consuming design to execute. You need to arrange for four groups, randomly select and assign participants to four conditions (three control and one experimental), and perform lots of testing. For many researchers, this kind of design is just not practical.

Internal and External Validity and Experimental Design

The different types of experimental designs previously mentioned in this chapter were outlined in the seminal work by Campbell and Stanley (1963), and if you intend to continue in your studies, you should read this short monograph. It's essential to understanding how research is, and should be, conducted. These researchers realized that it was not enough just to come up with different designs—a way in which to evaluate these designs was also needed. What outside criteria might one use to judge the usefulness of these different ways of approaching a problem?

What was their decision? They decided to use the criteria of internal and external validity; both measure how well the design does what it should.

Internal validity is the quality of an experimental design such that the results obtained are attributed to the manipulation of the independent variable. In other words, if what you see is a function of what you did, then the experiment has internal validity. For example, if you can show that a treatment works to increase the social skills of withdrawn children and if that treatment is the only apparent cause for the change, then the design (and the experiment) is said to be internally valid. If there are several different explanations for the outcomes of an experiment, the experiment does not have internal validity.

> Internal validity is synonymous with control.

External validity is the quality of an experimental design such that the results can be generalized from the original sample to another sample and then, by extension, to the population from which the sample originated. For example, if you can apply the treatment for increasing the social skills of withdrawn children to another group of withdrawn children, then the design (and the experiment) is said to have external validity.

> External validity is synonymous with generalizability.

Not all designs and experiments have acceptable levels of internal and external validity for a variety of reasons, which Campbell and Stanley call threats to internal and external validity. Once you understand what these threats are, you will be able to see which experimental designs are preferable and why.

Threats to Internal Validity

The following is a brief explanation of those threats to internal validity that lessen the likelihood that the results of an experiment are caused by the manipulation of the independent variable. Good scientists try to reduce or eliminate these threats.

History

Many experiments take place over an extended period of time (**history**), and other events can occur outside of the experiment that might affect its outcome. These events might offer a more potent explanation (other than the original treatment) for the differences observed between groups.

For example, a researcher wants to study the effect of two different diets on the school behavior of hyperactive children. Without the researcher's knowledge, some of the parents of the children in the experimental group have contacted their child's teacher, and together they have started an at-home program to reduce troublesome school behaviors. If there was a difference in school behavior for the kids on the diet plan, how would one know that it was not attributable to the teacher–parent collaboration? That outside influence (the teacher–parent activity) is an example of history as a threat to internal validity because the at-home program, not the diet plan, might account for any observed difference.

Maturation

Maturation can be defined as changes over time, often caused by biological or psychological forces. These changes might overshadow those that are the result of a treatment.

For example, a researcher is studying the effects of a year-long training program on increasing the strength of school-age children. At the end of the program, the researcher evaluates the children's strength and finds that the average strength score has increased over the year's time. The conclusion? The program worked. Correct? Maybe. However, as attractive as that explanation is, by the very nature of physical development, children's strength increases with age or maturation.

Selection

The basis of any experiment is the selection of subjects as participants. **Selection** is a threat to the internal validity of an experiment when the selection process is not random but instead contains a systematic bias that might make the participating groups different from each other.

For example, a researcher wants to determine how extended after-school child care affects family cohesion. As part of the experiment, the researcher forms an experimental group (those families whose children are in extended care) and a control group (those families whose children are not in extended care). Because the families were not randomly selected or randomly assigned to treatments, there is no way to tell whether they are equivalent to each other. The group of extended-care children might come from families with a positive or negative attitude toward the program before it even begins, thereby biasing the outcomes.

Testing

In many experiments, a pretest is part of the experiment. When the pretest affects performance on later measures (such as a posttest), **testing** can be a threat to internal validity.

For example, a researcher pretests a group of subjects on their eighth-grade math skills, and then teaches them (the treatment) a new way to solve simple equations. The posttest is administered, and there is an increase in the number of correct answers. Given this information, one does not know whether the increase is due to learning a new way to solve the simple equations or to the learning that might have taken place as the result of the pretest. The experience with the pretest alone might make the participants test-wise, and their performance reflects that, rather than the effectiveness of the treatment.

Instrumentation

When the scoring of an instrument itself is affected, any change in the scores might be caused by the scoring procedure, rather than the effects of the treatment.

For example, a researcher is using an essay test to judge the effectiveness of a writing skills program. There is little doubt that when he grades the 100th examination, a different set of criteria will be used than when he graded the first one. Even if the criteria do not change, simple fatigue is likely to cloud the scorer's judgment and result in differences due to **instrumentation**, not the actual effects of the program.

Regression

This is a really fascinating (and often misunderstood) threat. The world of probability is built in such a way that placement on either extreme of a continuum (such as a very high or very low score) will result in scores that regress toward the mean on subsequent testing (using the same test). In other words, when children score very high or very low on some measure, you can expect their scores on subsequent testing to move toward the mean, rather than away from it. This is true only if their original placement (in the extreme) resulted from their score on the test.

If you do not already realize it, regression occurs because of the unreliability of the test and the measurement error that is introduced, which places people more in the extremes than they probably belong. Given the lower probability that someone will end up in the extreme part of a distribution (whether high or low), the odds are greater that on additional testings, they will score in an area more central to the distribution. And for high or low scorers, moving toward the center of the distribution means moving toward the mean, which is what **regression** is all about.

For example, a teacher of children with severe physical disabilities designs a project to increase their self-care skills and pretests the group using anecdotal information compiled in September before the program begins. In June, she retests them and finds that their skills have increased. A solid argument could be made that the increase was due to regression, not to anything the teacher did; that is, children who were in the extremes to begin with (on the self-care skills test) would move toward the average score (and be less extreme) if nothing happened. The change takes place through regression alone and may have nothing to do with the treatment.

Mortality

One of the real-world issues in research is that subjects are sometimes difficult to find for **follow-up studies**. They move, refuse to participate any further, or are unavailable for other reasons. When this happens, the researcher must ask whether the composition of the group after participants dropped out is basically the same as the initial composition. **Mortality** (or attrition) is a threat to the internal validity of an experiment when the drop-outs change the nature of the group itself.

For example, research involving very young infants is fascinating but often can be frustrating. They usually arrive sleeping, or crying, or ready to eat, but rarely ready to play, and many have to be sent home and rescheduled or even dropped from the study. Those who are dropped may indeed be substantively different from those who remain, and thus the final sample of subjects may no longer be equivalent to the initial sample, which raises questions about the effectiveness of the treatment on this different sample.

Threats to External Validity

Just as there are threats to the internal validity of a design, so there are threats to a design's external validity. Once again, external validity is not concerned with whether the manipulation of the independent variable has any effect on the dependent variable (that is the province of internal validity), but whether the results of an experiment are generalizable to another setting. Threats to external validity, including definitions and examples, are discussed in the following. As with threats to internal validity, good scientists try to reduce the threat to external validity.

Multiple Treatment Interference

A set of subjects might receive an unintended treatment in addition to (hence, **multiple treatment interference**) the intended treatment, thereby decreasing the generalizability of the results to another setting where the unintended treatment may not be available.

For example, let's say that a group of nursing home residents is learning how to be more assertive, and the nursing aides pick up on the program and do a little teaching of their own. The results of the experiment would not be easily generalized to nursing home residents in another setting, and thus not generalizable, because the other settings may or may not have aides that are as industrious.

Reactive Arrangements

From 1927 through 1932, at the Cicero, Illinois Western Electric company Hawthorne plant, Elton Mayo, a Harvard business professor, measured the effects of changing certain environmental cues—lighting and working hours—on work production. The problem was that the participants in the study knew about Mayo's intent. Even when the lighting was worse and the working hours were longer, production increased for the experimental group. Why? Because the workers received special attention from the researchers, which resulted in changes in productivity; lighting and working-hour conditions were found to be secondary in importance. Unless subjects were studied within other settings (which would defeat the intent of the experiment), the external validity would be low, as would the generalizability.

Incidentally, this threat to external validity, called **reactive arrangements**, is also sometimes called, you guessed it, the **Hawthorne effect**.

Experimenter Effects

The Hawthorne effect shows how research must consider what participants know about a research experiment.

Another threat to external validity involves the researchers themselves. Imagine an experiment designed to reduce the anxiety associated with a visit to the dentist. What if the person conducting the desensitization training unintentionally winced each time the dentist's drill started. The results of such a training program cannot be generalized to another setting because another setting would require a trainer who would behave in a similar fashion. Otherwise, the nature of the experience is changed.

In other words, the training program might not be as effective without the trainer's emotional expressions, and hence the results of the training program might not be generalizable because the person conducting the training is not part of the program. In other words, **experimenter effects** might be responsible for any changes that are observed.

Pretest Sensitization

You have already seen how pretests can inform people about what is to come and thus affect their subsequent scores, thereby decreasing the internal validity of a study. In a similar fashion, the presence of a pretest can change the nature of the treatment, so that the treatment applied in another setting is less or more effective without the presence of the pretest (**pretest sensitization**). To make things equivalent and to maximize generalizability to other settings, the pretest would have to be part of the treatment, which, by definition, would change the nature of the treatment and the experiment's purpose.

Increasing Internal and External Validity

First, internal validity. It is no secret how to maximize the internal validity of an experiment: Randomly select participants from a population, randomly assign them to groups, and use a control group. In almost every design in which these characteristics are present, most threats to internal validity will be eliminated.

If you want to compensate for any threats to internal validity, use a control group and randomize, randomize, randomize.

Let's take the example of the children with severe physical disabilities and the project that begins in September to increase self-care skills. If a group that does not receive the program (the control group) is included, then the assumption is that both the control group and the experimental group will progress or regress equally, so any difference noted at the end of the year must be due to the self-care program.

Similarly, if the groups are equivalent to begin with (ensured through randomization), changes are the result of the treatment, not the lack of equivalence at the beginning of the experiment.

The inclusion of a control group and the use of randomization similarly take care of other threats, including testing, mortality, and maturation. Assuming that groups are equivalent to start with and are exposed to similar circumstances and experiences, the only differences between them would be a function of the treatment, right?

Ensuring external validity is a somewhat different story because it is more closely tied to the behavior of the people conducting the experiment, rather than to the design. For example, the only way to ensure that experimenter effects are not a threat to the external validity of the experiment is to be sure that the researcher who administers the treatment acts in a way that does not interfere with the outcome. In the example of desensitizing anxious dental patients, the trainer must not have any significant problems with the dentist's office setting.

Whereas most threats to internal validity are taken care of by the experiment's design, most threats to external validity need to be taken care of by the designer of the experiment.

Internal and External Validity: A Trade-off?

This might be a situation in which you can have your cake and eat it too, as long as you do not make a pig out of yourself! An experiment can be both internally and externally valid but with some degree of caution and balance. For example, internal validity in some ways is synonymous with control. The higher the internal validity, the more confident you can be that what you did (manipulate the independent variable) is responsible for the outcomes you observe. On the other hand, if there is too much control (such as very exacting experimental procedures with a very specifically defined sample of subjects), the results of the experiment might be difficult to generalize (hence lower external validity) to any other setting. This is true because the degree of control might be impossible to replicate, to say nothing of how difficult it might be to find a sample that is similar to the one that was originally used.

> An experiment must have both internal validity and external validity, and the two must be balanced.

The solution? Use your judgment. Strive to conduct your experiments in such a way as to ensure a moderate degree of internal validity by controlling extraneous sources of variance through randomization and a control group. The same goes for external validity. Unless you can generalize to other groups, the value of your research (depending on its purpose) may be limited.

TEST YOURSELF

In what type of experimental situation (what topics might you be investigating) internal validity is more important than external validity. How about the opposite? Keep in mind that both are always important, but there can be a slight trade-off.

Controlling Extraneous Variables

All this talk about extraneous variables! Just what are they? **Extraneous variables** are factors that can decrease the internal validity of a study. They are variables that, if not accounted for in some way, can confound the results. As you have read in this Chapter, results are confounded when you cannot separate the effects that different factors might have on some outcome. For example, a researcher is studying the effects of school breakfasts on student attendance. Parents who are more motivated might get their children to school for the breakfasts, which might make the difference between those who attend and those who do not. The breakfast, per se, might have nothing to do with any group difference. In this case, the treatment (the breakfast) is confounded with parents' motivation.

> Variables of importance cannot be ignored, even if they go directly untested.

Almost everywhere you look in experimental research there are variables that can potentially confound study results. These variables muddy the waters in a scientist's attempt to understand just what factors cause what outcomes. What is the solution to this problem? There are several. The general question becomes, "Which variables are important enough to worry about and which can be deemed unimportant?" Remember, that for any variable, it can be ignored (when it is really irrelevant), tested (when it is important and should be part of the experiment), or enrolled (when it may be important but for a variety of reasons cannot be tested).

For the variables that are of concern, what can be done to minimize the effect they might have on the outcomes of the experiment?

First, you can choose to ignore any variable that is unrelated to the dependent variable being measured. For example, if attendance is the primary dependent variable and offering school lunch is the primary independent variable, are factors such as gender of the child, gender of the teacher, class size, or parents' age important? Possibly. The only way you can tell is through a review of the literature and the development of some sound conceptual argument as to why the teacher's gender is or is not related to the child's attendance. For the most part, if you cannot make an argument for why a variable is related to the outcome you are studying, then it is probably best ignored.

Second, it is through the use of randomization that the effects of many different potential sources of variance can be controlled. Most important, randomization helps to ensure that the experimental and control groups are equivalent in a variety of different characteristics. In the example used before, randomly assigning children to the breakfast or nonbreakfast groups would ensure that parental motivation would be an equally probable influence for both groups and, therefore, it would not be a very attractive explanation for any observed difference.

Matching

In general, random assignment of subjects to groups is a good way to ensure equivalence between groups. The occasion may arise, however, when a researcher wants to make sure that the two groups are matched on a particular attribute, trait, or characteristic. For example, in the school breakfast program study, if parental influence is a concern and if the researcher does not think that random assignment will take care of the potential problem, matching is a technique that can be used.

Matching of subjects simply means that for every occurrence of an individual with a score of X in the experimental group, the researcher would make sure there is a person in the control group with a similar score. In general, the rule you want to remember is that the variable for which subjects are matched needs to be strongly related to the dependent variable of interest; otherwise, matching does not make much sense. Because this is the general rule, it comes as no surprise that the first step in the matching process is to get a measure of the variable to be matched before group assignment takes place. These scores are then ranked, and the pairs that are close together are selected. One subject from each pair is placed in each group, and the experiment continues.

What researchers are doing when they follow this strategy is stacking the cards in their favor to ensure that some important and potentially strong influences are not having an undue effect on the results of the study. Matching is a simple and effective way of ensuring this.

As you might suspect, there is a downside to matching. Matching can be expensive and time consuming, and you might not be able to find a match for all individuals. Suppose one set of parents is extremely motivated and the next most motivated set of parents is far down on the scale. Can you match those sets? It is doubtful. You would probably have to exclude the extreme scoring parents or find another with a similarly high score to whom those parents can be matched.

There's another downside as well (thanks to Amanda Blackmore, reviewer extraordinaire, for pointing this out)—when you match, you match on certain variables at the expense of establishing equivalence on others. But if you randomly assign participants to groups, and then match on groups (not variables), you have a better chance of getting equivalent groups.

Use of Homogeneous Groups

One of the best ways to ensure that extraneous variables will not be a factor is to use a homogeneous population, or one whose members are very much alike, from which to select a sample. In this way, most sources of differences (e.g., racial or ethnic backgrounds, education, political attitude) might automatically be controlled for. Once again, it is really important for the groups to be homogeneous only on those factors that might affect their scores on the dependent variable.

Analysis of Covariance

A final technique is a fairly sophisticated device called **analysis of covariance** (ANCOVA), a statistical tool that equalizes any initial differences that might exist. For example, let's say you are studying whether a specialized exercise program increases running speed. Because you know that running speed is somewhat related to strength, you want to make sure that the participants in the program are equal in strength. Let's say you try to match subjects but discover there is too wide a diversity to ensure that matching will equalize the groups. Instead, you use ANCOVA.

ANCOVA, on its simplest level, subtracts the influence of the relationship between the covariate (which in this case is strength) and the dependent variable (which in this case is speed) from the effect of one treatment. In other words, ANCOVA adjusts final speed scores to reflect where people started as far as strength is concerned. It is like playing golf with a handicap of a certain number of strokes—handicapping helps to equalize unequals. ANCOVA is an especially useful technique in quasi-experimental or causal-comparative designs when you cannot easily randomly assign people to groups, but you have information concerning variables that are related to the final outcome and on which people do differ.

Variables can play insignificant or quite major roles in experimental research. Why can't you control every variable in an experiment, and even if you could, why would that be a poor strategy?

Summary

Do you want to find out if A (almost) causes B? Experimental methods are the peaches, the max, the top of the line. They provide a degree of control that is difficult to approach by using any of the other methods discussed so far in this volume. The milestone work of Campbell and Stanley (1963) identified the various threats to these designs and provided tools to evaluate the internal validity and external validity of various pre-experimental and experimental designs. Through such techniques as matching, the use of homogeneous groups, and some statistical techniques, you can have a good deal of confidence that the difference between groups is the result of the manipulation of the independent variable, rather than some other source of differences. If cause and effect is the order of the day, you came to the right place when you read this chapter.

Exercises

1. Why can you assume the groups in a pretest posttest control group design are equivalent at the beginning of the experiment?

2. You are worried that having participants fill out a stressful life events scale might increase their stress levels by bringing attention to stressful aspects of life and therefore influence posttest scores on the scale. What research design can you use to ease your worries?

3. Give an example of a study that would be more internally valid than externally valid. Then, give an example of a study that would be more externally valid than internally valid.

4. Define each of the following threats to internal or external validity and provide an example of how each one might be a factor in an experiment.
   (a) Mortality
   (b) Instrumentation
   (c) Pretest sensitization
   (d) Reactive arrangements

5. So, this researcher is investigating the impact of singing on the language skills of young children. He takes a group of 100 children (a nice big sample, right?) and teaches them to sing when they are 3 years of age and comes back 5 years later and assesses their language skills. He cries "Eureka!" throughout his building once he analyzes the results. What's wrong here?

6. Why is a balance between external validity and internal validity necessary for acceptable research?

7. A group of children with emotional disorders is placed in a special program to improve the quality of their social interactions based on their extreme test scores. At the end of the program, the average increase in the quality of their interactions is 57%. What threat to internal validity negates the value of this finding, and what can you do to remedy the situation?

8. A physical trainer wants to compare the effects of two types of exercise programs on weight loss. He divides his clients into two groups: one focused on short-interval circuit training and one focused on a cardio warm-up followed by a free-weight workout. Without his knowledge, some of his clients have decided to cut out carbohydrates in their diet with the hope of increasing their weight loss. What type of threat to validity would the clients' diet change introduce?

9. For many standardized tests, scorers are asked to use grading rubrics to score essay sections. Which threat to validity might grading rubrics help reduce?

10. Why are the three types of randomization we mentioned at the beginning of this chapter important?

11. List the steps you would go through to ensure that two groups participating in a study of attitude toward divorce are equally matched.

12. Write an abstract that describes a study in which regression is a threat to the internal validity of the study. Be sure to describe what steps the researcher might take to account for regression as a threat.

13. What are the ethical considerations for assigning first graders to different experimental learning groups? Does it affect your ethical concerns if the assignment is random?

14. How does the inclusion of a control group help negate the potential threats that exist to the internal validity of an experiment?

15. A researcher is interested in finding out whether keeping live flowers at home affects scores on a hope scale. She divides participants into a flowers group and a no-flowers group, and she considers matching the participants in both groups based on race. Should she go ahead with the matching process? Why or why not?

16. What are some examples of pre-experimental research you see in the real world?

17. What are some benefits of using pretests?

18. If you go through all the efforts to randomize participants and groups, then why even consider using a pretest?

19. What are the threats to external validity? How could each threat affect you as a researcher? Come up with a research example for each threat to external validity. What are some methods to increase external validity?

20. What statistical technique would be helpful when you would like to equalize groups on Variable A, which is related to the dependent variable, but are unable to use the matching technique?

Online. . .

Find Out More About Experimental Design

Have even more fun (if that's possible) learning about experimental designs at http://www.itl.nist.gov/div898/handbook/pri/section3/pri3.htm.

A Glossary of Experimental Design

At http://www.stats.gla.ac.uk/steps/glossary/anova.html, Valerie J. Easton and John H. McColl bring you a concise and informative glossary of terms associated with experimental design. The experimental method is one way to determine the presence of cause-and-effect relationships.

Validity Threats and Research Design

Chong-ho Yu and Barbara Ohlund outline the important works of Campbell and Stanley (1963), Cook and Campbell (1979), and Shadish, Cook, and Campbell (2002) at http://www.creative-wisdom.com/teaching/WBI/threat.shtml. They also provide their own examples, which are helpful in showing how different designs may be vulnerable to different validity threats.

❖ ❖ ❖ Chapter 12 ❖ ❖ ❖

Quasi-Experimental Research: A Close Cousin to Experimental Research

In Chapter 11, you read about how an experimental design can be used to investigate the cause-and-effect relationship that might exist between two variables. Another type of research design also attempts to establish a cause-and-effect relationship but does not have the particular strength or power of the true experimental method. In this chapter, you will explore the quasi-experimental method as an alternative to the experimental designs about which you have already learned. Although the quasi-experimental method may not be as powerful as the true experimental method, it is the preferred (and often required) design when important cultural and ethical issues regarding design choice are introduced into the decision-making process. More about this last point in a moment.

The Quasi-Experimental Method

The quasi-experimental method differs from pre-experimental and experimental methods in one very important way. In **quasi-experimental research**, the hypothesized cause of differences you might observe between groups has already occurred. For example, if you looked at differences between males and females on verbal ability, the possible cause of differences in verbal ability (the independent variable, gender) has already "occurred." In other words, "group" assignment has already taken place. Another way to say the same thing is that in quasi-experimental designs, *preassignment to groups has already taken place.*

In the example we just gave, the researcher had no control over who would be in each group because gender is predetermined, as is age, ethnicity, eye color, and hundreds of other variables. In other words, there is a preassignment to groups based on some characteristic or experience of the group. When you use the true experimental method (as described in Chapter 11), you may have an infinite range of values of the independent variable from which to select. More important, as the researcher you assign the values of the various levels of the independent variables (such as 3, 5, or 7 hours of training each week). When you use the quasi-experimental method, you do not, nor does anyone else, have the same degree of control.

The values of the independent variable are simply there to begin with, such as in the case of gender (male, female), race (white, Asian, etc.), age

> **WHAT YOU'LL LEARN ABOUT IN THIS CHAPTER:**
>
> - The difference between experimental and causal-comparative designs
> - How quasi-experimental designs differ from pre-experimental and true experimental designs
> - How quasi-experimental designs differ from one another
> - The kinds of questions answered by developmental research
> - The advantages and disadvantages of the longitudinal and cross-sectional methods
> - The importance of age in developmental research
> - The use of single-subject designs in experiments

The quasi-experimental method does not have the same degree of power as the true experimental method

245

(under 18, 18 or over), and illness (history of heart disease, no history of heart disease).

This preassignment to groups (or treatments) introduces the major shortcoming of the quasi-experimental method compared with the classic true experimental method: less power in understanding the cause for any differences that might be observed in the dependent variable. For example, if differences are found between males and females on verbal ability, your conclusion that these differences are caused by gender differences might be correct, but conceptually the argument is left wanting. To what can this difference between the sexes be attributed? The way they were treated when younger? The experiences and opportunities they did or did not have? Hormonal differences that affect brain development? These are only three explanations that might account for the difference. To understand the nature of the differences fully, however, these other factors must be taken into consideration.

So, when does the quasi-experimental method come in handy and when is it even preferred? Despite the doubts just raised, the quasi-experimental method is essential for one reason: It allows exploration of topics that otherwise could not be investigated because of ethical, moral, and practical concerns. Look at some of the following research topics and try to think how you would understand their origins:

> The quasi-experimental method allows for the exploration of questions that otherwise could not be ethically investigated.

- Differences in the personalities of abused children compared with nonabused children
- The effects of malnutrition on infants
- The effects of maternal cocaine use during the third trimester of pregnancy on neonatal (newborn) behavior
- Differences in intellectual capacity between elderly people placed in nursing homes and those living with their spouses in their own homes

The list goes on and on. Can you spot the reason why quasi-experimental is preferred over the experimental method in these instances? All these examples include "treatments" or placement into groups that would be unethical for a researcher to arrange artificially. Placing one child in group A (which receives reading help) or group B (which does not) is one thing, but could you justify depriving a pregnant woman of sufficient nutrition to examine the effects on the child or moving an elderly person into a nursing home to determine the effects of the move on intellectual ability? Never.

Quasi-experimental studies allow us to look at the effects of such variables after the fact, which is why they are also referred to as **post hoc** (or after the fact) research.

As you shall see, quasi-experimental designs permit the random assignment of people to groups such as when you select 50 of 500 males to make up group A. You cannot, however, randomly assign "treatments" to groups (they are already assigned), which is the major shortcoming.

In terms of control and internal validity, quasi-experimental studies have a higher level of internal validity than do pre-experimental designs (which, as you remember, don't include a control group) but not as much as true experimental designs (which, you remember, have both a control group and random assignment of treatments to groups). Also, quasi-experimental designs can have substantial levels of external validity, perhaps as high as that of true experimental designs.

TEST YOURSELF

Basically, why is the quasi-experimental method of testing a hypothesis not as "true" as the true experimental method discussed earlier?

Quasi-Experimental Designs

The most desirable characteristics of any good research design are the random selection and assignment of subjects and the use of a control group. They are desirable because they ensure that groups will be equivalent to one another before the treatment is applied.

In some cases, however, randomization is simply impractical or impossible, and the use of a control group is impossible or too expensive or unreasonable. For example, you cannot randomly decide which expectant parents will have boys and which will have girls. Nor can you decide which children will attend preschool and which will not. Designs for which it is impossible to randomly assign participants to all groups are called quasi-experimental designs because they are not truly experimental. The argument for cause-and-effect relationships in quasi-experimental designs is simply not as strong as it is in true experimental designs.

In this section, you will read about some of the most commonly used quasi-experimental designs.

The Nonequivalent Control Group Design

The **nonequivalent control group design** is one of the most commonly used quasi-experimental designs, especially when it is impossible or difficult to assign subjects randomly to groups. For example, in an educational setting, children cannot be rearranged very easily into different classes, but you would like to be able to use them as part of a sample. Here's what the nonequivalent control group design looks like:

> The nonequivalent control group design is the most popular of all quasi-experimental designs.

Step 1	Step 2	Step 3	Step 4
Participants are assigned to the experimental group	A pretest is administered	A treatment is administered	A posttest is is administered
Participants are assigned to the control group	A pretest is administered	No treatment is administered	A posttest is administered

The first thing you may notice is how similar the design is to the pretest posttest control group design discussed in Chapter 11, except that there is no random selection or assignment here. The researcher uses intact groups, such as nursing home residents, a classroom of children, or factory workers. This situation immediately decreases the power of the design to establish a causal relationship because there are (always at least some) doubts about the equivalence of the groups before the experiment begins. That is why it is called a nonequivalent design.

The most serious threat to the internal validity of this design is selection because the groups might initially differ on characteristics that may be related to the dependent variable. With the inclusion of a pretest, you can compare pretest scores and determine whether the groups are equivalent. If they are (that is, if there is no significant difference between them), you should have less (but still some) concern about their equivalence. Statistically, differences can be worked with using such techniques as analysis of covariance (ANCOVA), which we discussed on page 241 in Chapter 11. But even if you can statistically equalize initial differences on the pretest, there still could be other factors (which randomization could take care of) that pose a threat to the internal validity of the experiment.

The nonequivalent control group design is the most frequently used design when randomization is not possible. It works because there is some control over the influence of extraneous variables (through the use of the control group). Some equivalence of groups, although not assured, is at least approachable.

The Static Group Comparison

What if you cannot randomize and also cannot administer a pretest? Then your choice of designs should be the **static group comparison design**, which looks like this:

Step 1	Step 3	Step 4
Participants are assigned to the experimental group	A treatment is administered	A posttest is administered
Participants are assigned to the control group	No treatment is administered	A posttest is administered

The static group comparison design is similar to the nonequivalent control group design, except there is no pretest. Under what conditions might you need the nonequivalent design? For whatever reason, there may not be time to administer a pretest, or it might be too expensive, or the sample might not be available before the treatment begins. These are just some examples where the static group comparison design might be appropriate.

Are there problems with this design? A bunch. One has little control over the major threats to internal validity, such as selection and mortality. As for external validity, all the threats (multiple treatment interference, reactive arrangements of setting, and experimenter effects) remain as well.

For example, let's say you are testing a treatment for nursing home residents to increase their social interaction. You are using three different nursing homes and have to use the same treatment (one of two treatment groups and one control group) for each of the homes. If you find a difference in social skills after the treatment, how do you know that the difference is not the result of some differences that existed before the experiment began? You do not. And because you have no pretest information, you cannot determine that either.

Why would you want to use this design? When you have no other choice—an important lesson to be learned about any of these less-than-optimal designs. They are used when circumstances prevent the use of true experimental designs, and the results of such experiments are interpreted within the framework of those limitations.

Single-Subject Design

Single-subject designs allow for an in-depth examination of specific behaviors.

The experimental method, as described throughout Chapter 11, is the most common way of testing whether cause-and-effect relationships exist; however, it is not the only way.

There is an entirely different approach to understanding causal relationships that looks at individuals rather than groups. **Single-subject research designs** are quite common to such fields as behavioral analysis and special education, but they are also useful in almost any setting in which a researcher wants to know the effects of manipulating an independent variable on the behavior of one individual. In fact, it is safe to say that, whereas group designs (such as those discussed by Campbell & Stanley,

1963) focus on one or more behaviors across many individuals, single-subject designs focus on one individual across many behaviors (of a similar type). The goal, however, is the same: to determine the effects of an independent variable on behavior.

It is not just the method that is different here but the entire view of behavior and what aspects are important to examine when conducting research. Single-subject design is very much rooted in the behavioral view of development, wherein changes in behavior are seen as a function of its consequences. This school of thought, popularized by the animal studies of B. F. Skinner, has helped provide substance to an entirely different view about the ways of behavior as well as the way in which behavior should be studied. No better or worse than the group method, the single-subject method goes about answering the important question of causality in a unique and creative fashion.

The method has been so creative that it has been successfully applied to other settings such as special education where the behavior of unique children is studied. Because these children's behaviors are unique and outside the bounds of "normal," it would be impossible to constitute a group of 30 or more where inference might play a role. Instead, the individual behaviors are examined, and the same objective rigor is applied—a different set of tools is used.

The basic method in a single-subject experiment is

1. To measure a behavior before the treatment
2. To apply a treatment
3. To withdraw the treatment (called a reversal)

The assumption is that if the behavior changes as a result of the treatment, when the treatment is withdrawn, the behavior will return to pretreatment levels. Therefore, if a researcher were interested in decreasing the level of verbal behavior of a particularly loud, outspoken child in a class, the researcher would do the following:

1. Measure the rate of verbal behavior every 5 minutes each hour for a period of 10 days. The researcher assumes this measurement scheme will result in a representative sampling of the child's verbal behavior. This first step is called the **baseline** because it is this measure against which the researcher will compare the results of the treatment to determine whether the verbal behavior increases.
2. Implement the treatment. Each time the child exhibits some inappropriate verbal behavior it is ignored, and strong verbal praise is offered when appropriate verbal behavior is demonstrated. Over a period of 10 days, the same type of record is kept.
3. As a final test of the efficacy of the treatment, the level of praise is increased for any verbal behavior, and the verbal behavior is once again measured.

A graph of what this experimental design might look like is shown in Figure 12.1. You can see that the frequency of the undesirable behavior decreased when the treatment was applied and that it increased when the treatment was withdrawn.

In single-subject design terminology, the baseline is labeled A and the treatment B. In the previous example, the design would be an ABA design. As you might expect, a whole variety of designs use the A and B conditions, such as the simplest AB design in which a baseline is established and a treatment is implemented. Then there is a set of ABAB designs in which there are alternating baseline and treatment conditions as well.

The primary advantage of the ABAB design over the AB and the ABA designs is that the former reduces concern about the ethical issue of introducing what is a potential correcting treatment (B) and then measuring only the effects of the withdrawal of the treatment. The ABAB design seeks to reintroduce the treatment and get the behavior back to where it was as the result of the first attempt at applying the treatment.

For example, if the child who had a low rate of appropriate verbal behavior were left in that situation, some questions might be raised as to whether this was an ethical

> ABA designs allow for the reapplication and testing of a potentially effective treatment.

Figure 12.1 A simple ABA design wherein a baseline is established, a treatment is applied, and then the treatment is withdrawn to observe if any effect has occurred.

decision. When it is easy to use an ABAB design and once again show the effectiveness of a treatment, why not make that choice and use that design?

Whether it's ABA or ABAB, single-subject design researchers have to be sure that the behavior they are focusing on is very well defined in operational terms (otherwise how could one effectively measure it), that the observers are well trained and inter-rater reliability is high, and most important, that the difference between conditions has practical application (such as showing that levels of aggression can be reduced).

Multiple Baseline Designs

If you've been paying attention (which we are sure you have), you might recognize a fundamental problem with any single-subject design: there is only one test of the effectiveness of the treatment. So many of the same threats to the internal validity of experimental and quasi-experimental designs remain threats.

That's where the multiple baseline design comes in very handy. In a multiple baseline design, two behaviors, two subjects, or two occasions are selected for study and a treatment is applied to only one of them. This is a variation on the ABA design. In this way, the behavior, participant, or situations in which a treatment is not present serves as a baseline against which the effects of the treatment can be determined. The second baseline is like a "control" baseline.

In the following example, two different individuals are being observed with the same behavioral goal. Let's say we are trying to reduce aggressive behavior in two children. Here's what we would do (as shown in Figure 12.2):

1. Chart the baseline rates for aggression in both participants (we'll call them Lew and Ron).
2. Apply the treatment (using a clear consequence, such as time-outs) to Lew.
3. Record the effectiveness of the treatment for Lew. If the treatment is effective, we go to the next step; otherwise, the study is stopped and a new treatment is considered.
4. Apply the same treatment to Ron, with the same consequence.
5. Record the effectiveness of the treatment for Ron.

The important comparison comes between Lew and Ron, when only one of them (Lew) is getting the treatment and the other (Ron) is not. You can see in Figure 12.2, the

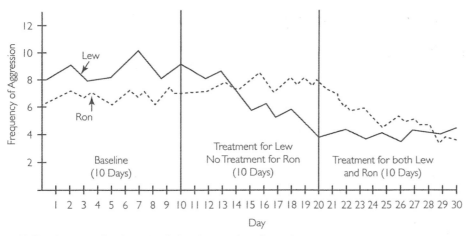

Figure 12.2 An example of a multiple baseline single-subject design.

treatment worked. Ron's level of aggression stays constant while not being treated, while Lew's decreases. Then, when Ron's aggression is treated, it decreases as Lew's continues to level out with treatment.

TEST YOURSELF

Single-subject designs are not just "another way to answer a question." They, indeed, depend upon the very rationale for asking the question in the first place. What is this rationale?

Evaluating Single-Subject Designs

You can apply the same criteria of internal and external validity as measures of the trustworthiness to single-subject designs as you did to other designs.

Most single-subject designs of the ABA and ABAB types have sufficient internal validity. They demonstrate that, by the manipulation of the independent variable (its presentation or withdrawal), a behavior will or will not change. Thus, what one observes is the result of what one did, which is the primary criterion for internal validity to be present.

External validity, or generalizability, is another story. Some critics of single-subject designs would claim that such experiments have limited generalizability because you cannot generalize beyond the results of a single subject. As you might expect, those critics are usually the ones who use the traditional group designs, which reflect a different view of how questions are formed. What these critics overlook is that traditional group designs also have problems with generalizability. In particular, many experiments do not have random assignment of groups, and their generalizability to another setting is often a bit of a stretch and a small leap of faith.

You can increase generalizability (external validity) by eliminating the threats discussed earlier in this chapter and by making your experiment as "naturally" occurring as possible, so that the results can easily be applied to another setting. The way in which the results of a single-subject design can be generalized depends on the extent to which the results of a single-subject experiment can be replicated, given identical or slightly varied conditions. For example, if the girl in our experiment were in fourth grade, would a single-subject experiment with a fifth grader and the same exact procedures increase the generalizability of the results so that one could talk about the independent variable and the experiment as having external validity? Probably so. And the greater the number of replications of varying kinds, the greater the external validity.

Developmental methods
examine changes over
time.

Developmental Research

The province of the developmental psychologist (and of many educators, pediatricians, anthropologists, and others) is to understand changes that occur throughout the process of development from conception through death. Two basic developmental research methods have evolved over the past 100 years to describe changes or differences in behavior within a framework of different ages or stages across the life span. In our discussion, we're considering age to be the independent variable and the assignment of people to age groups to be predetermined; hence, these are quasi-experimental in nature.

Let's take a look at each type, discuss an example, and then talk about the relative advantages and disadvantages of each type.

The Longitudinal Method

Longitudinal studies
examine age changes.

The **longitudinal method** assesses changes in behavior in one group of subjects at more than one point in time. In other words, if you were to test a group of 30-year-olds in 1960, then test the same group again in 1965 (when they were 35 years old) and again in 1970 (when they were 40 years old), and so on (as shown in Figure 12.3), you would be conducting a longitudinal study. The dashed line in Figure 12.3 illustrates the design for a longitudinal study in which the same group of study participants born in 1930 is tested five successive times at 5-year intervals.

Longitudinal studies are conducted to examine age changes over an extended period of time. For example, J. L. Singer, D. G. Singer, and W. Rapaczynski (1984) conducted a longitudinal study of television, imagination, and aggression. The purpose of the study was to examine television viewing within a family setting and the influences that such viewing might have on the social interaction patterns of the family.

The study tested various groups (or waves) of children from 1977 through 1982, with a final group of 84 children available at the end of the experiment. Parents were asked to keep a daily log of their children's television viewing, and researchers interviewed parents, analyzed school reports and measures of intelligence, interviewed the children, and obtained other information.

There are clear advantages to the longitudinal method. Most important, it allows for the study of development over an extended period of time. What is more, because the same people are studied at more than one point in time, the subjects act as their own controls. In other words, each person always brings the same (his or her own) background (genetic, ethnic, or otherwise) and experiences to the testing situation. This type of design is very powerful because intra-individual variability is minimized.

		Year of Testing				
		1960	1965	1970	1975	1980
	1940	20	25	30	35	40
	1935	25	30	35	40	45
Year of Birth	**1930**	30	35	40	45	50
	1925	35	40	45	50	55
	1920	40	45	50	55	60

Figure 12.3 The basic layout for a longitudinal and a cross-sectional developmental design indicating when participants are born, the years they are tested, and their age. Note: Age appears in italics.

There are some significant disadvantages as well. First, these types of studies are very expensive to conduct. Not only is it costly to keep track of people over a long period of time, but staff and overhead costs also increase from year to year. That is one reason why relatively few longitudinal designs are currently initiated, compared with many years ago when some of the classics began. One such study, the Terman study of gifted children, began in the 1920s and continues today (and costs lots of $$$).

Another disadvantage of longitudinal designs is that people drop out of experiments (often called mortality). Although you might assume that this dropout rate is random, there is often some concern that the dropout is systematic, which means that a particular type of person might drop out, thereby leaving the remaining sample substantively different in characteristics and qualities from the original sample. For example, the subgroup in the United States that moves most often is low-income families. When members of low-income families withdraw from an experiment, it skews the characteristics of the group.

The Cross-Sectional Method

Whereas the longitudinal method examines one group of people repeatedly over time, the **cross-sectional method** examines several groups of people at one point in time. In other words (see the solid line in Figure 12.3), if you examined age differences in 30-, 35-, 40-, 45-, and 50-year-olds (all born in different years) in the year 1970, you would be conducting a cross-sectional study. The cross-sectional method is used to examine age differences rather than age changes, as is done using the longitudinal method.

For example, to find out whom children of different ages ask for different types of advice when confronted with different types of problems, M. G. Wintre, R. Hocks, G. McVey, and J. Fox (1988) used the cross-sectional method. The study involved 48 subjects—24 males and 24 females aged 8, 11, 14, and 17 years—who were presented with three hypothetical problems. Researchers asked the children to select a familiar adult, an adult expert, a familiar peer, or a peer expert as a consultant. In this study, the researchers were examining age differences (not changes), and by selecting different age groups and evaluating their responses at the same point in time, the researchers' goal was accomplished.

As with the longitudinal approach, the cross-sectional approach has its advantages and disadvantages. One advantage is that this approach is much less expensive to conduct than the longitudinal method because testing takes place over a limited time period. Because the time period for testing is short, dropout is minimized. People tend to be located in the same place for a sufficient amount of time to complete this type of project. The disadvantages? The most serious is the lack of comparability of groups because the only thing they differ on is age. And as you will see in a moment, age is not a very useful independent variable.

Table 12.1 shows you a comparison of the advantages and disadvantages of longitudinal and cross-sectional research strategies.

> Cross-sectional studies examine age differences

TEST YOURSELF

How is confounding a serious problem in both longitudinal and cross-sectional studies and what can one do to avoid this problem?

The Utility of Follow-up Studies

The information in Table 12.1 gives you a pretty good idea as to the benefits and shortcomings of the longitudinal and cross-sectional methods. The decision as to which one you should use depends on such factors as available resources, time constraints, and, of course, the question you are asking.

> Follow-up studies can help answer developmental questions with less time and expense than a traditional longitudinal study.

Research Strategy	Advantages	Disadvantages
Cross-sectional method	• Inexpensive • Short time span • Low dropout rate • Requires no long-term administration or cooperation between staff and participants	• Limits comparability of groups • Gives no idea as to the direction of change that a group might take • Examines people of the same chronological age who may be of different maturational levels • Reveals nothing about the continuity of development on an individual basis
Longitudinal method	• Reveals extensive detail in the process of development • High comparability of (the same) groups • Allows for the study of continuity between widely differing groups • Allows for modified cause-and-effect speculation about the relationship between variables • High comparability of groups	• Expensive • Potential for high dropout rate

Table 12.1 Advantages and disadvantages of longitudinal and cross-sectional developmental designs

It is usually impractical for any type of longitudinal study to be completed as part of your undergraduate and graduate school experience because the time span for collection of data is usually too long. However, follow-up studies are highly feasible because data that have already been collected can be used as a basis for collecting additional data. In fact, this is a great way to get a potentially significant longitudinal study accomplished in a relatively short amount of time.

For example, look at H. M. Skeels' (1942) classic study of 25 infants reared in an orphanage where they received good basic care but very little human attention and affection. Thirteen of these infants were transferred from the orphanage to an institution for mentally retarded women, where the children were "adopted" by the women. He found that the children who were reared in the institution for women and received stimulation scored 28 points higher on IQ tests than did those children who were left in the orphanage. In a follow-up study (Skeels, 1966) 21 years later, Skeels examined whether there were any long-lasting effects of the different care that the groups of children had received. Much to his delight, he found that all 13 infants who had been part of the experimental group (those who had been transferred) were self-supporting, 11 were married, and 9 of those had children. Sadly, one-third of those children who did not receive any special experiences were still in institutions as adults, and only a few of the children who had remained in the orphanage were leading normal adult lives. Skeels did not follow these subjects throughout their lives, but he did conduct a follow-up study which provided information of a longitudinal nature.

The Role of Age in Studying Development

Age describes the process of development but does not do a very good job of explaining it.

Age is a tricky variable and one that people become very dependent on to help "explain" changes observed in a large variety of human behaviors. For example, although it might be convenient to describe changes in the way children use words at different ages as a function of age, it is probably more accurate if these changes are understood in terms of changes in cognitive complexity, experience, and the ability to manipulate symbols.

In other words, age has *descriptive* value but not necessarily any *explanatory* value. Although age can describe what is happening, age alone cannot tell us why. Donald Baer (1970) summarized this observation in a very persuasive article, "An Age Irrelevant Concept of Development." In this article, he argues that experience, not age, is the driving force behind the differences observed in development, and that studying these experiences is much more fruitful than studying behavior as a function of chronological or maturational age.

These observations and general concerns about the utility of age have led to additional types of developmental designs other than the longitudinal and cross-sectional methods just described. Some of these new techniques take into account such variables as when the behavior is measured (known as measurement effects) and cohort (or group) effects.

Take a basic cross-sectional study that examines groups of people born in different years who are tested on the same date. If you find differences between the groups (or age differences), how do you know that the differences are not due to the year in which they were born rather than their age? How could birth date contribute to such differences? Easy. What if one group of people was born before the discovery of a drug or technique or even a cultural event that makes learning easier or harder?

Take, for example, children born before and after *Sesame Street*, the intensive, preparatory cognitive enrichment program broadcast on public television. Watching that program might very well have an impact on language skills. In this case, cohort (year of birth) and age may be confounded (a great word!). Confounding occurs when two variables (such as date of birth and age) explain the same thing (differences in language skills), and you cannot separate the effects of the two.

Another example of confounding occurred with age and the time that the measurement took place in a study conducted by J. R. Nesselroade and Paul Baltes (1974). They examined personality changes in adolescence and found age-related declines in measures of superego strength, anxiety, and achievement. One might want to attribute those changes to age, but these scientists also found that, regardless of the child's age over the 3-year examination period (some went from 13 to 15 years, whereas others went from 16 to 18 years), the decline in scores was the same. The change in age evidently was irrelevant. What was relevant, however, was the "cultural moment" when the behaviors were assessed. This is an example of a historical influence. Whatever was going on during the time of testing seemed to affect children's scores regardless of their age.

Although developmental studies that use maturational or chronological age as the major dependent variable can do a good job of describing change over time, be cautious that other factors, such as those pointed out in the Nesselroade and Baltes study, are not attractive as sources of explanation.

Test Yourself

"Age correlates with everything and explains nothing." What are the implications of using age as an independent variable in light of this comment and what is one remedy?   .

Summary

This is the last chapter in the book that will discuss different types of experimental design. Now that you have the basics about how to design and carry out an experiment, the most important next step is learning about how to share the results of all your hard work. To do this, we turn to Chapters 13 and 14, which cover writing a research proposal and writing a research report.

Exercises

1. What is the primary difference between a quasi-experimental and a true experimental design and why would you use which and when?

2. Single-subject research is quite different from group experimental research. How do they differ, and under what conditions would you choose to use a single-subject design?

3. When are quasi-experimental studies appropriate?

4. Which of the following independent variables are appropriate for a quasi-experimental design and why?
   Blood type
   Reading group
   Level of abuse
   Math strategy
   Deprivation of food

5. In what way does quasi-experimental design differ from experimental design?

6. What are some examples of quasi-experimental research questions?

7. Rank these designs in order of level of internal validity, from lowest to highest:
   (a) pre-experimental design
   (b) true experimental design
   (c) quasi-experimental design

8. What is the difference between a nonequivalent control group design and a pretest posttest control group design?

9. Give an example of an ABAB single-subject design. What is an advantage to using ABAB over ABA or AB designs?

10. Propose a longitudinal study and a cross-sectional design being sure to identify the independent and dependent variables and discuss how you might be able to avoid the confounding that results from the presence of age in these quasi-experimental designs.

11. Here's a statement of the results of an experiment. "As the sample got older, from 50 to 70 years, lung volume decreased." Although this statement might be true, what might be one interpretation, given what you know of the use of age as an independent variable?

12. Find a journal article of a longitudinal study and outline the abstract. How could you change this study to a cross-sectional one?

13. Cohort effects are a threat to validity in which design: longitudinal or cross-sectional?

Online. . .

Real live case study reports of one study describing the treatment of dyslexic children can be found at http://www.readingsuccesslab.com/CaseStudies/.

Find out more about different types of single-subject designs and their evaluation at http://www.msu.edu/user/sw/ssd/issd01.htm, a site brought to us by Dr. Time Stocks.

Database of Longitudinal Studies

The National Institute on Aging has compiled a database of longitudinal studies available for viewing at http://www.nia.nih.gov/ResearchInformation/ScientificResources/LongitudinalStudies.htm

❖ ❖ ❖ Chapter 13 ❖ ❖ ❖
Writing a Research Proposal

If one of the requirements for this class is to write a research proposal, then you have come to the right place. This chapter will lead you through the process you need to take to write a research proposal. Even if you are not required to write a proposal for class, stick around anyway. What you learn here will be helpful in your research endeavors. You will learn what distinguishes acceptable proposals from unacceptable ones. You will also learn the importance of framing a question in a clear, logical manner so that it is easier to answer. In Chapter 3, there was a ton of information about reviewing the literature—both on and off line—an important part of preparing any research proposal. If you need to, review that now.

Writing a proposal is not an easy task for anyone, and it may be especially difficult if you have not written one before or if you have not done much writing. The job takes diligence, commitment, and hard work, but all the hard work is well worth it. You will end up with a product of which you can be proud, and that is only the beginning. If you actually follow through and complete the proposed research, you will be making a significant contribution to your field. With these words of encouragement, the following are the major steps to follow in the writing of a proposal, beginning with what a proposal looks like.

WHAT YOU'LL LEARN ABOUT IN THIS CHAPTER:

- Only one thing—How to write a proposal!

The Format of a Research Proposal

Knowing how to organize and present a proposal is an important part of the research craft. The very act of putting thoughts down on paper will help you clarify your research interests and ensure that you are saying what you mean. Remember the fellow on the television commercial who said, "Pay me now or pay me later"? The more work and thought you put into your proposal, the easier it will be to complete the research later. In fact, many supervising faculty suggest that a proposal's first two or three chapters be actually the same as the entire finished thesis or dissertation—putting you way ahead of the game.

The following is a basic outline of what should be contained in a research proposal and a few comments on each of these sections. Keep in mind that proposals can be organized differently and, whatever you do, be sure that your professor approves of your outline before you start writing.

    I. Introduction
       A. Problem statement
       B. Rationale for the research
          1. Statement of the research objectives
       C. Hypothesis
       D. Definitions of terms
       E. Summary, including a restatement of the problem
   II. Review of the relevant literature (the more complete it is, the better)
       A. Importance of the question being asked
       B. Current status of the topic
       C. Relationship between the literature and the problem statement
       D. Summary, including a restatement of the relationships between the important variables under consideration and how these relationships are important to the hypothesis proposed in the introduction
  III. Method
       A. Participants (including a description and selection procedures)
       B. Research design
       C. Data collection plans
          1. Operational definition of all variables
          2. Reliability and validity of instruments
          3. Results of pilot studies
       D. Proposed analysis of the data
       E. Results of the data
  IV. Implications and limitations
   V. Appendices
       A. Copies of instruments that will be used
       B. Results of pilot studies (actual data)
       C. IRB (Institutional Review Board) application and letter of approval
       D. Participant permission form
       E. Time line
       F. Actual data collected

If you have looked at someone else's thesis or dissertation, you might notice that this outline is organized around the same general sequence of chapter titles—introduction, review of literature, methodology, results, and discussion. Because this is only a proposal, the last two sections cannot present the analysis of the real data or discuss the findings. Instead, the proposal simply talks about the implications and limitations of the study, and the last part (V) contains all the important appendices.

The first three sections of the finished proposal form a guideline about what the proposal should contain: introduction, review of literature, and method. The rest of the material (implications and such) should be included at your own discretion and based on the wishes of your adviser or professor. Keep in mind that completing the first three sections is a lot of work. However, you will have to gather that information anyway, and doing it before you collect your data will give you more confidence in conducting your research as well as a very good start and a terrific road map as to where you are going with your research.

Appearance

Although the words in your proposal are important, the appearance of your proposal is also important. What you say is more important than how you say it, but there is a good deal of truth to Marshall McLuhan's statement that the medium is the message.

Here are some simple, straightforward tips about proposal preparation. If you have any doubts about presentation (and if you don't have any other class guidelines), follow the guidelines set forth in the sixth edition of the *Publication Manual of American Psychological Association* (APA, 2009), which is discussed and illustrated in Chapter 14.

- All pages should be typed with at least 1-inch margins on top, bottom, left, and right to allow sufficient room for comments.
- All pages should be double-spaced.
- All written materials should be proofread. This does not mean just using a spell checker. These marvels check only your typing skills (to, two, or too?), not your spelling or grammar. So, proofread your paper twice—once for content and once for spelling and grammatical errors. And, it would not be a bad idea to ask a fellow student to read it once.
- The final document should be paper clipped or stapled together, with no fancy covers or bindings (too expensive and unnecessary).
- All pages should be numbered with a running head (all of which is right justified) and a page number like this

Cognitive Style and Gender Differences/Salkind   15

As for the format of the contents, you cannot go wrong if you follow the example given in Chapter 14, which is written using the APA guidelines for manuscript presentation. There are some differences between what you are reading here and what you will see in Chapter 14, but nothing major. For example, APA guidelines do not require the author's name on each page because the review for journals is "blind." Your professor, however, needs your name on each page.

Evaluating the Studies You Read

When you begin to go through research articles in preparation for writing a proposal (or just to learn more about the research process), you want to be sure that you can read, understand, and evaluate the content.

As a beginning researcher, you might not be ready to take on the "experts" and start evaluating and criticizing the work of well-known researchers, right? Wrong! Even if you are relatively naive and inexperienced about the research process, you can still read and critically evaluate research articles. Even the most sophisticated research should be written in a way that is clear and understandable. Finally, even if you cannot answer all the questions listed below to your satisfaction at this point, they provide a great starting place for learning more. As you gain more experience, the answers will appear.

So what makes good research? B. W. Hall, A. W. Ward, and C. B. Comer (1988) asked that very question about 128 published research articles. Among a survey of research experts, they found the following shortcomings (in order of appearance) to be the most pressing criticisms. Even though this article is almost 16 years old, the findings are still relevant to *any* proposal.

- The data collection procedure was not carefully controlled.
- There were weaknesses in the design or plan of the research.
- The limitations of the study were not stated.
- The research design did not address the question being asked by the researcher(s).

- The method of selecting participants was not appropriate.
- The results of the study were not clearly presented.
- The wrong methods were used to analyze the information collected.
- The article was not clearly written.
- The assumptions on which the study was based were unclear.
- The methods used to conduct the study were not clearly described or not described at all.

This is quite a series of pitfalls. To help you avoid the worst of them, you might want to ask the following set of questions about any research article.

Criteria for Judging a Research Study

Review of Previous Research

1. How closely is the literature reviewed in the study related to previous literature?
2. Is the review recent? Are there any outstanding references you know about that were left out?

Problem and the Purpose

3. Can you understand the statement of the problem?
4. Is the purpose of the study clearly stated?
5. Does the purpose seem to be tied to the literature that is reviewed?
6. Is the objective of the study clearly stated?
7. Is there a conceptual rationale to which the hypotheses are grounded?
8. Is there a rationale for why the study is an important one to do?

Hypotheses

9. Are the research hypotheses clearly stated?
10. Are the research hypotheses explicitly stated?
11. Do the hypotheses state a clear association between variables?
12. Are the hypotheses grounded in theory or in a review and presentation of relevant literature?
13. Are the hypotheses testable?

Method

14. Are the independent and dependent variables clearly defined?
15. Are the definition and description of the variables complete?
16. Is it clear how the study was conducted?

Sample

17. Was the sample selected in such a way that you think it is representative of the population?
18. Is it clear where the sample came from and how it was selected?
19. How similar are the subjects in the study to those that have been used in other similar studies?

Results and Discussion

20. Does the author relate the results to the review of the literature?
21. Are the results related to the hypotheses?

22. Is the discussion of the results consistent with the results?
23. Does the discussion provide closure to the initial hypotheses presented by the author?

References

24. Is the list of references current?
25. Are the references consistent in their format?
26. Are the references complete?
27. Does the list of references reflect some of the most important reference sources in the field?
28. Does each reference cited in the body of the paper appear in the reference list?

General Comments About the Report

29. Is the report clearly written and understandable?
30. Is the language unbiased (nonsexist and relatively culture free)?
31. What are the strengths and weaknesses of the research?
32. What are the primary implications of the research?
33. What would you do to improve the research?

In my class, students are required to answer all 33 of these questions for a research article that reports about an experimental study in their discipline.

Planning the Actual Research

You are well on your way to formulating good, workable hypotheses, and you now know at least how to start reviewing the literature and making sense out of the hundreds of available resources. But what you may not know, especially if you have never participated in any kind of research endeavor, is how much time it will take you to progress from your very first visit to the library to your final examination or submission of the finished research report. That is what you will learn here.

Although you still have plenty to learn about the research process, now is a good time to get a feel for the other activities you will have to undertake in order to complete your research project. It is also helpful to get a sense of how much time these activities might take.

First the activities. Table 13.1 shows an example of a checklist of activities you probably need to complete in order to complete your proposal (or research). The activities are grouped by the general headings previously discussed.

Now for computing how much time the process will take. One effective way to do this is to estimate how much time each individual activity (writing the literature review, collecting data, etc.) will require, using some standard measure, such as days, keeping in mind that sometimes things go

- Just as planned
- Not as well as planned
- Not well at all (which usually is the rule, rather than the exception).

Now take the average of these values. To be more precise, let's break workdays into 4-hour chunks (for morning and evening) and call each chunk one unit of time. There are then 10 units of time in 1 week. If you enter Table 13.1 as a spreadsheet (using a program such as Excel), you can easily sum the columns as you fiddle and tinker with the amount of necessary time.

	Activity	Time Estimates		
		When Things Go Just as Planned	When Things Don't Go Exactly as Planned	When Things Don't Go Well at All
Introduction	• Search general sources and come up with an idea	_____	_____	_____
	• Formulate a research question	_____	_____	_____
	• Present a preliminary hypothesis	_____	_____	_____
Review of the Literature	• Search through secondary sources	_____	_____	_____
	• Search through primary sources	_____	_____	_____
	• Reconsider the literature and state the research hypothesis	_____	_____	_____
Methodology	• Identify and describe the dependent variables	_____	_____	_____
	• Identify and describe the independent variables	_____	_____	_____
	• Field test the dependent variables	_____	_____	_____
	• Create data entry forms	_____	_____	_____
	• Locate a suitable sample	_____	_____	_____
	• Pilot test the research hypothesis	_____	_____	_____
	• Distribute permission forms	_____	_____	_____
	• Collect data	_____	_____	_____
Results	• Analyze the data	_____	_____	_____
	• Report the results accompanied by tables and graphs, if useful	_____	_____	_____
Discussion	• Review the nature and purpose of the research	_____	_____	_____
	• Refer to the results in light of the question being asked	_____	_____	_____
	• Draw the appropriate conclusions about the confirmation or refutation of the research hypothesis	_____	_____	_____
	• Discuss the limitations of the study	_____	_____	_____
	• Discuss the implications of the study	_____	_____	_____
	• Discuss topics and directions for future research	_____	_____	_____

Table 13.1   A checklist of activities to help you complete your proposal or research

For example, let's look at a search through primary sources (as part of the literature review) and estimate that it will take you

- Four days, or 8 time units, if things go great
- Six days, or 12 units, if things do not go exactly as planned
- A whopping 8 days, or 16 units, if things do not go well at all

Once you have these estimates, average them for the activity, and you will have a singular estimate of how long any one activity should take, such as,

$$\frac{(8 + 12 + 16)}{3} = 12 \text{ units}$$

or 6 days, which is about one very full week's work (if you work on Saturday or Sunday).

If you want to be even more precise, weight the estimates. For example, let's say that you anticipate having trouble finding a sample, and at best you can expect things to go only okay. Writing the descriptive section, though, should be a snap. You should weight the "not as well as planned" estimate two or three times greater than the others.

These estimates can be computed for all the activities you see in Table 13.1 and then summed to get an estimate for the overall activity. Keep in mind that everything takes longer than you initially think, so be generous, even for your most optimistic estimate.

Selecting a Dependent Variable

You have read at several places in this volume how important it is to select a dependent variable or an outcome measure with a great deal of care. It is the link between all the hard preparation and thinking you have done and the actual behavior you want to measure. Even if you have a terrific idea for a research project and your hypothesis is right on target, a poorly chosen dependent variable will result in disaster.

The following nine items are important to remember when selecting such a variable. Use the following as a checklist when you search through previous studies to find what you need.

- Try to find measures that have been used before. This gives them credibility and allows you to support your choice by citing previous use in other research studies.
- Ensure that the validity of the measure has been established. Simply put, don't select dependent variables whose validity either has not yet been established or is low. Doing so will raise too many questions about the integrity of your entire study. Remember, you can find out if a test has been shown to be valid through a review of other studies where the test has been used or through an examination of any manuals that accompany the test or assessment tool.
- Ensure that the reliability of the measure has been established. As with validity, reliability is a crucial characteristic of a useful dependent variable.
- If the test requires special training, consider the time and the commitment it will take to learn how to use it. This does not mean simply reading the instructions and practicing the administration of a test. It means undergoing intense training such as that required for the administration of intelligence tests and several personality scales.
- Be sure you can get a sample of the test before you make any decision about whether you will use it. You might have read about it in a previous study, but you should not make a final decision until you examine its guidelines on the intended testing population, requirements for administration, costs, and so on. You can usually get a

sample packet either at no cost or at a minimal cost from the test developer or publisher (although you may need a letter from your adviser because several test companies will not send materials to just anyone who requests it).

- If you will need them, be sure that norms are available. Some tests do not require the use of norms, but if your intention is to compare the performance of different samples with scores from a more general population, you must have something to compare it with. As you will see later, norms are especially important for norm-referenced tests.

- Obtain the latest version of the test. Publishers are always changing test materials, whether it is a repackaging of the materials or a change in the actual normative or reliability and validity data. Just ask the simple question, "Is this the latest version available?"

- The test needs to be appropriate for the age group with which you are working. If a test measures something at age 10, it does not mean it will be equally reliable and valid at age 20, or even that it will measure the same underlying construct or behavior at that age. Look for other forms of the same test or another test that measures the same construct for the intended age group.

- Finally, look for reviews of the test in various journals and reference sources, such as at the Buros Institute (www.unl.edu/buros), which lists thousands of tests on just about everything, and the *Mental Measurement Yearbook* (14th ed.), which is also published by the Buros Institute. Both these publications contain extensive information about different types of tests including administration procedures, costs, critical reviews of the tests by outside experts, and so on. Examine these critical reviews before you decide to adopt an instrument.

Reviewing a Test

What follows is more about selecting dependent variables (or screening measures for assignment to groups as independent variables). At best, with all things going in your favor, it is difficult to find exactly the test you want to use to diagnose, evaluate, determine effects, use as a placement tool, and so on. The dependent variable you select may not even be a test in the formal sense of the word. But if it is, you need to be concerned about many different characteristics and qualities of the instrument.

With that in mind, the following outline of criteria will help you compare and contrast various tests. For each test you want to consider, complete the outline to the extent possible and then use this information to make a decision. Be sure to weigh each of the criteria accordingly. For example, although a test might be appropriate as far as its design and purpose, if it is prohibitively expensive or requires special training (which you do not have) to administer it, it is not likely that you will be able to use it.

Basic Information

1. Name of the test
2. Date of publication
3. Test author(s)
4. Publisher
5. Cost of all needed test materials
6. Cost of sample packet

General Test Information

7. Purpose of the test as stated by author(s)
8. Purpose of the test as used in other studies
9. Age levels included
10. Grades included
11. Special populations included
12. Method of administration (individual or group)
13. Method of scoring (manual or computer)
14. Amount of time required for administration
15. Ease of administration
16. Ease of scoring
17. Amount of training required for administration
18. Adequacy of test manual and other materials

Design and Appearance

19. Clear and straightforward directions
20. Design and production satisfactory
21. Arrangement of items on page
22. Ease of reading

Reliability

23. Reliability data provided
24. Type of reliability established (test–retest, parallel forms, etc.)
25. Independent studies used to establish reliability

Validity

26. Validity data provided
27. Type of validity established
28. Independent studies used to establish validity

Norms

29. Norms available
30. Description of norm groups
31. How norm groups were selected
32. Appropriateness of norm groups for your purpose

Evaluation

33. How used in the past
34. Summary of outside review(s)
35. Other evaluative information

Selecting a Sample

Many researchers feel that there is nothing more important than selecting a sample that accurately reflects the characteristics of the population they are interested in studying. Yet sample selection can sometimes be a risky business, with all kinds of questions needing to be answered before you can make any moves toward the sample selection process. Here is a list of factors to keep in mind:

1. Imagine yourself trying to find a suitable pool of candidates from which to select a sample, and multiply the number of other people trying to do the same thing in your community by 100. That is a small estimate of how many people in every university community are looking for a sample to include in their study. Where can you look? Try some of the following:
   - Church and synagogue groups
   - Boy and Girl Scouts
   - Retirement homes and communities
   - Preschools
   - Singles clubs
   - Special interest and hobby groups
   - Fraternal organizations

2. Remember, you do not want to select any group that is organized for a particular reason if that reason is even remotely related to what you are studying. For example, you would not select members from the Elks Club for a study of loyalty or friendship or parents who send their kids to private schools for a survey on attitudes toward supporting public education, unless the selection of such samples is an important part of your sampling plan.

3. Approach candidates with a crystal clear idea of what you want to do, how you want to do it, and what they will get in return (a free workshop, the results of the study, or anything else you think might be of benefit to them).

Similar to the previous point, the population must match the characteristics of those groups you want to study. It might go without saying (but I'll say it here anyway), but selecting a sample from a poorly identified population is the first major error in sample selection. If you want to study preschoolers, you cannot study first graders just because the two groups are close in age. The preschool and the first-grade experience differ substantially.

The type of research you do will depend on the type and size of sample you need. For example, if you are doing case study descriptive research, which involves long, intense interviews and has limited generalizability (which is not one of the purposes of the method), you will need very few participants in your sample. If you are doing a group differences study, you will need at least 30 participants for each group.

A highly reliable test will yield more accurate results than a homemade essay exam. The less reliable and valid your instruments, the larger the sample size that will be required to get an accurate picture of what you want.

Consider the amount of financial resources at your disposal. The more money (and resources in general) you have, the more participants you can test. Remember, the larger the sample (up to a point) the better, because larger samples come closer to approximating the population of which they are a part.

The number of variables you are studying and the number of groups you are using will affect the sample selection process. If you are simply looking at the difference in verbal skills between males and females, you can get away with 25–30 participants in each group. If you add age (5- and 10-year-olds) and socioeconomic status (high and low), you are up to six different possible combinations (such as

5-year-old girls of high socioeconomic status) and up to 6×30, or 180, subjects for an adequate sample size.

Data Collection and Analysis

If you are following the steps in this chapter, you can do the following:

- Understand the format of a research proposal
- Choose a problem of some significance in your field and specify what the variables of interest (both dependent and independent) will be
- Locate measures of the dependent variable that are both reliable and valid

Now you are ready to begin the data analysis stage.

In Chapters 7 and 8, you learned how to use some basic statistical tools to describe the characteristics of the data you collect during the early stages of your research.

At this point in your proposal, you want to address the following tasks and ensure that they are completed before you continue:

1. Development of a data collection form to help you with organization and accuracy.
2. Specification of which types of descriptive statistics you will use to describe the variables you are examining. At what level of measurement do they fall, and what level of measurement—nominal, ordinal, interval, or ratio—best reflects what you are trying to say?
3. Identification of the other kinds of information you need to present in this initial analysis of what your data look like. Maybe you need demographic information, such as the gender, age, socioeconomic status, or political affiliation, of the participants. Even if this information is not directly related to the question you are asking, it does not hurt to collect it at this point. Later on you might want to go back and look at some of the other information, and you will be glad you collected it. This does not mean that the demographic questionnaire you use is 10 pages long and contains more than 1,000 questions. It means that, within reason, you collect information related to, but not directly bearing upon, your main question.
4. Pilot data collection, so that you can practice the simple descriptive and inferential statistics discussed in Chapters 7 and 8. Treat the analysis as if it were the real thing and go through every step that you plan to go through for the final data analysis. In this way, you will know exactly what you do and do not understand and can get help if necessary. Do the data analysis both by hand using the formulas in this chapter and by using SPSS, which is illustrated in Appendix A.

Selecting an Inferential Statistic

Selecting an inferential test is a task that always takes care. When you are first starting out, the choice can be downright intimidating.

You can learn about some of the most common situations, such as testing the difference between the means of two or more groups and looking at the relationships between groups. In both cases, the same principles of testing for the significance of an outcome apply.

Now, do not think for a minute that (a) you can substitute a chart like the one you saw in Chapter 8 for a basic statistics course, or that (b) this is a statistics course (and this is a statistics book). Instead, that chart you see on page 187 offers some simple help to guide you toward a correct selection. You got a little bit of the why of inference in Chapter 8, but to get all of the why, enroll in that Statistics 1 class and make your adviser (and parents) happy.

Protecting Human Subjects

As you learned in Chapter 2, most organizations that sponsor research (such as universities) have some kind of committee that regularly reviews research proposals to ensure that humans (and animals) are not in any danger should they participate.

Before investigators begin their work, and as part of the proposal process, an informed consent form is completed and attached to the proposal. The committee reviews the information and either approves the project (and indicates that human subjects are not in danger) or tries its best to work with the investigator to change the proposed methods so that things proceed as planned.

Summary

When it comes time to write a proposal, here is the quote you want to paste over your desk:

> Pay me now or pay me later.

And that is the truth. Successful scientists will tell you that if you start out with a clear, well-thought-out question, the rest of your proposal, as well as the execution of your research, will fall into place. On the other hand, if your initial question is unclear, you will find yourself floundering and unable to focus on the real issue. Work on writing your proposal every day, read it over, let it sit for a while, have a friend or colleague glance at it and offer suggestions, write some more, let it sit some more. Get the message? Practice and work hard, and you will be well rewarded.

Exercises

1. Develop a demographic questionnaire with 6–8 items related to demographic variables. Be sure to include answer choices for categorical variables.

2. Go to the library and select a journal article that represents work in your field of interest. Apply each of the criteria that we specified in this chapter (see the section titled "Criteria for Judging a Research Study"). To make this exercise even more interesting, work on the task with a colleague, or select the same journal article as a colleague and compare your results.

3. What elements do you think should be part of a human experimentation or IRB form?

Online. . .

APA Style

Get a beginner's tutorial, a refresher, or even a summary of changes to the newest edition of the *American Psychological Association Publication Manual* at http://www.apastyle.org/.

Getting Funding for Research

S. Joseph Levine provides a very useful guide for writing research proposals at http://www.learnerassociates.net/proposal/. After all, once you know how to write a proposal for a research project, why not try and find funding for it?

The Grant Getter's Primer

More information about grants and the application process can be found at http://www.niaid.nih.gov/ncn/grants/default.htm, which is one of the many different institutes at the National Institutes of Health.

❖ ❖ ❖ Chapter 14 ❖ ❖ ❖

Writing a Research Manuscript

One day, you may have the opportunity to submit a manuscript by yourself or with a coauthor for publication. If you have lived right, the manuscript may be accepted, and won't you (and your parents and professor) be proud!

There are many ways to organize a manuscript, and most journals require that manuscripts be submitted according to specific guidelines. In the social and behavioral sciences, the *Publication Manual of the American Psychological Association* (6th ed., 2009) is the standard. This chapter is all about preparing a manuscript for submission according to those guidelines. Although there is no substitute for buying this manual (it costs about $29, but your department or adviser probably has one), this chapter provides the basics of how a manuscript should be organized, formatted, and mechanically prepared to meet APA guidelines.

To help you out, included is an example of pages from a manuscript prepared in the correct fashion. The manuscript (and the study on which it is based) was completed by one of the author's students who took a class very much like the one you are taking now. Following some general guidelines about manuscript preparation, you will see the manuscript, annotated with tips and hints. Just follow along. And, by the way, a terrific set of guidelines for how to use the APA format has been prepared and revised by Russ Dewey, Bill Scott, and Doc Scribe. You can find it at http://www.wooster.edu/psychology/apa-crib.html.

> **WHAT YOU'LL LEARN ABOUT IN THIS CHAPTER:**
>
> - The American Psychological Association's (APA's) *Publication Manual* and guidelines for manuscript preparation
>
> - The different parts of a manuscript and how they should be prepared
>
> - Formatting the manuscript using APA style

What a Manuscript Looks Like

Like a book, a report, or any other document that contains information, a research manuscript consists of different parts. Here is an outline of these parts and the order in which they are to be assembled (a description of what each contains follows):

- Title page
- Abstract
- Introduction
- Method
- Results
- Discussion
- References
- Appendices
- Author notes

- Footnotes
- Table captions
- Tables
- Figure captions
- Figures

This organization is fairly simple. The following subsections briefly describe the function of each part and what each part contains.

Title Page

The title page is the first thing the reader sees when considering the manuscript. It should contain information that is as clear and concise as possible. The title itself should be able to stand alone, convey the importance of the idea, and communicate the content of the manuscript. The title page is removed by the journal editor when the manuscript is sent out for review so the reviewers do not know who authored the manuscript.

The title should be concise and explanatory primarily because these titles are often used as the basis for index entries of the kind that were discussed in Chapter 3. If the title of a manuscript does not clearly reflect the content, a person using an index to find a study on a certain subject could easily miss the important work that has been done.

As you will see in the sample manuscript, the title page consists of the following components:

- A running head (appearing on each page) for the publication
- The title of the manuscript
- A byline or the authors listed in order of their contribution (not necessarily in alphabetical order) along with their institutional affiliation (for each author if different)

The running head, which appears on every page of the manuscript along with the page number, is used to identify the manuscript (because there is no other identifying information on the manuscript). Because many manuscripts are reviewed without knowing the author (or authors), something must be used for identification. The running head should be short.

Abstract

The abstract is a summary of the contents of the manuscript. It provides enough information for the reader to learn the purpose and the results of the research being reported and it does so in a concise, forthright fashion. No extras, no frills—just the facts—and in fewer than 120 words (editors do count them). The abstract should include the following specific information:

- A one-sentence statement of the purpose
- A description of the participants used in the research, including number, age, gender, ethnicity, special conditions, and other identifying characteristics
- The results
- Any conclusions being offered

The abstract should not be indented, should be titled Abstract in upper and lower case letters centered at the top of the page, and should include numerals as digits (such as 3) instead of words (such as three) to save space. The page should be numbered 2.

Introduction

The first page of the text begins with the title of the manuscript centered, with the first letter of each word capitalized (except for articles and prepositions). The introduction, unlike other sections in the manuscript, is not explicitly labeled as such; rather, it just begins after the manuscript title. The introduction provides a framework for the problem that is being studied and a context for the statement of the purpose of the study being reported.

A good introduction orients the reader to the importance of the problem by providing sufficient background material. This is not the place for an extensive historical review of the important literature. It should mention only the most important works that have been done and illuminate the important studies. Basically, the goal is to provide the reader with sufficient information to understand and appreciate the importance and scope of the problem.

Once the problem under study is stated and explained (and the stage is set), it is time to end the introduction with a clear statement of what will actually be done in the study, for example, "This descriptive study has three purposes. The first is . . . " Some writers also include a statement of the hypothesis.

Method

The method section of the manuscript describes how the study was conducted. This information is reported in sufficient detail so that anyone can refer to this section and duplicate the study exactly as it was originally done.

Because there are many different components to the method section, and they vary from manuscript to manuscript, different subheadings are used as well. The most common subheadings are Participants, Instruments, and Data Analysis.

In the method section, the participants are described in great detail, answering such questions as who participated in the study, how the participants were selected, and how many there were. The participants are further described by providing information on gender, ethnicity, location, age, marital status, and other potentially important descriptors. Which descriptors should be included? Whatever ones you think have some bearing on the nature of the study. For example, there are few studies using human participants in which gender would not be important to report, whereas there are few in which the participants' height would be important. In some cases, it is easier to compile a table of participant characteristics.

Results

Next in the text of the manuscript is the results section, wherein the reader can find which statistical techniques were used to analyze the data and what the results of the analysis were. This is not the place for a presentation of the actual results of the analysis, only information about how the analysis was done. It should specify which variables were used in the analysis and, if necessary, a rationale for why these particular procedures were selected.

This is the author's opportunity to report the actual results of the study, including numbers, numbers, and more numbers. As you can see, tables are used (such as Tables 1, 2, and 3 in the sample) to present the results visually, but a verbal description is provided as well.

Discussion

Finally, in the discussion section, the author of the manuscript is free to explore important relationships between past research, the purpose of the current study, the stated hypothesis, and the results of the current study. Now it is time for an evaluation of what has been done and a "measuring up" to determine whether the reported results fit the researcher's expectations. Sometimes the results and discussion sections are combined.

This is the researcher's opportunity to sum up the purpose and findings reported in the manuscript. It is here that you will find any statement as to what contribution might have been made by the current research and how well the original question was answered. The discussion section is also the place in which the implications and limitations of the current study are discussed, as well as suggestions for future research.

References

The references comprise the sources that were consulted during the course of the research and the writing of the manuscript. References can be anything from a book to a Web site, and all references must be entered in the reference list in a particular format (discussed later in this chapter).

Appendices

An appendix usually contains information that is not essential for understanding the content of the manuscript but is important to provide a thorough picture of what happened. Usually, an appendix will contain original data or drawings.

Author Notes

Author notes include any ancillary material that is important to understanding the content of the manuscript but does not belong to any of the previous sections.

Footnotes

Footnotes are used to elaborate on references or some other technical point in the manuscript.

Table Captions

Table captions identify each of the tables with a number and a title.

Tables

Tables are text arranged in columns or rows, and they are most often used in the results section. They are numbered consecutively (unless there is only one).

Figure Captions

Figure captions identify each of the figures with a number and a title.

Figures

This is where the actual figures for the manuscript are physically placed.

Nuts and Bolts

The content of a research manuscript is by far the most important part of the presentation. The format, however, takes on some importance as well, especially because most journals receive hundreds of manuscripts each year. Standardization of some kind helps streamline the process.

Here is a mini-guide to some of the most important format rules to keep in mind:

1. Make sure that the type is readable.
2. Use 12-point Times New Roman for text and Arial for figure captions.
3. All lines, including the headings, must be double spaced.
4. Allow 1 inch for a margin on the left, right, top, and bottom of the page.
5. Pages are numbered as follows:
   (a) The title page is a separate page, numbered 1.
   (b) The abstract is a separate page, numbered 2.
   (c) The text starts on a separate page, numbered 3.
   (d) The references, appendices, author notes, footnotes, and tables all start on separate pages, and the pages are continuously numbered. However, do not number artwork (figures and such).
6. The first line of each paragraph must be indented five to seven spaces or one-half inch.
7. The text should be left aligned, leaving a ragged right margin.
8. Headings are to be typed as follows. Here is an example of three different levels of headings, which are sufficient for most papers:
   (a) First-Level Headings are Centered, Upper and Lower Case.
   (b) Second-Level Headings are Flush Left, Upper and Lower Case.
   (c) **Third-level headings are indented, boldface, and lower case**.
9. Place one space after all punctuation (periods, commas, semicolons, etc.).
10. Do not indent the abstract.
11. Start the list of references on a new page.

Summary

That's it for preparing a manuscript according to APA guidelines and *Exploring Research* as well. I sincerely hope you enjoyed using the book as much as I have enjoyed writing it. My best wishes for success in all the years to come.

Running head → Family Engagement

1

Defining and Measuring

Title → Engagement Within the Family: Development of the Family

Engagement Behaviors Scale

Authors → Kristin Rasmussen Teasdale

Institutional Affiliation → University of Kansas

The Title is the main entry point and tells the reader the focus of the manuscript

Running head on each page → Family Engagement

2

No indent ↓

Abstract

To date, no assessment of family engagement—defined as the positive behaviors family members carry out to invest in and learn about the family unit and members, and to achieve individual and common family goals—exists within the field of positive psychology of the family. The aim of this study was to define more clearly the term "family engagement" and to develop a measure of this concept: The Family Engagement Behaviors Scale (FEBS). The participant sample includes 309 adults from diverse family backgrounds. Results show initial support for the internal consistency and test-retest reliability of the FEBS, as well as concurrent validity of the FEBS.

Keywords: family, engagement, strengths, assessment

The purpose of the abstract and the main findings are reported in the abstract

Level 1 heading → Defining and Measuring Engagement Within the Family: Development of the ⎤ *Title*

Indent one-half inch ↓ Family Engagement Behaviors Scale ⎦

All text is double spaced

Families have competencies they use to survive challenges, and individuals have strengths that influence their families. However, traditional family psychology, much like other psychology fields, generally has focused on assessment and treatment of family dysfunctions without examining the useful skills families already have in place or could adopt. To omit these competencies from the working model in assessment skews the overall view of the family unit and provides a less accurate picture of the family's situation. It also limits the resources families can seek to develop when trying to achieve goals.

The introductory part of the manuscript provides a background for the reader to understand the context in which the study was done.

Despite the call for positive family functioning assessment tools, and despite family literature's inclusion of engagement as a family strength *—1.5 inch margin —* (Sheridan, Dowd, & Eagle, 2004; Sheridan, Warnes, Cowan, Schemm, & Clarke, 2005), an extensive literature search failed to find an extant measure focused solely on the positive behaviors relating to family engagement as it is conceptualized in the present study. Measures of similar constructs are available, but none seems to speak to family engagement as a specific strengths-based, predictive, and action-oriented construct. Though traditionally sound family measures often address the feelings of cohesion and interactional styles families have, there seems to be an opening for a measure that looks specifically at the changeable behaviors families can enact frequently to improve their overall level of functioning, and that lends some more predictability to family interactions. Therefore, the purpose of the current study is to develop and work toward initial validation of a measure of engagement within the family: The Family Engagement Behaviors Scale (FEBS).

1.5 inch margin

One of the primary reasons for developing a measure focused on common behavioral aspects of family functioning is to provide a way to examine more closely the strengths-based facets of family functioning that are more dynamic and changeable than the feelings of closeness, which affect family functioning but seem to require more extensive intervention methods. The working model for the FEBS supposes that family engagement leads to the growth of strong positive feelings about family, which in turn contribute to more family engagement, in a circular, forward-feeding process.

Citations, such as the one seen here, provide a historical context within which important questions and assumptions can be addressed.

Reference to where Figure 1 should be placed

Insert Figure 1 about here

This model is derived from the one offered by DeFrain and the University of Nebraska-Lincoln for Families Writing Team (2007), whereby the authors propose loving actions toward family members influence the growth of loving feelings, which in return promote more loving actions. Between changing behaviors and changing feelings, intervening at the behavioral level seems to be the most amenable place to begin, which is why the FEBS specifically focuses on dynamic family behaviors rather than extant feelings about the family.

Despite family engagement's presence and stressed value in strengths-based family theory, few empirical studies have included family engagement as a construct. Possible reasons for this gap between theory and empirical research include the fact that researchers do not have a reliable and valid measure of family engagement to use, nor an agreed-upon definition to use. An aim of the current study is to address these two issues by offering a definition of family engagement and operationalizing the construct via development of a measure of engagement within the family, the FEBS. If, as hypothesized, the FEBS demonstrates adequate

The method section contains a sufficient amount of detail so that another researcher can replicate the research just as it was originally done.

internal consistency, test-retest reliability, and concurrent validity with measures of family quality of life and family strengths, conceivably it could provide insight about the actions families can take frequently to enhance their family wellbeing.

Method

Participants

Level 2 heading →

Participants in the initial sample included 309 family members who represent diverse ethnic, socioeconomic, education level, and age populations. They were recruited from Zoomerang, a Web-based survey program, in an attempt to find participants who more closely represent the national census demographically than do participants in previous normative samples for family assessments. Criteria for inclusion were broad: Respondents were required to be 18 years old or older and were required to be in a home including at least one parent and one child. Table 1 shows the breakdown in demographics of the participants of this study.

Tables are only one way to help summarize important information.

Reference to where tables should be placed

Insert Table 1 about here

A separate group of participants was recruited in order to examine initial test-retest reliability of the FEBS. In this sample of 29, participants were college students enrolled in an orientation seminar, and the majority of participants again were white and non-Hispanic.

The all important hypotheses are clearly stated within the context of the original research question.

Hypotheses

To address issues concerning the reliability and validity of the proposed measure of family engagement, it is hypothesized that the measure a) will be internally consistent, demonstrating a Cronbach alpha of .70 or higher, b) will show moderate to strong concurrent validity with the family interaction, parenting, emotional wellbeing, and physical/material wellbeing subscales of the Beach Center Family Quality of Life Scale (FQOL Scale; Hoffman, Marquis,

Poston, Summers, and Turnbull, 2006), demonstrating a significant Pearson product moment correlation at the $p < .01$ significance level, c) will show moderate to strong concurrent validity with the American Family Strengths Inventory (AFSI; DeFrain & Stinnett, 2002), demonstrating a significant Pearson product moment correlation at the $p < .01$ significance level, and d) will have adequate test-retest reliability, demonstrating a correlation coefficient of .70 or stronger that is significant at the $p < .01$ level.

Instruments

Family Engagement Behaviors Scale (FEBS). The measure of family engagement in this study reflects an attempt to unify related definitions of engagement and focus on their behavioral aspects. Consequently, the measure contains items that address behaviors that correspond to being involved within the family, focusing on role activities, actively investing in family members, and carrying out actions that lead to the achievement of common family goals. Several items were reverse-coded in the first draft of the FEBS, and in order to provide a validity check, multiple items
addressed the same engagement behavior in this draft.
The rating scale for each item is a 4-point Likert scale, where
1 = *unlike our family*, 2 = *somewhat unlike our family*, 3 = *somewhat like our family*, 4 = *like our family*. Internal consistency for the current sample was tested with Cronbach's alpha, and concurrent and face validity were evaluated as well. Additionally, an exploratory factor analysis was conducted to determine whether the measure was unidimensional or multidimensional.

Family Quality of Life Scale (FQOL Scale). The FQOL Scale (Hoffman et al., 2006) is a 25-item measure with five unidimensional subscales determined by factor analysis: Family interaction, parenting, emotional wellbeing, physical/material wellbeing, and disability-related support. The FQOL Scale has demonstrated ample internal consistency, test-retest reliability, and convergent validity.

American Family Strengths Inventory (AFSI). The AFSI (DeFrain & Stinnett, 2002) is an 86-item questionnaire divided into six subscales—appreciation and affection, commitment, positive communication, enjoyable time together, spiritual wellbeing, and effective management of stress and crisis—as well as a global measure of family strengths. This measures comes from research by Stinnett, DeFrain, and their colleagues within the international family strengths model, and it covers information obtained from more than 24,000 family members in 35 countries over the course of 35 years.

Demographic Questionnaire. All participants filled out a demographic questionnaire to provide information about their age, marital/relationship status, annual income, ethnicity, the number of children they currently have in their household, and any disabilities experienced by their family members.

Procedure

In developing the FEBS, the first step was to consult theory-based literature to review extensively family psychology theories and outcome-based research, and to determine how to conceptualize family engagement in a way that is consistent with theory, easily defined, and relatable to clinicians and family members alike. Also at this time, experts on family strengths, after being given a definition of family engagement, were asked to provide information about the components of family life they see as being most relevant to family engagement. Consistent with the literature and with descriptions from experts in positive family functioning, the current study's definition of family engagement is the positive behaviors family members carry out to invest in and learn about the family unit and members, and to achieve individual and common family goals. Initial FEBS items were based on the information gathered from experts and the review of theories.

Before data collection with the study sample occurred, a group of 10 individuals participated in a pilot study to give feedback about the time requirement, wording, and item content of the measure. Based on the feedback, items were revised before the study sample completed the FEBS. Also at this point, four experts in the field of family-centered positive psychology who are knowledgeable about family engagement reviewed the measure to determine its face validity. They rated each item on a Likert scale ranging from 1: *Absolutely does not relate to the construct* to 5: *Absolutely relates to the construct.* Based on pilot study data analysis, pilot study feedback, and expert feedback, item revisions were made before administration to the study sample.

A sample of 309 participants completed the measure in the revised format, along with completing a demographic questionnaire, the FEBS, the AFSI, and the family interaction, parenting, emotional wellbeing, and physical/material wellbeing scales of the FQOL Scale. Initial concurrent validity was assessed, and Cronbach's alpha was used to measure the internal consistency of the FEBS with this sample as well. Also, on two occasions, one month apart, 29 participants completed a revised version of the FEBS to assess initial test-retest reliability.

Following the initial administration to a sample of 309, the author completed an exploratory factor analysis to determine the number of factors appropriate for the final scale, and items with the highest factor loadings that appeared to be most relevant to theory remained in the final version of the FEBS.

The results section provides a summary of the results of the analysis and any other pertinent information that will later be discussed.

Results

A factor analysis was performed to look at the number and nature of appropriate factors for the created measure. As no literature is available to support positive hypotheses about separate factors of family engagement, the factor analysis was an exploratory one, rather than a confirmatory one, and no hypothesis was made about the number of factors. The dimensionality of the 104 initial items from the Family Engagement Behaviors Scale (FEBS) was analyzed using maximum likelihood factor analysis. Two criteria were used to determine the number of factors to rotate: the scree test and the interpretability of the factor solution. Based on the scree plot, two factors were rotated using a Varimax rotation procedure. Figure 2 shows the scree plot for the 27-item version, which holds the same shape as the original scree plot from the 104-item measure.

Insert Figure 2 about here

The rotated solution, as shown in Table 2, yielded two interpretable factors: family engagement and active disengagement with family. From the initial 104 items, the items with the lowest factor ratings and items correlating strongly with other items were removed one at a time, and new rotations were completed to yield the final 27 items. The family engagement factor accounted for 49.84% of the item variance and the active disengagement factor accounted for 10.04% of the item variance; a total of 59.88% of the variance was accounted for with the two factors. No items loaded strongly on both factors.

It is sometimes easier and more concise to combine both the results and the discussion sections of a paper.

Insert Table 2 about here

The internal consistency estimate of reliability for the FEBS was evaluated with the coefficient alpha. The final 27-item version of the FEBS demonstrated an alpha of .96, indicating strong internal consistency. This analysis supports Hypothesis 1, which states the FEBS will have a

Cronbach's alpha of .70 or stronger. Internal consistency of each subscale was also examined. Factor 1, family engagement, demonstrated an alpha of .97, while Factor 2, active disengagement, demonstrated an alpha of .84.

To determine whether the FQOL Scale and AFSI demonstrated internal consistency with the sample of this study, Cronbach's alpha was evaluated for both measures. Both measures demonstrated strong internal consistency in this study; the alpha for the FQOL Scale was .966, and the alpha for the AFSI was .972.

Test-retest reliability, as addressed in Hypothesis 2, was evaluated with a Pearson product moment correlation between 29 participants' responses at Time 1 and their responses exactly one month later. The Pearson product moment correlation for this analysis was .811, $p < .001$, demonstrating strong test-retest reliability.

The third and fourth hypotheses address concurrent validity evaluation of the FEBS. These hypotheses state that the Pearson product moment correlations between the FEBS and the FQOL Scale (Hoffman et al., 2006), and the FEBS and the AFSI (DeFrain & Stinnett, 2002), would be moderate to strong correlations and would be significant at the $p < .01$ level. Both hypotheses were supported. The correlation between the FEBS and the FQOL Scale was .781, $p < .001$, which is classified as strong (Cohen, 1988). The correlation between the FEBS and the AFSI was .623, $p < .001$, which is classified as a moderate to strong correlation (Cohen, 1988).

Discussion

The aim of this study was to define more clearly the term "family engagement" and to develop a measure of this concept: The Family Engagement Behaviors Scale (FEBS). Results show initial support for the internal consistency and test-retest reliability of the FEBS, as well as concurrent validity of the FEBS when correlated with existing strengths-based family assessments.

The all important discussion section ties together the separate sections of the manuscript and especially the introduction and the results. It is also the location of any future research direction the author of the manuscript thinks is worth consideration.

   The factor analysis conducted with the original 104 items of the FEBS, which led to the removal of items with the weakest factor loadings, designates which 23 behaviors are the strongest indicators of family engagement and which four behaviors are the strongest barriers to family engagement. While the 23 behaviors can be thought of as strengths in the area of family engagement, the four items (all reverse-coded) on Factor 2 can be thought of as indicators of active disengagement. In other words, while some family members may have a lower base rate of family engagement—whether due to a lack of knowledge, skills, or opportunities to practice the skills—other family members may participate in avoidance behaviors that appear to be more hurtful to the family.

Limitations and Considerations in Interpreting Results

   Regarding data analysis, concurrent validity and test-retest reliability analyses warrant some caution in interpretation. Since no validated measure of family engagement was found to use as a measure of concurrent validity, concurrent validity in this study was only able to be Guns and Chewing Gum demonstrated with measures of related and more general constructs, and not with a previously validated instrument aimed specifically at engagement within the family. Furthermore, the coding of "not applicable" items on the AFSI to neutral responses could have affected results of the concurrent validity. The test-retest reliability shown in the results should be interpreted with caution as well, as the sample for this analysis is small and homogeneous, and as respondents answered the 27 items within the 104-item version of the FEBS. The 27-item version should be examined with larger more heterogeneous sample in the future.

Implications for a New Measure of Family Engagement: Addressing the "So What" Question

   Even with initial reliability and validity support for the FEBS, the question remains: How is the introduction of this measure relevant and helpful for scholars, clinicians, and families? In short, this study addresses to some degree three problems commonly identified by scholars and clinicians working with families and family assessments. The first issue is the tendency for family assessments to be deficit-focused while ignoring competencies that could be just as helpful in making positive changes in the family. The second issue is that within family strengths literature and even among family assessments, many constructs have remained vaguely defined or undefined, with little connection to theory (Krysan, Moore, & Zill, 1990; Turnbull, Summers, Lee, & Kyzar, 2007; Walsh, 1993). The third issue identified is the problem of continuing to use older measures that initially were normed on white, middle-class, homogeneous samples to assess families that do not share demographic characteristics with the initial norming samples (Krysan et al., 1990; Turnbull et al., 2007).

The FEBS appears to meet the goals of focusing on strengths, clarifying a definition, connecting to theory, and diversifying sampling methods reasonably well. As a result, this instrument may be useful for a wide range of families and the clinicians who work with them. It can aid family clinicians in assessing and developing short- and long-term goals with family members. It also may help with intervention planning by revealing behavioral strengths family members can call upon to overcome present and future challenges. When families are experiencing situational problems but still score high on the FEBS, clinicians can use the results to reinforce the skills families already have in place. With families who acquire nearly any score on the measure, clinicians can use responses to generate conversations (e.g., "Look at these skills you have; you are doing these things right. Now what can we add to them?").

The FEBS is a new assessment tool that is consistent with the current directions of the field of positive psychology of the family. It addresses common concerns scholars and clinicians have expressed, and it fills a gap between theory and assessment. It is applicable to families and clinicians alike, and family engagement is a relatively easy concept for families to grasp. The hope of the FEBS author is that these qualities will contribute to the usefulness of the instrument in enhancing everyday family life.

Family Engagement

13

Level 1
heading → **References**

Book
reference → Cohen, J. (1988). Statistical power analysis for the behavioral sciences

(2nd ed.). Hillsdale, NJ: Lawrence Earlbaum Associates.

DeFrain, J. & Stinnett, N. (2002). Family strengths. In J. J. Ponzetti et a ;

(Eds.), International encyclopedia of marriage and family (2nd ed.).

Journal   New York: Macmillan.
article
reference → Hoffman, L., Marquis, J.G., Poston, D.J., Summers, J.A., & Turnbull, A.

(2006). Assessing family outcomes: Psychometric evaluation of the

family quality of life scale. Journal of Marriage and Family, 68,

1069-1083.

Report
reference → Krysan, M., Moore, K., & Zill, N. (1990). Identifying successful families:

An overview of constructs and selected measures. United States

Department of Health and Human Services.

Sheridan, S., Dowd, S., & Eagle, J. (2005). Families as contexts for

children's adaptation. In S. Goldstein & R. Brooks (Eds.), Handbook of

resiliency in children. New York: Kluwer/Plenum.

Sheridan, S., Warnes, E., Cowan, R., Schemm, A., & Clarke, B. (2004).

Family-centered positive psychology: Focusing on strengths to build

student success. Psychology in the Schools, 41, 7-17.

Turnbull, A., Summers, J., Lee, S., & Kyzar, K. (2007). Conceptualization

and measurement of family outcomes associated with families of

individuals with intellectual disabilities. Mental Retardation and

Developmental Disabilities Research Reviews, 13, 326-356.

Walsh, F. (Ed.). (1993). Normal family processes. New York: Guilford

Press.

Appendix A

The Family Engagement Behavioral Scale—Original Items

Please circle the response that best answers the question, "How much does this sound like your family?"

Appendices provide additional information which makes the presentation more complete and useful for the reader.

1 = unlike our family
2 = somewhat unlike our family
3 = somewhat like our family
4 = like our family

1. Whether messy or clean, we try to keep our home welcoming and comfortable.
2. The parents in our family are available to help with homework and projects if needed.
3. The parents in our family give space for the children to engage in their own fun projects.
4. We frequently talk to each other about what we enjoy about school/work.
5. We talk frequently about the satisfaction we get from our accomplishments.
6. The parents in our family complain to the family about the daily stresses of work.
7. We express our appreciation of each other.
8. When we experience a crisis, we talk together about how to cope.
9. We show our support for each other.
10. We let each other make reasonable mistakes.
11. We recognize when a family member needs help.
12. We offer our assistance when we feel we can help a family member.
13. We try not to impose many rules on family members.
14. We avoid blaming others for our own mistakes.
15. We have had to ask a family member to leave our family.
16. We value the stories the grandparents in our family have shared.
17. Members of our family understand what we expect of them.
18. We maintain reasonable expectations for each member of our family.
19. When a family member needs help from someone outside the family, we rarely seek it.
20. We give specific compliments to each other.
21. We frequently tell each other funny stories.
22. We frequently disagree about important issues.
23. We make an effort to "pick our battles" and choose confrontations carefully.
24. When family members are in a disagreement, one of us usually ends up leaving "huffing and puffing."
25. When we're in a rough patch, we demonstrate our faith in a brighter future.
26. The children in our family often come up with their own ideas of fun projects.
27. The children in our family make up their own games to play.
28. We encourage each other to take reasonable risks and rise to challenges.
29. We outwardly express our support for each other.
30. We give many more compliments to each other than we do criticisms.
31. We typically act in ways that are consistent with what we say.
32. We find ways to honor and learn about family members who have died.
33. We find ways to keep up with family members who live far away.
34. The parents in our family tell stories about their past.
35. The children in our family enjoy hearing about their parents' past experiences.

36. We frequently express what makes each member a good person.
37. We have some kind of fun together on most days.
38. We frequently talk about good memories together.
39. We learn about each other's goals.
40. We think about ways we can help other family members achieve their goals.
41. We have trouble coming up with family activities every member can enjoy.
42. We say please and thank you to each other.
43. We plan times in the future to get together for fun reunions or activities.
44. When a family member accomplishes something positive, we celebrate the effort the family member put forth.
45. Laughter is a very common occurrence in our home.
46. We apologize when we have hurt a family member's feelings.
47. We try to explain our actions when another family member has trouble understanding them.
48. When we spend time together, it is usually focused more on required activities than things we want to do.
49. We know what resources we have and what resources each member can use for his or her wellbeing.
50. When our arguments get heated, we make an attempt to calm down.
51. When we get in a disagreement, we try to avoid saying spiteful things.
52. The parents in our family differ significantly in their parenting styles.
53. We value the role other family members play in our own wellbeing.
54. When a family member fails in some way, we do not regard the member as a failure in general.
55. We have people outside the family whom we can rely on when we need support.
56. We encourage each other to take chances, even if a reasonable risk of failure is involved.
57. We prioritize work over family.
58. We prioritize our family over our friends.
59. We forgive each other when we have been wronged.
60. When one of us needs help, we talk to a family member about it.
61. When a family member suggests something to us, we usually take it into consideration.
62. We schedule family activities every member wants to attend.
63. We talk about who will fill each responsibility in our home.
64. Members of our family tend to criticize each other's character.
65. We talk about the positive results that arise when a family member has worked hard.
66. We record our family experiences, whether it's by video, scrapbook, growth chart, journal, etc.
67. When a member is away from home, we keep up frequent positive correspondence.
68. We work together on our spiritual enrichment, whether it is through religious practices, connectedness with nature, or another form
69. We take part in lots of outdoor activities.
70. We take part in lots of indoor activities.
71. Parents teach the children how to enjoy the city, town, or countryside we live in.
72. We make our home the kind of place where neighbors are comfortable visiting.
73. We have interesting guests visit our home from time to time.
74. In the future, we will probably be too busy to spend time as a family.
75. We recognize the unique talents each member has.
76. When things get tough, we try not to blame each other.

77. When we disagree with each other, we attempt to compromise.
78. We are truthful with each other.
79. When one of us says we will do something for the family, we do what we can to follow through.
80. When a family member is struggling, we express our understanding.
81. When we experience sudden change, we open up discussion about it.
82. The parents in our family model sound decision-making.
83. When members of our family argue, we often stop listening to what the other member is saying.
84. We are familiar with the friends and other important people who influence each family member's life.
85. When two members of our family disagree, the other members often take sides.
86. We have interesting things to play with and work with around the home (e.g., an old broken phone, paintbrushes, sand, building materials, gardens, pets)
87. The parents in our family tend to be too busy to attend to the children's specific needs.
88. Everybody has a space of their own in our home, no matter how small or large.
89. We invent games to play.
90. Even if we don't have a lot of money, we can almost always find fun stuff to do around our home.
91. We have traditions that are unique to our family.
92. We find many reasons to celebrate together.
93. We attend family members' performances or athletic events.
94. If one of us were to be presented with an award, we would want our other family members to be there.
95. We express gratitude.
96. We introduce family members to other people we know.
97. We talk about our hobbies.
98. We keep a lot of secrets from each other.
99. When a family member is struggling, we express our love.
100. We usually know where every member of the family is.
101. Family members frequently leave the home without telling each other.
102. We display drawings or other works created by family members.
103. We offer to help each other with unpleasant tasks around the home.
104. We have fun with animals, whether it's with a pet, at the zoo, or with the insects and frogs in our yard.

Appendix B

The Family Engagement Behavioral Scale

Please circle the response that best answers the question, "How much does this sound like your family?"

1 = unlike our family
2 = somewhat unlike our family
3 = somewhat like our family
4 = like our family

1. We forgive each other when we have been wronged.	1 2 3 4
2. We express our appreciation of each other.	1 2 3 4
3. When we experience a crisis, we talk together about how to cope.	1 2 3 4
4. We offer our assistance when we feel we can help a family member.	1 2 3 4
5. We give specific compliments to each other.	1 2 3 4
6. The parents in our family tend to be too busy to attend to the children's specific needs.	1 2 3 4
7. We outwardly express our support for each other.	1 2 3 4
8. We frequently talk about good memories together.	1 2 3 4
9. We learn about each other's goals.	1 2 3 4
10. When a family member is struggling, we express our love.	1 2 3 4
11. Laughter is a very common occurrence in our home.	1 2 3 4
12. We apologize when we have hurt a family member's feelings.	1 2 3 4
13. Family members frequently leave the home without telling each other.	1 2 3 4
14. We value the role other family members play in our own wellbeing.	1 2 3 4
15. We frequently express what makes each member a good person.	1 2 3 4
16. When a family member suggests something to us, we usually take it into consideration.	1 2 3 4
17. We talk about the positive results that arise when a family member has worked hard.	1 2 3 4
18. In the future, we will probably be too busy to spend time as a family.	1 2 3 4
19. We recognize the unique talents each member has.	1 2 3 4
20. When we disagree with each other, we attempt to compromise.	1 2 3 4
21. When a family member is struggling, we express our understanding.	1 2 3 4
22. When we experience sudden change, we open up discussion about it.	1 2 3 4
23. We express gratitude.	1 2 3 4
24. We keep a lot of secrets from each other.	1 2 3 4
25. We give many more compliments to each other than we do criticisms.	1 2 3 4
26. When a family member accomplishes something positive, we celebrate the effort the family member put forth.	1 2 3 4
27. We think about ways we can help other family members achieve their goals.	1 2 3 4

Table Title→

Table 1

Demographic Breakdown of the Initial Sample of Participants

Gender	
Male	44 %
Female	56%
Age	
18 – 24	16%
25 – 34	24%
35 – 44	19%
45 – 54	22%
55 – 64	10%
65 or older	9%
Marital Status	
Single	16%
Committed relationship	7%
Engaged	3%
Married	60%
Separated	1%
Divorced	10%
Widowed	3%
Annual Household Income	
Under $20,000	19%
$20,000 - $39,999	30%
$40,000 - $59,999	19%
$60,000 - $79,999	13%
$80,000 - $99,999	6%
$100,000 or more	12%
Ethnicity	
Black	8%
Asian	5%
Latino(a)	1%
White, not Hispanic	85%
American Indian or Alaska Native	1%
Native Hawaiian or other Pacific Islander	1%
Do You Consider Your Family Biracial or Multiracial?	
Yes	15%
No	85%
Does Your Family Include a Member or Members with a Disability or Disabilities?	
Yes	23%
No	77%

Table 2

FEBS Factor Loadings

Scale/Items	Engagement	Active Disengagement
We express gratitude.	.814	.171
We outwardly express our support for each other.	.797	.160
The parents in our family tend to be too busy to attend to the children's specific needs (reversed).	.112	.797
When a family member is struggling, we express our love.	.793	.232
We think about ways we can help other family members achieve their goals.	.782	.099
We forgive each other when we have been wronged.	.780	.161
We value the role other family members play in our own wellbeing.	.775	.079
We express our appreciation of each other.	.767	.166
We apologize when we have hurt a family member's feelings.	.767	.137
When a family member is struggling, we express our understanding.	.765	.177
When we experience a sudden change, we open up discussion about it.	.764	.141
When we disagree with each other, we attempt to compromise.	.763	.086
We recognize the unique talents each member has.	.762	.221
We frequently talk about good memories together.	.761	.113
We frequently express what makes each member a good person.	.755	.045
Laughter is a very common occurrence in our home.	.753	.123
We learn about each other's goals.	.747	.118
When a family member suggests something to us, we typically take it into consideration.	.746	.149

Scale/Items	Engagement	Active Disengagement
Family members frequently leave the home without telling each other (reversed).	.008	.744
We keep a lot of secrets from each other (reversed).	.249	.742
When a family member accomplishes something positive, we celebrate the effort the family member put forth.	.742	.122
We give specific compliments to each other.	.742	.060
We offer our assistance when we feel we can help a family member.	.740	.173
We talk about the positive results that arise when a family member has worked hard.	.739	.208
When we experience a crisis, we talk together about how to cope.	.734	.137
We give many more compliments to each other than we do criticisms.	.730	.074
In the future, we will probably be too busy to spend time together as a family (reversed).	.165	.698

Table 14.2 *Continued*

Family Engagement

21

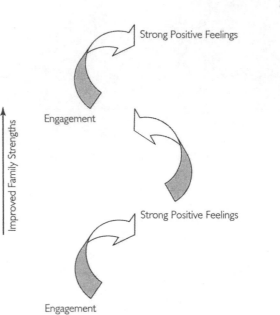

Figure title → **Figure 1**   The forward-feeding process of engagement and positive feelings within the family.

↑
*Figure number
in Italics*

Family Engagement

22

Figure 2 Scree plot for factors of the Family Engagement Behaviors Scale.

Appendix A

An Introduction
to SPSS 19.x

Lesson 1
Starting SPSS

After This Lesson, You Will Know

*   How to start SPSS
*   What the opening SPSS screen looks like

With this lesson you will start your journey on learning how to use SPSS, the most powerful and easiest-to-use data analysis package available.

Keep in mind that throughout these lessons we expect you to work along with us. It's only through hands-on experiences that you will master the basic and advanced features of this program.

Starting SPSS

SPSS is started by clicking the icon (or the name representing the program) that represents the application either on the Start Menu in Windows or on the desktop on the Macintosh.

The SPSS Opening Window

As you can see in Figure 1, the opening window presents a series of options that allow you to select from running the SPSS tutorial, entering data, run an established query, or opening an existing source of data (an existing file). Should you not want to see this screen each time you open SPSS, then click on the Don't show this dialog in the future box in the lower left corner of the window.

Figure I   The Opening SPSS Window.

The SPSS for Windows Dialog Box

For our purposes, we will click the Type in data option since it is likely to be the one you first select upon opening and learning SPSS. Once you do this, the **Data View** window (also called the **Data Editor**) you see in Figure 2 becomes active. This is where you enter data you want to use with SPSS once that data has been defined. Although you cannot see it when SPSS first opens, there is another open (but not active) window as well. This is the **Variable View** where variables are defined and the parameters for those variables are set. We will cover the Data and Variable Views in Lesson 5.

The **Viewer** displays statistical results and charts that you create. An example of the Viewer window is shown in Figure 3. A data set is created using the Data Editor and once the set is analyzed or graphed, you examine the results of the analysis in the Viewer.

Figure 2   The Data View window.

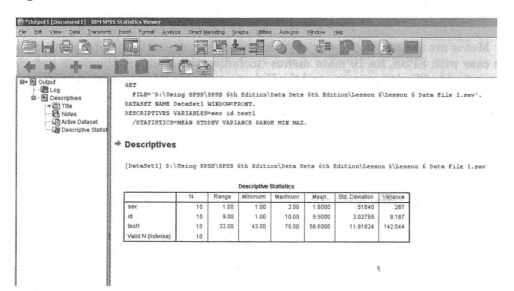

Figure 3   The Viewer.

If you think the Data Editor is similar to a spreadsheet in form and function, you are right. In form, it certainly is, since the Data Editor consists of rows and columns just like in Excel and Lotus 2-3. Values can be entered and then manipulated. In function as well, the Data Editor is much like a spreadsheet. Values that are entered can be transformed, sorted, rearranged, and more. In addition, SPSS can use formulas to compute new variables and values from existing ones, as you will learn in Lesson 12.

As you will learn in Lesson 10, one of the many conveniences of SPSS is its ability to import data from a spreadsheet accurately and efficiently. This ability makes SPSS particularly well suited and powerful for further analysis of data already in spreadsheet form.

Lesson 2
The SPSS Main Menus and Toolbar

After This Lesson, You Will Know

- Each of the SPSS main menus and what the commands on the menus do
- The icons on the toolbar

Key Words

- Analyze menu
- Data menu
- Edit menu
- File menu
- Graphs menu
- Open dialog box
- Status Bar
- Toolbar
- Transform menu
- Utilities menu
- View menu

Menus are the key to operating any Windows or Mac application, and that is certainly the case with SPSS. Its 10 main menus (including the standard Windows and Help menus for the Windows version and the Help menu for the Mac version) provide access to every tool and feature that SPSS has to offer. In this lesson, we will review the contents of each of these menus and introduce you to the toolbar, a set of icons that takes the place of menu commands. The icons make it quick and easy to do anything, from saving a file to printing a chart.

The SPSS Main Menus

SPSS comes to you with 12 main menus, as you see in the opening screen in Figure 4.

While you think you may know all about the File menu and what options are available on it, stick with us through the rest of this lesson to see exactly what the File menu, and the other nine menus, can do for you.

| File | Edit | View | Data | Transform | Analyze | Direct Marketing | Graphs | Utilities | Add-ons | Window | Help |

Figure 4 The SPSS menus.

The File Menu

The purpose of the **File menu** is to work with files. Using the options on this menu, you create new files, open existing ones, save files in a variety of formats, display information about a file, print a file, and exit SPSS. The File menu also lists the last few documents that were accessed (File -> Recently used files), so you can quickly return to a previous document.

For example, when it comes time to start working with the file named "Teacher Scale Results," you would select Open from the File menu and then select the file name from the Open dialog box. You will learn more about this process in Lesson 7.

The Edit Menu

When it comes time to cut or copy data and paste it in another location in the current, or another, data file, you will go to the **Edit menu**. You will also seek out options on the Edit menu to search for data or text, replace text, and set SPSS preferences (or default settings). All these activities and more are found on the Edit menu.

Tip: When items on a menu are dimmed, it means they are not available.

For example, if you wanted to find what Mary Jones scored on test 1, you could search for "Mary Jones" and then read across the file to find her score on the variable named test 1. You would use the Find command on the Edit menu to search for that information.

The View Menu

Here's a chance to customize your SPSS desktop. Using various commands on the **View menu**, you can choose to show or hide toolbars, **Status bar**, and grid lines in the Data Editor, change fonts, and use Value Labels.

Tip: If you use labels for your variables, make sure that the Value Labels option is checked on the View menu. Otherwise, you won't see them at all.

For example, if we didn't want to use labels for variables, we would be sure that the Value Labels option was not selected.

The Data Menu

Variables and their values are the central element in any SPSS analysis, and you need powerful tools to work with variables. You have them on SPSS. On the **Data menu** you can see commands that allow you to define and sort variables, work with templates, go to a specific case, merge and aggregate files, and weigh cases as you see fit.

Tip: When a menu options is followed by three dots (called an ellipsis), clicking on that option opens an additional dialog box with other options.

For example, if we want to insert a new variable after data has already been entered, this is the menu you would use and the Insert Variable options is the menu options that would be selected.

The Transform Menu

There will be times when a variable value needs to be transformed or converted to another form or another value. That's where the commands on the **Transform menu** come in handy. On this menu, you will find commands that allow you to compute new values, create a set of random values, recode values, replace missing values, and do more.

For example, you could easily compute a new variable that represents the mean of a set of items using the Compute command on the Transform menu.

The Analyze Menu

There are 23 different options on the **Analyze menu** that lead to almost any statistical analysis technique you might want to use. These range from a simple computation of a mean and standard deviation to time series analysis and multiple regression.

For example, if you wanted to determine if there is a significant difference between the average rating that Professor 6 received on a teaching evaluation form versus the average rating received by Professor 4, you could look to the Compare Means option on the Analyze menu.

The Direct Marketing Menu

The **Direct marketing menu** is a specialized menu that uses SPSS add-ons.

The Graphs Menu

Want to see what those numbers *really* look like? Go to the **Graphs menu** where you can create 16 types of graphs. Graphs make numbers come alive, and you should pay special attention to later lessons where we show you how to create, edit, and print them.

For example, if you want to see test scores as a function of gender, a bar graph (on the Graphs menu) could do it quite nicely.

The Utilities Menu

On the **Utilities menu**, you can find out information about variables and files, and you can define and use sets of variables.

For example, the File Info option (for File Information) on the Utilities menu can tell us that the file named "Teacher Scores" contains 50 cases and 8 variables.

The Add-ons Menu

Add-ons is kind of a catch all menu for commands that do not conveniently fit wlesehwere. For example, there information on SPSS consulting and SPSS tutlorias.

The Window and Help Menus

These two menus function much like any other Windows application menus. The **Window menu** helps you switch from one window to another and minimize the SPSS Data Editor or Viewer.

The **Help menu** provides online help. We will focus on the Help menu in the next lesson.

Variable	Definition	Range
id_prof	professor's identification number	1–10
Sex_prof	professor's gender	1 or 2
Age	professor's age	33–64
Rank	professor's rank	Assistant, Associate, or Full Professor
School	professor's school	Liberal Arts, Business School
crab1	Score on item 1 on the Crab Scale	
crab2	Score on item 2 on the Crab Scale	
crab3	Score on item 3 on the Crab Scale	
crab4	Score on item 4 on the Crab Scale	
crab5	Score on item 5 on the Crab Scale	
crab6	Score on item 6 on the Crab Scale	

Table 1   Crab Scale Summary

The SPSS Toolbar and Status Bar

What's the easiest way to use SPSS? Clearly, through the use of the **toolbar**, the set of icons that are underneath the menus. Click on the icon, and the command is performed. So, instead of going to the Utilities menu to select variables, you can just click on the Variables icon on the toolbar. Table 1 presents the toolbar icon, its title and what it does.

Different screens have different toolbars. For example, as you will see in Lesson 15, when you create a chart, a new set of icons becomes available on the toolbar.

Tip: You can always find out what an icon does by placing the mouse cursor on top of it. A toolbar tip should popup.

Another useful tool is the Status Bar located at the bottom of the SPSS window. Here, you can see a one-line report as to what activity SPSS is currently involved in. Messages such as "SPSS Processor is ready" tell you that SPSS is ready for your directions or input of data. Or, "Running Means . . . " tells you that SPSS is in the middle of the procedure named "Means."

The Data Files

An important part of learning how to use SPSS and using this book, is using the sample files located at the Prentice Hall Web site (http://www.pearsonhighered.com/salkind). Throughout we will use two separate sets of data to illustrate various SPSS features, such as entering and working with data. These are described in the following.

Tip: If you are performing an analysis and nothing seems to be happening, look in the Status Bar before you panic and conclude that SPSS or Windows has locked up. Large numbers and complex analyses often take computer resources and time to complete.

The Crab Scale File

The first data set is a collection of scores on the Crab Scale and some biographical information for 10 college professors who completed a measure of crabbiness. Table 1 gives a summary of the variables, their definition and their range of values.

The Crab Scale includes the following six items:

1. I generally feel crabby if someone tries to help me.
2. I generally feel happy when I watch the news.
3. I generally feel crabby when I watch mothers and fathers talk baby talk to their babies.
4. I generally feel happy when I am able to make sarcastic comments.
5. I generally feel crabby when I am on a family vacation.
6. I generally feel happy when I am beating someone at a game.

A teacher responds to each item on the following 5-point scale:

1. Totally agree
2. Agree
3. In a quandary
4. Disagree
5. Vicious lies

The Crab Scale yields two scores:

1. *The Cross-Situational Crab Index:* This index tries to assess whether individuals refuse to be happy regardless of the situation.
2. *The True Crab Scale:* This index attempts to assess whether an individual is acting in a true crablike fashion: crabby when confronted with a pleasant stimulus and happy when confronted with an unpleasant stimulus.

Items 1–6 are summed to yield a total score. For the Cross-Situational Crabbiness Index, all scores are summed together. Items 2, 4, and 6 are happiness items, and the scores on these items must be reversed so that higher scores indicate more crabbiness as shown here.

Original Scoring	Recoded Scoring
1	5
2	4
3	3
4	2
5	1

You can see the actual set of data as Crab Scale Results.

The Teacher Scale File

No teacher escapes being rated by students. The second set of data we will deal with in Part I of *Using SPSS for Analyzing and Understanding Data for Windows and the Macintosh* is a set of responses by students concerning the performance of these 10 professors.

The second data set is a collection of scores on the Teacher Scale and some biographical information for 50 students who completed the Teacher Scale.

Table 2 shows the biographical information we collected on each student and their responses to the 5-point scale. We will be using them in examples throughout this part of the book.

The Teacher Scale contains the following five items:

1. I love that teacher.
2. My teacher says good stuff.

Variable	Name	Range
id_stud	student's identification number	1–50
id_prof	professor's identification number	1–5
Sex_stud	student's gender	1 or 2
teacher1	score for item 1 on the Teacher Scale	1–5
teacher2	score for item 2 on the Teacher Scale	1–5
teacher3	score for item 3 on the Teacher Scale	1–5
teacher4	score for item 4 on the Teacher Scale	1–5
teacher5	score for item 5 on the Teacher Scale	1–5

Table 2   Teacher Scale Summary

3. The teacher has trouble talking.
4. The teacher is a jerk.
5. My teacher made the boring lively, the unthinkable thinkable, the undoable doable.

Items 3 and 4 must be reversed so that higher scores indicate effectiveness as follows:

Original Scoring	Recoded Scoring
1	5
2	4
3	3
4	2
5	1

Lesson 3
Using SPSS Help

After This Lesson, You Will Know

- About the contents of the SPSS Help menu
- How to use the F1 function key for help
- What Help options are available
- How to use the Find option to search for particular words

Key Words

- Ask Me
- Contents
- F1 function key
- Find
- Help menu
- Index
- SPSS Help
- Topics

If you need help, you've come to the right place. SPSS offers help that is only a few mouse clicks away. It is especially useful when you are in the middle of creating a data file and need information about a specific SPSS feature. Help is so comprehensive that even if you're a novice SPSS user, SPSS Help can show you the way.

How to Get Help

You can get help in SPSS in several ways. The easiest and most direct is by pressing the **F1 function** key or by using the **Help menu.** Unlike earlier versions of SPSS, Help is now entirely web based so you need an Internet connection to access it.

As you can see, there are ten options on the Help menu.

- **Topics** lists the topics for which you can get help. You can click on any one of these. As you enter the topic, SPSS searches its internal database to find what you need.
- **Tutorial** takes you through a step-by-step tutorial for major SPSS topics.
- **Case Studies** provides you with hands-on examples of how to use SPSS.
- **Statistics Coach** walks you through the steps you need to determine what type of analysis you want to conduct.
- **Command Syntax Reference** provides you with information on SPSS programming language. (Note: This option does not appear in the Macintosh version of SPSS.)
- **Developer Central** is for those brave folks who want to develop add-ons or products which use SPSS as a platform.
- **About** tells you the version of SPSS that you are currently using.
- **Algorithms** tells you about how SPSS does its work in the background.
- **SPSS Home** uses your Internet connection to take you to the home page of SPSS on the Internet. Syntax Guide provides you with help using SPSS' powerful syntax feature.
- **Check for Updates** does just that—it checks to make sure that your version of SPSS is current.

Figure 5   The F1 Help options.

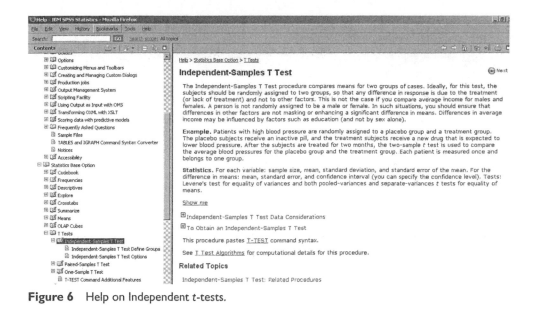

Figure 6   Help on Independent *t*-tests.

Using the F1 Function Key

The F1 function key is a quick way to get help, and open the **Help** window you see in Figure 5. It is not context sensitive. In other words, it produces the same outcomes as the HelpfiTopics click combination.

In the Help window you can select from the several options on the Help menu in the Data Editor Windows such as Help, Tutorial Case Studies, Statistics Coach, and Add-ons. For example, in Figure 6, you can see the help screen for an independent *t*-test.

Lesson 4
A Brief SPSS Tour

After This Lesson, You Will Know

- How to open a file
- Some of the basic functions that SPSS can perform

Key Words

- Fonts
- Open

In the first three lessons of *Using SPSS*, you learned how to start SPSS, took a look at the SPSS main menus, and found out how to use SPSS Help.

Now, sit back and enjoy a brief tour of SPSS activities. Nothing fancy here. Just creating some new variables, simple descriptions of data, a test of significance, and a graph or two. What we're trying to show you is how easy it is to use SPSS. We will spend all of Part II of *Using SPSS* concentrating on exactly how to use SPSS' analytic procedures.

Figure 7 Opening a File.

Opening a File

You can enter your own data to create a new SPSS data file, use an existing file, or even import data from such applications as Microsoft Excel into SPSS. Any way you do it, you need to have data to work with. In Figure 7 you can see we have a screen full of data, the Teacher Scale Results file mentioned earlier. We opened it using the Open option on the File menu.

If you use a spreadsheet application, then the structure of the data file appears familiar; it has rows and columns, with cases for rows and variables for columns.

Working with Appearance

Everyone has his or her preference on how things look. In Figure 7, the data appear in a sans serif font named Arial and 10 points (with one point being equal to 1/72 of an inch) in size. For whatever reason, you may want to select another font and change the style in which the values or headings appear.

> *Tip: If you want to open saved output, then you have to select the Output option on the File → Open menu, or the Syntax or Script option or whatever you want to open.*

Simply by using the Fonts option on the View menu, we changed the font to Times New Roman 12 point. We also used the Grid Lines option on the View menu to turn off the grid lines. The partial screen showing the data file appears in Figure 8.

> *Tip: A quick way to change the appearance of data in the Data Editor is to right click in any cell and click Grid Font. Then select the font, size, and style.*

Creating a New Variable

As you know, the Teacher Scale is a five-item measure of teacher effectiveness. Let's assume that we want to compute a new variable that is the average of the five items, so that each student's ratings have an average score.

Figure 8 Changing the appearance of data.

Figure 9   Using the Compute Command to create a new variable.

To create a new variable, we use the Compute Variable option on the Transform menu. The finished result (the new variable named "Average") is shown in Figure 9.

A Simple Table

Now it's time to get to the reason why we're using SPSS in the first place, the various analytical tools that are available. First, let's say we want to know the general distribution of males and females. That's all, just a count of how many males and how many females are in the total sample.

In Figure 10, you can see an output window that provides exactly the information we asked for, which was the frequency of the number of males and females. We clicked AnalyzefiDescriptive StatisticsfiFrequencies to compute these values. We could have

Statistics

Sex of Student

N	Valid	50
	Missing	0

Sex of Student

		Frequency	Percent	Valid Percent	Cumulative Percent
Valid	Male	28	56.0	56.0	56.0
	Female	22	44.0	44.0	100.0
	Total	50	100.0	100.0	

Figure 10   A simple SPSS table.

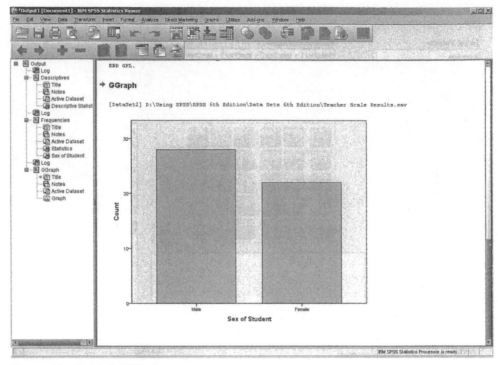

Figure 11 A simple SPSS chart.

computed several other descriptive statistics, but just the count is fine for now. Here's your first look at real SPSS output, contained in the Viewer window and the outline pane on the left which lists all the output available.

Guess what? With just another few clicks, we can create the bar chart you see in Figure 11). Also, you should notice that as additional items are added to the Viewer, the outline pane to the left of the viewer lists those as well.

A Simple Analysis

Let's see if males and females differ in their average Teach scores. This is a simple analysis requiring a *t*-test for independent samples. You may already know about this procedure from another statistics class you have had, or it may be entirely new. The procedure is a comparison between the mean for the group of males and the mean for the group of females.

In Figure 12, you can see a partial summary of the results of the *t*-test. Notice that the listing in the left pane of the Viewer now shows the Frequencies, Graph, and *t*-test procedures listed. To see any part of the output, all we need to do is click on that element, in the left pane of the Viewer, as we did with Frequencies. The large arrow (which appears in red on the screen) indicates which of the various outputs you have highlighted in the output pane.

Figure 12 A simple SPSS analysis.

Lesson 5
Defining Variables

After This Lesson, You Will Know

- How to open a new data file
- How to define an SPSS variable's characteristics

Key Words

- Column
- Row
- Variable View window
- Data View window
- Variable information bar

Here's where all the work begins, with the entry of data into the SPSS spreadsheet like structure, the Data View. When you first open SPSS, the Data Editor window is labeled "Untitled - SPSS Data Editor," and it's ready for you to enter variables as well as cases. You can just begin entering data in Row 1, Column 1 and as you can see in Figure 13, SPSS will record that as the first data point for var00001 (which SPSS will automatically name the column or variable). In SPSS, rows always represent cases and columns always represent variables.

Creating an SPSS New Window

If you are already working within SPSS and want to create a new Data View window, follow this step.

1. Click **File → New → Data**. You will see a blank Data View window and you are ready to either define or enter data.

Having SPSS Define Variables

Now that the new data window is open, you can do one of two things. The first is to enter data into any cell in the Data View Window and press the Enter key (which is the

Figure 13   Entering Data in Data View Window.

Figure 14   SPSS can automatically define variables.

standard way of entering data). For example, you could enter the value 87 in row 1, column 1 and press the Enter key. Since SPSS must have a variable name to work with, SPSS will automatically name the variable var00001. If you did this in row 1, column 5 (where the value 52 was entered), then SPSS would name the variable var00005 and also number the other columns sequentially, as you see in Figure 14.

Note also that right below the main menu in the upper left-hand corner of the Data View window is an indicator of what cell is being highlighted. For example, in Figure 25, you can see that 1:var00005 represents row 1, variable 5.

Custom Defining Variables: Using the Variable View Window

However, a critical part of dealing with data is defining those variables that you intend to enter. And by defining, we mean everything from providing a name for the variable (or the column in the Data View window), the type of variable it is, how many decimal places it will use and so forth.

In order to define a variable, one must first go to the Variable View Windows by clicking the Variable View tab at the bottom of the SPSS screen. Once that is done, you will see the Variable View window as shown in Figure 15 and be able to define any one variable as you see fit.

Once in the Variable View window, you can define variables along the following parameters:

- **Name** provides a name for a variable up to eight characters
- **Type** defines the type of variable such as text, numeric, string, scientific notation, etc.
- **Width** defines the number of characters wide the column housing the variable will occupy.
- **Decimals** defines the number of decimals that will appear in the Data View.
- **Label** defined as a label up to 256 characters for the variable.
- **Values** defines the labels that correspond to certain numerical values (such as 1 for male and 2 for female).
- **Missing** indicates how missing data will be dealt with.
- **Columns** defines the number of spaces allocated for the variable in the Data View window.
- **Align** defines how the data is to appear in the cell (right, left or enter aligned).

Figure 15   The Variable View Window.

Figure 16 The Variable View of the Crab Scale Results file.

- **Measure** defines the scale of measurement that best characterizes the variable (nominal, ordinal, or interval).
- **Role** defines the type of variable it is (Input, Target, etc.)

The general way in which these characteristics of a variable are defined is by clicking on the cell for that particular variable (variable 1, variable 2, etc.) and then specifying the particulars of those characteristics for the variable under question.

Each of these is described as follows. We use the file named "Crab Scale Results" and discuss how we defined these available. The Variable View of their file is shown in Figure 16.

Defining Variable Names

To define the name of a variable, follow these steps:

1. Click on a cell in the **Name column** in the Variable View window.
2. Press the Enter key. The name for the first variable was "id_prof."

Defining Variable Types

If you click on a cell in the Type button, and the ellipsis in it (see Figure 17), you see the Variable Type dialog box. Its variable definitions include numeric (e.g., 3435.45),

Figure 17 Defining the type of variable.

Figure 18   Changing the width of a variable.

comma (e.g., 3,435.45), dot (e.g., 3.43545), scientific notation (e.g., 3.4E+03), date (e.g., 12-FEB-1996), dollar (e.g., $3,435.45), custom currency (as you design it), or a string (such as William). In our example, all variables are defined as numeric.

Defining Variable Widths

To define the width of a variable, follow these steps:

1. Click on a cell in the **Width column** for the corresponding variable (in the Variable View screen).
2. Enter the number of characters you want to use to define the variable or click on the up and down triangles (see Figure 18) to change the value (which in this example is for age).

Defining Variable Decimals

To define the number of decimals used to define variable, follow these steps:

1. Click on the **Decimal column** for the corresponding variable
2. Enter the number of characters you want to use to define the number of decimals or click on the up and down triangles to change the number in the cell.

Defining Variable Labels

To define the Label used for a variable, follow these steps:

1. Click on the **Label column** for the corresponding variable.

Enter up to 256 characters for the label, including spaces. Labels appear in SPSS output and are not visible in the Data View window.

Defining Variable Values

Values are used to represent the contents of a variable in the Data View window. For example, we will show you how we defined the sex of the teacher using 1's and 2's and 3's for the variable named "rank," while those 1's and 2's and 3's appear as assistant, associate, and full professor in the Data View window.

In general, it makes more sense to work with numbers than with string or alphanumeric variables in an analysis. In other words, values such as 1 for assistant professor, 2 for associate professor, and 3 for full professor provide more information than the actual text that describes the levels of the variable named rank.

Just the same, it sure is a lot easier to look at a data file and see words rather than numbers. Just think about the difference between a data file with numbers representing various levels (such as 1, 2, and 3) of a variable and the actual values (such as assistant professor, associate professor, or full professor).

To define the Values used for a variable, follow these steps:

1. Click on the **Values column** for the corresponding variable. In this case, we are using rank as the example.
2. Click on the **ellipsis** to open the Value Labels dialog box as shown in Figure 19.
3. Enter a value for the variable. This is what will appear in the data file window, such as 1, 2, or 3.
4. Enter the value label for the value such as assistant, associate or full.
5. Click **Add**.
6. Click **Continue**. When you finish your business in the Define Labels dialog box, click **OK**, and the new labels will take effect.

Tip: Once a variable is defined, you can easily change the value by just clicking on the arrow of a highlighted cell in the Data View.

Defining Missing Values for a Variable

To define the Values used for a variable, follow these steps:

1. Click on the **Missing column** for the corresponding variable
2. Click the **ellipsis** and you will see the Missing Values dialog box. The various options you can select are as follows:

   - The No missing values option treats all values as being valid, such that no missing values are present in the data file.
   - The Discrete missing values option allows you to enter up to three values for a missing variable.

Figure 19 The Value Labels dialog box.

- The Range plus one discrete missing value option will identify as missing all the values between the low and high values you identify, plus one additional value outside the range.

Defining Variable Columns

To define the variable Columns Values follow these steps:

1. Click on the **Columns** column for the corresponding variable
2. Enter the value you want for the width of the column or click on one of the up or down triangle to set the width.

   Tip: Don't confuse variable width and variable columns defining character-istics. Width refers to the number of characters used to define the display in the Data View window. Columns refers to the number of columns used to define the variable.

   Tip: To change the width of a column (in the Data View or Variable View windows), you can drag on the vertical lines that separate the columns from one another.

Defining Variable Alignment

To define the alignment used for a variable, follow these steps:

1. Click on the **Align** column for the corresponding variable.
2. From the drop down menu, select Left, Right, or Center.

Defining Variable Measure

To define the Measure used for a variable, follow these steps:

1. Click on the **Measure column** for the corresponding variable.
2. From the drop down menu, select Scale, Ordinal, or Nominal as the level of measurement you want to use for this variable.

   In sum, we have defined 11 different variables as shown in Figure 27. Each has particular set of characteristics and any of these can be changed quickly and easily be clicking on the Variable View window tab and then changing the variable attribute you want.

Lesson 6
Entering and Editing Data

After This Lesson, You Will Know

- How to enter data into an SPSS Data Editor window
- About editing data in SPSS

Figure 20   A simple data file.

Key Words

- Active cell
- Save File As dialog box
- Save Data As dialog box

You just learned how to define a set of variables. Now it's time to enter data that correspond to the set of variables. We'll also learn how to edit data. The file that you will create consists of 10 cases and three variables (id, sex, and test1), and you can see what it looks like in Figure 20.

Getting Ready for Data

Let's start at the beginning. First, we'll define each of the three variables in the data file you see in Figure 20. Start with an empty Data Editor window.

1. Click the **Variable View tab** in the opening window.
2. In cell 1, row 1, type the variable name id.
3. Press the Enter key and you will see SPSS complete the default definition for each of the variables characteristics.
4. In cell 1, row 2, type the variable name sex.
5. Press the Enter key and you will see SPSS complete the default definition for each of the variables characteristics.
6. In cell 1, row 2, type the variable name test.
7. Press the Enter key and you will see SPSS complete the default definition for each of the variables characteristics. Each row (representing a variable) should contain the information necessary to define three variables; id, sex, and test as you see in Figure 21.
8. Click on the **Data View tab** to return to the Data Editor window.

Figure 21   Defining three variables.

Entering Data

Entering data into the Data Editor window and creating a data file is as simple as entering data in a spreadsheet or creating a table using a word processor. You just click in the cell where you want to enter data (which then appears as outlined), click, and type away. Let's enter data for the first case.

1. Place the cursor on row 1, column 1.
2. Click once. The cell borders of the individual cell in the data file will be outlined.
3. Type 1 for id.
4. Press Tab to move to the next variable in the current case. You can also press the down arrow (↓) key to move to the next case within the same variable. SPSS will enter the value 1.00 since the default format is two decimal places. The next cell in the row will then be highlighted. You'll notice that as you enter values into cells in the Data Editor the value appears in the data entry information bar right above the column headings.

    The cell in the Data Editor that is highlighted and that shows the value in the information bar is the active cell. In Figure 22 the active cell has a value of 1.
5. Type 1 for sex.
6. Press the tab key to move to the column labeled "test." The Shift+Tab key combination moves one cell to the left.
7. Type 45. To get to the next case, press the Home key and the down arrow (↓) key. Compare your Data Editor to the one you see in Figure 34 to be sure you are entering data in the correct locations.
8. Continue entering data in the Data Editor until all the data you see (all 10 cases) are entered.

    If you make an error, just backspace. Or, just don't worry about it! You will learn how to correct such errors in the next section in this lesson.

Editing Data

Editing data in a data file is simply a matter of locating the data you want to edit and then changing them. There are several techniques you can use to do this, including a simple click and edit or cutting and pasting. You'll learn about them all in this part of the lesson.

Changing a Cell Value

Let's say that you want to change the value of test for case 3 from 44 to 54. You made an error in data entry and want to correct it. Here's how.

1. Click on the cell you want to change, which in this case is the cell in test1, case 3 with a value of 44. When you click on the cell, its value will appear in the data information bar or the cell editor area.
2. Type 54. As you begin typing the new value, it replaces the old one.

Figure 22 Entering the first data point in the Data Editor.

3. Press Enter. The new value is now part of the data file.

Tip: As with any Windows operation, double clicking on the contents of a cell selects all the material in that cell. You can just double click and type the replacement.

Editing a Cell Value

You can also edit an existing value without replacing it. For example, you may want to change the test1 value for case 1 from 45 to 40, and you just want to change the last digit rather than replace the entire value. Here's how.

1. Click the cell containing the value you want to edit. In this case it is the cell for test1, case 1, which contains the value 45.
2. Click to the right of the last digit in the data entry information bar. A blinking horizontal line will appear in the cell editor following the last digit of the cell entry.
3. Backspace once to delete the 5.
4. Type 0.
5. Press Enter or move to another cell. The new value is now part of the data file.

If you wanted to change a value such as 4565 to 4665, you would use the mouse pointer to insert the blinking cursor between the first 5 and the 6, press the backspace key once, and then enter the new value. If you wanted to insert a value in an existing one (such as changing 198 to 1298), you would place the cursor where you want the new values to be inserted and just enter them.

Saving a Data File

This is the easiest operation of all, but it may be the most important. As you know from your experience with other applications, saving the files that you create is essential. First, saving allows you to recall the file to work on at a later time. Second, saving allows you to back up files. Finally, you can save a file under a new name and use the copy for a purpose different from the original purpose.

Don't wait to save until your data file is entered and you are sure there are no errors. Why should you save a file before it is entered exactly as you want it? It's a matter of being "safe rather than sorry."

Tip: How often should you save? You should save after a set amount of work (either time or pages worth). One general rule is to save as often as necessary so that you can easily recreate any work you might lose between saves—every time you finish entering 10 cases or after 30 minutes of work might be a good starting guideline.

When you are creating a data file document (and before you save it for the first time), the only "copy" of it is stored in the computer's memory. If, for some reason, the computer malfunctions or the power (and the computer) goes off, whatever is stored in this temporary memory will be lost. It literally disappears, whether it is a data file with three variables and 10 cases or 300 variables and 10,000 cases. Save data files as you work!

Before saving a file for the first time, however, the first order of business is deciding on a name for the file.

To save a data file, you must assign a unique file name to it. For example, if you were to name a file "data" you might find it confusing, because you will surely be creating more than one file, and "data" describes virtually all of them. Also, should you try to save a file to a directory containing an identically named file with different contents, the new file will overwrite the original file. You lose the original file and all your work.

For these reasons, use a name that describes the contents of the data file. SPSS also automatically attaches the .sav extension to all saved files.

With Windows, file names can be up to 225 characters long, so you shouldn't have any difficulty being sufficiently descriptive, although being wordy has problems, too. Try to find a middle ground between describing the file and not having a name so long that it can't easily fit on the screen.

To save the data document that is active, follow these steps:

1. Click **File → Save**. When you do this, you will see the Save Data As dialog box which you should be familiar with by now.
2. Select the directory in which you want to save the data. If you are saving to a hard drive and you are working in a computer lab, be sure you have permission. If you are saving to a floppy disk, select drive a or drive b.
3. Enter the file name you want to use in the File Name text box to save the data that has been entered.
4. Click OK.

The data you entered will then be saved as a data file, and the name of the file will appear in the title bar of the Data Editor window. The next time you select Save Data from the File menu, you will not see the Save Data As dialog box. SPSS will just save the changes under the name you originally assigned to the data file. And remember, SPSS will save the data in the active directory. In most cases, that will be the same directory that contains SPSS, a situation you may or may not want.

Tip: You can have Windows hide file extensions by going to the Explorer, right clicking, selecting properties and asking Windows to hide extensions.

The Save As option on the file menu allows you to save a file under another name or under another format. For example, if you select the Save As options, you can select from such formats as Excel and Lotus 2-3—very handy for exporting your SPSS file to another application.

Tip: Unlike other Windows applications, you must first enter data before you can save the data as an SPSS file. SPSS will not let you save a blank Data Editor window.

Saving a File in a New Location

You can easily select any other location to save a file. Perhaps you want to keep the application and data files separate. For example, many SPSS users have a separate directory for each project. That way, files from different projects don't get mixed together. Or, you may want to save a file to a floppy disk and then take the disk home for safekeeping.

Here's how to save a file to another location:

1. Click **File → Save As**. You'll see the Save Data As dialog box.
2. Enter the name of the file in the File Name text box.
3. In the Save In section of the Save As dialog box, click the directory where you want the file saved. For example, if you want to save the file to a disk in drive B, click [-b-].
4. Click OK, and the file is saved to the new location.

You can save to any location by clicking a series of drives and directories.

Figure 23   The Open File dialog box.

Opening a File

Once a file is saved, you have to open or retrieve it when you want to use it again. The steps are simple.

1. Click the File icon or **File → Open → Data** (and the kind of file you want to open), and you will see the Open File dialog box as you see in Figure 23.
2. Find the file you want to open, and double click on the file name to open it or highlight the file name and click OK.

Lesson 7

Inserting and Deleting Cases and Variables

After This Lesson, You Will Know

- How to insert and delete a case
- How to insert and delete a variable
- How to delete multiple cases and variables

Key Words

- Insert
- Delete

More often than not, the data you first enter to create a data file need to be changed. For example, you may need to add a variable or delete a case. You learned in the last lesson how to enter and edit data and then save all the data as a data file. But the simple editing may not be enough.

There are times when you want to add one or more cases, or even an entirely new variable, to a data set. A subject might drop out of an experiment and you may choose to delete a case, or for measurement or design reasons an entire variable may no longer be

Figure 24   Data File.

useful and need to be deleted from a data file. In this lesson, we will show you how to insert and delete both cases and variables.

The SPSS file we'll work with in this lesson is shown in Figure 24. It contains three variables (age in years, social class, and preference for soft drink).

Inserting a Case

Notice in Figure 24 that the cases are sorted by age in ascending order from the youngest subject (aged 44) to the oldest subject (age 67). Let's say we want to add a new case. We'll place it between the second and third cases.

> *Tip: When inserting a case, you can select any cell in the row above which you want to insert the case.*

1. Select a cell in the row above which you want to insert the new case. In this example, it is row 3 since we want the new case to appear right above row 3. You can select any cell in the row.
2. Click **Edit → Insert Cases**, or click the Insert Case button on the toolbar. As you can see in Figure 25 an entire new row opens up, providing room to enter the data for the new case.

You'll notice that when you add a case, dots appear in the blank cells indicating that there are missing data. Now you can enter the data that make up the new case. Enter any data you want.

Figure 25   Inserting a case.

Inserting a Variable

Now let's say that you need to add an additional variable to the data file. For example, you want to add the variable weight in pounds so that it appears before the variable labeled "pref," for preference.

1. Select a cell in the column to the right of where you want to insert the new variable. We selected a cell in column 3 (labeled pref) since we want to insert a new variable just to the left of pref.
2. Click **Edit → Insert Variable**, or click the Insert Variable button on the toolbar. As you can see in Figure 26, an entire new column opens up providing room to enter the data for the new variable. As you can also see, the new variable is automatically named by SPSS as "var00001."

Deleting a Case

Now it comes time to learn how to delete a case that you no longer want to be part of the data file.

1. Click on the case number (not any cell in the row) to highlight the entire row.
2. Click **Edit → Clear**. You can also press the Del key, or right click and click Clear, and the case will be deleted.

Tip: Oops! Inadvertently delete something? Select the Undo command on the Edit menu or use the Ctrl → Z key combination to undo the last action.

Deleting a Variable

We're sure you know what's next, deleting a variable. Needing to delete a variable is probably a rare occurrence; you would have thought through your data collection procedures well enough to avoid collecting data you don't need. Nonetheless, the situation does arise.

Tip: To delete more than one case or more than one variable, drag over the cases or variables and select them all and then press the Del key.

For example, perhaps you find out after the fact that data you collected (such as social class) are confidential and cannot be used. You therefore need to delete the variable across all cases. Here's how.

Figure 26 Inserting a new variable.

1. Click on the variable or column to highlight the entire column.
2. Click the **Edit → Clear**. You can also press the Del key, and the variable will be deleted, or right click and click Clear.

Lesson 8
Selecting, Copying, Cutting, and Pasting Data

After This Lesson, You Will Know

- How to select data
- How Cut and Copy and Paste can be used in a data file
- How to cut and paste data
- How to copy and paste data
- What the clipboard does, and what its limitations are

Key Words

- Buffer
- Clipboard
- Copy
- Cut
- Paste

This last lesson on editing a data file has to do with some Windows techniques that you may already be familiar with: selecting, cutting, copying, and pasting. In fact, these simple operations can save you time and trouble, especially when you want to move the value of one or more cells from one location to another, or to repeat columns or rows.

Copying, Cutting, and Pasting

With the Cut, Copy, and Paste tools located on the Edit menu, you can easily move cell entries (be it one or more cells) from one part of a data file to another part of the same data file. You can also move cell entries from one data file to another entirely different data file or even to another Windows application!

In general, the steps you take to cut or copy and paste are as follows:

1. Select the data you want to cut or copy by dragging over the data with the mouse pointer. It can be an individual cell, row, column, or more than one row or column. Rows and columns can also be selected by clicking on them at the top (for a column) or at the left (for a row). A range of cells defines a rectangular- or square-shaped set of cells.

   Tip: The Shift+arrow key combination can be used to select a range of cells as well. Click in an "anchor" cell, the use the Shift up, down, right or left arrows to select what you want.

Figure 27 Data File.

2. Click **Edit** → **Cut** or Copy. Unfortunately, unlike in other Windows applications, there are not cut, copy, and paste buttons on the toolbar.
3. Select the destination, or target cell, where you want the data pasted. The destination, or target cell, you select will act as the upper left-hand anchor if you are cutting or copying more than one cell.
4. Click **Edit** → **Paste**.

The selected data will appear in the new location. Here is an example of cutting and pasting and copying and pasting—the data that we're using, which you see in Figure 27. It consists of five cases of three variables (weight in pounds, height in inches, and strength ranking).

Selecting Data

Before you can cut, copy, or paste anything, you first have to highlight what you want to cut or copy. You are probably used to the most direct way of highlighting data, which is through the drag technique. For example, if you want to highlight a particular section of a data file, just drag the mouse pointer over that section.

Thus, any set of data, cases, or variables can be highlighted by just dragging over the information using the mouse. An individual cell is automatically highlighted when you click on that cell.

What if you're not a mouser? Not to worry. Here's an easy-to-use summary (Table 3) that will tell you how to use the keyboard to select any amount of text you want.

To select	Use these keys
One cell down	↓ or the Enter key
One cell up	↑
One cell to the right	→
One cell to the left	←
The first cell in a case	Home
The last cell in a case	End
The first case in a variable	Ctrl + ↑
The last case in a variable	Ctrl + ↓
An entire case	Shift + Space
An entire variable	Ctrl + Space
a block of cells	Shift + ↑ or ↓ or ← or →

Table 3 Keyboard strokes for selecting

Figure 28   Highlighting a variable to be moved.

Cutting and Pasting

Data are cut from a data file when you want to remove them from their original locations and paste them into another location.

Here's an example of cutting data to rearrange the order in which variables appear. We'll be showing you this activity in Figures 28 and 29 where part of the data file is copied to a new location. Specifically, we'll move the height variable so that it is after strength.

1. Highlight the data you want to cut as you see in Figure 28. In this example, we are highlighting the variable (and not just the data in that column) named "height." Remember, when data are cut, they disappear from the original location. When you select, be sure to click on the variable name.
2. Click **Edit → Cut**. When you do this, the variable height disappears from the Data View window.
3. Move the insertion point to the location where you want to insert, or paste, the data and create a new place for a variable. Click at the top of the column where the new variable name will appear so you highlight the entire column.
4. Click **Edit → Paste**. The data that were cut will then appear as you see in Figure 29. This is a pretty efficient way of getting data from one place to another.

   Tip: When cutting, copying, and pasting, SPSS has right-click features where you can highlight and then right click to select Cut, Copy, or Paste. You can also use keyboard command to Copy (Ctrl + C), Cut (Ctrl + X), and paste (Ctrl + V). If you use a Mac, use the Apple key instead of Ctrl.

This is an example of cutting and pasting text within the same data file. Should you want to cut and paste between data files, the process is much the same. Here are the general steps.

Figure 29   Pasting a variable in a new location.

1. Highlight the data you want to cut and paste.
2. Click **Edit → Cut**.
3. Open a new data file or the one into which you want the data pasted.
4. Move the insertion point to the location where you want to insert, or paste, the data.
5. Click **Edit → Paste**. Data will appear in the new location as shown in Figure 29.

Copying and Pasting

Copying data is not much different from cutting data, except that the data remain in their original locations. Copying is the ideal tool when you want to duplicate data within a document or between documents.

> *Tip: Want to paste the same data in several locations? Just continue to select the Paste option from the File menu or the right-click menu.*

For example, the weight, strength, and height data may be part of one data file, and you want to copy only the first two variables (weight and strength) to a new data file. You will add additional variables and cases to the new file, but you want to preserve the original.

The steps for copying and pasting are basically the same as cutting and pasting except for one different command. Here are the steps.

1. Highlight the data you want to copy. Remember, when data is copied, the data remains where it was originally located.
2. Click **Edit → Copy**.
3. Move the insertion point to the target cell where you want to insert or paste the copied data.
4. Click **Edit → Paste**. The data that were copied will then appear.

A good use of copy and paste would be to copy data from a master data file that you want to use over and over, don't want to change, and need to borrow from in the future. Using copy and paste will leave the master document intact while you copy what you need.

Where Copy or Cut Data Go

What happens to data that you cut or copy? When you cut or copy data, they are placed in a buffer, an area reserved for temporary memory. This buffer is called the clipboard. The data are retrieved from the buffer when you select Paste. In fact, whatever information is in the buffer stays there until it is replaced with something else.

For this reason you can paste the contents of the buffer into documents over and over again until something new has been cut or copied, replacing what was in the buffer. That's why the Paste button is always darkened (or active) since it's ready to paste whatever is in the buffer.

Want to see the contents of the clipboard? Here's how.

1. Click **Start → Programs → Accessories → Clipboard Viewer**. You'll see the current contents of the clipboard.

It's useful to remember some things about the clipboard.

First, this buffer can hold only one thing at a time. As soon as you cut or copy something new, the new data replace whatever was first in there.

Second, when you quit SPSS, the contents of the clipboard disappear. The clipboard is a temporary place so anything you want to save permanently, you should save to a file with a unique name.

Lesson 9
Printing and Exiting an SPSS File

After This Lesson, You Will Know

- How to print a data file
- How to print a selection from a data file
- How to print output from an analysis or a chart

Key Word

- Print dialog box

Once you've created a data file or completed any type of analysis or chart, you probably will want to print a hard copy for safekeeping or for inclusion in a report or paper. When your SPSS document is printed and you want to stop working, it's time to exit SPSS. You probably already know the way to exit an application is not by turning off the computer! Rather, you need to give your application (and your operating system) time to do any necessary housekeeping (closing and ordering files, and so forth). In this lesson, we will show you how to print and safely exit SPSS.

Printing with SPSS

Printing is almost as important a process as editing and saving data files. If you can't print, you have little to take away from your work session. You can export data from an SPSS file to another application, but getting a hard copy right from SPSS is often more timely and more important.

In SPSS, you can print either an entire data file or a selection from that file. We'll show you how to do both.

Printing an SPSS Data File

Let's begin with data files. It's simple to print a data file.

1. Be sure that the data file you want to print is the active window.
2. Click **File → Print**. When you do this, you will see the Print dialog box shown in Figure 30.

Figure 30 The Print dialog box.

```
┌─────────────────────────────────────────────┐
│              Lesson 9 Data File 1             │
│                                               │
│         ┌──┬────────┬────────┬──────────┐     │
│         │  │ weight │ height │ strength │     │
│         ├──┼────────┼────────┼──────────┤     │
│         │ 1│   132  │   68   │     5    │     │
│         │ 2│   155  │   71   │     4    │     │
│         │ 3│   215  │   76   │     1    │     │
│         │ 4│   165  │   72   │     2    │     │
│         │ 5│   178  │   71   │     3    │     │
│         └──┴────────┴────────┴──────────┘     │
│                                               │
│ 12/05/05 09:41:15 AM                    1/1   │
└─────────────────────────────────────────────┘
```

Figure 31 SPSS Output.

Tip: You can easily print a file with one click; just click the Print icon on the toolbar.

As you can see, you can choose to print the entire document or a specific selection (which you would have already made in the Data Editor window), and increase the number of copies from 1 to 9999 (that's the limit).

3. Click OK and whatever is active will print.

Look at the printed output in Figure 31, and then read the comments in the following.

First, you can see the title of the name assigned to the data file at the top of the page. In this case, it's Lesson 9 Data File 1. This is a convenient reminder of what's being printed.

Second, a footer with the date and time and page numbers is automatically generated and printed at the bottom of the page.

Third, the default is to print gridlines. If you do not want the grid lines to print, click Grid Lines from the View menu (so it is not checked) and the grid lines will not appear, either on screen or on the hard copy. If you want value labels printed, then select Value Labels from the View menu, and those labels will appear in cells, rather than the actual value you entered.

Finally, the default for the orientation is to print in Portrait, which means the short edge of the paper is horizontal. If you want to switch to Landscape, you have to select Properties from the Print dialog box and then click Landscape on the Paper tab.

Tip: The Properties dialog box (File → Print → Properties) allows youth do some pretty cool things. For example, you can print output so that there are two or four pages on a sheet. Perfect for reviewing the results of an analysis before it is printed up for the final draft of an article or report. (Note: You will not find this dialog box in the Mac version.)

Printing a Selection from an SPSS Data File

Printing a selection from a data file follows exactly the steps that we listed for printing a data file, except that in the Print dialog box, you click the Selection option in the Print dialog box.

1. Be sure that the data you want to print is selected (using the techniques we discussed in the last lesson).
2. Click **File → Print** or click the Print icon on the toolbar. When you do this, you will see the Print dialog box.

3. Click Selection if it is not already selected.
4. Click **OK**, and whatever you selected will be printed.

Printing from the Viewer Window

When you complete any type of analysis in SPSS or create a chart, the results appear in the Viewer window. To print the output from such a window, follow exactly the same procedures as you did for printing any data file.

Clicking OK in the Print dialog box will print all the contents of the Viewer. To print a selection from the Viewer, first make the selection by either clicking on the actual material in the right pane of the Navigator, or clicking on the name of the material you want to print in the left pane of the Viewer. Then select the Print option from the File menu and click Selection in the Print dialog box. If the Selection option is dimmed in the Print dialog box, it means that you didn't make a selection and, therefore, cannot print it.

> *Tip: You can select more than one item from the Viewer by holding down the Ctrl key as you select different output elements.*

> *Tip: The Page Setup menu on the File menu (when the Viewer is active) allows you a great deal of flexibility in printing out the contents of the Viewer window. You can set margins and orientation, and even click the Options button and create a highly customized header or footer.*

Exiting SPSS

How do you end your SPSS session and close up shop for the day? Easy.

1. Click **File → Exit SPSS**. SPSS will be sure that you get the chance to save any unsaved or edited windows and will then close. (Note: For the Mac, click File and then click Quit.)

Lesson 10
Exporting and Importing SPSS Data

After This Lesson, You Will Know

- How to export a data file to another application
- How to export a chart to another application
- How to import data from another application

Key Words

- Export
- Import

You already know how to open an SPSS data file by selecting Open from the File menu, locating the file, and clicking OK. But what if you created a file in another application, such as Excel or Lotus 2-3 or Word for Windows, and want to use that file as a data file in SPSS? Or what if you want to use an SPSS data file or a chart in a report you created with Word for Windows? Does that mean reentering all the data? Not at all. SPSS lets you export and import data, and in this lesson you will learn how to do both.

Tip: You export data from SPSS to another application and import data from another application to SPSS.

Getting Started Exporting and Importing Data

When you export an SPSS data file, you are sending it to another application. Just as one country exports products to other countries, so you are exporting data from SPSS to another application.

When you import data from another application, you are going to use it with SPSS. It may be a file created in Word or Excel or dBase. Just as one country imports products from other countries, so you are importing data from another application to SPSS.

Tip: If you have trouble exporting a file created with another application to SPSS, try and convert the file to a text or ASCII file within the application where it was originally created. SPSS can more easily read ASCII files than any others.

In general, the more commercially popular an application is, the more different types of data it supports. For example, Word can translate more than 30 different data formats. SPSS was designed for a more narrow audience than such a popular word processor, so fewer applications can directly read SPSS files. With the increasing popularity of SPSS and with the release of version 11 however, SPSS is more compatible with other applications than ever before.

Exporting Data

Here's just the situation where you would be interested in exporting data. You have been using SPSS to analyze data, and you want to use the results of the analysis in another application. To do so, you want to export data from SPSS. Let's go through the steps of both exporting data, exporting an analysis of that data, and exporting a chart.

Why might you want to export data? One good example is when you want to create an appendix of the raw data used in the analysis. You could just print the data file but, SPSS is limited in that you cannot use more than eight characters to name a variable or change the height of rows (or cases). You, however, want longer variable names or taller rows. So, you'll export the data to Microsoft Excel, which has much greater flexibility in formatting. And since you are writing your report in Microsoft Word for Windows, an Excel-generated appendix is completely compatible.

The first and most important thing to remember about exporting data to another application is the SPSS data must be saved in a format that the other application can understand. Fortunately, SPSS can save data files under a wide variety of formats. Just by examining Table 4, you can get a general idea as to what applications data files can be exported to. The SPSS data file must be saved using the appropriate extension for the application you are exporting to.

Let's go through some examples, beginning with exporting the file we named "Teacher Scale Results" to Excel for Windows.

Application	Extension
SPSS	.sav
SPSS/PC+	.sys
SPSS Portable	.por
Tab Delimited	.dat
Fixed ASCII	.dat
Excel	.xls
2-3 Release	.skl (v3), .wkl (v2), wks (v1)
Sylk	.slk
dBase	.dbf

Table 4   Exporting SPSS data

1. Be sure the data file you want to export is active.
2. Click **File → Save As**.
3. In the "Save as type" area type scores, select the format used by the application you are exporting to. When you make the selection, the file extension changes. In this example, it would be .xlsx (for Excel). Be sure to provide a name for the new file. In this case, it is "scores," and the file will be saved as scores.xlsx.
4. Click **OK**. A new file is created under the file name scores.xls, which can now be read by Excel. When you do export a file, SPSS confirms the export by giving you a message Internet the Viewer window regarding the number of variables and number of cases exported. It's a nice confirmation.
5. Open Excel.
6. In Excel, click **File → Open**.
7. Open the new exported file. Excel displays the file as shown in Figure 32.

What if the application you want to export data into is not listed in the above table? Almost every application can read Tab Delimited or Fixed ASCII data. For example, let's say you wanted to export an SPSS data file into Word for Windows (which saves files with a .doc extension). You could save it as a Tab Delimited file, and then have Word read it. Now, it "ain't purty," but the information is all there. With some changing of font size and spacing, it could appear quite nice and fit well into any document.

SPSS has some pretty terrific charting features. You saw what an SPSS chart looks like in Lesson 4, and you'll learn more about them later in Part I of *Using SPSS*. It won't be uncommon for you to need to create a chart and export it into another application. Let's export a graph into a Word file.

Figure 32   An SPSS file exported into Excel.

1. Create the graph you want to export. Be sure it is active.
2. Click on the actual graph in the right pane of the Viewer. When the graph is selected and ready to be exported, it will be surrounded with a thin black line.
3. Click **Edit → Copy**, or right click, and click then Copy or Copy objects (depending upon the application).
4. Open the application into which you want to export the chart. In this example, the application is Word.
5. Click **File → Paste** or Paste Special (depending upon the application), or right click, and then click Paste. The chart should appear in the new document.

Exporting the Results of SPSS Output

Here's the situation. You've just done a simple *t*-test using SPSS, and you want to export the results of that analysis into another document. In effect, output is treated just like text. It can be cut or copied and pasted, and exporting output is identical to what you just did with a chart.

Why retype all that information when you can just paste it right in? Here's how.

1. Run the analysis you want.
2. Right click on the output you want to export in the right pane of the Viewer.
3. Click **Edit → Copy**, or right click, then click Copy or Copy objects depending on how you want the format of the copied results to appear. If you chose Copy, then the contents of the output will be copied without any special format, and these contents can be edited. If you chose Copy objects, then the exact format you see in the output will be copied.

   Tip: SPSS creates objects as output and cannot be directly edited when exported. They need to be edited within SPSS or exported using the simple copy command.

4. Open the document into which you want to paste the output.
5. Click Edit fi Paste, or right click, and then click Paste.

Here's an important caution, however. If you copy results as an object, then you will not be able to edit it in the new application. An object is a bit-mapped image, much like a picture. If you simply copy them (and not use the Copy objects option), the data will be exported as text and you can edit it, but it will lose it's original format. The best advice? Make your SPSS results to be exactly as you would like (by double clicking on, editing the table within SPSS) them to appear and then copy them as an object.

Importing Data

Here's the situation. You are a user of Excel or Lotus 2-3 and you've entered your data into one of these spreadsheets. Or perhaps you choose to enter your data into one of the many word processors available, such as Word for Windows or WordPerfect. Now you want to analyze the data using SPSS.

This might be the situation if you did not have access to SPSS when it came time to enter the original data or if you just feel more comfortable using some other application to enter data.

1. Click **File → Open**.
2. Locate the file you want to import, highlight it, select the type of file it is from the drop-down file type menu and then click OK. When you do this, you will see the data in the SPSS Data Editor window appearing exactly as it would if you entered directly into SPSS.

Just as you can export from SPSS to other applications, so you can import from a variety of different applications. A word of caution, however. Even though SPSS can read certain file formats (such as .xls for Excel files), it may not mean that SPSS can read the latest version of Excel. Revisions of many products occur, so often it is impossible for them all to stay synchronized as far as versions are concerned. So, before you start entering loads of data to import, check to see if it's even possible.

The most important thing to remember about exporting and importing is finding the right format. You need to save a file in the right format so it can easily be exported or imported. Almost any set of data can be imported and exported as an ASCII file. When you want the data to remain intact as far as format and such, you'll have to look for a different format and experiment to see which format works best. At the very least, you should be able to simply select the data and import or export it to and from SPSS using the Copy and Paste commands available on the main menu and when you right click.

Lesson 11
Finding Values, Variables, and Cases

After This Lesson, You Will Know

- How to find variables, cases, and values
- How to find text

Key Words

- Case
- Case sensitive
- Go To Case dialog box
- Search for Data dialog box
- Value
- Variable
- Variables dialog box

Just imagine you have a data file that contains 500 cases and 10 variables. You know that the entry for age (one of the 10 variables) for case 147 was entered incorrectly. You can either scroll down to find that case or use one of the many find tools that SPSS provides. We'll go through those tools and how to use them in this lesson.

Finding Things

Before we begin showing you how to find things, let's pause for a moment to distinguish among variables, cases, and values. Even if we've covered some of this before, it's a good idea to see all of it in one place.

A value (also called a cell entry) is any entry in a cell, or the intersection of a row and a column. Values can be numerical such as 3, 56.89 or $432.12, or alphanumerical or text such as Sam, Sara, or Julie.

A variable is something that can take on more than one value. Age, weight, name, score on test1, and time measured in seconds are all variables. Variables are defined in SPSS by columns.

Tip: Any search operation requires you to enter the search information in a dialog box, which may block your view of the data editor. You'll have to move the dialog box to view the results of the search. Do this by dragging on the title bar.

A case is a collection of values that belong to a unique unit in the data file, such as a person or a teacher or a school. Cases are defined in SPSS by rows.

With a small data file, you can just eyeball what is on the screen to find what you need. With a large data file, however, you could spend a good deal of time trying to find a case or variable, and even more time trying to find a particular value. If you have 10 variables and 500 cases and no missing data, you have 5,000 cell entries (all of which are values). Trying to find a particular one could take all day! Thus, the SPSS features that can find variables, cases, and values are most welcome.

Finding Variables

For the example in this lesson, we'll use the data file named "Crab Scale Results." Open that file now. We'll find the variable named "rank."

1. Make sure the data file is active.
2. Click **Utilities → Variables**. When you do this, you will see the Variables dialog box, as shown in Figure 33.
3. Click **Rank**. The Variables dialog box provides a good deal of information about the variable, including its name, label, type, missing values that are included, and value labels (Assistant Professor, etc.).
4. Click **Go To**, and SPSS will highlight the first cell in the column containing the variable.

You're now ready to perform any type of operation on that variable, such as working with labels, transformation, recoding, and more.

Finding Cases

Now that you know how to find any variable in a data file, it's time to see how you can find any case. In the Crab Scale Results example, let's assume that you need to locate case 8. You can do that by scrolling through the data file, which is simple enough. If the cases number in the hundreds, however, it's not so simple a task. To save you time and trouble, SPSS finds cases like this.

1. Click **Edit → Go To Case**. When you do this, you will see the Go To Case dialog box, as shown in Figure 34.
2. Type 8.
3. Click **OK**. SPSS will highlight the row corresponding to the number you entered, for whatever column or variable the cursor is currently located in. For example, if we

Figure 33 The Variables dialog box.

Figure 34   The Go To Case dialog box.

just found the variable named rank and then (as a separate operation) located case 8, the highlighted cell would be the rank for case 8, which is Assistant Professor.

Finding Values

Finding values is the most useful of all the search tools, but in one important way it also is the most limited. It's the most useful because any data file has more values than it does variables or cases. It's the most limited because it can only search for a value within one variable.

For example, let's say we want to find the case with an age value of 36.

1. Click the column labeled age. You may highlight any cell in the variable (or column) in which you want to search for the value, such as age.
2. Click **Edit → Find**. When you do this, you will see the Find Data in Variable Age dialog box, as you see in Figure 35.
3. Type 36. You can search either forward or backward through the variable. If you highlighted the first cell in the column, you cannot search backwards since there's no place to go.
4. Click **Find Next** to search through the variable. SPSS will highlight the value when it is found. If SPSS cannot find the value, you will get a Not Found message.

You can also use the Search for Data option to search for values entered as numbers but appearing as text (if they have been assigned labels). For example, if you wanted to find the first occurrence of Female in the variable named sex_prof, you would do as follows:

1. Highlight any cell in the variable (or column) named sex_prof.
2. Click **Edit → Find**.
3. Type Female in the Search for Data dialog box.
4. Click **Find Next**. SPSS will highlight the first occurrence of the value Female.

Figure 35   The Find Data in Variable dialog box.

The value Female was not originally entered in the cell. Instead, the value 2 was entered, and through the definition of the variable the label Female was assigned to that value. If you searched for the value 2 in the same column (sex_prof), SPSS would stop on all occurrences of what you now read as Female. That's because SPSS is looking for *data*, and not necessarily for numbers or text, and Female and 2 are both data. And, if you entered the value female, SPSS would find Female as well, since it looks for whatever it can find that corresponds to what you enter in the Find Data dialog box.

If you want the search to be case sensitive (where upper and lower case letters are distinguished from one another such as Doctor and doctor), then be sure the Ignore case of text in strings box is checked.

Lesson 12
Recoding Data and Computing Variables

After This Lesson, You Will Know

- How to recode data and create new variables
- How to compute new values
- How to recode into Same Variables dialog box
- How to recode into Same Variables: Old and New Values dialog box

Key Words

- Compute
- Compute Variable dialog box
- Formula
- Function
- Recode

There are often situations where you need to take existing data and convert them into a different variable, or to take existing variables and combine them to form an additional variable. For example, you may want to compute the mean or standard deviation for a set of variables and enter those values as a separate variable in the data file. Or you may want to recode data so that, for example, all values of 10 or greater equal 1, and all values less than 10 equal 0. Your needs for transforming or recoding data will depend on the nature of your data and the purpose of your analysis. In either case, SPSS provides some easy-to-use and powerful tools to accomplish both tasks, which we will show you in this lesson.

Recoding Data

You can recode data in one of two ways. First, you can recode a variable to create a new variable. Or you can recode a variable and modify the variable that has already been entered. In this lesson you will use the data saved in the file named "Crab Scale Results."

As you may remember, the Crab Scale includes the following six items:

1. I generally feel crabby if someone tries to help me.
2. I generally feel happy when I watch the news.
3. I generally feel crabby when I watch mothers and fathers talk baby talk to their babies.

Original response	Recorded response
1	5
2	4
3	3
4	2
5	1

Table 5   Reversed Crab Scale Scores

4. I generally feel happy when I am able to make sarcastic comments.
5. I generally feel crabby when I am on a family vacation.
6. I generally feel happy when I am beating someone at a game.

Each item is ranked on the following 5-point scale:

1. Totally agree
2. Agree
3. In a quandary
4. Disagree
5. Vicious lies

   Since some of the crabbiness items (2, 4, and 6) are reversed, these items need to be recoded. For example, if someone totally agrees (a value of 1) with item 2, it means they are happy when they watch the news. Since we are measuring crabbiness and since the lower the score the more crabby someone is, the accurate scoring of this item should be reversed, as shown in Table 5.
   Here's how to do just that.

1. Be sure the file named "Crab Scale Results" is active.
2. Click **Transform → Recode → Into Same Variables**, since we want the transformed variable to replace the values in the current variable that is being transformed. You should see the Recode into Same Variables dialog box, as shown in Figure 36.
3. Double click crab2 to move the variable into the Numeric Variables box.
4. Click the **Old and New Values** ... button, and you will see the Recode into Same Variables: Old and New Values dialog box, as shown in Figure 37.
5. Type 5 in the Value area under Old Values.

Figure 36   The Recode into Same Variables dialog box.

Figure 37 Recode into Same Variables: Old and New Values dialog box.

Figure 38 The Old → New Values dialog box.

6. Type 1 in the Value area under New Values.
7. Click **Add**. The variable is added to the Old—New box, as you see in Figure 38. When SPSS encounters a 5 for variable 2, it will recode it as a 1.
8. Click **Continue**, and you will be returned to the Recode into Same Variables: Old and New Values dialog box.
9. Click **OK**, and the actual values entered in the cells will change according to the way in which they were recorded. For example, if someone responded with a 5 to item 2 on the Crab Scale (as was the case for Professor 3), the recorded value would be 1.

To recode more than one variable at a time (such as items 2, 4, and 6), just add all of them to the Numeric Variables box in the Recode into Same Variables dialog box.

Computing Values

Computing a value means taking existing data and using them to create a new variable in the form of a numeric expression.

To show you how to do that, we will compute a total score for any one individual on the crabbiness scale based on a custom formula. To do this, we will simply add together the scores for variables crab1 through crab5. Keep in mind that SPSS comes with 70

Figure 39 The Compute Variable dialog box.

predesigned functions (a predesigned formula) that will automatically perform a specific computation.

For example, we could tell SPSS to compute a new variable that is the addition of items crab1, crab2, crab3, crab4, and crab5. Or, we could use the SUM function that SPSS provides to accomplish the same end. We'll show you how to do both.

Creating a Formula

Let's create a formula that will add together the values of all five crabbiness items.

1. Click **Transform → Compute Variable**. When you do this, you will see the Compute Variable dialog box, as shown in Figure 39.
2. Click the **Target Variable text box** and enter the name of the new variable to be created. We named it tot_crab, which is the sum of items 1–6 on the Crab Scale.
3. Click the **Numeric Expression text box**.
4. Click **crab1**, the first variable you want to include in the formula.
5. Click the • to add it to the Numeric Expression text box.
6. Type +.
7. Continue adding variables and using the + key to add them together. The completed formula looks like this.

    crab1 + crab2 + crab3 + crab4 + crab5 + crab6

8. Click **OK** and the variable named "tot_crab" was added to the existing data file.

For example, the tot_crab score for case 1 is 16, the simple addition of all the crab items (appropriately recoded, we might add!). If you wanted the average, you could just edit the formula in the Numeric Expression text box to read as

(crab1 + crab2 + crab3 + crab4 + crab5 + crab6)/6

In fact, you can perform any type of mathematical computation you see fit.

Using a Function

Functions are predesigned formulas. So instead of

crab1 + crab2 + crab3 + crab4 + crab5 + crab6

you can enter

$$SUM(crab1,crab2,crab3,crab4,crab5,crab6)$$

which will accomplish the same thing.

There are more than 70 different functions including arithmetic functions, statistical functions, distribution functions, logical functions, date and time functions, cross-case functions, and string functions. It's beyond the scope of *Using SPSS* to go into each one and provide examples, but regardless of how complex or simple functions are, they are all used the same way.

We'll show you how to use one of the most simple and common functions, SUM, which adds a group of values together.

1. Click **Transform → Compute Variable**. If the dialog box is not clear, click Reset.
2. Type tot_crab in the Target Variable text box.
3. In the list of functions, scroll down (if necessary) and find the function you want to use as shown in Figure 40.
4. Double click on that function to place it in the Numerical Expression box.

Figure 40 Entering and using an SPSS function.

5. Now, add variables by double clicking them or by typing their names.
6. Click **OK** and the new variable is created.

An alternative to typing in each variable in the list is to use the "to" operator. Instead of crab1, crab2, ... through crab6, you could type crab1 to crab6 so you have

$$SUM(crab1\ to\ crab6)$$

as the operators in the Numeric Expression box.

Lesson 13
Sorting, Transposing, and Ranking Data

After This Lesson, You Will Know

- The differences among sorting, transposing, and ranking data
- How to sort cases on one or more than one variable
- How to transpose a data file
- How to rank data

Key Words

- Data
- Rank
- Sort Cases
- Transpose

As you have seen in the last few lessons, working with data includes importing, transforming, and recoding data. Working with data also involves sorting, transposing, and ranking data—techniques every SPSS user needs to know to create a data file that exactly fits data analysis needs. We'll look at each of these techniques in this lesson.

Sorting Data

The first of the three data tools is sorting. Sorting data involves reordering of data given the value of one or more variables. Sorting is an invaluable tool when it comes to organizing information.

For example, if you wanted the data for the Crab Scale Results organized by the variable named "rank," you would sort on that variable. If you wanted to sort on more than one variable, you can do that easily as well, such as a sex within rank sort.

Sorting Data on One Variable

Sorting data is as simple as identifying the variable on which you want to sort and directing SPSS to sort.

1. If it is not already opened, open the file named "Crab Scale Results."
2. Click **Data → Sort Cases**. When you do this, you will see the Sort Cases dialog box, shown in Figure 41.

Figure 41   The Sort Cases dialog box.

3. Double click Rank to move rank from the variable list to the Sort by: text box. The Ascending that appears next to rank in the sort box means that the variable will be sorted in ascending order and ascending is the default condition. If you want, select descending order by clicking in the Descending button.
4. Click **OK**.

In Figure 42, you can see the data sorted by rank. After the sort, assistant, associate, and full professors are grouped together. As you can see, when alphanumeric information is sorted in ascending order, the sort is from A to Z.

Tip: When you sort, the results are sorted according to the values in the cells (such 1 for male and 2 for female) and not the labels. If it were sorted according to the labels, then the sort would be with females first since ascending order for text is A through Z.

Sorting Data on More Than One Variable

Sorting data on more than one variable follows exactly the same procedure as the one just outlined, except that you need to select more than one variable to sort on. SPSS will sort in the order they appear in the Sort by list in the Sort Cases dialog box. For

	id_prof	sex_prof	age	rank
1	1.00	Male	33.00	Assistant Professor
2	4.00	Female	36.00	Assistant Professor
3	7.00	Female	29.00	Assistant Professor
4	5.00	Female	42.00	Associate Professor
5	8.00	Male	64.00	Associate Professor
6	9.00	Male	37.00	Associate Professor
7	2.00	Male	58.00	Full Professor
8	3.00	Male	45.00	Full Professor
9	6.00	Male	59.00	Full Professor
10	10.00	Male	42.00	Full Professor

Figure 42   A completed ascending sort on one variable (rank).

example, if you want to sort on gender within rank, then rank should be the first selection in the Sort Cases dialog box and gender (sex_prof) would be the second.

1. Click **Data → Sort Cases**.
2. Click **Rank** to move rank from the variable list to the Sort by: text box.
3. Select whether you want to sort in ascending or descending order.
4. Double click **Sex of Teacher** to move sex_prof from the variable list to the Sort by text box.
5. Select whether you want to sort in ascending or descending order.
6. Click **OK**.

The cases have been sorted on the variable named "rank," such that assistant, associate, and full professors are grouped together, and within rank they are sorted on sex_prof.

Transposing Cases and Variables

As you already know, an SPSS data file is constructed with cases represented by rows and variables represented by columns. This is the way that most data are entered in any type of data collection form, including spreadsheets and other data collection applications.

There may be occasions, however, where you want cases listed as columns and variables listed as rows. In other words, you want variables and cases transposed. This is most often the case when you are importing data (see lesson 10) from a spreadsheet where the data were not entered as cases (rows) and variables (columns). Now that you've imported the data, you want to switch them to fit the conventional SPSS format. Here's how to do it.

1. Click **Data → Transpose**.
2. In the Transpose dialog box, click the variable name and then the [[[-3859]]] button to insert the variable in the Variables text box. Note that you cannot double click to move the variable name as you can in other dialog boxes.
3. Repeat steps 2 and 3 until all the variables that you want to become cases have been entered.
4. Click **OK**. All the variables that were not transposed will be lost, so if you transpose either all the variables in the data file or just some, the ones you don't will not appear after the operation is performed.

Ranking Data

The final data manipulation technique we will deal with is ranking data. Let's say that we used the Compute feature (on the Transform menu) to create a sum of all Crab scores as we did earlier.

Tip: When you want to use a procedure using the same dialog box, use the Recall dialog box button on the toolbar and select the dialog box you want to use.

Now let's say that we are not interested in the absolute value of the Crab score, but rather in the relative rank of professors according to their Crab score. Here's how to do it.

1. If you have not done so already, create a new variable (using the Compute command on the Data menu) named tot_crab, a total of all six crab item scores.
2. Click **Transform → Rank Cases**. You'll see the Rank Cases dialog box, as shown in Figure 43.

Figure 43 The Rank Cases dialog box.

Figure 44 The completed ranking of data.

3. Click on **tot_crab** and move the variable into the Variable(s): text box.
4. Click on the **Largest value** button in the Assign Rank 1 to area.
5. Click **OK**, and a new variable, named Rtot_cra, will be created, as you see in Figure 44, reflecting the ranking of all cases (from 1 through 10) on the variable tot_crab. Cases 2 and 5 have the same tot_crab score (13), and, therefore, the same rank (5.5).

If you select more than one variable on which cases will be ranked, then a separate and new variable will be created for each one of those rankings, and the relative rankings will be listed as well.

Tip: If you want to clear entries in any Variables dialog box, click on the Reset button.

Lesson 14
Splitting and Merging Files

After This Lesson, You Will Know

- How to split a file
- How to merge more than one file and more than one case

Key Words

- Add Cases From dialog box
- Add Cases: Read File dialog box

- Add Variables Fromdialog box
- Add Variables: Read File dialog box
- Merge
- Split
- Split File dialog box

The last skills you need to master before you move on to creating and working with SPSS charts are how to split and merge files. When you **split** a file, you are dividing it into two new and separate files for separate analysis. When you **merge** files, you are combining two files keyed on the same variable or variables, or the same cases using different variables. In this lesson, we'll look at how to do each of these.

Splitting Files

Tip: You can tell that a file has been split when the words Split File On are showing in the right-hand side of the Status Bar.

Throughout this first part of Using SPSS, you have used the Crab Scale Results and Teacher Scale Results to perform simple and complex procedures. We'll use the file named Teacher Scale Results to demonstrate how to split a file.

In general, you split a file when you want to create two separate files, both having at least one variable in common. Creating two separate files might be a choice if you want to produce individual listings of data or prepare data in a way that a particular section, split or organized by using a particular variable, can be cut or copied.

For example, in this lesson, we will split the Teacher Scale Results file using the variable named sex_stud into two separate files. One file will be named Sex Males, and the other will be Sex Females. Then we can do analysis of variance or regression on the separate files.

Splitting a file is not a particularly difficult process. In fact, it's only a matter of selecting the variable on which you want to split.

For example, for the Teacher Scale Results we'll split on sex_stud by following these steps:

1. Open the file named Teacher Scale Results.
2. Click **Data → Split File**. When you do this, you will see the **Split File dialog box**, as shown in Figure 45.

Figure 45　The Split File dialog Box.

Sex of Student = Male

Descriptive Statistics[a]

	N	Minimum	Maximum	Mean	Std. Deviation
teacher1	28	1.00	5.00	3.6429	1.31133
Valid N (listwise)	28				

a. Sex of Student = Male

Sex of Student = Female

Descriptive Statistics[a]

	N	Minimum	Maximum	Mean	Std. Deviation
teacher1	22	1.00	5.00	3.1818	1.09702
Valid N (listwise)	22				

a. Sex of Student = Female

Figure 46 Split Results.

3. Click **Organize Output By Groups** since you are presumably splitting the files to create data for two separate analyses.
4. Double click **Sex_of Student** and move it to the Groups based on box.
5. Click **OK**. The file will then be organized such that all male students are grouped together as are all female students.

Once the split is completed, SPSS will not create two physically separate files. Rather, for the rest of the SPSS session, SPSS will perform every procedure as if the file was physically split into two separate files. A simple descriptive analysis results in descriptive statistics for both males and females.

For example, if you calculate simple descriptive statistics on the variable named teacher1, then you will get separate output for both males and females without having to identify an independent variable named sex_stud. The results of such an analysis are shown in the Viewer in Figure 46. Notice that the analysis was automatically done for both males and females.

Any analysis is performed on each split of the file. For example, if you split on sex_stud (2 levels) and id_prof (10 levels), you would have 20 different descriptive analyses.

Tip: Just as you can sort on more than one variable, you can split on more than one as well. Just enter them into the Split file dialog box in the order you want the entire file split.

Merging Files

Merging files is just as useful as splitting files. Files can be merged, or combined, in two different ways.

First, you can combine two files that contain the same variable or variables but different cases. This would be the setting if more than one researcher were collecting data on the same variables but for different cases (or subjects), and you need to combine the two data files. For example, the Teacher Scale Results survey could have been administered to more than one group of students, and we eventually might want to combine the results of each administration.

Second, you can combine two files that contain different variables but the same cases. For example, you might be having one person collect data with a certain sample and then another person collecting a different set of data on the same sample. Then you want these two combined. Let's look at these possibilities.

Merging Same Variables and Different Cases

In this example, we are going to combine, merge, or add (your choice of words) a new set of five cases of Teacher Scale data to the existing file named Teacher Scale Results. These data are named Teacher Scale Results—Add Data. Be sure that the file named Teacher Scale Results is still open or if not, open it now.

In this example, one researcher collected data on 50 students, and another researcher collected data on five students. The Teacher Scale Results should be open.

1. Click **Data → Merge Files**, then click **Add Cases**. When you do this, you will see the **Add Cases to Teacher Scale Results** (note that SPSS will add the name of the open file to which you are adding to to the dialog box title). There are two options.

   If there is another file open to be added to an existing file, you can specify that in the dialog box by double clicking on that file name.

   If another file is not open, you can browse for the file you want to add, which is the case in this example.
2. Click the Browse button in the Add Cases to Teacher Aclae Results dialog box and find the file names Teacher Scale—Add Data.
3. Click **Continue**. You will see the **Add Cases from Teacher Scale** dialog box.
4. Click **OK**, and the file named Teacher Scale Results—Additional Data is added to the file named Teacher Scale Results, and the total file now has 55 cases (50 cases from Teacher Scale Results and 5 from Teacher Scale Results—Additional Data).

Merging Different Variables and Same Cases

Now we have the example where you have two files that contain a different set of variables for the same cases. For example, we want to combine the Teacher Scale Results—Additional Data and Crab Scale Results files where the common variable is id_prof.

What SPSS will do in this case is combine cases in the Teacher Scale Results file with cases in the Crab Scale Results file, using the variable named id_prof as a common link.

1. Be sure that the original file named Teacher Scale Results is open.
2. Click **Data → Merge Files**, then click **Add Variables**. You will see the **Add Variables: Read File** dialog box.
3. Browse for the file named Crab Scale Results using the An external SPSS data file option.
4. Click **Continue** and you will see the **Add Variables to Teacher Scale Results**.
5. SPSS has already identified that id_prof is common to the two files and has listed it in the Excluded Variables area.
6. Click **OK**.

The result of this merging is a file larger than either of the two files that share the variable named id_prof. If you recall, the file named Teacher Scale Results does not contain any demographic information, such as gender or age, but the merged file including Teacher Scale information does, since it was merged with the Crab Scale data.

Lesson 16
Creating an SPSS Graph

After This Lesson, You Will Know

- How to create a simple line graph
- About some of the different graphs that you can create with SPSS

Key Words

- Area graph
- Bar graph
- Define Simple Line dialog box
- Line Graphs dialog box
- Pie graph
- .spo

SPSS offers you just the features to create graphs that bring the results of your analyses to life. In this lesson, we will go through the steps to create several different types of graphs and provide examples of different graphs. In Lesson 16, we'll show you how to modify a graph by adding a graph title, adding labels to axes, modifying scales, and working with patterns, fonts, and more. Throughout this unit of *Using SPSS*, we'll use the words graph and chart interchangeably.

Tip: Although the main menu for creating a graph in SPSS is labeled Graphs, you may also notice that the word chart isused in dialog boxes. No matter, they both mean the same thing—the visual presentation of data.

Creating a Simple Graph

The one thing that all graphs have in common is that they are based on data. Although you may import data to create a graph, in this example we'll use the data you see here to create a line graph of test scores by grade. These data are available and named Lesson 16 Data File 1.

Grade	Score
1	45
2	56
3	49
4	57
5	67
6	72

Creating a Line Graph

The steps for creating any graph are basically the same. You first enter the data you want to use in the graph, select the type of graph you want from the Graph menu, define

Figure 47   A Simple Line graph.

how the graph should appear, and then click **OK**. Here are the steps we followed to create the graph you see in Figure 47. We did some enhancing as well which we will describe more later in this appendix.

1. Enter the data you want to use to create the graph.
2. Click **Graphs → Legacy Dialogs → Line**. When you do this, you will see the **Line Charts dialog box**, as shown in Figure 48.
3. Click **Simple** and then click **Define**. You will see the **Define Simple Line dialog box**.
4. Click **Grade**, click to move the variable to the Category Axis: area.
5. Click the **Other Statistic** button.
6. Click **Score**, and then click to move the variable to the Variable: area. Now is the time to enter a title or subtitle in any graph by clicking the Titles button in the Define dialog box and entering what titles, subtitles, and footnotes you want.
7. Click **OK**, and you see the graph in the Output Navigator.

This is the default graph with no additions, changes, or edits.

Figure 48   The Line Charts dialog box.

Saving a Graph

A graph is only one possible component of the Output Navigator window. The graph is not a separate entity that stands by itself, but part of all the output generated and displayed in the Viewer. To save a graph, you have to save the entire contents of the Output Navigator. To do so, follow these steps:

1. In the Output Navigator window, click **File → Save**.
2. Provide a name for the Output Navigator window.
3. Click **OK**. The Output Navigator is saved under the name that you provide with an **.spo** extension (attached to all Viewer files). If you want to open this file later, you have to select this extension from the Files of type drop-down menu.

Printing a Graph

There are several ways to print a graph. The first way is to print from the Output Navigator by selecting the graph and then selecting Print.

> *Tip: You can print only one or more elements in the Viewer by first selecting the element by clicking on it once and then select FilePrint, click Selection, and then click OK. To select more than one, hold down the Ctrl key as you click.*

1. Be sure that the graph you want to print is in the active Viewer window.
2. Click on the graph so that it is selected.
3. Click on the Print icon on the Toolbar or click **File → Print** and then **OK**. The graph will be printed.

Different SPSS Graphs

SPSS offers many different types of graphs all of which you can see at **Graphs → Legacy Dialogs**.

While some types of graphs may be used in lieu of others, each has its own purpose. The purpose depends on the type of data being graphed as well as the research question being asked. It's beyond the scope of this book to detail each graph and all the possible combinations (for help, just click on any icon in the Graphs Builder help area), but the following are examples of some of the more simple graphs. Keep in mind that there is an almost infinite number of variations of the graphs you can create by using SPSS. You'll learn about modifying graphs in Lesson 16. All sample graphs that follow appear as they were first created, with no modification.

The Bar Graph

A **bar graph** represents values as separate bars, with each bar corresponding to the value in the Data Editor. Bar graphs are often used because they are easy to understand

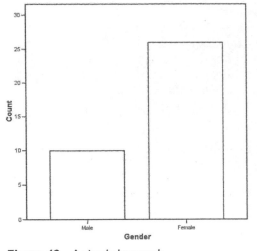

Figure 49   A simple bar graph.

and require little attention to detail. In Figure 49, you can see an example of a bar graph of the number of males and females.

The Area Graph

An **area graph** represents the proportions of the whole that each data point contributes. In Figure 50, you can see an example of average product preference as a function of earning power (high, moderate, and low).

The Pie Graph

The **pie graph** is a circle divided into wedges, with each wedge representing a proportion of the whole. Pie graphs provide a clear picture of the relative contribution that a data point makes to the overall body of information. In Figure 51, you can see a simple pie graph for expenses (rent, insurance, and miscellaneous).

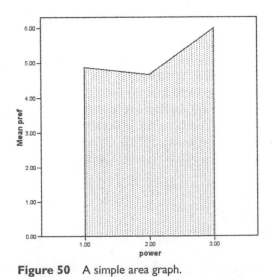

Figure 50   A simple area graph.

Figure 51   A simple pie graph.

Keep in mind that when you first create a graph, all the SPSS defaults are used. You can easily change type size and font and many other characteristics. You will learn how to do that in the next lesson.

Lesson 17
Enhancing SPSS Graphs

After This Lesson, You Will Know

- How to modify chart elements, including titles, axes, colors, and patterns

Key Words

- Category Axis
- Category Axis dialog box
- Colors dialog box
- Pattern dialog box
- Scale Axis
- Scale Axis dialog box
- SPSS Chart Editor
- Text Styles dialog box
- Titles dialog box

A picture might be worth a thousand words, but if your pictures or graphs don't say what you want, what good are they? Once you create a chart, as we showed you in the last lesson, you can finish the job by editing the chart to reflect exactly your meaning. Color, shapes, scales, fonts, text, and more can be altered, and that is what you'll do in this lesson. We'll be working with the line chart that was first shown to you earlier.

Modifying a Chart

The first in the modification of any chart is to double click anywhere inside of the chart in the Output Navigator to access the **SPSS Chart Editor** and then click the maximize button on the Application title bar. As you can see in Figure 52, there is a Chart toolbar containing a set of buttons across the top of the chart.

Tip: Graphs can be easily copied (use the Edit menu) and pasted into other Windows applications.

One cautionary note before we begin. The most basic reason for modifying a chart should be to increase the chart's ability to communicate your message. If you get caught up in Chart Junk (a close cousin to Font Junk), you'll have a mess on your hands. Modify to make better, not to show your reader that you know how to use SPSS.

Some instructional notes before we begin. The general strategy for changing any element in a chart is to select the chart element and then make the change. You select a chart element much as you select any Windows element, by clicking on it. If you single click, you then must select the menu command for the item you want to change. If you double click, in some cases, you will go immediately to the dialog box in which you can make the change. And, there are usually several different eways to

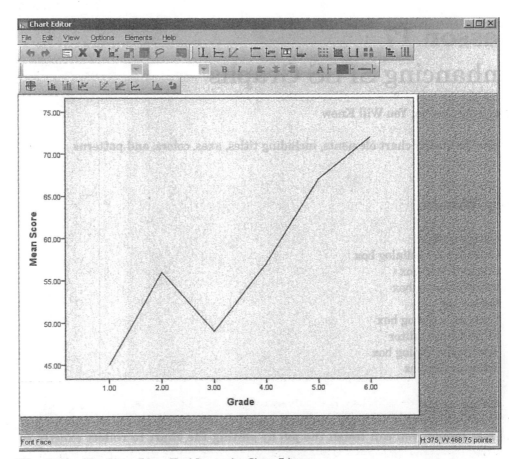

Figure 52   The Chart Editor Tool Bar in the Chart Editor.

change a chart element. You can usually double click on the element (such as the Y-axis) and make approriate changes or use a corresponding tool on the toolbar. And, most parts of a graph have a Properties dialog associated with it where you can fine tune graph edits.

Tip: The first step in changing any graph elment is to click on that element in the Chart Editor. The second step is to make the changes in the Properties box associated with that element. The final step is to click the Apply button.

Working with Titles and Subtitles

Our first task is to modify the title and subtitle for the chart.

1. With the Chart Editor open, **click Options → Title**. When you do this, the Title area is highlighted as you see in Figure 53. You can also see how a Properites box opens up where can also make adjustments to the title.
2. Edit the title (or subtitle or footnote) as you would any other text and make whatever edits as necessary.
3. Once you are done, click anywhere else in the Chart Editor outside of the title area.

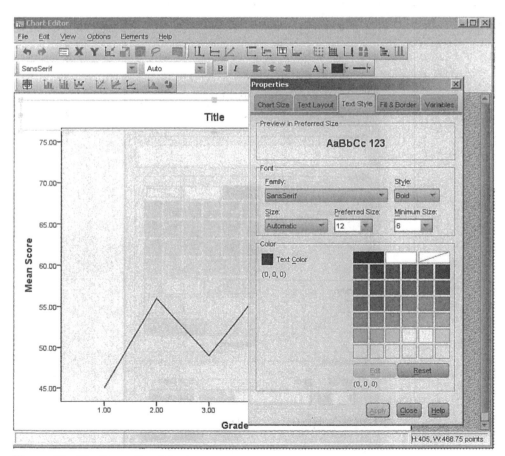

Figure 53 The Properties dialog box.

Working with Fonts

Now it's time to work with the font used for text in the chart. You can do this one of two ways, with each way yielding the same dialog box used to change fonts:

Tip: You can also access the Properties window by using the CTRLT key combination after you have highlighted the element you want to modify.

1. Select the area of the chart containing the text you want to change. When you select text, it appears with a solid line around it. In this example, we selected the title of the chart, Score by Grade. Once selected, it appears with a box around it.
2. To change a font's properties, double click on the title and you will see the Properties box as shown in Figure 54.
3. Make the changes that you want. In this example, we changed it to 14-point Arial Italic.
4. Click the **Apply** button, and the font will change in the chart. The Properties dialog box will remain on the screen until you close it. That way you can change the chart size and other characteristics of the chart without having to reselect the Properties dialog box.

You can highlight more than one text area at a time by holding down the CTRL key as you click with the mouse.

Figure 54   The Properties dialog box.

Working with Axes

The X- and Y-axes provide the calibration for the independent (usually the X-axis) variable and the dependent (usually the Y-axis) variable. SPSS names the Y-axis the **Scale Axis** and the X-axis the **Category Axis**. Each of these axes can be modified in a variety of ways. To modify either axis, double click on the title of the axis and you will see the Properties dialog box for that axis.

How to Modify the Scale (Y) Axis

For example, to modify the Y-axis, follow these steps:

1. Double click on the line representing the Y-axis (the axis will turn blue) and you will see the Properties dialog box as shown in Figure 55.
2. Select the options you want from the dialog box. We clicked the Number Format tab and made sure that there were no decimals.

How to Modify the Category (X) Axis

Working with the X-axis is exactly the same as working with the Y-axis. Here's how the X-axis was modified:

1. Double click on the label of the X-axis. The Properties dialog box opens as shown in Figure 56.
2. Select the options you want from the Properties dialog box.

Figure 55   The Properties dialog box.

Figure 56 The Properties dialog box.

Our finished and modified line chart (with a few more changes) is shown in Figure 47 and while none of these changes are dramatic, they do show how easy these enhancement tools are to use.

We got back to the output window by closing the Chart Editor when we were done modifying the chart. The only other change we made was left justifying the footnote and italicizing it by using the font options we saw in the Properties dialog box once we double clicked on the footnote.

Appendix B

Sample Data Set

ID No.	Gender*	Grade	Building	Reading Score	Mathematics Score
1	2	8	1	55	60
2	2	2	6	41	44
3	1	8	6	46	37
4	2	4	6	56	59
5	2	10	6	45	32
6	1	10	6	46	33
7	2	8	6	58	58
8	2	6	6	41	43
9	2	8	6	50	45
10	1	2	6	35	41
11	1	4	6	56	58
12	1	6	1	47	33
13	1	2	6	43	44
14	2	2	6	44	39
15	1	6	6	48	37
16	1	8	6	50	51
17	2	4	6	48	54
18	1	2	6	45	44
19	2	6	6	58	59
20	1	4	6	57	53
21	2	6	4	32	36
22	2	4	6	60	60
23	1	4	6	57	52
24	2	2	6	40	42
25	1	2	6	44	44
26	2	6	6	58	60
27	2	2	6	43	44
28	1	8	6	47	53
29	1	10	3	55	49
30	1	2	6	40	44
31	2	6	6	50	55
32	2	8	6	51	58
33	2	2	6	44	43
34	2	8	6	56	59
35	1	4	6	45	43
36	1	8	6	57	54
37	1	10	6	58	59
38	1	10	6	47	20
39	2	4	6	48	43
40	1	2	5	31	34
41	1	8	6	60	59
42	1	8	6	41	42
43	1	10	6	54	55
44	1	10	6	56	57

ID No.	Gender*	Grade	Building	Reading Score	Mathematics Score
45	2	6	6	56	57
46	1	6	6	48	46
47	2	2	6	43	40
48	1	6	6	58	60
49	1	6	6	45	47
50	1	6	6	50	56
51	2	10	6	51	41
52	2	6	6	50	45
53	2	8	6	54	54
54	1	8	4	38	22
55	1	4	6	53	51
56	2	4	2	53	47
57	2	2	6	42	45
58	1	2	6	43	41
59	2	6	6	57	57
60	2	2	6	38	45
61	2	6	6	56	57
62	2	10	6	50	44
63	1	6	5	53	56
64	1	2	6	41	41
65	2	4	6	48	53
66	1	4	4	39	45
67	1	2	6	44	39
68	2	6	6	55	58
69	2	4	6	50	57
70	1	8	6	31	31
71	2	8	6	59	57
72	1	6	6	51	50
73	2	2	6	44	43
74	2	8	6	52	40
75	1	8	6	58	59
76	2	8	6	42	48
77	2	8	6	51	49
78	1	10	6	58	59
79	1	2	6	43	38
80	1	4	6	55	58
81	2	10	6	58	57
82	2	10	6	49	23
83	1	2	6	33	35
84	2	6	6	53	39
85	2	6	6	56	60
86	2	10	6	54	53
87	1	4	6	49	54
88	1	8	6	58	56

Table Continued

ID No.	Gender*	Grade	Building	Reading Score	Mathematics Score
89	1	6	6	48	51
90	1	2	6	43	40
91	2	4	6	52	43
92	1	6	6	58	57
93	2	2	6	45	45
94	2	4	6	49	55
95	2	4	6	55	55
96	1	4	6	54	54
97	2	10	6	53	41
98	1	4	6	53	53
99	2	2	6	41	41
100	1	6	6	51	56
101	1	10	4	48	30
102	2	4	6	57	57
103	2	4	6	56	59
104	2	6	6	57	60
105	2	10	6	56	45
106	2	2	6	37	45
107	1	8	6	47	39
108	2	4	6	56	51
109	2	2	6	42	44
110	1	8	6	55	59
111	2	6	6	52	56
112	1	8	6	58	60
113	2	6	5	54	53
114	1	2	6	39	29
115	1	10	6	49	45
116	2	10	6	47	40
117	1	8	6	54	53
118	1	4	6	51	54
119	2	8	4	55	48
120	1	4	6	49	53
121	1	2	6	45	44
122	2	2	3	42	42
123	2	4	6	42	46
124	2	4	6	49	43
125	1	8	6	56	59
126	1	2	6	40	43
127	2	4	6	55	60
128	2	10	6	54	58
129	2	6	6	47	50
130	2	6	6	56	58
131	2	4	3	43	38
132	2	6	6	41	45

ID No.	Gender*	Grade	Building	Reading Score	Mathematics Score
133	1	8	6	47	57
134	1	6	6	55	55
135	2	2	6	41	44
136	1	10	6	47	29
137	2	8	6	52	37
138	1	4	6	51	48
139	1	6	6	59	59
140	1	8	6	36	47
141	1	4	6	53	58
142	2	2	6	37	37
143	1	6	6	49	55
144	2	8	6	55	57
145	2	10	6	40	47
146	2	10	6	53	56
147	2	4	6	57	59
148	1	2	6	45	44
149	2	4	6	56	57
150	1	4	6	46	50
151	1	8	6	48	36
152	2	6	6	43	41
153	2	6	6	51	54
154	2	8	6	41	52
155	1	4	4	41	30
156	2	2	6	45	42
157	2	10	4	39	19
158	2	6	6	57	59
159	1	8	4	58	59
160	2	4	6	52	48
161	2	10	6	27	18
162	1	2	6	40	43
163	1	10	6	41	15
164	1	6	6	51	53
165	1	6	4	39	52
166	2	6	6	58	60
167	2	2	6	42	41
168	2	6	6	52	51
169	1	10	6	41	39
170	2	6	6	38	23
171	2	10	6	55	59
172	2	6	6	59	59
173	1	10	6	31	31
174	2	6	6	50	55
175	1	8	6	59	59
176	1	10	4	49	19

Table Continued

ID No.	Gender*	Grade	Building	Reading Score	Mathematics Score
177	1	2	6	36	37
178	2	10	6	54	50
179	1	10	6	46	41
180	2	4	6	35	38
181	2	6	6	45	57
182	2	6	4	40	31
183	1	10	6	54	47
184	1	8	6	57	52
185	2	2	6	41	42
186	1	10	6	52	47
187	1	10	6	55	57
188	2	8	6	36	33
189	2	6	6	39	43
190	1	2	6	45	45
191	2	6	6	49	42
192	2	6	6	51	51
193	2	8	6	55	43
194	1	2	4	38	33
195	1	10	6	50	45
196	1	8	6	55	59
197	2	8	6	58	53
198	1	8	6	52	54
199	2	8	6	52	48
200	1	6	6	42	53

*1 = male, 2 = female

Appendix C

Answers to End-of-Chapter Exercises

Chapter 1

1. This is an exploratory exercise and answers will vary.
2. This is an exploratory exercise and answers will vary.
3. A hypothesis is a testable statement about a relationship between two variables and is specific to one research question. A theory represents a body of related works.
4. This is an exploratory exercise and answers will vary.
5. This is an exploratory exercise and answers will vary.
6. This is an exploratory exercise and answers will vary.
7. Some (of many) correct answers include: height, number of siblings, parents' education levels, adoption status, presence of a genetic disorder, and history of vaccinations.
8. This is an exploratory exercise and answers will vary.
9. This is an exploratory exercise and answers will vary.
10. A correlation between variables indicates only an association, not a cause-and-effect relationship. In correlational research it is always possible for other variables to be the true cause of the effect. For instance, strength may be the result of differences in nutrition and exercise, not age. Even if one variable does affect the other, a correlational study can never reveal which is the cause and which is the effect.
11. Definitions of science often include some of these elements:
    A system for seeking knowledge
    A measurement process or component
    A research activity
    Asking questions within the framework of a theory
12. The best rule of thumb is, "What question are you trying to answer?"
13. This is an exploratory exercise and answers will vary.
14. Some (of many) correct answers include: the value of generating new questions, checking the results of others, and increasing the likelihood that results did not occur by chance. Also, a replication helps to clarify the equivocal nature of certain findings, where several different studies may report results that are opposite or contradictory to one another.
15. Most directly, by providing us with the tools that we need to collect valuable and valid data that can be used in the decision-making process.
16. Good research is based on the work of others, can be replicated, is generalizable, is based on some logical rationale and tied to theory, is doable, generates new questions or is cyclical in nature, is incremental, and is an apolitical activity that should be undertaken for the betterment of society.
17. (a) Some (of many) correct answers include: What is the relationship between parental education level and reading skills among 6-year-olds? Does the amount of time spent practicing reading at home affect reading skills as evaluated at school for 6-year-olds? What is the relationship between IQ and reading skills among 6-year-olds?
    (b) Following the scientific method, reconsidering the theory can be beneficial to the researcher between examining data and asking a new research question.
18. This is an exploratory exercise and answers will vary.
19. *Historical research* relates to events that have occurred in the past to current events. It addresses the nature of events that have happened in the past. *Correlational research* provides an indication as to how two or more things are related to one another, or how well a specific outcome might be predicted by one or more pieces of information. *Quasi-experimental (or Post hoc) research* takes place after the assignment of participants to groups. Therefore the researcher has a high degree of control, but not the highest degree of control over the cause of whatever effects are being examined.
20. Here we go . . .
    Yes—Differences
    Yes—Participants preassigned (their country of origin)
    Yes—Quasi-experimental

Chapter 2

1. a. The independent variables are the individuals in the sample (children) and the type of fitness program. The dependent variable is strength.

   b. The independent variables are the various smoking cessation treatments (of which there are five). The dependent variable is the number of cigarettes smoked each day.

   c. The independent variable is the various methods used to teach the material. The dependent variable is the measure used to assess student learning of the material, such as a comprehensive final exam.

2. a. Tutoring for the independent variable and test scores for the dependent variable

   b. Party preference for the independent variable and candidate voted for, for the dependent variable

   c. Participation in a drug and alcohol treatment program for the independent variable and recidivism or rate of return for the dependent variable.

3. Some correct answers include: dependent variable, criterion variable, results variable, and "y."

4. The null hypothesis is always a statement of equality because, without any other knowledge, the researcher assumes that the starting point for investigating a relationship is that groups are equal. The research hypothesis can take on many forms because there are so many different questions that can be asked if one assumes that the null hypothesis is not the most attractive explanation for any observed differences.

5. Null Hypothesis: Attitudes toward work and family will be the same for middle-aged men who have children as for those who do not. Research Hypothesis: The attitudes toward work and family will differ between middle-aged men who have children and those who do not.

6. A null could be as follows: There is no difference in later achievement between children who participate in an early intervention program during their first 3 years and those who do not participate. A directional research hypothesis could be as follows: Children who participate in an early intervention program during their first 3 years of life will score higher on tests of academic achievement later in their school years than those children who do not participate.

7. Some (of many) advantages to having a hypothesis that is linked to literature and theory include: knowing what variables are of interest to people studying the same topic, having a novel hypothesis and increasing the chances of bettering the theory, saving time and energy by drawing on previous work, having a more accurate guess for the direction of the hypothesis, and having somewhere to return should the results not support the hypothesis.

8. Using a "fishing-trip" approach can produce too many results to sort out cleanly, no results at all, results that are difficult to interpret, or results that have little practical utility and do not contribute anything useful to existing theory and literature. Furthermore, reputable journals are unlikely to publish a study that uses the "fishing-trip" approach.

9. This is an exploratory exercise and answers will vary.

10. Statistical significance is the probability associated with the rejection of the null hypothesis when it is true—it's a "goof." But, the reason why it is important is because it allows us to recognize that inference is not perfect and no matter how much confidence we have in the outcome, there is always a chance we may be wrong. What's so cool about this is that we can set this level and design our studies appropriately.

11. What is not significant is as important a contribution as being aware of what is, especially when the results are from a well-conducted study. It is information that provides a perspective.

12. a. The sample includes every 10th household listed in the phonebook, or in other words, every household contacted to participate.
    b. The population includes every household in Howard County.

13. a. The color of Lew's hair (C)
    b. Age in years (V)
    c. Number of windows in your residence (C)
    d. The color of any late-model car (V)
    e. Current time of day (C)
    f. Number of possible correct answers on this week's quiz (C)
    g. Number of signers of the Declaration of Independence (C)
    h. Name of the fifth girl in the third row (C)
    i. Today's date (C)
    j. Number of words remembered on a memory test (V)

14. a. The sample may not represent the population (i.e., Kindergarteners or fifth graders may have different perceptions of the school than do third graders).
    b. Consequently, the results lack generalizability, and the principal cannot adequately infer information about opinions from students in other grades.

15. Researcher B has the best way of measuring the dependent variable of test performance because the measurement is more specific. (Chapter 5 contains more information about levels of measurement and why specific measurements are more helpful in measuring the true outcome of interest.)

16. In the example, the experience of Hurricane Katrina is an extraneous variable. That is, the researcher cannot be sure that significant differences in avoidance strategies between residents of New Orleans and residents from Church Point are due to the place of residence and not to the exposure to Hurricane Katrina.

17. This is an exploratory exercise and answers will vary.

18. A good hypothesis is stated in declarative form and posits an expected relationship between variables. Good hypotheses reflect the theory and literature upon which they are based and are brief, to the point, and testable.

Chapter 3A

Questions 1 through 9 are library activities and answers will depend on individual student selections and interests.

10. Some (of many) correct answers include: think it over for a few days, talk to other students, talk to an adviser or another professor, think of other ideas and compare them to the first idea.

12. a. Allows the searcher to find contact information for a person or business
    b. Serves as a wild card, allowing the search to return results with a related root but with different prefixes or suffixes, etc.
    c. Weights the search toward the repeated word and allows the searcher to find a different set of results on the same topic

13. Some (of many) advantages to reading peer-reviewed journal articles include: Information in peer-reviewed journals has to meet strict guidelines and pass multiple reviews, journal articles have "blind" reviewers to reduce bias, journal articles typically include literature reviews and are based in theory, journal articles typically have a Method section that is helpful for replication of the study, and journal articles require citations and references. Some advantages to using Wikipedia include: Wikipedia has a

wide breadth of articles and topics, it is largely trustworthy, it is revisable, and its site contains related informational tools (Wiktionary, Wikinews, Wikiquotes, etc.).

14. a. *Encyclopedia of Psychology* (S)
    b. *Time* magazine (G)
    c. *Statistics for People Who (Think They) Hate Statistics* (S)
    d. *Journal of Sport Health* (P)
    e. Facts on File (G)
    f. A review of Freud's dream interpretations (S)
    g. Dissertation abstracts online (P)

15. Answers to this question will vary. Several (of many) correct answers include: Repeat the study with participants from a different grade level, repeat the study with adults who have graduated college, replace the outcome variable of career decision-making efficacy with another career-related outcome variable.

16. At press time, the three titles appearing in the Google Scholar search were:
    a. Test anxiety and direction of attention
    b. Correlates, causes, effects, and treatment of test anxiety
    c. Cognitive and emotional components of text anxiety: a distinction and some initial data

17. Answers to this question will vary. Several (of many) correct answers include: number of children, number of previous divorces, length of marriage, gender of divorcee, children's attitudes toward divorce.

18. Some (of many) correct answers include: A literature review reduces the chances of selecting a research question that already has been answered, reduces the chances of selecting a trivial research question, provides a framework for answering questions, shows you which ideas have been retained and which have been rejected, and encourages a well-documented report.

Chapter 3B

1. The decision to use deception in a study must be justified. That is, if the researcher reasonably can complete the study without the use of deception, deception should not be a part of the study. Likewise, the study's potential benefits need to outweigh the use of deception. The deception should be kept to the minimal amount needed to derive benefits from the study, and all participants should be debriefed at the conclusion of the individual intervention or the conclusion of all data collection.

2. This is an exploratory exercise and results will be specific to your college or university.

3. Electronic consent is allowable when participants are at least 18 years old, when the study poses no or low risks to participants, and when the online consent form is broken into steps so participants can address each part of consent one at a time.

4. In most cases, researchers are responsible for their behavior to the institution to which they belong and there are usually review boards (such as an IRB) who would act as a judge in determining whether there was a violation and what action should be taken. Similarly, professional organizations such as The American Psychological Association in the case of members would also take some remedial action. Such action can range from removal of membership privileges to, if the action results in a violation of law, prosecution and civil or criminal punishment.

5. You will have to chose these for yourself, but this exercise will demonstrate how similar many of these guidelines are meaning that most scientists are cognizant of the same ethical issues when research is involved.

Chapter 4

1. a. Define the population from which I want to draw a sample; in this case, high school students.
    b. Compose a list of all the high school students.
    c. Assign each student a number.
    d. Decide on some criterion not related to the study, such as a table of random numbers, to select individuals for the sample.
2. This researcher is using convenience sampling. Finding the sample and eliciting participation may be easy, but her sample is not random and may not be representative of her population of interest.
3. The numbers in the table appear in random order and are unrelated to any characteristics of the population from which the sample is being drawn.
4. He's asking a very biased sample of people and how will he ever determine what those who do not buy fast food think?
5. Probability sampling is a strategy used when the likelihood of any member of the population being selected is known. For example, if there are 300 centers playing college basketball out of a total 2000 players, the odds of selecting one center as part of the sample is 300 out of 2000, or .15.

    In a nonprobability sampling strategy, the likelihood of selecting any one member from the population is unknown. For example, if we do not know how many mothers consume alcohol during their pregnancy, we cannot compute the likelihood of any one such mother being selected.

    The advantage of a probability strategy is that selection is based on chance factors, thus eliminating determination by nonsystematic and random rules and increasing the chance that the sample will be representative of the population. The main advantage of a nonprobability strategy of sampling is that it is relatively convenient and inexpensive, and it ensures some degree of representativeness in the population. However, the disadvantage is that the results may be questionable with regard to representativeness because the true probability was never known.
6. The easiest way to reduce sampling error is to use good selection procedures and increase the size of the sample.

    There is an inverse relationship between sampling error and the generalizability of the results of the study. As sampling error increases the generalizability decreases and vice versa, because sampling error, in part, reflects the degree of variability in the sample. If the sample is large, the implication is that the population is diverse, which means that the results may not be very generalizable. If the sample size is increased, sampling error will decrease because as the sample gets larger it approaches the size and representativeness of the actual population, which includes some of the diversity that can elevate sampling error.
7. Because the number of individuals is unequal to begin with in the population, in order to select a representative sample where n 5 150, one might use a stratified sampling strategy with two variables stratified. If 150 children will be selected from a population of 10,000, this represents 1.5%. This percentage is to be multiplied by the percentages representative of non-whites, whites, single-parent and dual-parent families in the population of 10,000. For example, there are 5,700 single-parent children, and the sample of 150 should include 85.5 children from single-parent families (1.5% $\times$ 5700). Using this strategy, in the sample of 150 children, 64.5 of the children have dual-parent families, 45 are non-white, and 105 are White.
8. When sending surveys by mail, increasing your sample size by about 40% to 50% helps to account for nonresponders and mail error. Therefore, with an original sample of 100, you would want to increase your sample size by 40 or 50, for a total sample size of 140–150.

9. In order to represent the population more accurately, the sample size should increase when a greater amount of variability within groups exists and a smaller difference between groups exists.

10. You expect there to be an even distribution of males and females in the sample because there is an even number of males and females in the population.

11. When a sample is too small, it may not be representative of the population, which adds to the error of your study. This can be overcome by taking a larger sample, but if the sample is too large, one is sure to find significant differences among groups which may not be "truth." This is due to the power and nature of statistical inference. For this reason, using too large a sample might be uneconomical and self-defeating.

12. Big enough to provide a representative sample but not too large to expend a great deal of resources for a marginal benefit.

13. a. It is not economical.
    b. The researcher is not taking advantage of the power of inference.

14. Cluster sampling should be used when the population consists of units rather than individuals, whereas simple random sampling should be used when the population members or individuals are similar to one another.

15. In this example, political party affiliation may or may not be related to the researcher's topic of study. If political party affiliation is related, the researcher should use stratified sampling in order to improve the sample's representation of the strata in the population.

16. Systematic sampling is easy and includes a sample that is representative of the population. However, it is less precise than some other sampling methods, and it violates the assumption that each member of the population will have an equal chance to be selected for participation. In other words, the sample is less random than with other sampling methods.

17. The employee in this example is using quota sampling. The employee is enlisting participation from people with the characteristics (i.e., 20 males and 20 females) the boss has requested, yet he is not randomly selecting participants. Shoppers who do not make eye contact with the employee do not have the same chance of being selected as do shoppers who make eye contact.

18. It is a lack of fit between the sample and the population or the difference between the characteristics of the population from which the sample was selected. A good researcher wants to reduce sampling error and have a sample that is representative of the population.

    This is important in order to have research results that can be effectively generalized back to the population. If a sampling error is too large, the results can be effectively generalized only to the population from which the sample was taken, and even then, without a great deal of confidence.

Chapter 5

1. (a) interval
    (b) nominal
    (c) interval or ratio
    (d) ratio
    (e) interval
    (f) nominal
    (g) ratio
    (h) nominal
    (i) interval
    (j) ordinal

2. a. t
    b. m
    c. m
    d. m
    e. t

3. • Test–retest. The same test is given at two points in time to the same group of individuals. The two sets of scores are correlated with each other to measure consistency over time.
    • Parallel forms. Two different tests made from the same general pool of possible questions are given to one group of people.
    • Internal consistency. A test is designed so that the items are unidimensional in nature.

4. In this example, your car would be considered reliable according to the definition of reliability in this chapter. Although you may be frustrated with the fact that your engine stalls three times every time you drive the car, the car is still consistent in its performance; you can predict that each and every time you drive the car, the engine will stall three times.

5. Set A appears to have items that are more internally consistent. Each of the items in Set A relates to views on the rightness or wrongness of the death penalty. The items in Set B hang together somewhat, as they relate to law, crime, and punishment, though they are not as closely related as are the items in Set A.

6. Content validity, and one way to establish it is to have experts in the area of history examine the questions and pass on their appropriateness for inclusion in the test.

7. Tests of moderate difficulty most accurately reflect the picture of an individual's performance. Having a test that is too easy does not give you information about how well the individual might do with more difficult questions. Likewise, having a test that is too difficult tells you what types of questions the individual cannot answer correctly but tells you little to nothing about what the individual *can* do with regard to the construct being tested.

8. Answers might include ACT, SAT, GRE, and (perhaps) intelligence tests.

9. When Mr. Barnes and Mrs. Fletcher give different instructions to their students, they create a threat to reliability. In some types of multiple-choice tests, more than one answer can be correct technically while only one answer is the best or "most correct" answer. Mr. Barnes's students may have chosen answer alternative "a" if it were technically correct and not even looked at answer "c" which contained the best answer for the item. If his students had been instructed to choose the best answer, they may have performed differently on the test—a sign of threat to reliability.

10. In the initial example, Professor Lee is evaluating parallel forms reliability, as he is using two different but comparable versions of the same test. If he were to use the same test twice, he would be evaluating test–retest reliability.

11. Level of measurement is the scale representing a hierarchy of precision on which a variable is assessed.

12. (a) Nominal–Gender
    (b) Ordinal–Place/rank in a competitio
    (c) Interval–Intelligence test scores
    (d) Ratio–Time in days

13. A test can be reliable without being valid but a test cannot be valid without first being reliable.

14. Asking an expert on the topic you are researching whether the items in your instrument assess what you intend for them to assess is a good way to establish content validity.

15. In this example, you have established discriminant validity. You can say that the items on your instrument are not simply measuring social desirability.

Chapter 6

1. The fact that the difficulty of items varies and that test takers are not expected to be able to answer every question suggests the test will be good at differentiating people from one another with regard to performance on the items designed to measure intelligence.
2. Standardized tests are tests produced by commercial publishers that come with their own standard set of instructions and scoring procedures. They differ from researcher- or teacher-made tests in that they may be administered to broad groups of people for broad purposes.
3. a. This example describes a criterion-referenced test, as test takers must meet the criterion of answering 70% of questions correctly, and as each individual's chances of receiving a passing score are unaffected by other individuals taking the test.
   b. This example describes a norm-referenced test, as test takers chances of receiving a passing score depend on the norms of other individuals who have taken the test.
4. Increasing or decreasing the attractiveness of the alternatives changes the difficulty level of the test items. It also will change the discrimination value.
5. a. Discrimination score = .34
   b. Difficulty score = .26
   c. Discrimination score = −.08
   d. Difficulty score = .21
6. Have a classmate check your items for clarity and understandability and when you do the same for a colleague, be sure that you look for every element that might contribute to the unreliability of the test.
7. This is an exploratory exercise and answers will vary.
8. a. Moderate difficulty and poor discrimination
   b. Easy item and acceptable discrimination
9. a. Questions that are clear and not too personal
   b. Coverage in a clear, concise manner
   c. Interesting questions
10. a. If you keep it anonymous, individuals will be more willing to be truthful.
    b. You can survey a larger geographic area by using the mail.
    c. Questionnaires are less expensive than using personal interviews.
11. When scoring Likert-type instruments, maintaining one direction is important. When some items are in a positive direction (e.g., "The plot was interesting.") and some are in a negative direction (e.g., "Most of the scenes were boring."), items in one direction must be reverse scored. For example, the 2 response of "Most of the scenes were boring" should be changed to a 4, as a 2 on a negative item indicates a favorable response toward the movie. Therefore, we add up 4+4+4+4 to equal 16. The scorer also might move all positive responses to a negative direction, in which case the total score would be 2+2+2+2 to equal 8, though this change would require more work from the scorer. In either case, the scorer should consistently score in one direction for each survey administered.

Chapter 7

1. Optical scanners are quite fast and save a lot of time compared to hand scoring. They also tend to be more accurate than hand-scoring processes. Additionally, scanned responses enable you to perform functions with the data (e.g., calculating item difficulty and discrimination) beyond simply scoring responses. The primary disadvantage to using an optical scanner is the cost. Also, though optical scanners

     tend to be reliable, in recent years some companies have reported mistakes made by optical scanners.

2.   Using digits makes data analysis easier, as digits are more precise than letters or words, and as digits are shorter than words. Also, some statistical software programs recognize only digits when dealing with nominal data.

3.   As data collection is one of the most daunting and time-consuming parts of completing research, searching for participants should begin as soon as possible in the research process. Keep in mind that the institutional review board should give approval for the study before the researcher seeks participation of any kind.

4.   a.   Visiting 20 classes for 30 minutes each takes approximately 600 (20 × 30) minutes, or 10 hours. However, allowing for 25% to 50% in your schedule is wise, in order to compensate for unplanned time-consuming events that are likely to occur. For 10 hours of estimated data collection, adding 25% to 50% of the time would add another 2.5 to 5 hours. Therefore, you should allot approximately 12.5 to 15 hours to data collection. (Responses may vary from this answer, as additional predictable events such as travel consume time as well.)

       b.   Answers may vary. In addition to allocating extra time for unforeseen events, when estimating how much time data collection will require, you should account for students who arrive tardy to class (especially if the questionnaire will be given at the beginning of class), students who read more slowly or are more careful in responding, time taken to have the instructor introduce you (and why on earth you are invading the class!), time taken to hand out the questionnaires and any required informed consent, time taken for you to answer any questions about participation, and any travel time to and from the classes.

5.   Failing to follow up with participants who did not show up for their scheduled participation might result in a sample size that is smaller than desirable or needed. Additionally, the possibility exists that the individuals who drop out or do not show up differ on one or more variables from the individuals who participate, creating a potential confound in the results.

6.   Your form will probably look different from those of others; just be sure it contains the important information.

7.   This will be of your own creation, but here's what some data might look like. The independent variables are gender and group, and test 1 and test 2 scores are dependent.

ID	Gender	Group	Test 1	Test 2
1	1	1	7	7
2	2	2	8	7
3	2	2	7	6
4	2	2	6	6
5	1	2	6	5
6	2	2	6	6
7	1	2	5	7
8	1	1	4	6
9	2	1	5	5
10	2	1	6	5
11	1	1	5	4
12	1	1	4	3
13	1	1	5	4
14	2	2	6	8
15	2	2	5	7

ID	Gender	Group	Test 1	Test 2
16	2	1	8	6
17	1	1	7	7
18	1	2	6	5
19	1	2	7	4
20	2	1	8	6

8. The median is best suited for ordinal (ranked) data. It is also appropriate in cases where the sample includes extreme scores.

9. a. .2
   b. 2.4
   c. −.6
   d. 97.5
   e. 106
   f. 110.6

   z-scores allow us to compare performances on tests which use different scoring systems. They indicate where a score falls on the normal curve associated with a particular test.

10. range = 5, s = 1.703, s^2 = 2.9

11. a. For math:
    b. Claire's z-score = 2.24
    c. Noah's z-score = 1.18
    d. For science:
    e. Claire's z-score = .70
    f. Noah's z-score = .96
    g. The best performance overall is Claire's on the math test.
    h. Based on z-scores alone, Claire is the better student overall.

12. Because they use the same measure of variability, the standard score, making them directly comparable.

13. A z-score of 0 indicates performance exactly at the mean and, if normally distributed, the student did better than 50% of the other students.

14. Because the few mega-millionaires would make the mean far above what most people earn, the median is usually reported as the average income.

15. 16%

16. The mean is the average of all of the scores. The median is the middle score. The mode is the most frequently seen score.

17. The mode is the only measure of central tendency that is usable with nominal (categorical) data.

18. The mean and the standard deviation are the two most important measures of central tendency for fully understanding the distribution of data and the distribution's meaning.

19. To obtain the standard deviation value from the variance value, you must take the square root of the variance. The square root of 64 is 8, which is the standard deviation in this example.

20.

Mean (Group 1) = 2.5	Mean (Group 2) = 5
Median (Group 1) = 2	Median (Group 2) = 4
Mode (Group 1) = 1	Mode (Group 2) = 3

21. Your printout should include the data you entered plus the values for the average at the bottom of the columns for the variables named test 1 and test 2.

Chapter 8

1. Chance is the random occurrence of events, and it is the most plausible explanation for any outcome given no other information. Its role in inferential statistics is that it becomes a yardstick against which we measure observed outcomes to see if they differ from one another.

2. When you begin studying the variables that you think are responsible for any observation, including differences, you have no evidence to support such assumptions. The only explanation that you can choose that is not presumptuous is that the differences are caused by chance.

3. When a sample size is less than 30, the central limit theorem will not uphold, meaning the means of the samples may not be normally distributed. Therefore, data may need to be analyzed with nonparametric statistical tests, which do not require an assumption of a normal distribution.

4. The null hypothesis cannot be rejected. According to the table of critical values, with 60 (closest to 53) degrees of freedom at the .01, in order to reject the null hypothesis the t value must be greater than or equal to 2.660.

5. Statistical significance means that the findings indicate that the null hypothesis is not the best explanation for the observed differences. It is possible that even if the findings are significant, they may not be meaningful for a variety of reasons. First, even if the treatment from which change is implied produces significant changes, are the changes large enough to warrant spending taxpayer money, investing millions, and so on?

   Second, significant findings may not be meaningful in another context. It seems prudent to assess significant findings in the arena of a cost/benefit analysis in order to determine meaningfulness.

6. They are the same thing! The level of significance is a way to express the chance of making a Type I error.

7. The central limit theorem posits that regardless of how a characteristic is distributed in the population, through repeated sampling a normal distribution of scores will represent the population. This is the critical link in inferential statistics, because although it would not be possible to ever truly know how the distribution is shaped in the population, the central limit theorem allows the researcher to generalize back to the population distribution. Without it, the researcher would be heavily restricted in generalizing back to the population.

8. a. Mean of the entire population = 3.23
   b. Mean of all five means computed = 3.16
   c. The central limit theorem explains why these means of the means are so close to the mean of all 30 scores: Repeated samples will produce a normal distribution of means whether or not they are normally distributed in the population. By taking the mean of the means, and because it is so close to the mean of all the scores, it is implied that the means are normally distributed about the true mean of the population.
   d. This example illustrates the power of the central limit theorem when it comes to making inferences from samples to populations, because it reveals how the researcher need not know the true state of affairs existing in the population in order to make generalizations to it from the findings generated from a sample.

9. To say that findings are statistically significant is to say that the observed differences between groups are owing to factors other than chance, primarily a treatment effect. The researcher sets a level on the odds of observing a value and once it is equaled or surpassed, the findings are considered statistically significant.

10. One would be where there is a very small difference (almost negligible) between two independent groups (say two groups of voters), yet the samples were large enough so

that the difference is significant. Let's say that Group 1 voted for candidate Bob (57%) and Group 2 voted for candidate Karen (56.99%), yet the sample is so large and the errors associated with voting so small that the difference is significant. Meaningful? I don't think so.

11. When the null hypothesis is rejected because the critical value equals or surpasses the value needed for rejection, the research hypothesis may be accepted as a likely alternative to account for the observed group differences. The research hypothesis can never be proved because what is being tested is the null hypothesis.

12. Increasing the sample size helps reduce the chances of making a Type II error. (Increasing the significance level also reduces the chances of making a Type II error, but this strategy may not be desirable if your goal is to avoid making a Type I error.)

13. a. Statement of the null hypothesis: There will be no differences in attachment between infants in child care and those cared for at home up to 11 months.
   b. Level of risk: $p < .05$
   c. Selection of test statistic: t-test for independent means
   d. Computation of test statistic value
   e. Determine the value needed to reject the null hypothesis using an appropriate table of critical values for t-test statistic
   f. Compare the obtained value with the critical value
   g. Either accept or fail to accept the null hypothesis based on comparison of the critical value with the obtained value.
   h. Draw conclusions based on the most attractive explanation. For example, if the critical value was not surpassed, then the most attractive explanation for any differences in attachment between infants in child care and infants cared for at home is chance factors. On the other hand, if the critical value was equaled or surpassed, then the null hypothesis can be rejected and the research hypothesis can be accepted as a possible explanation for the differences in attachment.

14. Type I error is rejecting a null hypothesis when it's true. Type II error is accepting a null hypothesis when it's false.

15. The p in this example stands for probability. The expression $p < .01$ means a 1% chance (or less) exists that you have made a Type I error, or rejected the null hypothesis even though it is true and your outcome is due to chance.

16. Waiting to choose a level of significance until you view the results of data analysis puts you at risk for bias in interpreting your results. Instead, consider important factors when choosing whether to hold a .01 or .05 significance level. The Web site listed in the *Online* section in this chapter provides an overview of factors to consider in this decision.

17. You should reject the null hypothesis when the obtained value is more extreme than the critical value.

18. The sample becomes more like the population as sample size increases. Therefore, the difference needed between the obtained value and the critical value in order to reject the null hypothesis is not as great.

19. Multivariate analysis of variance (MANOVA) is appropriate to use with multiple dependent variables.

20. Analysis of variance (alternative c), because you are comparing the averages of more than two groups.

21. Meta-analysis is the analysis of results from several studies and it allows us to understand general trends.

22. Effect size is a standard unit, which means it allows researchers to make comparisons between different groups and outcomes regardless of the different methods and samples used in previous studies. The effect size tells us something about how strong the relationship between variables is, and as it increases, we know the difference between groups is greater.

Chapter 9

1. a. How many people intend to vote for a tax raise to fund the new athletic fields?
   b. How can doctors better satisfy their patients?
   c. What are the favorite strategies that teachers use to teach?
   d. What is the favorite work of nonfiction among young adults?
   e. Who are the most popular students in school?
2. Among many advantages to interviews are that they can provide more rich information about people's feelings and perceptions, they allow for greater flexibility than some other methods, they allow the researcher to set the tone of the data collection, and they allow the researcher directly to observe qualities about the setting of the interview and the interviewee's behavior. Among many disadvantages to interview are that they can be time consuming and expensive, they limit the anonymity of the interviewee, they lack standardization, and they may be prone to the researcher's biases.
3. Answers will vary. Examples include:
   a. What advantages do you see to keeping score in a children's sports game?
   b. How might keeping score be a negative experience for child athletes?
   c. How do you think keeping score at a sports event might affect children's competitiveness in other areas of life?
4. The five steps of developing an interview are as follows:
   a. Identify the purpose of the interview and review relevant literature.
   b. Select an appropriate sample for your study.
   c. Develop appropriate interview questions and field-test them.
   d. Train the interviewers to ask the questions in the manner you prefer.
   e. Conduct the interview.
5. .78, 2.67, .53, .21, 2.01
6. The fault with this argument is that there is no reason to think that a relationship between two variables is causal. One does not necessarily cause the other. There may be other factors that contribute to the relationship between study time and test performance. Without controlling for other important variables, such as amount of sleep, test anxiety, and the style of the teacher, one cannot assume from the information that lack of study time causes poor performance.
7. a. Positive
   b. Negative
   c. No relationship
   d. Negative
8. a. As people get taller they get stronger.
   b. As test takers go slower, they make fewer mistakes.
   c. As puzzle solvers need fewer moves to solve the puzzle, the higher their score.
9. a. No
   b. Yes
   c. Yes
   d. Yo
   e. No
10. Many correct answers are possible. For question (a), the interviewer should break up the initial question into two separate questions. The interviewee might have different attitudes toward teenage cigarette smoking than toward teenage drinking. Additionally, the interviewer may want to specify further the group term "teenagers," as smoking cigarettes, for example, is illegal for a 13-year-old but not for a 19-year-old. The interviewer might get more information by using an open-ended question rather than a closed one. For question (b), "colloquialism" is too formal a word for an interview question, particularly for a question aimed at junior high students. The interviewer should consider using a simpler word, such as "slang."

11. The purpose of descriptive research is to assess the current status of a set of things, people, events, or constructs. It provides a descriptive account of phenomena and often serves as a catalyst for other research ideas. Descriptive research simply describes a phenomenon, it does not explain or attribute cause-and-effect relationships to variables.

12. Descriptive research would be appropriate when someone is trying to describe certain conditions in a setting. For example, I am interested in knowing the average number of parents who show up on teacher–parent night and break that down by grade and by those children who participate in extracurricular activities.

13. C is the only one that is not true.

14. In large enough samples, there will always be enough variance to share between variables such that the correlations will be statistically significant. But, that says nothing about meaningfulness. For example, the correlation between problem-solving skills and the number of the school bus that the child rides each day may be significant in a sample of 5,000 elementary school children, but certainly not meaningful.

15. Though the correlation of .25 is significant in this example, correlations between .2 and .4 are considered weak. Therefore, the relationship between drinking milk during dinner and wetting the bed overnight is not very meaningful and may have more to do with outside factors (such as a large sample size) than with a true connection between these events. In this example, the researcher certainly would not want to advise mothers to withhold milk from their children (which also assumes causality!) based on a clinically significant but weak correlation.

16. The coefficient of determination represents the amount of variance accounted for in one variable by the other. For variables with a correlation of .60, the coefficient of determination would be .36 ($.60 \times .60$), meaning 36% of the variance in one variable can be explained by the other variable. This leaves 64% (100–36) of the variance unexplained, or a coefficient of alienation of .64.

Chapter 10

1. You would consult the primary types of sources mentioned in this chapter as well as those mentioned in Chapter 3: general, secondary, and primary.
2. Here are just some of the options:
   a. Interviews with living participants
   b. Newspaper articles
   c. Photographs
   d. Tape recordings
   e. Police and other law-related documents
3. They differ in the type of data that are collected and the underlying philosophy of the method. Both can work quite well to answer similar questions, but the major difference is whether the richness of the context within which the behavior is occurring is of interest to the research; hence, qualitative methods are more appropriate.
4. Here are three of many possibilities:
   a. The effectiveness of implementing a program for children with special needs
   b. A simple case study of a single child over the school year
   c. The efficiency of an athletic director in dealing with the media
5. Some are of the fact that historical research deals with events that have occurred in the past and also deals with primary and secondary sources. Another is that historical research uses as criteria authenticity and accuracy.
6. To be answered individually.
7. a. What are some of the positive comments and negative comments that parents have about the use of vouchers in public schools?

    b.   How can families create a better and more supportive environment for their children?

    c.   What are the most efficient intervention programs and how do parents contribute to their effectiveness?

    d.   How might older adults learn best?

    e.   How has the implementation of equal-access laws influenced the development of new school policies?

8. In focus groups, distinct groups should remain separated. Therefore, in this example, separating the women from their husbands would be desirable. In this way, both the men and the women are more likely to express their true opinions rather than adjusting their expressions because of the presence of their spouses.

9. This is an exploratory exercise, and answers will vary.

10. This is an exploratory exercise, and answers will vary.

11. This conclusion is causal one. Drawing causal conclusions from case studies is inappropriate, as a sample size of one yields insufficient data for a causal conclusion, and as case studies are not designed with the purpose of examining cause and effect.

12. This ethnographer likely did not spend enough time in the culture for the culture to get used to her presence and represent typical cultural experiences rather than the ones the ethnographer's presence offers. She has neglected the ethnography practice of prolonged field activity, which can take years!

Chapter 11

1. You can assume the groups are equivalent because participants are assigned randomly, which reduces the likelihood the groups will have significant differences between them.

2. A Solomon four-group design would be a good choice, as it allows you to determine whether taking the pretest influences posttest scores.

3. Answers will vary. An example of a more internally valid study would be a study on a depression medication intervention that includes only participants with a single diagnosis who are stable enough (i.e., not actively suicidal) to participate in a double-blind study at a lab. An example of a more externally valid study would be a study to develop SAT norms that occurs in a high school, where other students are taking the test in the same room and the potential for a few people to walk down the hallways outside exists.

4. *Mortality*—The dropout rate or reduction in a sample size over time. One example would be when families move out of the area during the experiment in which they are participating.

     Instrumentation—Changes in the system used to score the dependent variable. One example would be the evaluation of drawings and how the criteria for acceptable and nonacceptable change as the drawings are scored.

     Pretest sensitization—Subjects increase or decrease performance because of exposure to a pretest. One example would be a pretest to measure self-esteem in young people, which might awaken thoughts which had not surfaced before. The new thought patterns could affect performance during treatment.

     Reactive arrangements—Simply knowing that one is being observed affects performance. In many experiments, subjects are not told the true nature of the study until its conclusion.

5. Quite clearly, the children's language skills would improve anyway (you could have them sleep with a dictionary under their pillow) and the results would have been the same. It is the lack of a control group that does not allow a true comparison.

6. Results should be both attributable to the hypothesized cause and generalizable to other populations.

7. Regression is a threat. The children were placed in the extreme owing to the measurement error associated with the instrument, and on subsequent testings it is highly likely that the scores will become less extreme, that is, approach the mean.

8. The clients' diet change would introduce the threat of history.

9. Grading rubrics help reduce the threat of instrumentation. They promote standard scoring.

10. a. Randomly select participants from a population.
    b. Randomly assign participants to groups.
    c. Randomly assign the conditions to groups.

11. Some steps could be:
    a. Random assignment of subjects to groups
    b. Random assignment of groups to treatments
    c. Relevant variables on which to match might be: gender, parental income, parental level of education

12. One possible abstract would be as follows: A researcher wishes to measure the effect of a new memory-enhancing drug on the intelligence of rats, as measured by the speed at which they learn a new maze. The researcher chooses the 10 slowest, or "dumbest," rats out of a group of 100, administers the drug to them, and is pleased to see that their learning speed has increased.

13. This is an exploratory exercise and answers will vary.

14. Simply and elegantly, and by providing a condition where the treatment is not present. If all other variables are controlled, then the only difference between the control and experimental group should be the effects of the treatment.

15. The decision to use the matching process depends on whether race is significantly correlated with levels of hope. If previous research indicates the relationship between these two variables is significant, the researcher should go ahead with matching. Otherwise, random assignment would do the trick.

16. Answers might include: superstitions, unproved betting systems, and behaviors meant to bring good luck.

17. Answers might include: a comparison with posttest to allow for a measure of change, and establishing a criterion for equalizing initial differences.

18. Because we're not perfect and there may very well be some contamination or confounding by a variable on which we assumed that groups were equal on, but in reality they are not.

19. a. *Multiple treatment interference*—Subjects may receive an additional treatment besides the intended treatment, which decreases the researcher's ability to generalize results to other settings in which the additional treatment may not be available.
    b. *Reactive arrangements*—If subjects know about the researcher's intent, they may act differently, thus reducing the generalizability of the study.
    c. Experimental effects—If the experimenter becomes actively involved in the research, he or she can become a treatment variable. This would reduce the generalizability of the study.
    d. *Pretest sensitization*—When the researcher informs subjects about what is to come or what is expected, it can affect their subsequent scores and decrease the internal validity of the study.

20. ANCOVA

Chapter 12

1. The primary difference is that in a quasi-experimental design, there is reassignment to groups. The experiment has no control over group membership on at least one independent variable.

2. Group design generally measures one behavior over a group of individuals, whereas single-subject design measures one individual over a group of behaviors. Single-subject design is best used when there is a limited availability of subjects or when the condition being studied is rare or unique.

3. Quasi-experimental research is conducted when the independent variables cannot be manipulated experimentally because of ethical or natural limitations. Examples might include the effect of different parenting styles, differences in salary based on gender, or a nation's gross national product as a function of employment rate.

4. Blood type, level of abuse, and food deprivation must be studied using the quasi-experimental method because participants are already assigned to "treatments."

5. In quasi-experimental design, the differences you might observe between the groups have already occurred, whereas in experimental design you control the assignment of groups.

6. Here are three examples:
   a. How does gender affect assertiveness?
   b. Does religion influence career choice?
   c. Does ethnicity/race affect age of marriage?

7. From lowest to highest:
   a. Pre-experimental design,
   b. Quasi-experimental design,
   c. True experimental design.

8. The pretest posttest control group design has random selection and assignment while the nonequivalent control group design does not.

9. One possible example is:
   a. Establishing baseline for stimming (self-stimulating) behaviors for a child with Asperger's disorder,
   b. Treatment for the stimming behaviors,
   c. Reversal (removal of the treatment),
   d. Reintroducing the treatment. Each step would include observation and recording of stimming behaviors for certain period of time.

10. Here's one example. Over a 30-year period, an experimenter studied the impact of membership in social groups on mental health. Rather than looking at only the age of the participants, the experimenter should look at the social activities (and other possible variables) over that time specifically as a correlate of age.

11. Sure, there's a relationship between lung volume and age, but it's not an increase in age that causes lung volume to be less. Rather, there are a host of other factors including elasticity of the lungs, previous lung volumes, general health, tobacco use, etc.—all of which do a much better job than age.

12. This exercise is exploratory and answers will vary.

13. Cohort effects are a threat to validity in cross-sectional designs. Participants of the same age likely have similar histories and experiences, which may confound with age.

Chapter 13

1. Questions 1 through 3 are library and do-it-on-your-own exercises.

Bibliography

American Psychological Association (1992). *Ethical Principles of Psychologists and Code of Conduct,* vol. 47: 1597–1611. Washington, DC: PA.

———— (2001). *Publication Manual of the American Psychological Association,* 5th ed. Washington, DC: PA.

———— (2009). *Publication Manual of the American Psychological Association*, 6th ed. Washington, DC: Author.

Baer, D. (1970). "An Age Irrelevant Concept of Development." *Merrill-Palmer Quarterly, 16,* 238–245.

Burton, N., & L. Jones (1982). "Recent Trends in Achievement Levels of Black and White Youth." *Educational Researcher, 11,* 10–14.

Calishain, T., & R. Dornfest (2003). *Google Hacks.* Sebastopol, CA: O'Reilly Associates.

Campbell, D. T., & J. Stanley (1963). "Experimental and Quasi-Experimental Design for Research on Teaching." In *Handbook of Research on Teaching,* edited by N. L. Gage, 171–246. New York: Macmillan.

Castro, G., & M. A. Mastropieri (1988). "The Efficacy of Early Intervention Programs: A Meta-Analysis." *Exceptional Children, 52,* 417–424.

Chaffin, M., J. Silovsky, B. Funderburk, L. Valle, E. Brestan, T. Balachova, S. Jackson, J. Lensgraf, & B. Bonner (2004). "Parent Child Interaction Therapy with Physically Abusive Parents: Efficacy for Reducing Future Abuse Reports." *Journal of Consulting and Clinical Psychology, 72,* 500–510.

Chen, C., & H. Stevenson (1989). "Homework: A Cross-cultural Examination." *Child Development, 60,* 551–561.

Cohen, J. (1988). *Statistical Power Analysis for the Behavioral Sciences,* 2nd ed., xxi, 567. Hillsdale, NJ: Erlbaum.

Cole, D. A., T. Vandercook, & J. Rynders (1987). "Dyadic Interactions Between Children With and Without Mental Retardation: Effects of Age Discrepancy." *American Journal of Mental Deficiency, 92*(2), 194–202.

Conoley, J. C., & J. J. Kramer, eds. (1989). *The 10th Mental Measurements Yearbook.* Lincoln, NE: Buros Institute of Mental Measurements.

Cook, T., & Campbell, D. (1979). *Quasi-experimentation: Design and Analysis Issues for Field Settings.* Boston, MA: Houghton Mifflin.

Csikszentmihalyi, M., & R. Larson (1987). "Validity and Reliability of the Experience-Sampling Method." *Journal of Nervous and Mental Diseases, 175,* 526–536.

Curtiss, S. (1977). *Genie: A Psycholinguistic Study of a Modern Day "Wild Child."* New York: Academic Press.

Damon, W., & R. Lerner, eds. (2000). *Handbook of Child Psychology.* New York: Wiley.

Duckett, E., & M. Richards (1989). "Maternal Employment and Young Adolescents' Daily Experiences in Single-Mother Families." Paper presented at the Society for Research in Child Development, Kansas City, MO.

Fleming, A. S., E. Klein, & C. Corter (1992). "The Effects of a Social Support Group on Depression, Maternal Attitudes, and Behavior in New Mothers." *Journal of Child Psychology and Psychiatry, 33,* 685–698.

Gardner, H. (1983). *Frames of Mind: The Theory of Multiple Intelligence.* New York: Basic Books.

Goodwin, L. (1986). "Use of Microcomputers with Preschoolers: A Review of the Literature." *Early Childhood Research Quarterly, 1*(3): 269–286.

Goodwin, C., & M. H. Goodwin (1966). "Seeing as a Situated Activity: Formulating Planes." In *Cognition and Communication at Work,* edited by Y. Englström & D. Middleton, 61–95. Cambridge, UK: Cambridge University Press.

Hall, B. W., A. W. Ward, & C. B. Comer (1988). "Published Educational Research: An Empirical Study of Its Qualities." *Journal of Educational Research, 81*(3), 182–189.

Hanna, Eleanor, Hsiao-ye Yi, Mary Dufour, & Christine Whitmore (2001). "The Relationship of Early-Onset Regular Smoking to Alcohol Use, Depression, Illicit Drug Use, and Other Risky Behaviors During Early Adolescence: Results from the Youth Supplement to the Third National Health and Nutrition Examination Survey." *Journal of Substance Abuse, 13*(3), 265–282.

Hanson, S. L., & A. L. Ginsburg (1988). "Gaining Ground: Values and High School Success." *American Educational Research Association, 25,* 334–365.

Jordan, T. E. (1987). *Victorian Childhood: Themes and Variations*. New York: State University of New York Press.

Kaufman, A. S., & N. L. Kaufman (1983). *Kaufman Assessment Battery for Children*. Circle Pines, MN: American Guidance Service.

Kazdin, A. ed. (2000). *Encyclopedia of Psychology*. New York: Oxford University Press.

Kidder, T. (1989). *Among School Children*. New York: Random House.

Klaczynski, P., K. Goold, & J. Mudry (2004). "Culture, Obesity Stereotypes, Self Esteem, and the 'Thin Ideal': A Social Identity Perspective." *Journal of Youth and Adolescence, 33,* 307–317.

Krohn, E. J., R. E. Lamp, & C. G. Phelps (1988). "Validity of the K ABC for a Black Preschool Population." *Psychology in the Schools, 25,* 15–21.

Lampl, M., M. L. Veldhuis, & M. L. Johnson (1992). "Saltation and Stasis: A Model of Human Growth." *Science, 258,* 801–803.

Likert, R. (1932). "A Technique for the Measurement of Attitudes." *Archives of Psychology, 140,* 55.

Mitchell, J. V. ed. (1983). *Tests in Print III: An Index to Tests, Test Reviews, and the Literature on Specific Tests*. Lincoln, NE: Buros Institute of Mental Measurements.

Neill, A. S. (1960). *Summerhill*. New York: Hart.

Nesselroade, J. R., & P. Baltes (1974). "Adolescent Personality Development and Historical Change: 1970–1972." *Monographs of the Society for Research in Child Development, 39*(1, serial no. 154), 1–79.

O'Neil, B. (1994, Mar. 6). "The History of a Hoax." *New York Times Magazine,* 46–49.

Radin, N., & R. Harold Goldsmith (1989). "The Involvement of Selected Unemployed and Employed Men with Their Children." *Child Development, 60,* 454–459.

Sarasm, S. (1959). *Psychological Problems in Mental Deficiency*. Minneapolis, MN: Arc Resource Center.

Shadish, W. R., Cook, T. D., & Campbell, D. T. (2002). *Experimental and Quasi-Experimental Designs for Generalized Causal Inference*. Boston, MA: Houghton-Mifflin.

Singer, J. L., D. G. Singer, & W. Rapaczynski (1984). "Children's Imagination As Predicted by Family Patterns and Television Viewing: A Longitudinal Study." *Genetic Psychology Monographs, 110,* 43–69.

Skeels, H. M. (1942). "A Study of the Effects of Differential Stimulation on Mentally Retarded Children: A Follow-up Report." *American Journal of Mental Deficiency, 46,* 340–350.

——— (1966). "Adult Status of Children with Contrasting Early Life Experiences: A Follow Up Study." *Monographs of the Society for Research in Child Development, 31,* 340–350.

Skeels, H. M., & H. A. Dye (1939). "A Study of the Effects of Differential Stimulation on Mentally Retarded Children: A Follow-up Report." *American Journal of Mental Deficiency, 46,* 114–136.

——— (1966). "Adult Status of Children with Contrasting Early life Experiences: A Follow-up Study." *Monographs of the Society for Research in Child Development, 31,* 340–350.

Smith, M., & G. Glass (1977). "Meta-Analysis of Psychotherapy Outcome Studies." *American Psychologist, 32,* 752–760.

Smith, M. L., & L. A. Shepard (1988). "Kindergarten Readiness and Retention: A Qualitative Study of Teachers' Beliefs and Practices." *American Educational Research Association, 25,* 307–333.

Solomon, D., M. Watson, K. Delucci, E. Schaps, & K. A. Battistich (1988). "Enhancing Children's Prosocial Behavior in the Classroom." *American Educational Research Journal, 25,* 527–554.

Stevens, S. S. (1951). "Mathematics, Measurement, and Psychophysics." In *Handbook of Experimental Psychology,* edited by S. S. Stevens, 1–49. New York: Wiley.

Terrance, L., & M. Johnson (1978). "Ratings of Educational and Psychological Journals." *Educational Researcher, 19,* 8–10.

Thurstone, L. L., & E. J. Chave (1929). *The Measurement of Attitudes.* Chicago, IL: University of Chicago Press.

Tuttle, W. (1995). *Daddy's Gone to War.* New York: Oxford University Press.

Vellman, P. F., & L. Wilkinson (1993). "Nominal, Ordinal, Interval, and Ratio Typologies Are Misleading." *American Statistician, 47,* 65–72.

Wigfield, A., & J. Eccles (1989). "Test Anxiety in Elementary and Secondary School Students." *Educational Psychologist, 24,* 159–183.

Wintre, M. G., R. Hocks, G. McVey, & J. Fox (1988). "Age and Sex Differences in Choice of Consultant for Various Types of Problems." *Child Development, 59,* 1046–1055.

Glossary

ABD "All but dissertation," which characterizes a surprisingly large number of graduate students who finish everything but the final document.

abstract A brief summary of a journal article which appears before the actual article or in a collection of abstracts.

accuracy A measure of the degree of trustworthiness of a historical data source.

achievement tests Tests used to measure knowledge in a specific content area, such as math or reading.

alternatives The variety of answers available for a multiple choice question.

analysis of covariance (ANCOVA) A statistical tool that equalizes any initial differences that may exist.

applied research Research that has an immediate application.

archival records Data associated with a certain event which has been stored under conditions where they are maintained, preserved, and made accessible to researchers.

attitude tests Tests that assess an individual's feelings or preferences about objects, events, and people.

authenticity Genuineness of a historical data source.

average A measure of central tendency represented as the mean, median, or mode.

baseline Level of behavior associated with a subject before an experiment begins.

basic research Pure research which adds to the base of information in a field but has no immediate application.

blind review The process through which journal articles are reviewed wherein the reviews don't know or are "blind" to the identity of the article's author(s).

browser A software tool used to tour and work with the World Wide Web.

case study A descriptive research method used to study an individual in a unique setting or situation in an intense manner.

categorical variable A variable characterized by only qualitative differences.

causal-comparative design Research in which subjects are assigned to groups based on a characteristic beyond the control of the experimenter, such as gender or age; also another name for post hoc or quasi-experimental research.

central limit theorem The theorem in inferential statistics which states that regardless of the shape of the population distribution, repeated samples from it will produce means that are normally distributed.

chance The unassuming explanation for differences between groups that implies that the differences are accounted for by variables other than those being studied.

closed-ended questions Interview questions which have a clear and apparent focus and a clearly called for answer (same as structured questions).

cluster sampling A probability sampling procedure wherein units of subjects are selected, rather than the subjects themselves.

coding Using numbers to represent data.

coefficient of alienation The amount of variance that is unaccounted for in the relationship between variables.

coefficient of determination The squared correlation coefficient, which indicates the amount of variance in one variable that is accounted for by the other.

concurrent validity   A type of criterion validity.

confounding   When variables compete to explain the effects found in a study.

construct validity   The extent to which a test truly measures a proposed psychological ability or skill and is related to an underlying theory or model of behavior.

content validity   The extent to which a test fairly represents the universe of all possible questions that might be asked.

continuous recording   Recording behavior on a continuous basis.

continuous variable   A variable that has an underlying continuum that can take on any value.

control group   The group that does not receive the treatment but may receive the other condition.

control variable   A variable that has a potential influence on the dependent variable.

convenience sampling   A nonprobability sampling procedure wherein the selected sample represents a captive audience; for example, sophomore college students in an introductory psychology class.

convergent validity   A component of construct validity in which method variance is shared when measuring the same trait.

correlation coefficient   An index of the strength of a relationship between two variables; it ranges in value from +1.00 to –1.00 and can be positive or negative.

correlational research   A method of research used to determine relationships between two or more variables.

criterion-referenced test   A test that measures mastery of specific definitions of performance for an individual in a particular content domain.

criterion validity   How well a test estimates (concurrent validity) or predicts (predictive validity) performance outside of the testing situation.

critical value   The tabled value at which point the null hypothesis cannot be accepted; the minimum value you would expect the test statistic to yield if the null hypothesis is true.

cross-sectional method   A method of developmental research used to examine age differences rather than age changes.

data collection form   A form used to record raw data and often used to facilitate entry into the computer.

data point   Each score for each individual on a test or in an experiment.

degrees of freedom   The leeway for variation a statistical value has; they help determine the critical value of the test statistic.

dependent variable   The outcome variable of research; dependent variables are observed for effects resulting from the influence of another factor, the independent variable(s).

descriptive research   Research that describes a phenomenon without attempting to determine what causes the phenomenon.

descriptive statistics   Simple measures of a distribution's central tendency and variability.

developmental research   Methods of research that examine changes over time.

difficulty index   The percentage of test takers who correctly answer a multiple-choice item.

direct observation   Activity that includes observation of behavior in the environment in which the behavior or outcome occurs.

directional research hypothesis   A research hypothesis that posits an inequality between groups with direction to that difference (such as more than or less than).

discrete variable   A variable that can take on one of several mutually exclusive values.

discriminant validity   A component of construct validity in which trait variance is shared when using the same method.

discrimination index   An index that describes how well a multiple-choice item differentiates between high scorers and low scorers on a test.

distracters   Answers to a multiple-choice question that are attractive enough that a person who does not know the right answer might find them plausible.

distribution of scores   The general shape of data which includes a mean, median, and mode.

documentation   Information or evidence in the form of media (paper, tape, data) which helps support an argument.

duration recording   Recording behavior based on the amount of time it lasts.

effect size   The notion that the stronger the effects of a treatment, the smaller the required sample size.

electronic mail (e-mail)   A method of communicating and sharing information electronically.

electronic newsgroups   Places where information can be posted and shared among Internet users.

equal- appearing intervals   Reference to the Thurstone scale.

error score   The part of an individual's observed score that is attributable to method or trait variance or error.

ethnography   A study of a culture or subculture.

experimental group   The group that receives the treatment.

experimental research   Research that examines cause-and-effect relationships through the use of control and treatment groups.

experimental research method   The method used to test the cause-and-effect relationship between variables.

experimenter effects   A threat to the internal validity of study whereby the presence of an experimenter can change the effectiveness of the treatment.

external criticism   The evaluative criterion used in historical research to establish the authenticity or validity of sources.

external validity   The extent to which the results of an experiment can be generalized.

extraneous variable   A variable that has an unpredictable impact on the dependent variable.

face-sheet information   The first or top sheet of a survey that is usually included and used to collect demographic information.

factor analysis   An advanced statistical technique that allows for the reduction of variables representing a particular construct and then uses factor scores as dependent variables.

factorial design   A research design in which more than one independent variable is studied in various combinations with others.

flow plan   A general plan for survey research of what activities will occur when.

focus group   A group of participants who are asked to make a judgment about a particular event or object.

follow-up studies   Studies that use the databases of previous research as a method for the collection of additional data.

frequency recording   Recording behavior based on the incidence or frequency of the occurrence of a particular behavior.

general sources   General information usually available through newspapers, periodicals, or broad indices.

generalizability   The ability to draw inferences and conclusions from data.

Hawthorne effect   The effect that knowledge of the experiment by the participants can have on the outcomes.

historical research   A methodology for examining how events that have occurred in the past affect events in the present and future.

historiography   Another name for historical research.

history   Uncontrolled outside influences on subjects during the course of an experiment.

hypothesis   An educated guess to be tested.

independent variable   A variable controlled by the researcher in an attempt to test the effects on some outcome, the dependent variable. Independent variables are also known as treatment variables owing to their manipulation and exposure to groups and individuals at the discretion of the researcher.

inferential statistics   Procedures that allow inferences to be made from a sample to the population from which the sample was drawn.

institutional review board   A group of people who review research proposals for the safety and confidentiality of participants.

instrumentation   Those conditions within a testing situation, other than the abilities of the subject, which might affect performance.

internal consistency   A measure of reliability which examines the unidimensional nature of a test.

internal criticism   An evaluative criterion used in historical research to establish the accuracy or trustworthiness of a data source.

internal validity   The accuracy in concluding that the outcome of an experiment is due to the independent variable.

internet   A worldwide online network of networks.

inter-rater reliability   Consistency of results produced by the same test given by different people.

interval level of measurement   Measurement that assigns values representing equal distances between points but that does not allow for proportional comparisons.

interval recording   Recording behavior that occurs during a particular interval of time (also called time sampling).

interview   A method of collecting data that is similar to an oral questionnaire. An interview can be informal and flexible or structured and focused.

interviewer bias   Bias introduced when the interviewer subtly influences the interviewee's responses.

item analysis   A process of evaluating multiple-choice items by using difficulty level and the ability of the item to discriminate or differentiate between group performance.

level of measurement   The scale representing a hierarchy of precision on which a certain type of variable might be assessed.

level of significance   The Type I error rate or the probability that a null hypothesis will be rejected when it is false.

Likert scale   A method used in attitude scales that requires the individual to agree or disagree to a set of statements using a five-point scale.

listserv   An automated mailing list for receiving mail and information about a particular topic.

longitudinal method   A method of developmental research that assesses changes in behavior in one group of subjects at more than one point in time.

matching   A method in which participants are matched on similar characteristics to help account for unexplained variance.

maturation   Changes caused by natural development, which may threaten the internal validity of an experiment.

mean   The sum of all the scores in a distribution divided by the number of observations.

measurement   Assignment of values to objects, events, or outcomes according to rules.

measures of central tendency   Measures of central tendency represented as the mean, median, or mode.

median   The score at which 50% of the scores in the distribution fall above it and 50% fall below it.

meta-analysis   A procedure that allows for the examination of trends and patterns that may exist in many different groups in many different studies.

method error   The part of an individual's error score that is due to characteristics of the test or the testing situation.

method of equal-appearing intervals   Thurstone scale.

method of summated ratings   Likert scale.

mode   The most frequently occurring score.

moderator variable   A variable that is related to the variables of interest masking the true relationship between the independent and dependent variables.

mortality   A threat to the internal validity of a study based on the dropping out or removal of participants from the experiment.

multiple treatment interference   A threat to internal validity when several treatments occur simultaneously.

multitrait-multimethod matrix   Various traits are measured using various methods. Regardless of how they are measured the scores are related. Thus, if the same trait is measured using different methods, the scores should be related, and if different traits are measured using the same methods, the scores should not be related.

multivariate analysis of variance (MANOVA)   Statistical procedures used to examine group differences that occur on more than one dependent variable.

net   Another name for the Internet.

network   A collection of computers that are connected to one another.

newsgroup   A discussion group on the Internet.

news reader   A software program (usually part of an Internet browser such as Explorer or Netscape) which allows you to access and read news.

nominal   The most general level of measurement characterized by the placement of objects in categories and the use of non-numerical labels.

nominal level of measurement   Measurement that assigns labels that do not suggest quantity.

nondirectional research hypothesis   A research hypothesis that posits an inequality (such as a difference between groups) but makes no suggestion of the direction of that difference (such as more than or less than).

nonequivalent control group design   A pre-experimental design in which groups are not equivalent at the beginning of the research and which generally lacks a suitable degree of internal validity.

nonexperimental research   Research in which no manipulation of variables is involved and no cause-and-effect relationship is studied.

nonprobability sampling   When the likelihood of selecting any one member of the population is unknown.

normal curve   The distribution of a set of scores such that it is characterized by being symmetrical about the mean; the mode, mean and median being equal; and the tails asymptotic.

norm-referenced test   A test in which the individual's performance is compared with the results of a larger group of peers.

null hypothesis   A statement of equality between groups in an investigation. The null hypothesis serves as a starting point for observing the effects of the independent variable(s) on the dependent variable and as a benchmark for the comparison of chance versus significant differences between groups.

observed score   True score plus error score.

obtained value   The value obtained by applying a statistical test of significance.

one-group pretest posttest design   A type of experimental design in which one group receives both a pretest and posttest.

one-shot case study design   A type of experimental design in which one group receives only one test.

open-ended questions   Interview questions that provide a broad opportunity for the participant to respond.

optical scanner   A special computer that reads optical scoring sheets.

optical scoring sheet   A specially printed scoring sheet that can be read and scored by computer.

ordinal level of measurement   Measurement that assigns only rank order to outcomes.

parallel-forms reliability   The relationship of two tests made from the same pool of items.

participant observation   Activity where individuals who take part in an experiment or a research project have the potential to affect the outcomes of the research.

Pearson product moment correlation coefficient   An index of the relationship between variables.

personality tests   Tests that assess stable individual behavior patterns.

physical artifacts   Objects that relate to a particular period of time and/or a phenomenon under study.

population   The entirety of some group.

post hoc   Research that is done "after the fact" or after treatments have been assigned to groups. Also known as quasi-experimental research.

posttest-only control group design   A true experimental design with a high degree of internal validity in which posttests are the only measures taken.

predictive validity   A type of criterion validity.

pre-experimental designs   Research designs that are characterized by a lack of random selection and assignment.

pretest posttest control group design   A true experimental design with a high degree of internal validity.

pretest sensitization   When the experience of taking a pretest is related to the effectiveness of the independent variable.

primary sources   People or documentation which presents firsthand information.

probability sampling   The type of sampling used when the likelihood of selecting any one member of the population is known.

projective tests   Personality tests that ask the participant to respond to an ambiguous stimulus. It is assumed that participants will "project" their worldview onto the stimulus.

proportional stratified sampling   A stratified random sampling procedure wherein subjects in the sample are selected in proportion to how they are represented in the population.

qualitative research   Research that examines phenomena within the cultural and social context in which it takes place.

quasi-experimental research   Research that is done when groups are preassigned to "treatments," such as gender, social class, and neighborhood. Also known as post hoc research.

questionnaires   Sets of structured, focused questions that employ a self-reporting, paper-and-pencil format.

quota sampling   A nonprobability sampling procedure similar to stratified random sampling in that a particular stratum is the focus; however, a specified number is set to be selected and once that number is met, no further selection occurs.

range   The distance between the highest and lowest score in a distribution.

ratio level of measurement   Measurement that allows for proportional comparison and a meaningful zero.

raw data   Data that are unorganized.

reactive arrangements   The Hawthorne effect.

regression   The tendency for extreme scorers to move toward more typical levels of performance when retested.

reliability   Consistency in performance or prediction.

reliability coefficient   A numerical index of the relationship between a set of variables.

research   An organized process for collecting knowledge.

research design   The method and structure of an investigation chosen by the researcher to conduct data collection and analysis.

research hypothesis   A statement of inequality between groups in an investigation. Research hypotheses suggest directional or nondirectional relationships between variables.

researcher-made tests   Tests designed for a specific purpose with specific scoring and instructions for that purpose.

sample   A representative portion of a population.

sampling error   The magnitude of the difference between the characteristics of the sample and the characteristics of the population from which it was selected.

scattergram   A plot of scores or data points which indicates the relationship between variables.

scientific method   A set of steps followed by scientists to ensure a common basis for conducting research.

secondary sources   Secondhand sources of historical data, such as newspaper clippings and summary statistics.

selection   A threat to the internal validity of a study based on a biased selection of participants.

significance level   The amount of risk one is willing to take that the null hypothesis is true even though it is rejected.

simple random sampling   A sampling procedure allowing for the equal and independent chance of subjects being selected as part of the sample.

single-subject research designs   Observing one subject over a variety of behaviors.

smartphone   A cellular phone that has many of the same features as personal computers in terms of capacity, computational power and applications.

Solomon four-group design   A traditional experimental design in which there are four different groups of participants, and many different questions can be answered simultaneously with some relatively simple comparisons.

standard deviation   Average distance of each score in a distribution from the mean.

standard scores   Scores that have been derived to create a common reference point and the same standard deviation to allow for easy comparison.

standardized tests   Tests with standard instructions and scoring procedures which are used for all administrations of the test.

static group comparison design   A pre-experimental design with limited internal validity.

statistical significance   The degree of risk you are willing to take that you will reject a null hypothesis when it is actually true.

stem   The leading part of a multiple choice question.

stratified random sampling   A random sampling procedure used when subjects are known to be unequal on some variable in the population.

stratified sampling   The process of selecting a sample that represents different groups or levels of a population.

structured questions   Interview questions that have a clear and apparent focus and a clearly called for answer (same as closed-ended questions).

structured tests   Tests that contain items with fixed responses.

Survey research   A type of research that uses a written or oral survet forom as its primary tool for the collection of information.

systematic sampling   A random sampling procedure in which increments determine who becomes part of the sample; for example, every third person is selected.

table of random numbers   An unbiased criterion used in the selection of subjects for a sample.

test   A measurement technique used to assess individual differences in various content areas.

testing   A threat to the internal validity of a study based on the sensitization of the group owing to the administration of a pretest.

test of statistical significance   The application of a statistical procedure to determine whether observed differences exceed the critical value, indicating that chance is not the most attractive explanation for the results.

test–retest reliability   The stability of a test over time.

theory   A group of logically related statements that explains things that have occurred in the past and predicts things that will occur in the future.

Thurstone scale   A method used in constructing attitude tests in which all of the items are assigned an attitude score. It is made up of nearly equal intervals for individuals to agree or disagree with various statements.

time sampling Recording behavior that occurs during a particular interval of time. Also called interval recording.

trait error The part of an individual's error score that is attributable to characteristics of the individual.

true experimental research method Research in which a cause and effect is unambiguously tested.

true score The actual score for someone on some test.

Type I error Same as the level of statistical significance—the level of risk you are willing to take that the null hypothesis is rejected when it is true.

Type II error The acceptance of a false null hypothesis. The probability that a Type II error will occur can be reduced by increasing the size of the sample.

unstructured questions Interview questions that provide a broad opportunity for the participant to respond. Open-ended questions are one example.

URL (universal resource locator) An address on the World Wide Web.

validity The truthfulness or accuracy within the score of a test or interpretation of an experiment.

variability The spread of scores in a distribution.

variable A class of outcomes that can take on more than one value. Variables are what researchers study.

variance A measure of the degree of dispersion or variability in a distribution of scores. The variance is the standard deviation squared (s^2).

World Wide Web (or WWW) A collection of graphically illustrated locations on the Internet.

z-score A standard score based on a distribution with a mean of 0 and a standard deviation of 1.

Index

Note: Letters 'f' and 't' following the locators refer to figures and tables cited in the text.

(Continued)